A Block in Time

A Block in Time

A NEW YORK CITY HISTORY AT THE CORNER OF FIFTH AVENUE AND TWENTY-THIRD STREET

CHRISTIANE BIRD

BLOOMSBURY PUBLISHING

NEW YORK · LONDON · OXFORD · NEW DELHI · SYDNEY

BLOOMSBURY PUBLISHING
Bloomsbury Publishing Inc.
1385 Broadway, New York, NY 10018, USA

BLOOMSBURY, BLOOMSBURY PUBLISHING, and the Diana logo are trademarks
of Bloomsbury Publishing Plc

First published in the United States 2022

LIBRARY OF CONGRESS CATALOGING-IN-PUBLICATION DATA IS AVAILABLE

ISBN: HB: 978-1-63286-742-1; EBOOK: 978-1-63286-744-5

2 4 6 8 10 9 7 5 3 1

Typeset by Westchester Publishing Services
Printed in the U.S.A.

To find out more about our authors and books visit www.bloomsbury.com and sign up
for our newsletters.

Bloomsbury books may be purchased for business or promotional use. For information on
bulk purchases please contact Macmillan Corporate and Premium Sales Department at
specialmarkets@macmillan.com.

For Simone and Silvie

CONTENTS

PREFACE

On the part of the floodplain that will one day become the island of *Mannahatta*, a shaggy mastodon throws back his tusks—fourteen feet of danger spiraling out. A smaller mastodon with smaller tusks turns and retreats . . .

CUT TO:

A group of Lenape men and women deliberately set fire to a swath of Mannahatta's forest, flushing out a herd of deer. The men pull back their bows, arrows fly, deer drop . . .

CUT TO:

Dutch settlers explore the island with their Lenape guides. They walk along the Wickquasgeck Trail, heading north. One hundred years later, much of this path will be known as Broadway . . .

CUT TO:

The Dutch have left the island. The English have arrived. They grant a tract of land in the lower middle of Manhattan, to the west of the Wickquasgeck Trail, to a former Black slave . . .

CUT TO:

A Dutch family now owns the Black man's land. Outside the windows of their yellow farmhouse hulks the so-called House of Refuge, where youths huddle together, waiting for a bowl of gruel. They've been labeled thieves, swindlers, and prostitutes, but most are simply poor . . .

CUT TO:

The yellow farmhouse has been converted into a raucous stagecoach stop. Nervous travelers down mugs of mead before venturing into "the upper wilds of Manhattan" . . .

CUT TO:

Shouts, curses, and cries pour out of a two-story hippodrome, built on the site of the former stagecoach stop. An audience of "blacklegs, gamblers, rowdies, and the whole miscellanea of polite roguery" are urging a half dozen ostriches on . . .

CUT TO:

High society swishes in and out of the city's poshest hotel, which has replaced the hippodrome. Voluminous skirts are swirling, gold-topped canes are gleaming, well-dressed thieves are lurking . . .

CUT TO:

In boardinghouses behind the hotel, prostitutes paint their faces, getting ready for the night. Competition is fierce. The whole neighborhood is packed with debauched yet alluring disorderly houses, concert saloons, dance halls, gambling joints . . .

CUT TO:

The hotel and boardinghouses are gone, replaced by office-and-loft buildings. Young women hunch over sewing machines, churning out shirtwaists and undergarments; young men hawk furniture, china, and glass . . .

CUT TO:

The Sixth Avenue Elevated railway screeches past the office-and-loft buildings, raining cinders and soot. In its cars and beneath its shadows lurk secrets and sorrows . . .

CUT TO:

Toy manufacturers from all over the country gather at the world's biggest toy center, built on the site of the former posh hotel. Lionel trains, Monopoly, hula hoops . . . What will be the next big thing? . . .

CUT TO:

A sprawling Italian marketplace fills the ground floor of the former toy center. Overflowing with food shops and restaurants, it is packed with hungry hordes from morning till night . . .

CUT TO:

Above the Italian marketplace, a social media company thrives. On its website, visitors take quizzes, read posts about cats, and vote on articles with bright yellow buttons: LOL, OMG, WTF? . . .

CUT TO:

Sirens wail. Shops and offices close. Sidewalks are empty . . . BLACK LIVES
MATTER, JUSTICE FOR GEORGE, reads graffiti spray-painted on splintering
wood . . .

CUT TO:

Vaccines arrive. Businesses are reopening. Life is returning to normal . . .

CUT TO:

???

*   *   *

This is the story of New York City, told through the prism of a single block
and the lives of the people who lived and worked there. Bordered by
Twenty-third Street to the south, Twenty-fourth Street to the north, Sixth
Avenue to the west, and Fifth Avenue and Broadway to the east, the block
once lay far north of the settled city, then at its epicenter, and then on
its cultural periphery once again. It's a story of forest and cement, bird
cries and taxi horns, Native Americans and Europeans, farmhouses and
hotels, theaters and brothels, publishing houses and clothing manufacturers, toys and gourmet foods. It's a story of high life and low life, immigrants and tourists, factory workers and aristocrats, newly independent
women and newly reinvented African Americans, crooked cops and moral
reformers. It's a story of the flow of history.

Often, the block's denizens have not been what they seemed. Often,
there have been secrets and scandals. At times, the block has seemed
to embody all that is best in human nature. At other times, it has seemed to
embody all that is worst. Much like New York City itself, and its celebrated
poet Walt Whitman, it has contained multitudes.

Wealth and want, greed and generosity, guilt and innocence, extravagance and degradation—all have flourished on this one Manhattan block,
emblematic of the metropolis as a whole.

*   *   *

The germ of the idea behind this book first came to me twenty-five years
ago when I was a graduate student in American studies at Columbia
University. I had taken a course in urban history with New York City historian Kenneth Jackson and written my master's thesis on New York's

Tenderloin, the notorious red-light and entertainment district that initially
stretched between Twenty-third and Forty-second streets, Fifth and Eighth
avenues, in the second half of the nineteenth century. Filled with an impossible number of improbable tales, the Tenderloin was the embodiment of
all the abovementioned contradictions, and those juxtapositions fascinated
me. There was a book there, I knew it.

But I couldn't figure out how to frame it. I didn't want to write a scholarly work, or an account of one of the Tenderloin's major events, or a biography of one or two of its central figures. I simply wanted to write about
the neighborhood and its unusual history, but that subject was too amor-
phous to shape into a compelling narrative—it had no glue. I brought up
my problem with my friend and editor Nancy Miller, but she saw no way
to frame the material effectively either, and I dropped the idea. For decades.

But I never forgot about it. In between other books and jobs and the
frenetic rush of daily life, the idea would come back to me. The Tenderloin. What a dazzling, unnerving neighborhood it had been.

About six years ago, I brought up the Tenderloin with Nancy once
again. Can you tell the history of the district in one or more buildings?
she asked me. I thought for a moment. One building came immediately to
mind: the Fifth Avenue Hotel, which had formerly stood at the corner of
Twenty-third Street and Fifth Avenue, on the far eastern edge of the
Tenderloin. For fifty years, from 1859 to 1909, it had served as an important
social, cultural, and political center, as well as the haunt of prostitutes and
con men. But the Fifth Avenue Hotel told only one part of the Tenderloin's
story and had been torn down decades before, as had most of the district's
other emblematic buildings.

Then I had another thought. How about concentrating on a single
block?

I worked out some of the details of the book. It would focus on the block
that had once held the Fifth Avenue Hotel, but would cover much more
than its nineteenth-century history. A work of narrative nonfiction, of
stories, it would begin in the Ice Age and end in the present. As much as
possible, too, it would use the evolution of the block to tell the larger story
of the city. I was off—

—to encounter problems I hadn't anticipated.

First, although I already had mountains of information about the nineteenth century and some about the eighteenth, finding detailed information specific to the block, as opposed to Manhattan in general, before then was difficult. That wasn't particularly surprising, given the nature of historical records, but it was frustrating to realize that I couldn't paint as complete a portrait of the block pre-1800 as I had hoped. There were no real stories to bring it alive—just an outline of basic facts. The world of its earliest residents, including that of a freed Black slave and his family, would have to remain shrouded in shadow.

Later in my research, I was surprised to encounter a similar problem when probing the block's twentieth- and twenty-first-century history. For the modern era, facts were abundant—I could easily find out what buildings had gone up when and who was renting what to whom—but captivating stories of the kind that had drawn me to the nineteenth century were much harder to find.

Only slowly did it dawn on me why that was so, though the answer was obvious. From the mid-nineteenth century through the early twentieth century, the block was at the center of the city. New York had moved uptown to Madison Square in the mid-1800s, and for the rest of the century, the whole area was bursting with hotels, restaurants, theaters, gambling dens, bars, and bordellos. The block itself contained not only the Fifth Avenue Hotel but also a first-class theater, mansions built by some of the city's most powerful and complex citizens, and boardinghouses inhabited by some of its least respectable and poorest ones.

During that period, too, the city was in the throes of enormous change. New York was metamorphizing from a small city into a financial capital, the nouveau riche were challenging old money, and societal mores were evolving at a rapid clip.

By the second decade of the twentieth century, in contrast, Manhattan had moved farther uptown and the block had lost its centrality, along with most of its residents. Its mansions, boardinghouses, and Fifth Avenue Hotel were gone, replaced by handsome but anonymous office-and-loft buildings that housed light manufacturing, apparel, and wholesale companies. Some of these buildings did hold fascinating tales, but the larger-than-life characters who had roamed the block in earlier days were gone. History had moved on, as it always does, pulling down what it had built up, pummeling what had once been viewed as permanent into oblivion.

The block reached a nadir in the 1970s and early 1980s, when New York City, suffering from financial crisis, became awash in homelessness and crime, but it regained some of its former glory in the 2000s as new-economy wealth flooded in and the area was revitalized. The only constant on the block through the centuries has been change—a hallmark of the city at large, which has always been too restless to stay still for long.

And so, by default, I was back almost to where I had started, writing a book that does cover the entire history of the block, but focuses on the second half of the nineteenth century, when the Tenderloin was flourishing. Almost all physical evidence of that era on the block is gone, but its ghosts linger.

The next series of questions I asked myself was, What is a history of a block really all about? What do I want to concentrate on? How can I best corral the enormous amount of information I have about the block and shape it into a meaningful, story-driven narrative that says something about the city at large?

Once again, the answer when it came to me was obvious: people. History is about people and the historical events that they made happen. I cared less about the buildings that had gone up or come down on the block than about the people associated with those buildings. The book would therefore be less a history of New York as told through the block than a history of the city as told through the lives of the people on the block.

Of course, most of those people did not live and work exclusively on the block. They roamed throughout the city and the world, interconnecting with others in myriad ways; to tell their stories with any resonance, I would have to widen my lens to include other places. This had the danger of softening the book's focus, but upon reflection, I realized that no other approach was possible. The block was interconnected too. What happened on the block affected the neighborhood and city, just as what happened in the neighborhood and city affected the block.

Some of the people associated with the block, most notably James Fisk and Stanford White, are well-known figures whose stories have been told many times. Others, such as the former slave Solomon Pieters, the real estate mogul Amos Eno, and the social climber Marietta Stevens, are more obscure, and still others—thousands of them—are completely unknown. Their lives, too, had bearing on the block, but their stories have been lost, at least until some future scholar uncovers them.

In the end, this book is only one of many histories that could have been written about the block between Twenty-third and Twenty-fourth streets, Fifth and Sixth avenues. Some authors might have focused more on land usage and the buying and selling of the block's lots. Others might have focused on architecture, technological developments, or sociology. Still others might have found a different cast of characters with tales to tell. Herewith my offering.

CHAPTER I

In the Land of the Real People

In the beginning, there was silence. For millennia, the fleck of land that would one day become the New York City block between Twenty-third and Twenty-fourth streets, Fifth and Sixth avenues, lay smothered beneath tons upon tons of glittering glacial ice. Entombed at the southernmost end of the vast Laurentide ice sheet that extended down from the Arctic, it and the 22.82-square-mile plot of earth that is now Manhattan felt no sunlight and saw no moonlight. The ice was thousands of feet thick.

Back then, the future block lay 120 miles away from the Atlantic Ocean. Sea levels were three hundred feet lower than they are today, and to the south and east stretched miles of exposed continental shelf on which mastodons, saber-toothed cats, and other animals of the Ice Age roamed. To the west knifed the canyon that would one day become the Hudson River.

Like the rest of Manhattan before the Ice Age, the block had once been part of a seabed and part of a mountain range, close to the equator and close to Africa. For a period, too, the block had belonged to a valley spanning the area between today's Thirtieth and Canal streets. On either side of the valley soared stark serrated mountains as tall as the Alps, made of metamorphic rock pushed up from the former sea floor by volcanoes. Millions of years later, those mountains, worn away by erosion and glaciers, became the bedrock of schist on which today's Midtown and downtown skyscrapers stand. That same bedrock underlies the city blocks that once lay in the valley but is buried much deeper below the island's surface, part of the reason—along with zoning laws—why there are far fewer skyscrapers in the lower middle part of the island than there are in Midtown or Lower Manhattan. The tallest building on the Twenty-third Street block is 19 stories high. Midtown's Empire State Building is 102 stories high, and Lower Manhattan's Freedom Tower, 104 stories high.

The Laurentide ice sheet began to retreat about twenty thousand years ago, in the wake of worldwide warming, and as it did, life appeared. First came mosses and lichens, then shrubs and bushes, then coniferous forests of spruce, fir, and pine. The mastodons, saber-toothed cats, and other animals of the Ice Age wandered in from the continental shelf, and thereafter, humankind appeared.

                              *   *   *

Where once there was silence, now there was noise. Howls, roars, barks, birdsongs, chirps, buzzes, splashes, crashes, groans, screams. The land that the early humans encountered was plush with marshes, ponds, rivers, and forests, interspersed with open areas of tundra where herds of moose, elk, caribou, and mastodons roamed. In the forests lived giant beavers, bear, and fox, while the rivers and ponds hosted multitudes of frolicking fish. The Atlantic Ocean was still many miles away though, and there was no New York Harbor. Sea levels were at least 150 feet below what they are today—it would take another six thousand years before they reached present levels.

New York's first known people were the Paleoindians, small-boned, dark-haired nomads who carried their belongings on their backs. Venturing into the region about twelve thousand years ago, they had probably come from the south or west and may have been descendants of small groups of migrating peoples who had crossed over to North America on the Bering land bridge between Siberia and Alaska. Archaeologists disagree on when exactly the Paleoindians arrived on the continent and on whether they even were the first people here, but they are the earliest people for whom archaeological evidence has been found.

The Paleoindians usually set up their encampments along shorelines, but they may have passed through the future Twenty-third Street block when gathering fruits and nuts or hunting game. Caribou, fox, and hare were their most common prey, but they also pursued larger animals, including mastodons. Scientists believe that the magnificent pachyderms, standing seven to twelve feet tall and weighing four to eight tons, were once as common on the continent as deer are today.

From the Paleoindians descended the Lenni Lenape, the "real people" or "original people," honored as the oldest of the northeastern Algonquin Indian cultures. Most spoke Munsee, a language that is now extinct. The word *Manhattan* comes from the Munsee word *mannahatta*, which may have meant "island of many hills," or "cluster of islands with channels everywhere," or "place where timber is procured for bows and arrows."

Lenapehoking, the "land of the Lenni Lenape," stretched from western Connecticut to Delaware, included most of New Jersey and southeastern New York, and was home to over a dozen Lenape subgroups. Northernmost among them were the Catskills, Wappingers, and Esopus. A little farther south, in what is now Westchester, the Bronx, and northern Manhattan, lived the Wickquasgecks. The Canarsees were in Brooklyn, the Raritans on Staten Island and around Raritan Bay, the Hackensacks in the Hackensack River valley, the Tappans in northern New Jersey, and the Rockaways, Matinecocks, Massapequas, and Merricks, among others, on Long Island.

No one is really sure how many Lenape were living in what became the greater New York City area when the Europeans arrived. The number may have been as high as fifteen thousand, but only a fraction of that figure—perhaps three hundred to twelve hundred—lived on Manhattan. The Indians probably used the island mostly as hunting and gathering grounds and as a base for fishing camps. Archaeologists have found about eighty Lenape settlement sites in the five boroughs, with only about fifteen of those in Manhattan. One was an encampment near a deep spring-fed pond, later known as Collect Pond, on the edge of today's Chinatown; another, a large fishing and planting site called Sapokanikan, in today's Meatpacking District in the West Village. Most of the other Manhattan sites were in the northernmost part of the island, in the areas now known as Washington Heights and Inwood.

Archaeologists have found no evidence of Lenape settlements on the Twenty-third Street block, but the island's most important Native American trail ran along its eastern edge. Known as the Wickquasgeck because it led to land of the Wickquasgecks in northern Manhattan, the trail traveled north from the southern tip of the island on what is now Broadway, veered east on today's Park Row, and then ran northwest on a diagonal more or less along today's Bowery, Fourth Avenue, and Broadway to the present junction of Twenty-third Street, Fifth Avenue, and Broadway—the southeast corner of the Twenty-third Street block. It then veered east a second time and traveled up the east-central side of Manhattan before returning to the west side and linking up with today's Broadway once again.

Throughout the region, the Lenape moved from place to place with the seasons. In the spring and summer, they camped near the shore, fishing and digging for oysters and clams; in the autumn, they moved inland to hunt and gather and harvest the fields of corn, beans, and squash they had planted in the late spring. In the winter, they moved yet farther inland, to less exposed areas in the Bronx and Queens, where they holed up in multi-family longhouses made of bark and grass, hunted for fox and hare, wove baskets and repaired nets, and told stories around campfires. A deeply spiritual people, the Lenape believed that their ancient grandparents governed the four directions of the wind, and that when the grandparents gambled, the seasons changed. Heaven was somewhere in the southwest sky, and when a person died, he or she traveled along the Milky Way, each footprint a star.

The Lenape were loosely organized into small, independent bands that ranged from a few dozen to several hundred people. Heading each was a sachem, who led through the consensus of the group. There was no hierarchy of command, and warfare was all but unknown. "It is a great fight where seven or eight is slain," declared one English colonist scornfully many decades later.

There was also no private ownership of land. The Lenape held their land communally, through families and bands. Each band had its own general territory in which to hunt and fish and plant, but other bands could ask for, and were usually granted, the right to use that territory at times in exchange for gifts.

Though the Lenape probably never inhabited the future Twenty-third Street block, they, like the Paleoindians before them, must have roamed over it in search of game, fruits, and nuts. Over the centuries, too, they would have burned its underbrush periodically to make it easier to hunt in and pass through. Landscape ecologists believe that in the two hundred years before Henry Hudson's arrival, 80 to 90 percent of Manhattan was deliberately set on fire, with the middle area, including the Twenty-third Street block, burned between two and ten times. The fires killed the island's shrubs, bushes, and saplings but left its canopy of oak, hickory, and red maple untouched. "An extraordinary and spectacular event," wrote Dutch lawyer Adriaen van der Donck about the fires in his 1655 book, *A Description of New Netherland*. "Seen from a distance it would seem that not only the leaves, weeds, and deadwood are being consumed, but that all the trees and the whole of the surrounding forest are falling prey to the flames . . . it is terrifying to watch."

*   *   *

The Wickquasgeck Trail usually followed Mannahatta's highest elevations, passing by lime-green marshes, shadow-dappled forests, shimmering meadows, hushed ponds, and tumbling brooks along the way. All were bursting with a splendiferous multitude of flora and fauna. Manhattan lies in a most unusual geographic position: it sits at the crossroads of northern and southern climate zones and at a spot where freshwater mixes with saltwater, meaning that thousands of species can flourish here. In the centuries before the arrival of the Europeans, the island held more ecological communities per acre than today's Yellowstone, more native plant species per acre than Yosemite, and more bird species than the Great Smoky Mountains National Park.

When the early Dutch settlers arrived in Mannahatta, they couldn't praise the glory of the island highly enough. They wrote of woods so filled with birds that "men can scarcely go through them for the whistling, the noise and the chattering"; of bays swarming "with fish, both large and small, whales, tunnies, and porpoises"; of "foxes in abundance, multitudes of wolves, wild cats, squirrels . . . beavers in great numbers, minks, otters, polecats, bears"; and of tall grasses, towering trees, pears larger than a man's fist, wild turkeys so big and numerous that they shut out the sunshine, and oysters a foot long.

Compared with much of the island at the time, the future Twenty-third Street block was relatively flat and probably lacked any distinguishing features. Still, it was likely thick with a mix of red maple, black cherry, American chestnut, sweetgum, red oak, and tulip trees, along with Virginia creeper, woodfern, panic grass, black haw, and sumac. Berries of all sorts—strawberries, huckleberries, chokeberries, blackberries, blueberries, ground cherries—would have flourished in its soil, while in its underbrush and canopy rustled such gentle creatures as deer mice, white-footed mice, salamanders, wood ducks, and flying squirrels. Larger mammals such as wolves and bear must also have passed over the block from time to time.

*　*　*

Among the many probable furry residents to the immediate east of the Twenty-third Street block, where Madison Square Park is today, was a remarkable creature, the beaver. Chomping down trees, carrying mud and stones in its forepaws, this toothy rodent, the second largest on earth, after the capybara of South America, worked hard from dusk to dawn to build dams that blocked up streams that created ponds in which the beaver then lived. In winter the ponds froze a solid icy blue, and in spring and summer turned a murky green, with cattails, pondweeds, and bladderworts sprouting up along their edges.

The streams carried rich silt down from the hillsides, and eventually, the built-up silt drowned the ponds, forcing the beaver to move on. The ponds then dried up and became marshland that became meadow that became forest that—in more modern times—became farmland that became city blocks, covered with pavement and pounded by an endless march of pedestrian feet. A beaver's ability to transform a landscape is second only to a human's.

Everyone from the ancient Romans to the early Europeans believed that the beaver had strange, magical powers. The first-century Roman naturalist and philosopher Pliny the Elder, echoing a still earlier Aesop tale, states that the beaver's testes have many medicinal uses, and that when beavers are cornered by trappers, they bite their testes off and throw them at the hunters to save their lives.

Van der Donck devotes a whole chapter of *A Description of New Netherland* to the "Nature, Amazing Ways, and Properties of the Beavers." In it he relates Pliny's tale and carefully chronicles the many medicinal powers of castoreum, a mucus then thought to be produced by the beaver's testes, but now known to come from two castor glands near its anus. According to Van der Donck, castoreum was "useful in treating lunatics" and cured dizziness, trembling, gout, paralysis, epilepsy, constipation, toothaches, menstrual cramps, and stomachaches.

Other seventeenth-century Europeans were interested in the beaver for a much more prosaic reason: its fur. Beaver coats and hats were highly fashionable in Europe at the time, and its once reliable supplier, Russia, was no longer delivering, as its beaver population had been depleted. The demand for beaver was then so high that a single ship carrying a cargo of furs could provide a man with a profit so grand that he could live on it handsomely for an entire year.

And so it was that one year after Hudson "discovered" the New York region in 1609, several merchants from Amsterdam sent a trading ship to the river "called Manhattes from the savage nation that dwells at its mouth" in search of beaver fur. Other traders soon followed, and by the early 1620s, the Dutch were shipping 1,500 beaver skins to Europe annually. That number escalated rapidly: in 1625 alone, the traders sent 5,295 beaver pelts back home. By the early 1700s, Manhattan's beavers would disappear, and for centuries, there would be no sign of them anywhere in the greater New York City region. When a pair of beavers was spotted in the Bronx River in 2007, it made headline news.

* * *

In 1621 the Dutch government established the West India Company and granted it a monopoly in trade in the Americas—part of a larger political agenda to wage economic warfare against Spain. The company was also granted the right to establish colonies, negotiate alliances with local leaders, and appoint governors, but that was secondary. The firm's overriding purpose was trade. Company profits came first.

The first shipload of settlers arrived in New Netherland in 1624, after eight rough, terrifying weeks at sea. On board were thirty families, most of them Walloons, or French-speaking Protestant refugees from Catholic Spain living in what is now Belgium. The families had been promised land and cheap livestock in exchange for six years of service to the West India Company, during which time they had to go where they were sent, plant what they were told, and otherwise obey all company orders.

Eighteen of the families were dispatched to Fort Orange, a trading post near today's Albany, and others to outposts along the Connecticut and Delaware rivers. Eight men were stationed off the coast of Mannahatta on Noten (Nut) Island, now Governors Island, named for its many hickory, oak, and chestnut trees. Today, the New York State Legislature recognizes Governors Island as the birthplace of New York State.

In 1626 confident, scrappy Peter Minuit, the colony's new director general, arrived to make the most famous purchase in U.S. history: he bought Mannahatta from the Lenape for sixty guilders' worth of beads and other items, probably including hatchets, cloth, and fishhooks. (Nineteenth-century historians equated that sixty guilders with twenty-four dollars, a number that is still widely quoted today, but its true relative worth is difficult to calculate. Items such as hatchets were invaluable to the Lenape, and the Europeans purchased other tracts of North American wilderness— then viewed as inexhaustible—for similar prices.) No deed documenting the sale exists, but the transaction was recorded in a November 7, 1626, letter addressed to the directors of the West India Company by one Peter Schagen. "High and Mighty Lords," he wrote. "Yesterday the ship the Arms of Amsterdam arrived here . . . They report that our people are in good spirit and live in peace. The women also have borne some children there. They have purchased the Island Manhattes from the Indians for the value of 60 guilders. It is 11,000 morgens in size [about 22,000 acres]."

The Dutch thought they now owned the island and, before long, began buying and selling large pieces of it, just as if they were back home in Europe. But to the Lenape, the agreement was a treaty, not a sale, allowing the Europeans to use the land, as one band allowed another band to use its territory.

Minuit next set about constructing Fort Amsterdam at the island's southern tip, along with simple houses built largely of tree bark, a horse-powered mill with a room above it for religious services, and a stone counting house for the West India Company. He also sent his men out to explore the rest of Manhattan. An account written between 1628 and 1630 speaks of good farmland to be found on the island's north and east sides, and mentions six West India Company farms, or "bouweries" as the Dutch called them, that had already been established to the immediate northeast of the settlement.

Meanwhile, through it all, the future Twenty-third Street block lay quiet and still, too far away to be much affected by the activity farther south, and too rocky and infertile to be a top choice for farmland. But the block was already witnessing change. Traffic along the Wickquasgeck Trail at its eastern edge was increasing exponentially. The Lenape had used the trail to travel from one end of the island to the other for generations, and now the Europeans, with the Indians as their guides, were using it too. Soon, the Dutch would establish farms in Harlem and on the island's east side, and use the trail for sending foodstuffs south to New Amsterdam, as the settlement surrounding Fort Amsterdam had been named.

*   *   *

After "selling" Manhattan to the Europeans, the Munsee, as the Europeans called the Lenape on the island, continued to occupy it, and for a decade or so, the two communities lived together in relative peace. Considered an integral part of New Amsterdam, the Munsee were a constant presence in town, and the colonists relied on them as helpmates and guides. The two groups shared meals, and some Indian women and European men lived together in informal marriages.

Already by the late 1630s, however, peace between the two groups was fraying. Cultural misunderstandings, internecine fighting among the Indians over furs and European goods, and the widespread use of guns and alcohol had led to increasing violence, with much of the trouble centered on land and animals. The Europeans' pigs and cattle were wandering about freely, trampling the Munsee planting fields, and the Munsee dogs were hounding the European cattle. The settlers were cutting down the Indians' hunting grounds, and the Indians were ignoring the settlers' property lines.

In 1638 Willem Kieft took over as the colony's new director general. The son of a merchant and a politician's daughter, he was well connected, learned, and tempestuous—Washington Irving called him "William the Testy"—and prone to using a walking stick that came up to his chin. He had nothing but disdain for the Munsee. He forbade the settlers from selling them guns and alcohol, and aggressively encroached on their hunting grounds by issuing large land grants to farmers.

Kieft disdained most of New Amsterdam's settlers too. By then numbering around four hundred, only about half were Dutch. The rest were Walloon, English, French, Polish, Irish, Swedish, Danish, Italian, and German. Most were also poor and uneducated, some with criminal backgrounds, and almost all were men. In contrast to the colonists in New England and Virginia, who had fled their homeland in search of religious freedom, the New Amsterdam settlers, like their employer the West India Company, were in the Americas for only one thing—making money.

Which had its positive side. United by business interests rather than religion or creed, the men lived and let live. As in the Dutch Republic, then the most progressive society in Europe, multiculturalism and a tolerance of differences were characteristic of New Amsterdam from the start. When the Jesuit missionary Father Isaac Jogues visited the colony in 1643, he found its people speaking eighteen different languages—a foreshadowing of the over six hundred different languages being spoken in New York City today.

One year after arriving in New Amsterdam, Kieft came up with an outlandish plan: he would levy a tax on the Munsee to pay for the "protection" that the West India Company was providing them against other Indian groups. The Lenape nation was outraged. Kieft "must be a very mean fellow to come to this country without being invited by them, and now wish to compel them to give him their corn for nothing," protested the Tappans, a Lenape subgroup living north of New Amsterdam in today's Orange County.

The following year, Kieft sent troops to look for hog thieves on Staten Island, and they attacked a Raritan village for no apparent reason, killing several Indians. The Raritans retaliated by burning a Dutch farm and killing four farmhands.

Anger over the incident was just dying down when in August 1641 incendiary news raced down the Wickquasgeck Trail, whooshing past the still-slumbering future Twenty-third Street block. Startled birds took to flight; four-footed creatures scampered to find places in which to hide. "Claes Swits is dead! Claes Swits is dead! Beheaded by an Indian brave!"

New Amsterdam erupted in rage. Claes Swits was well known in the settlement. A kindly older man who had once worked as a wheelwright, he owned property at today's Forty-seventh Street and Second Avenue, where he ran a small trading shop and roadhouse. On that fateful morning, a twenty-seven-year-old Indian had arrived at his doorstep with furs to trade. Swits knew the young man, who had once worked for his son, and invited him in, offering him food and drink. He then bent over a chest to pull out goods to trade, and the brave cut off his head with an axe.

To the Europeans, the incident seemed entirely unprovoked. But to the Wickquasgeck, it was an act of revenge. Fifteen years earlier, a small group of Wickquasgeck had been on their way down the island to trade beaver pelts when they were attacked and massacred by a group of Europeans. Only one twelve-year-old boy—now the twenty-seven-year-old brave—had escaped.

The Lenape refused to give up the young man for punishment, and Kieft went to war. One bloody incident followed another, with the violence rising to a crescendo on February 25, 1643, during the Month of the Frog Moon. On that day, against the counsel of other New Amsterdam leaders and the explicit commands of the West India Company, Kieft ordered a night attack on an Indian encampment at Pavonia (today's Jersey City). Made up of Lenape refugee families who had fled a violent Lenape-Mahican conflict farther north, the encampment lay quiet as the soldiers crept in. Unsuspecting men, women, and children were breathing their last.

The horror began around midnight. David de Vries, an influential colonist who had vehemently condemned the attack, wrote, "I heard a great shrieking, and I ran to the ramparts of [Fort Amsterdam], and looked over to Pavonia. Saw nothing but firing, and heard the shrieks of the savages murdered in their sleep . . . infants were torn from their mother's breasts, and hacked to pieces in the presence of the parents, and the pieces thrown into the fire . . . Some came to our people in the country with their hands, some with their legs cut off, and some holding their entrails in their arms."

From then on, there was no turning back. Raids and counter-raids began. The Lenape bands of the lower Hudson Valley united and attacked the colonists, burning their farms, destroying their settlements, killing, and taking captives. The colonists attacked in kind until finally, in August 1645, a peace treaty was signed "under the blue canopy of heaven."

The Lenape might have survived the war, in which they lost about sixteen hundred, had it not been for the catastrophic epidemics ravaging their nation before, during, and after the conflict. Traveling over trade routes and spreading from person to person within seconds, measles, typhus, diphtheria, and especially smallpox felled the Indians by the thousands. Modern historians estimate that the Europeans' diseases killed anywhere from 50 percent to 91 percent of the Lenape population; between the 1620s and 1700, the Lenape may have been struck by as many as seventeen separate epidemics.

By the end of the 1600s, the Munsee would be all but gone from Mannahatta, and by the middle of the 1700s, the Lenape would be all but gone from Lenapehoking. The first displaced groups fled to New Jersey, Delaware, and western New York, but as the Europeans began arriving in greater numbers, the Indians headed still farther west in search of a new homeland. Evidence of their passing can be found in the place-names they left behind—Muncie, Indiana; Lenapah, Oklahoma; Munceytown, Ontario—but otherwise, they have been all but forgotten. The Munsee language died out at the beginning of the 1800s.

Within less than a century, the Europeans had succeeded in displacing two of Mannahatta's most important populations, one animal, the other human. Neither would be coming back.

CHAPTER 2

Half Freedom

In June 1679 two unassuming Dutchmen sailed aboard the *Charles* from Amsterdam to New York. Traveling under pseudonyms, they were members of a small communal sect, the Labadists, dedicated to simple living, the gospels, and personal prayer. The sect was being persecuted in Europe, and the men—Jasper Danckaerts and Peter Sluyter—had a secret mission: to find a safe place in which to establish a new community. They eventually found one in Bohemia Manor, Maryland, where they set up America's first communal colony, but before doing so, they spent much time in Manhattan. Danckaerts kept a journal of their trip, which was not discovered until almost two centuries later, in 1864, by a man from Long Island browsing in an old bookstore in Amsterdam.

While in Manhattan, Danckaerts and Sluyter hiked the length of the island from south to north, almost certainly following the Wickquasgeck Trail and so walking along the eastern edge of the future Twenty-third Street block. Along the way, they passed mulberry trees with leaves as big as plates and peach and apple trees so laden with fruit that it seemed they bore more fruit than leaves. At times, too, the men were brought up short, because, Danckaerts wrote, "in passing through this island we sometimes encountered such a sweet smell in the air that we stood still, because we did not know what it was we were meeting."

As they hiked, the men noted that the country they were passing through was "almost entirely taken up, that is, the land is held by private owners." Already the island that had so beguiled the earliest settlers was changing character, from a dazzling natural jewel into a land of farms and fences, piers and pastures, buildings and roads. A tract that included the future Twenty-third Street block was being laid out and surveyed in the same year the Labadists passed by, and the following year it was part of a land grant awarded to a member of one of the island's most disenfranchised peoples, both then and for centuries to come, a Black man named Solomon Pieters.

*   *   *

Both free and enslaved Africans and biracial peoples had been part of New Amsterdam from the start. A decade before the white Europeans settled on the island, an African Portuguese man named Jan (Juan) Rodrigues, raised in the Spanish town of Santo Domingo in the Dominican Republic, took up residence. Known for his linguistic talents, he had been working on a Dutch ship exploring the Hudson River in 1613 when he and several other crewmen were dumped on Mannahatta after a mutiny. The other crewmen sailed off on other ships the following spring, but Rodrigues stayed on, became fluent in the Native American languages, and helped facilitate trade between the Indians and the Europeans. Eventually, he married a woman from the Rockaway tribe and may have been living on the island as late as the 1640s, planting corn, raising livestock, fishing, and hunting.

One of the first slaves to be brought to the colony, in 1626, the same year that Peter Minuit arrived, was Pieter Santomee, the father of the first owner of the Twenty-third Street block. Along with ten other captured men, Pieter had probably been shipped from the Portuguese slave-trading island of São Tomé—hence his last name—off the coast of central West Africa, near the Dutch-controlled regions of Angola and the Congo. Among his fellow enslaved travelers were Manuel de Gerrit de Reus, Paulo Angola, Simon Congo, and Anthony Portuguese. Two years later, the island's first three enslaved women arrived from Angola. All fourteen were "owned" by the West India Company.

Some of these early slaves may have been of mixed African and European heritage, others purely African. Their Christian first names would have been conferred on them either at birth or after their capture, and their last names reflected the wily intentions of savvy traders hoping to sell them at good prices. The Europeans of that era regarded Angolan and Congolese slaves as docile, complacent, and talented in the mechanical arts.

More Africans arrived in the colony in the decade that followed, but until the mid-1650s, there were never more than a few dozen slaves living in all of New Netherland, including Long Island and the Hudson Valley. Many of the early Dutch were uncomfortable with the idea of owning their fellow human beings, and in the colony's earliest years, the West India Company's directors were uncomfortable, too, even consulting theologians on the matter.

As company property, Pieter Santomee and the other enslaved men were the backbone of the colony's labor force, commanded to help build Fort Amsterdam, cut timber and firewood, clear the land for roads, farm the fields, herd livestock, remove dead animals from the streets, and burn limestone and oyster shells to make the lime used in outhouses and in burying the dead. Enslaved men were also sent to retrieve runaways, and a slave named Pieter, perhaps Pieter Santomee, had the unbearable, heart-numbing job of whipping, maiming, and executing criminals, white and Black. The women slaves were probably employed mostly as the domestic servants of company officials.

In the 1630s the West India Company set up slave quarters in a camp called Quartier van de Swarten (Quarter of the Blacks) on the shores of the East River near Seventy-fifth Street, about five miles north of town. Here the captured peoples formed families and had children, shared their African beliefs and traditions, and celebrated their diverse heritages through dance, music, and song.

The colony's slaves were worked from dawn to dusk and often badly treated, but they still had considerably more rights and freedoms than they would in later years under the British and early Americans. They could testify in court and take legal action against whites, earn wages, own property and farmland, marry and baptize their children in the Dutch Reformed Church, and bear arms during emergencies—the latter a testament to how much they were trusted. In 1639, de Reus, aka "the Giant," who had arrived on the same boat as Pieter Santomee and worked for Kieft, brought a case against settler Henric Fredericksen van Bunninck, claiming that the white man owed him fifteen guilders for his labor; de Reus won. Sometime later, the court found English colonist Jan Celes guilty of cutting slave Cleijn Manuel's cow with a knife, and ordered the white man to pay the Black man for damages.

In 1641, when New Amsterdam's entire population still numbered fewer than five hundred, the community was riveted by an incident involving eight slaves, all accused of killing another slave in the woods near their homes by the East River. Shrewdly, the men all pleaded guilty, knowing that the colony could not afford to lose eight able-bodied men. The men were then ordered to draw straws, and the unlucky lot fell to Manuel the Giant. The execution date was set, and one cold January day, a throng of settlers gathered to watch him hang. The executioner tied two strong nooses around his neck and shoved him off the ladder. Both ropes broke, and the Giant fell unhurt to the ground. Stunned, the crowd shouted for mercy. The court listened. De Reus and the other accused men went back to work without further punishment.

Three years later, de Reus, who must have been an outsized presence in the community in more ways than one, appeared in court again, this time with ten other enslaved men, including Pieter Santomee. The men had a surprising request. Having served the West India Company for eighteen years, they argued, it was now time for them and their wives to be set free. They had always considered their enslavement to be temporary anyway and needed their freedom to better provide for their families.

Even more surprisingly, Kieft endorsed their petition, and on February 25, 1644, with the war against the Lenape still raging, the court granted the slaves' request under certain conditions, which became known as "half freedom": the men would pay dues, grain, and one fat hog to the company every year, they would assist the company when needed, and their children would remain enslaved. The first two constraints were similar to those placed on the colony's white settlers, but the last was a different matter altogether. The newly half freed protested vehemently, to no avail. However, the regulation was not widely enforced, and many children continued to live freely with their parents.

Not long thereafter, a dozen or so other enslaved men and women petitioned for, and were granted, their half freedom as well. The arrangement had advantages for the West India Company—Kieft's surprising humanitarian gesture was not so altruistic after all. Under half freedom, the company no longer had to care for some of its older and less productive slaves yet could still demand their services when needed. Also, because the half-freed families were given land grants north of the area settled by whites, the company benefited from both an increase in food production and the added protection the farms provided against Indian attacks.

Some of the "Negroes' farms," as they were known, lay just north of today's City Hall, near Collect Pond, the large body of fresh water where the Lenape had had an encampment. Others lay above what is now Houston Street between Lafayette Street and the Bowery, and still others in today's Greenwich Village and near Washington Square Park. Most of the grants were small, between two and eighteen acres, but they were large enough to keep a couple of cattle and raise enough wheat and vegetables to feed a family. By 1664, there were about thirty Black landowners in Manhattan.

Observed Danckaerts, the incognito Labadist, on his trek uptown, "We went from the city following the Broadway, over the *valley*, or the fresh water. Upon both sides of this way were many habitations of negroes, mulattoes and whites. These negroes were formerly the proper slaves of the (West India) company, but, in consequence of the frequent changes and conquests of the country, they have obtained their freedom and settled themselves down where they have thought proper, and thus on this road, where they have ground enough to live on with their families."

To Pieter Santomee, Kieft granted land near the Bowery on December 15, 1644. Bordering a plot granted to another half-freed slave, Simon Congo, the property ran along the sides of a swamp and amounted "in all to about 6 acres or 3 morgen and 84 rods." That does not sound as if it were particularly desirable property, but it was fertile—and, to a former slave, a dazzling, life-altering prize. When Santomee awoke in his humble thatched-roof home surrounded by fields every morning, he must have praised whatever god or gods he believed in for his reversal of fortune, which was both so small and so momentous. He had his freedom, circumscribed though it was, and he had property. Congo, whom he had known ever since their forced Atlantic crossing together nearly two decades before, lived next door, and other half-freed families lived nearby. In the evenings and on Sundays, they could congregate in each other's homes and enjoy some semblance of a normal life.

Santomee had three sons: Lucas, Solomon, and Mathias. There are no records of their births, or of Lucas's baptism, but Solomon was baptized in the Dutch Reformed Church on November 30, 1642, with no recorded witnesses, and Mathias was baptized three years later, with witnesses "Groot Emanuel, negro, Susanna Congoy, negress." As was customary in the church's baptismal records, the name of their mother was not recorded.

As Santomee's sons grew up, Solomon became known as Solomon Pieters and Lucas as Lucas Pieters. Their last name was derived from their father's first name, then a common custom in both the Dutch Republic and some parts of West Africa. What happened to Mathias is unclear; his name disappeared from the records, and he may have died while still a child.

*   *   *

In 1647 Peter Stuyvesant arrived in New Amsterdam to take over as director general from the disgraced Kieft, recalled for igniting the disastrous Lenape war. The autocratic son of a Calvinist minister, expelled from his university for seducing his landlord's daughter, Stuyvesant had come to New Amsterdam from Curaçao, where he had served as acting governor and taken part in a siege against the Spaniards in Saint Martin. During the assault, an enemy cannonball crushed his right leg. Doctors amputated it just below the knee, and Stuyvesant had it replaced with a wooden leg, bound in silver, which became his trademark.

Stuyvesant and his family sailed into New Amsterdam one bright, sunny day in May 1647, accompanied by four ships filled with soldiers. Everyone was at the landing to greet them—officials, traders, farmers, slaves, and the unhappy Kieft, who would soon be sailing home to Europe, only to drown in a shipwreck en route. But the new director general, stomping boldly off the boat on his peg leg, barely acknowledged the crowd before him and, after a brief ceremony, during which he sat while everyone else stood, headed straight for his new home inside Fort Amsterdam. He had no time for pleasantries. He had work to do.

Thereupon began a seemingly endless string of commands. People must mend their fences, keep their animals in, remove garbage from the streets, repair the fort, and tear down ugly huts and sheds. And that was just the beginning. During his first decade in office, Stuyvesant also turned the town's paths and lanes into regular streets, created a municipal market, and established the city's first hospital, post office, poorhouse, orphanage, Latin school, night watch, and garbage dumps. The colony was growing, and New Amsterdam was no longer an outpost of mostly single men working for the company; by 1664, its population would number over fifteen hundred men, women, and children.

Working in concert with Stuyvesant's strict management style was his intolerance. The only religious services he allowed were those of the Dutch Reformed Church, and he tried to prevent Jews from settling in the colony, for which the West India Company emphatically rebuked him. Jews had invested much capital in the firm; moreover, some of the company's officers in Amsterdam were Jewish. Chagrined, Stuyvesant was forced to let the Jewish newcomers stay, but he harassed them continuously and forbade them from building a synagogue.

It was under Stuyvesant's watch, too, that the colony's slave population increased exponentially. Before his governance, slaves had arrived on the island in small groups, usually brought in by privateers. But in 1655, with Stuyvesant's enthused endorsement, the first slave ship, the *Witte Paard* (White Horse), sailed into New York Harbor carrying nearly four hundred terrified, grieving souls, bound and shackled in a noxious hold. A few weeks later, the slaves were sold at auction for good prices, and avaricious merchants and West India Company officials took note; the Dutch were no longer so uncomfortable with the idea of owning their fellow kind. Other slavers followed, and by the end of Dutch rule in 1664, New Amsterdam was North America's largest slave port. Its slave population numbered 325, with Stuyvesant himself owning 40 slaves, far more than anyone else in town. Anger, sorrow, and despair must have flooded the hearts and minds of Pieter Santomee, Manuel the Giant, and the town's other seventy-odd free and half-free Black men and women.

Along the northern end of white-settled New Amsterdam ran a wall (now Wall Street) erected by slaves at the direction of company officials in 1653. Constructed of logs twelve feet long and sharpened at the top, the wall was built to protect the town from a possible attack coming from New England. The Dutch and the English had gone to war the year before, largely over the sea trade, and troubles between the two colonies had continued, with frequent border disputes and an alarming number of English people moving out of rocky New England and into fertile Dutch lands. By the early 1660s, there were thirteen English communities and only five Dutch ones on supposedly Dutch-controlled Long Island.

When the British attack finally came in August 1664, however, it was not by land but by sea. Four English warships carrying nearly two thousand soldiers under the command of Colonel Richard Nicolls appeared in the harbor, alarming all on shore. Anchoring his forces in Gravesend Bay, opposite Manhattan, Nicolls ordered Stuyvesant to surrender, but offered generous terms, promising that after the takeover, all New Netherland citizens would remain free and in possession of their homes and businesses. Stuyvesant wanted to fight, and tried to rally an army, but the colonists begged him to accept Britain's terms. Stuyvesant capitulated, and on September 8, 1664, the British captured the city with no loss of life. New Netherland was now New York.

*   *   *

Stuyvesant may have been New Amsterdam's largest slave owner and a devoted supporter of the slave trade, but he was also a man of contradictions. Nine months before the British takeover, he had granted half freedom to eight sons of the first generation of half-freed slaves, and three months after the takeover, while the British were allowing him to complete unfinished business, he granted those same eight their full freedom. Among them was Solomon Pieters.

Solomon was now twenty-two years old and engaged to Maria Anthony, whom he married later that year. The daughter of Anthony Portuguese, another of the colony's first slaves and half-freed men, Maria had technically grown up as a slave, but whether that was ever enforced is unclear, and after her marriage to Solomon, she was free as well.

Three years later, the patriarch Pieter Santomee passed away, and Solomon and his brother Lucas inherited their father's Bowery property. "Well known in the colony," according to early land ownership documents, the two brothers were also well prepared to take over their father's responsibilities. Lucas, and likely Solomon as well, had attended a school for boys set up by the Dutch Reformed Church and the West India Company to "train the youth of the Dutch and the Blacks in the knowledge of Jesus Christ" and so were literate men, better educated than most of their peers, white or Black. (The school later evolved into today's Collegiate School, the oldest independent school in the United States, still serving boys only.) Lucas was employed as a barber-surgeon, and Solomon went to work for Sir Edmund Andros, the new British governor of New York, not long after his arrival in the colony in 1674.

A soldier and aristocrat, Andros spoke fluent Dutch and, like other British governors of New York before and after him, was scrupulous in carrying out the peaceful terms of Britain's takeover. He ensured that the Dutch retained their property rights and freedom of religion, and formed an alliance with the Iroquois of upstate New York. But he was recalled to England in 1681 following complaints from English merchants, who accused him of favoring the Dutch traders, taking bribes, and pocketing taxes.

Be that as it may, one month before leaving New York, on December 14, 1680, Andros awarded Solomon Pieters the largest land grant ever given to a Black man: "30 Acres of Upland" stretching approximately between today's Twenty-first and Twenty-sixth streets, Broadway and midway between Sixth and Seventh avenues. The land abutted the Wickquasgeck Trail and included the future Twenty-third Street block.

At the time, Solomon and Maria were living on family property on the Bowery, next door to neighbors they had known since childhood, and it is unclear whether they ever moved to their new land grant. Many settlers of that period preferred to live together in a community, rather than in widely separated farmhouses, and to travel to their fields daily. Solomon may have done the same, rising in the dark predawn hours to eat a hearty breakfast before hiking uptown on the peaceful dirt-grass extension of the Bowery that led to Twenty-third Street, surrounded by birdsong. Or perhaps he hired others to work his land, or dispatched his sons when they were grown, and traveled uptown only periodically to inspect what was going on. He was a relatively wealthy man for colonial New York. Between 1695 and 1699, when a pig cost about two shillings, he was assessed in the Bowery Ward on property worth between fifty and sixty pounds (one pound = twenty shillings). He and Maria were also pillars of the free Black community and members of the Dutch Reformed Church on the Bowery near their home, where they worshipped together with whites—a practice that would be unheard of just two decades later.

As a new property owner, Solomon would almost certainly have grazed livestock on his land and likely cleared and prepared part of it for agriculture, perhaps with the help of oxen. Then, like most colonial New York farmers, he probably planted much corn—food for both people and animals—along with smaller amounts of barley, oats, rye, and wheat. During the spring, he would have tilled and planted the fields, and during the fall, he would have harvested the crops. He may have planted a small orchard, too, and year round, chopped wood, tended to his animals, mended fences, and made repairs, while Maria worked at home, caring for the couple's many children (according to baptismal records, they had nine, but some may not have survived early childhood), preparing meals, managing a vegetable garden, canning fruits, smoking meats, making soap and candles, sewing and mending clothes, and more. Colonial New Yorkers worked nonstop.

Solomon may also have erected some sort of building on his new land, perhaps on the future Twenty-third Street block. A shed or barn likely went up, and maybe a simple house with a dirt floor and thatched roof. Later, too, his children may have lived on the uptown land grant, as it was in their family for over three decades.

Six years after Solomon received his patent, the Dongan Charter of 1686 granted the city a huge tract of Common Lands in the middle of Manhattan abutting the Pieters property. Originally stretching between about Twenty-third and Ninetieth streets, the land was rocky in some parts, swampy in others, and generally unfit for cultivation. The city leased it out to farmers, who used it primarily for grazing. Official cowherds blowing horns would collect the cattle from their barns downtown in the mornings, herd them north to the Common Lands, and bring them back again in the evenings.

Leading to and through the Common Lands was the Boston Post Road, also known as the Eastern Post Road. Opened by King Charles II in 1673, it began at the Battery, ran north along the Bowery, swerved west and north to today's Twenty-third Street and Fifth Avenue, ran northeast through Madison Square Park, and then continued along the island's east side, past Harlem and the Bronx, to Boston. Post riders carried mail along it until the 1840s, when the railroad arrived, and thereafter the road was gradually swallowed up by the growing city. Its vestiges can still be seen in the broad diagonal walkway that runs southwest–northeast through Madison Square Park.

When Solomon died in 1694, at the age of fifty-two, he left all his household goods to Maria, with the provision that upon her death, those goods go to his four daughters. He also left his wife all his real estate and property, with the stipulation that if she remarried, she would get only one half and the rest would go to his children. To his four sons, he bequeathed his "Iron Tooles Implements & utensils of husbandry" and all his guns, swords, and pistols.

On May 15, 1716, the Pieters family sold their uptown tract to a Dutchman and that same year sold their Bowery property as well. Only thirty-five years had passed since Governor Andros granted Solomon his uptown land, but times had changed and changed radically on two major fronts. Black New Yorkers' rights had become severely circumscribed, and the city's real estate had escalated in value. Already by 1700, most African-owned land around Collect Pond had been sold to people of European descent, and by the time Maria sold her land, there were virtually no other "free Negro lots" left in the city. Africans freed after 1712 were not even allowed to own land, meaning that Maria and her children were forbidden by law to pass their property on to their descendants.

The new property law was part of the Black Code of 1712, which was a response to the colony's first slave rebellion earlier that year. The island's slave population had increased exponentially, to about one thousand out of a total population of six thousand, with a busy slave market at the foot of Wall Street by the East River. Conditions for many Africans had become extremely harsh, and whippings were common. Slaves who "misbehaved" were at times tied and dragged through the streets by cart.

Finally, a group of two dozen slaves recently arrived from Africa had had enough. At two A.M. on April 6, 1712, a Sunday morning, they rubbed themselves with a powder provided by a free Black sorcerer in hopes of making themselves invincible and gathered by an orchard on Maiden Lane. Armed with muskets, axes, and knives, they set fire to an outhouse, and when whites rushed to put it out, they ambushed them. Nine whites were killed and seven others wounded. The rioters fled north, and soldiers swept the streets, to discover some of the slaves hiding near Canal Street. At least six slit their throats to avoid capture, and others were imprisoned. Forty slaves—many of them innocent—were then brought to trial, and twenty-six found guilty. Most were hanged, and three were burned alive, with one roasted over a slow fire "in Torment for Eight or ten hours," according to one contemporary account. Another was chained and starved to death, and still another broken alive on a wheel, his bones smashed one by one with a crowbar, while his executioner refreshed himself now and again with a mug of beer. A pregnant woman was kept alive until she gave birth and then executed.

The Black Code of 1712 formalized the already increasingly poisoned race relations rampant in New York City. The code not only barred slaves freed after 1712 from owning land but also allowed masters to punish slaves at their full discretion, forbade slaves from going out after dark without a lantern, forbade slaves from owning firearms, and made manumission prohibitively expensive. The colony's assembly defended this last restriction by asserting, "It is found by Experience that the free Negroes in this colony are an Idle Slothful people and prove very often a charge on the place where they are."

Many prescient free Blacks fled the city soon after the Black Code became law. Most of the Pieters family moved to New Jersey and the Hudson River Valley, where some married into the Ramapo Lenape tribe and flourished. Those who remained in Manhattan were not so lucky. City records show that in 1738, Lucas Pieters, the great-grandson of Pieter

Santomee and grandnephew of Solomon Pieters, was living as an indentured servant, meaning that he had lost not only his material possessions but also the freedom hard-won by his forebears. His ailing wife was forced to enter an almshouse. His family's land was gone. The future Twenty-third Street block now belonged to the Dutch.

CHAPTER 3

The John Horne Farm

In the wilderness of the Hudson Valley, amid small settlements of mostly Dutch and English farms, there once lived a man named Jacob Horne. Together with a friend, he leased some land near the village of Kingston in 1685. Two years later, the local authorities ordered him and all other residents of the Hudson Valley to take the British oath of allegiance. He refused—he was Dutch. His original name may have been Jacobus Hoörne.

What the repercussions of Jacob's refusal were is unclear, but he may have been forced to leave the valley, because six years later he was living in Flushing, New York. Here he signed on to the *Adventure Galley*, a square-rigged, thirty-two-gun vessel commandeered by the dashing Scotsman Captain William Kidd. Setting sail from New York Harbor on September 6, 1696, the ship voyaged across the Atlantic and around the tip of Africa to India, where Captain Kidd, hitherto a highly respected privateer with a mandate to hunt enemy ships and pirates, turned pirate himself.

There is no evidence that Horne participated in Kidd's raids or even returned to New York—he may have died at sea—but he left behind a son, John Horne, the man who would purchase the land encompassing the future Twenty-third Street block from the Pieters family in 1716. The Horne family would then own that land for more than one hundred years.

* * *

John Horne was about ten years old when his father set sail with Captain Kidd. The boy had spent his earliest years in Kingston, but by 1700, when he was about fourteen, was living in Manhattan. His mother, Sarah, had apprenticed him to the wheelwright Peter Minthorne, also previously of Kingston and perhaps a relative or family friend. Minthorne had agreed to teach the youth the ins and outs of the wheelwright trade and how to "Read and Write perfectly the English Tongue." In return, John had pledged to work for him for six years.

Like most apprentices of the day, John likely lived in his master's home, sleeping in an attic or outbuilding, and was provided with meals. The use of apprentices was widespread in the New York colony, with some masters, including Minthorne, serving as kindhearted surrogate parents and others viciously abusing their young charges, beating or overworking them until they ran away, to sleep in the streets, barefoot and half starving. New York has never been kind to runaways.

By the time young John arrived in Manhattan, it was already well on its way to becoming anglicized. Most of its Dutch men and women had accepted their English conquerors, and many had learned to speak the English language. Most had also embraced a new legal system that combined elements of English and Dutch law, and honored the Dutch land grants, thereby solidifying the ties between the new British authorities and the old well-to-do Dutch families. Unlike in New England, no democratic town meetings or elected assemblies were established, but also unlike in New England, all religions and ethnicities continued to be welcomed. The harassment of Jews instituted under Stuyvesant ended, an influx of French Huguenots fleeing persecution had arrived, and most of the city's diverse populations—Blacks being a glaring exception—were flourishing.

Settled Manhattan now extended as far north as Maiden Lane. The wall at Wall Street had been torn down, exposing a noxious garbage dump behind it, while farther north, the once peaceful and pristine Collect Pond festered, completely despoiled. The waters in which the Lenape had fished were now a rotting, malarial swamp and the only place in the city where the slaughtering of animals was allowed. Butchers and hide tanners operated along its shores, and an island in its middle was used for executions.

With the wall finally gone, Wall Street was serving as the town's commercial heart. A new City Hall stood at the corner of Wall and Broad,

Trinity Church stood at Wall and Broadway, and a bustling wharf extended
from the street into the East River. In New York Harbor nested a resident
fleet of more than 160 river boats, ships, and sloops, hulls creaking as men
scuttled along gangplanks carrying chests and casks.

As young John went about his daily life, learning how to bend wood
and insert spokes into wheels, running errands, and delivering work to
clients, he would have rubbed shoulders with everyone from wealthy
merchants and British officials to brick makers and shipwrights to ne'er-
do-wells and the many pirates then roaming the streets. Their presence had
been a given in the city since the early 1690s, when Britain was at war with
France and both countries relied on privateers to capture enemy ships and
their cargoes. The practice had proved so profitable that many privateers,
like Captain Kidd, had turned pirate and were now attacking vessels of
any country, for their own personal gain. Boston had started refusing entry
to pirate ships, but New York, ever tolerant, especially when it came to
money, was still embracing them—and their spoils.

Among the pirates' biggest fans was New York's own governor, Benjamin
Fletcher, who not only allowed the pirates to swagger about unmolested
but entertained them in his home. When pirate Thomas Tew sailed into
New York Harbor in 1694, Fletcher invited him to dinner, took him out
for a night on the town, and gave him a gold watch in the hope that he
would return. When Captain Edward Coates arrived in port with an estimated sixteen thousand pounds of stolen goods, he gave the governor his
ship as a gift. And even when the murderous Captain Richard Glover, who
had burned alive the crews of two East India Company ships, dropped
anchor, Fletcher remained jovial and serene, the perfect host.

Young John probably listened wide-eyed to all the fantastic tales about
the outlaws, but the pirate who would have interested him most must have
been Captain Kidd. In addition to Kidd's connection to John's father, the
privateer had lived in New York for years before his fateful expedition,
forming friendships with powerful men, marrying a wealthy widow, setting
up housekeeping on Pearl Street, and buying a coveted pew in Trinity
Church. Many New Yorkers felt as if they knew him personally, and John,
along with everyone else in the city, must have devoured every bit of news

about the once dashing captain, from his arrest in Boston Harbor in July 1699 to his death by hanging in London on May 23, 1701.

*   *   *

When John was about twenty-seven, he married a cousin of the wife of his master Peter Minthorne. The bride was a young widow, Rachel (Webber) Swansten, whose parents owned property on the Bowery, and who was related to Deacon Webber, a well-respected man of the cloth.

The couple prospered, and three years after their marriage, on May 15, 1716, John and his brother-in-law Cornelius Webber bought the same thirty acres of upland that Governor Andros had granted to Solomon Pieters in 1680. Along its eastern edge now ran a new road, Blooming-dale Road, opened only thirteen years before. An unpaved dirt lane about sixty-five feet wide, it began at today's Twenty-third Street and Fifth Avenue, where the Bowery then ended, and continued at a northwest diagonal to about 114th Street, following the old Wickquasgeck Trail in parts. It would be widened in 1760, and extended in 1795 to 147th Street, where it would be merged into Kingsbridge Road in the Bronx. Down-town, it connected to Broadway, the name that would later be adopted for the entire route.

Not surprisingly, Bloomingdale Road led to Bloomingdale, a hamlet centered roughly on today's One Hundredth Street. First settled by a few Dutch farmers, its name was a corruption of the Dutch word *Bloemen-dael*, meaning "vale of flowers." Washington Irving described the haven as "a sweet and rural valley, beautiful with many a bright wild flower, refreshed by many a pure streamlet, and enlivened here and there by a delec-table little Dutch cottage." The name "Bloomingdale" was also used to refer to the entire sparsely settled west side of Manhattan north of about today's Forty-second Street.

Much of Manhattan was by then all but denuded of its once magnificent forest. Many of the several million trees that had covered 80 to 85 percent of the island when the Dutch arrived had been burned as fuel, either directly for heating and cooking or indirectly as charcoal for creating the high temperatures needed for metalworking, brickmaking, and glassmaking.

Only a small percentage of the forest had been used for building homes, ships, and fences.

Much of the island's larger wildlife was also gone. In 1686, the colonists had been given license to hunt and destroy wolves, the last of the big predators still roaming Manhattan, and the late-night howling that had once driven fear into homesteads had been silenced. Pigs, chickens, and cattle could now rout, peck, and graze without fear.

In the mid-1700s, other hamlets would emerge along Bloomingdale Road, to flourish until around the time of the Civil War. Among them were Great Kill, centered near today's Times Square and named for a deep, cool stream that emptied into the Hudson (*kill* was Dutch for "waterbed" or "stream"); Harsenville, around today's Seventieth to Seventy-fifth streets; and Striker's Bay, around today's Ninetieth to Ninety-ninth streets by the Hudson. Most of the families who lived along the road were Dutch, or "Knickerbockers," as they were colloquially known, a term coined by Irving in reference to the pants rolled up just below the knees that the early Dutch male settlers wore.

Still occupying the center of Manhattan directly across from the Horne-Webber purchase were the city-owned Common Lands, leased out to farmers for grazing. Not until after the American Revolution would the city, strapped for cash, begin selling the lands to private owners.

Like Solomon and Maria Pieters before them, John and Rachel Horne probably continued to live in lower Manhattan in the years immediately after their uptown purchase, with John traveling along the Bowery to Bloomingdale Road regularly to work or inspect his new fields. The couple also owned land on the Bowery and must have still been living there in 1727 when John was elected collector of the Bowery Division of the Out Ward. They did move uptown soon thereafter, though, building a home in the center of today's Fifth Avenue just south of Twenty-third Street.

*   *   *

The Horne home would have been small and simple at first, constructed of wood, with only two or three rooms, dirt floors, unglazed windows, and a large hearth and walk-in fireplace where a cauldron of stew could bubble above an open fire. Later, the Hornes would add more rooms and fireplaces, a wooden floor, an attic, a root cellar, and a wide veranda. Out back they erected a barn, from which John, dressed in a starched linen shirt and dark-colored breeches, hitched up a wagon on Sunday mornings to take the family to services at the Dutch Reformed Church on the Bowery, the same church where the Pieters family had once worshipped.

By 1736 the Hornes had expanded their farm further, to include a successful wagon-building and wheel-making shop. Stagecoaches, mail couriers, and travelers on horseback were constantly passing by and were often in need of services.

To the south of the Horne property, along what is now about Twenty-first Street, ran Abingdon Road, also known as Love Lane, a tranquil, isolated route that led west and then south to Greenwich Village. Some of the land between John Horne's property and Abingdon Road was city owned, but he blithely ignored that fact by fencing it in and using it to graze cattle. Decades later, his son Jacob Horne would do the same and, when issued a summons for the encroachment, would cavalierly respond that he "had a Small Patent [for the land] which he could not find at present."

As the years went by, John, Rachel, and their growing family continued to prosper, as did colonists all over the island. More vessels were docking in port each year, more wharfs were being built, and the pastures south of Collect Pond were being laid out with streets, homes, and businesses. New taverns, coffeehouses, and inns had sprouted up, and retail shops were buzzing with customers. Among the many items the Hornes could have purchased in the 1720s and 1730s were imported furniture and window glass, pipes and snuff, Canary wine and olive oil, coffee and tea, books and stationery goods, and wigs and stays (corsets). Rachel might have visited Mrs. Edwards's cosmetic shop, which offered "An admirable Beautifying Wash, for Hands Face and Neck [that] makes the Skin soft, smooth and plump," or convinced John to buy one of Nichols Bailey's chairs specifically designed for the ladies. The couple might also have perused the many fine items being crafted by the city's growing number of goldsmiths, watchmakers, and jewelers.

Much of the reason for the city's prosperity was its bustling trade with the West Indies, which had largely come about because of England's insatiable hunger for sugar. Once a luxury enjoyed only by the wealthy, sugar was now considered an essential foodstuff for people of every class. By 1720, half the ships entering New York Harbor were directly on their way to or from the Caribbean sugar plantations, and another one quarter en route to the Caribbean via other North American colonies.

All of this had led to yet more explosive growth in the city's slave industry. By 1746, New York's African population numbered nearly 2,500, or about 20 percent of the city's overall population of 11,700, and by 1750, New York City was home to more slaves than any other North American city except Charleston, South Carolina, and New Orleans. Between 40 and 50 percent of all New York households held a slave—including, in all probability, the Hornes, as census records show the family owning slaves by 1790. The tract of land that had once been filled with the hopes and dreams of a newly freed Black family now held the country's greatest evil. New York did not abolish slavery until 1827, long after most other northern states.

*　　*　　*

By 1760, the John Horne farm was in the hands of his son Jacob, who married Dutchwoman Annatje Somerendyk. The couple had three children, including a son named John after his grandfather. The younger John Horne, known as John the Second, would inherit the family farm, expand its operations exponentially, and die on the property in 1815 at the then ripe old age of seventy. Around 1800, the family changed the spelling of their last name to "Horn."

As a teenager, John the Second mustered under a Captain John Grant for a year and, as a young man, served in the American Revolution. Before the war began, he married Jemima Hopper of Great Kill Farm farther north on Bloomingdale Road and may have crept behind enemy lines to visit her during the conflict. Bloomingdale Road, like the rest of Manhattan, was under British control for almost the entire duration of the war.

"No taxation without representation"—the rebellious cries had begun in Boston in the 1750s and 1760s, but were soon picked up by colonists in New York. Troops from George Washington's Continental Army arrived in the city in January 1776, to secure the East River with forts on both banks, build Fort Washington on Manhattan's northern tip, and surround Brooklyn Heights, the key to the city's defenses, with protective entrenchments.

The following June and July, over one hundred British ships carrying thousands of soldiers anchored in the waters off Staten Island. New Yorkers were astonished. Such a large fleet had never been seen before in North America: "I could not believe my eyes. I declare that I thought all London was afloat," declared one astounded rifleman. Under the command of General Sir William Howe, the troops were intent on not only taking the city but making it their headquarters. The British military had maintained a presence in Manhattan for decades and felt at home on the island. British officers enjoyed its many urban pleasures: oyster bars serving bivalves seven or eight inches long, taverns offering cheap liquor and plentiful prostitutes, bowling fields, cricket fields, horse racing, bullbaiting, and a plethora of shops. They also enjoyed spending their weekends in the countryside north of the city, traveling along the Bowery and Bloomingdale Road, past the John Horne farm, and stopping for a glass or two of mead at lively roadside cottages.

Howe's forces landed at Gravesend Bay, Brooklyn, on August 22, 1776, and four days later, his troops drove the revolutionaries back to their first line of entrenchments in Brooklyn Heights. But on the night of August 29, under the cover of rain and fog, 9,500 rebel troops—likely including John the Second—loaded all their stores and equipment onto small boats and crossed over to Manhattan. The men were forbidden to speak or even cough. The British didn't even realize they were gone until the following morning.

Two weeks later, Howe attacked Manhattan. The Continental Army fell back, and the British pushed quickly forward, to halt at the northern end of Central Park. The next day, Washington's troops poured down from Harlem Heights. The British retreated, but casualties were heavy, and Washington, fearing British reinforcements, evacuated the city.

Manhattan was now in British hands and would remain so for seven years. Thousands of British Loyalists who had fled returned, to be joined in the years that followed by thousands more Loyalists from other colonies and thousands of Black slaves who had been promised their freedom in return for supporting the king. By 1782, an estimated fifty thousand

Loyalist civilians were living behind British lines in and around the city, along with tens of thousands of Tory troops and camp followers.

New York became a city divided, with many of its residents cheering the Tories on and others engaging in subversive activity. Some merchants made a good living selling to the British military, and with food scarce, many farmers, likely including the Hornes, were forced to surrender their crops to the redcoats in return for certificates of payment. The certificates rarely paid what the foodstuffs were worth, and soon the farmers were surreptitiously selling their crops on a burgeoning black market. A vicious guerrilla war—cattle rustling, the burning of crops, robbery, abduction—spread over the countryside.

The war in effect ended on October 19, 1781, when the British General Lord Cornwallis surrendered to the Continental Army at Yorktown, but the last redcoats did not leave the city for another two years. Not until the morning of November 25, 1783 did troops led by General Washington, General Henry Knox, and Governor George Clinton begin marching south from Harlem, tramping along the Boston Post Road to the Horne farm before turning onto the Bowery and continuing farther south.

All the Horne family must have turned out to watch the procession pass—a ragtag group of men and youth of all ages, dressed in dusty blue or gray coats, tricornered hats, and knee-length breeches, carrying muskets and powder horns. John the Second may have been home with his family by then, or he may have been proudly marching with the troops, waving to his wife and children as he passed by.

*   *   *

After the war, General Washington took up residence in Manhattan and on April 30, 1789 was inaugurated as the first president of the United States at Federal Hall on Wall Street. The city served as the nation's capital until July 1790, when it was moved to Philadelphia.

Like many New Yorkers and the British brass before him, Washington relaxed by taking drives in the countryside. His favorite excursion was "The Fourteen Miles Around," which started at the northwest corner of Franklin Square and Cherry Street, proceeded up the Boston Post Road to Apthorp's Lane at about Ninetieth Street, crossed to Bloomingdale Road, and then returned to its starting point, passing the John Horne farm on the way. Various stagecoach operators offered the excursion, as well as shorter tours, including one that just went "around the tour by Horn's."

The first federal census of 1790 found the Horne household containing four white males age sixteen and older, three white males under age sixteen, eight white females, and two slaves, gender not stated. Ten years later, the census listed the Horne household as containing two white males under age sixteen, one white male between twenty-six and forty-five, one white male over forty-five (presumably John the Second), one female between sixteen and twenty-six, three females over forty-five, and one slave, again gender not stated.

When John the Second died in 1815, he left behind a farm that included eleven dwelling houses, two shops, six stables, a barn, and about thirty-four acres. Some outbuildings stood on the future Twenty-third Street block, while the family home with the wide veranda remained in the middle of Fifth Avenue just south of Twenty-third Street. A lane shaded by "venerable and stately sycamore trees" led from the house to the road. John the Second had done his great-grandfather Jacobus Hoörne proud.

CHAPTER 4

The Making of Block 825

He was just twenty-one when he started, a young, inexperienced, dark-haired man with a temper and a passion for details and math. From a large, close-knit Irish family in Albany, he was the son of a brass founder and jeweler who had fought in the American Revolution, been captured by the British, and survived incarceration in a brutal prison in Halifax, Canada, showing a grit and determination that he passed on to his son.

For thirteen years, the son toiled, operating out of a field office at the corner of Christopher and Herring (now Bleecker) streets in Greenwich Village, then still a rural area. Almost every day, he passed by the Herring Street home of Thomas Paine, author of *Common Sense* and *The Age of Reason*, whom he greatly admired and often observed sitting by an open window, a book before him, a decanter filled with an amber-colored liquid at his elbow.

From Greenwich Village, the young man tramped farther north, to and through the future Twenty-third Street block and beyond. Along the way, he took meticulous measurements and pounded almost sixteen hundred bolts and markers into rock and earth, inscribing what would become the most famous grid in the world upon the land. Often working alone, he walked for many miles in all kinds of weather, cutting his way through underbrush and trespassing on private lands. He must have looked like a tramp or even a criminal to some, but by the time his project was finished, he was JOHN RANDEL JR., a nationally recognized figure.

The idea for the Commissioners' Plan of 1811, as Randel's grid was formally known, had begun years earlier, when it became apparent that in order to thrive, New York needed to expand in an orderly fashion. A commission of three prominent citizens (John Rutherfurd, Gouverneur Morris, and Simeon De Witt) was appointed in 1807 and given three years in which to come up with a plan. The commissioners considered a "natural city" layout that would take into account the contours of the land, and a "square block" plan, with all sides of each block the same length, but rejected them both. Then one day, while walking beside Cedar Creek in the future Madison Square Park across from the future Twenty-third Street block, or so legend has it, the commissioners saw a shadow cast by a wire screen that workmen were using to sift sand. The shadow showed wide lines of wire running north–south and narrower lines running east–west—the apparent inspiration for Manhattan's broad north–south avenues and thinner east–west streets.

Using a grid plan to lay out a city was nothing new. It had been used for centuries in Europe, Central America, and Asia, and was already in place in some American cities, including Philadelphia and Albany. But New York's grid was designed on a grand and sophisticated scale, the likes of which had never been seen before. Randel needed three years just to survey the island's still largely undeveloped 11,400 acres north of today's Canal Street and draw a map, a detailed document nearly nine feet long. Then he took another six years to measure elevations and mark each future intersection of streets with a white marble marker four feet tall. He used advanced instruments that he had designed himself, and carefully recorded everything in forty-five thick notebooks. Finally, he and his wife devoted more years to drawing what became known as the Randel Farm Maps—ninety-two detailed colored maps that overlaid the island's natural topography and property lines with the proposed grid.

After Randel, New York was never the same. "The year 1811 marks the end of the little old city and the beginning of the great modern metropolis," wrote I. N. Phelps Stokes in his monumental *The Iconography of Manhattan Island, 1498–1909*, published in six volumes between 1915 and 1928, and still considered the most important history of the city ever written.

*   *   *

Implemented largely as it was envisioned, the Commissioners' Plan divided Manhattan north of Houston Street into a neat rectangular grid of twelve one-hundred-foot-wide avenues crossed every two hundred feet by sixty-foot-wide crosstown streets. The heaviest traffic was expected to run east–west, off the docks, and the crosstown streets were expected to carry breezes from the rivers into the island's interior. At the time, there were no street cars and only a handful of carriages, and most buildings were under three stories tall.

The exacting grid was visionary, but also suffocating and ruthless. It made no allowance for the natural contours of the land or for any existing streets, including the Bloomingdale and Boston Post roads. There were to be very few parks or public spaces, and no circles, ovals, or curved streets, only right-angled ones. All the island's many hills, some as high as 154 feet, were to be leveled, and its valleys, swamps, and ponds filled in. Furthermore, each of the grid's two thousand or so blocks was to be given a number and subdivided into standardized lots of about twenty-five by one hundred feet, which would make them easier to buy and sell. The Twenty-third Street block's number was, and still is, 825.

In many ways, the grid suited Manhattan's utilitarian, profit-driven nature. Right-angled roads and structures were the cheapest and most practical to build, and the most efficient to navigate. Let other cities, such as the then much-maligned Washington, D.C., embrace the romanticism of circular drives, leisurely boulevards, and pastoral vistas. New York had no time for such nonsense. It was a city on the move.

Randel's map extended to 155th Street, a fact that "caused a good deal of merriment" among ordinary citizens, who poked fun at the grid's commissioners for their optimism, for which the commissioners "felt called upon to apologize." Yet their idea was that the grid would take many decades to implement and would grow gradually as the city expanded, a bold outlook at the time.

At first, many New Yorkers supported the 1811 grid plan, seeing it as a necessary remedy for the chaos of Lower Manhattan. But as the years passed and the grid began to grow, so did anger and bitterness against it. In 1818, one of Chelsea's earliest and most prominent residents, Clement Clarke Moore, railed, "The natural inequalities of the ground are destroyed . . . These are men who would have cut down the seven hills of Rome."

Adjustments to the Commissioners' Plan were made. Bloomingdale Road was allowed to remain, and squares were opened up at those points where it crossed the avenues. More parks were added, most notably the city's signature Central Park, created decades after the grid. Designed by Frederick Law Olmsted and Calvert Vaux, the park embraced all the romantic ideals that Randel eschewed—curves and ovals, hills and valleys, rocks and trees.

As for Randel, he went on to become chief engineer for the Chesapeake & Delaware Canal Company. It was a highly coveted post, but while there, he made a shocking error. He underestimated the cost of building the canal by some 82 percent and was summarily dismissed. Not one to take a hit lying down, Randel filed for breach of contract and was awarded $226,885.84, a staggering sum for the time (about $5 million today). He and his wife retired to a one-thousand-acre farm in Maryland that they named after themselves, Randelia.

It was the beginning of the end for the grid's creator, as in the ensuing decades, he made other miscalculations and filed more lawsuits until he was widely regarded as an erratic, self-aggrandizing, and unpleasant man. Yet through it all, Randel remained a visionary. In 1846 he proposed building an elevated railroad over Broadway that would lead to a leafy suburb stretching north of 155th Street—then a fabulously inventive idea, to be taken up decades later by other engineers. The city came close to accepting Randel's plan, but in the end turned it down.

A dozen or so years later, Randel and his wife, who had already lost much of their fortune, became embroiled in a lawsuit with a neighbor. All their possessions, including a family carriage, two cows, seven hogs, a piano, a looking glass, clothing, and a clock, were seized. Then their only surviving child, a son in his twenties, died. Broke and bereft, Randel again tried to interest the city in building an elevated railroad, and again was rejected. He died on August 2, 1865, of "brain inflammation," and his name disappeared into the history books even as his grid grew in size and stature.

*   *   *

Though the commissioners' original grid did not include many parks or public squares, it did include some, the largest of which was the Grand Parade, to be carved out of the Common Lands and neighboring tracts. Initially planned to stretch between Twenty-third and Thirty-fourth streets, Third and Seventh avenues, and thus encompass block 825, the Grand Parade was to be used primarily for military purposes. Three years later, however, the commissioners revised their plan, shrunk the parade by almost two thirds, and named it Madison Square, in honor of President James Madison. Later still, the square was reduced to its current size, covering 6.8 acres between Twenty-third and Twenty-sixth streets, Fifth and Madison avenues.

At the time the Grand Parade was envisioned, the Common Lands contained a stone-and-brick U.S. Arsenal, diagonally across Bloomingdale Road to the north of the Twenty-third Street block. Enclosed by a high, forbidding wall, and built far away from the settled town because its munitions had the unfortunate habit of exploding, the arsenal had been erected in 1807 as part of the city's defense system against the British in the War of 1812. The war never reached the city, however, and ended three years after it began.

To the east of the arsenal stretched a potter's field, where the unknown, the destitute, and victims of yellow fever were buried until 1797, when a new potter's field was opened in Washington Square. The Bellevue Institution (now Bellevue Hospital), named for the "Bell Vue" farm on which it stood, was conveniently located nearby and contained a "pesthouse" where the yellow fever victims were sent. Rickety carts, piled high with bodies wrapped in yellow sheets to alert their handlers of the contagion, were a common sight along the roads near the Horne farm, and the family must have kept a close eye on them.

Two of John the Second's sons, Joseph and Jacob, must also have kept a close eye on the arsenal and marched in militias on the parade grounds.

They had both enlisted in the War of 1812, and Joseph, a major, had built some of the war's fortifications, including a tower at 123rd Street and Amsterdam Avenue that was named after him, Fort Horn.

Per John the Second's will, his farm had been divided into eight lots, one for each of his children, daughters as well as sons. To his daughter Margaret—perhaps a favorite child—and her husband, Christopher Mildeberger, he had bequeathed an especially attractive tract that included most of the eastern third of the Twenty-third Street block and the family home that stood in the middle of Fifth Avenue below Twenty-third Street. The couple moved in, in 1820.

Margaret had married well. Mildeberger, a courtly man of fine manners, was a wealthy merchant and "leather dresser"—someone who smooths and finishes leather. His offices were downtown in the heart of "the Swamp," as the headquarters of the leather trade was known. Stretching between today's John and Franklin streets, the area was named for its soft, low, wet ground, the result of the overflow of the industry's enormous tanning vats.

Some of Margaret's siblings may have been displeased that Mildeberger was of Bavarian, not Dutch, extraction, but he *was* the grandson of a captain in the Royal Guards of the King of Bavaria, who had come to America on a visit in 1735 and liked it so much he stayed. His father, Oliver, had made a fortune in the leather business, and Christopher had inherited most of his fortune. He and Margaret had six children, and when they died, were buried in the cemetery at St. Mark's Church in the Bowery, as befitted their solid social status.

John the Second left the other two thirds of the Twenty-third Street block in equal-sized parcels to three of his other children. His daughter Mary, nicknamed Polly, inherited the land to the immediate west of Margaret's land. She, too, had married well. Her husband, James Striker, was the son of Gerrit Striker, a well-to-do farmer from an old Dutch family who had built a mansion, Striker's Bay, near the foot of today's Ninety-sixth Street, overlooking the Hudson. The elder Striker had died before the Revolutionary War began and left everything to James, then still a teenager, but before James could take up the farm's management, he was conscripted into the British Army. He escaped at the first chance he got and fled to New Jersey, where he joined George Washington's Light Horse

Troop. Then, in the summer of 1780, longing for home, he disguised himself as a yeoman and slipped over the Hudson by boat to marry his sweetheart and first wife, Mary Hopper, also of Bloomingdale Road.

Soon thereafter, James returned to war and Mary moved into Striker's Bay, where James's mother still lived. One year later, the British took over the mansion and forced Mary, James's mother, and the other women in the household to cook their meals, mend their clothes, and polish their boots and bayonets. The women seethed, but obeyed.

After the war was over, Mary died of natural causes, leaving three children behind, and in 1790, James married Polly Horne. Being his second wife must have been hard for her at first—after all, her husband had risked his life for his first wife, who'd been a heroic survivor of British occupation. Nonetheless, Polly moved into Striker's Bay, where she had eight children, and leased the land she had inherited from her father to other farmers.

Among the Hornes' closest neighbors was the Varian family, who owned farms to both the north (around today's Twenty-sixth Street) and south (Eighteenth to Twentieth streets) of their property. Isaac Varian had purchased his northern farm, carved out of the original Horne-Webber purchase, from the Hornes in the 1780s and built a house partly made out of a ship's cabin that remained a Bloomingdale Road landmark for years. His son Isaac Leggett Varian would later serve as New York City's mayor from 1839 to 1841 and as state senator from 1842 to 1845.

Other nearby neighbors included the Dyckmans, Grenzebacks, Semlers, and Oodhoudts, while farther north lived the Hoppers, Webbers, Somerindycks, Strikers, and more Dyckmans, as well as the Harsens, Motts, Cozines, and Havemeyers—most descendants of early Dutch settlers. The families had known each other for generations and were closely entwined through culture, friendship, and marriage. Wrote one of the descendants of the Striker, Hopper, and Mott families in 1908, "Following the old-time custom, when to marry an outsider was seldom heard of, and intermarriages among cousins usual, the old residents were so connected that from present Union Square to Bloomingdale village (One Hundredth Street) the Dutch settlers were joined by ties of consanguinity little understood in these days."

Life along Bloomingdale Road was pastoral, but not quiet. Stage-coaches, private carriages, horsemen, and carts heaped high with agricultural goods bound for the settled city farther south passed by day and night, kicking up dust in summer, splashing through puddles and mud in spring and fall. In the winter, sleighs with loudly ringing bells, filled with carousing weekenders, shot past—perhaps by the hundreds, because in 1847, one Bloomingdale Road family sitting on their piazza counted 1,160 sleighs passing by in a single hour. Some were brightly colored cutters driven by gentlemen in fur caps, bearskins on their laps; others were large family sleighs wrapped in animal skins tied on with red ribbons.

Tradespeople also wandered up and down the road, hawking their wares, along with chimney sweeps, small African American boys dressed in rags led by a master in tailcoats and a tall hat. "Sweep, O-O-O-O! From the bottom to the top, without a ladder or a rope. Sweep, O-O-O-O!" the boys cried in a refrain that became romanticized by songwriters and poets of the day. But cleaning chimneys was dirty, hard, and dangerous work. The flues had to be scraped by hand to prevent them from catching fire, and only children were small enough to crawl through the narrow, often zigzagging and hot passageways. Dressed in underwear and stocking caps with slits for eyes, the boys used their blankets, under which they slept at night, to collect the soot, which was then sold as fertilizer. Their skin became leathery and covered with cuts, and eye infections, tuberculosis, and lashings by masters were constant dangers.

A favorite stop among weekend revelers was the Buck's Horn Tavern, on Abingdon Road a few hundred feet below Twenty-third Street and a stone's throw away from the Horne family home. Set back from the street on a ten-foot-high hill, with the head and horns of a buck at its entrance, the roadhouse was already "old and well-known" by 1816. City folk liked to take a drive north on the Bowery and Bloomingdale Road, stop on their way back at the roadhouse for refreshment, head west on Abingdon Road, travel south through Greenwich Village, and return to the city through Lispenard Meadows, a drained salt marsh near today's Greenwich and Spring streets. Filled with wildflowers in spring and summer, snowy vistas in winter, the meadows were a favorite spot for lovers.

Even so, some might have shivered as they passed through the meadows, as an infamous murder had occurred there a generation earlier. The crime, which led to what is widely regarded as the first murder trial in U.S. history, had involved a beautiful young woman named Gulielma Sands, or Elma for short, and her lover Levi Weeks, a carpenter and the brother of a well-known architect. The two lived in separate rooms at a boarding-house on Greenwich Street and were planning to elope on the night of December 22, 1799, or so Elma told her sister and a friend a few days before she disappeared.

On January 2, 1800, Elma's body was discovered at the bottom of a well near Lispenard Meadows. Her neck was broken. Levi was arrested and quickly indicted, though the evidence against him was circumstantial and slim.

With the help of his brother, Levi retained the legal services of Alexander Hamilton and Aaron Burr, then working together as a team. Most New Yorkers thought Levi was guilty, but the defense team raised doubts, and after a two-day trial and five minutes of jury deliberation, he was acquitted. He promptly left the city and moved to Natchez, Mississippi, where he prospered.

*   *   *

In 1823, the arsenal in Madison Square across Bloomingdale Road from the Horn farms was abandoned, and the building and land sold for $6,000 (about $150,000 today) to the Society for the Reformation of Juvenile Delinquents, which erected the first juvenile reformatory in the country on the site. Known as the House of Refuge, it held only 6 boys and 3 girls at first, but soon expanded to contain about 300 youths, with 1,678 inmates admitted in its first decade. Most had been arrested for petty crime or vagrancy—that is, poverty.

Looking out at the House of Refuge from their farmland, the Horns—now spelling their name without the *e*—would have seen two stone buildings, each 150 feet long and two stories high, surrounded by a stone wall 17 feet high and more than 2 feet thick. One of the buildings was for boys and the other for girls; a high wooden fence separated the two. Also on the property was a brick building for the superintendent and his family, a foundry, a bakery, a stable and carriage house, an exercise yard, and flower and vegetable gardens.

Bells rang throughout the day. The first pealed at sunrise, rousing the young inmates from their beds in locked, windowless five-by-eight cells, and the second rang fifteen minutes later, when guards unlocked the cells and herded the youth into washrooms. From there, it was on to the chapel for prayers, to the dining rooms for breakfast, and to the workshops, where labor began at seven thirty A.M. The boys toiled for eight hours a day making brushes, cane chairs, brass nails, saddles, and shoes, while the girls worked in the laundry, sewed clothes, and performed general domestic tasks. A four-tier badge system separated the children according to their "moral conduct," and the badges had to be worn on the left arm at all times.

The inmates also attended school for four hours a day, where they learned how to read and write, and received copious instruction in the Protestant religion. The goal was to turn them into responsible workers who would "earn an honest living, and become, from degraded outcasts, useful and reputable citizens of this Republic." After a youth was deemed reformed, he or she was usually bound out as an apprentice. Most of the boys were sent to work on farms or whaling ships, and most of the girls became domestic servants.

Among the earliest residents of the Girls' Refuge were C.A., a fifteen- or sixteen-year-old epileptic, the daughter of a "depraved mother" who had been arrested for stealing a watch; J.M.C., a "vicious and criminal" twelve-year-old thief whose mother was living in an almshouse; and J.G., a sixteen- or seventeen-year-old who had formed "evil" associates and was a "seducer of young females." Among the earliest residents of the Boys' Refuge were S.C.B., a fourteen-year-old orphan and "one of the most extraordinary instances of juvenile depravity" that the board had ever seen (he had already served two terms for stealing in the city's adult penitentiary); D.B.L., a fifteen-year-old tambourine player who had performed in dance halls and was arrested "on suspicion of having stolen a shawl"; and J.P., a youth of about fourteen, who "stole a goose from on board a sloop."

And then there was Austin Reed, inmate number 1221. An African American youth who entered the reformatory in 1833, Reed later wrote an extraordinary memoir, discovered only in 2009 at an estate sale in

Rochester, New York. Published in 2016, *The Life and Adventures of a Haunted Convict* tells the story of man who spent much of his life incarcerated, first at the House of Refuge and later at New York's infamous Auburn state prison.

Reed had started out in an unusually good position for an African American child in the early 1800s, as he was born into a middle-class family in the booming upstate town of Rochester. But after his father died when he was six, his mother, struggling to make ends meet, hired him out as an indentured servant to a white farmer. Unhappy and rebellious, with "home still hanging in mind," Reed refused to work and was dragged to a barn and whipped—a visceral reminder of the slavery era, which had ended in New York just a few years before. Reed retaliated by trying to set fire to one of the farmer's barns, and was arrested, convicted, and sentenced to ten years at the House of Refuge, which admitted youths from all over the state. He was eleven years old.

At first, Reed was housed together with all the other boys, but after his first year, the superintendent moved him into a new separate dormitory built for children of color; the lines of racial segregation in the city were tightening once again. Nonetheless, Reed's best friends remained two Irish boys, the sons of recent immigrants, and the threesome ran away one rainy Sunday in 1836 or 1837, crossing a meadow before coming out on Bloomingdale Road and continuing about fifteen miles farther north. They spent the night in a farmer's barn and the next day headed to a landing to catch a steamboat for Albany. But just as they were stepping aboard, or so writes Reed in a story that sounds apocryphal or at least embellished, the feared High Constable Jacob Hays appeared, "grasped us and lock us in the black Mariah and order the driver to drive directly up to the House of Refuge with us."

Jacob Hays was a legendary figure in mid-nineteenth-century New York. The city's chief marshal for almost fifty years, he was a short, stocky, and aggressive man with a craggy visage who prowled the streets in a black suit and stovepipe hat, a white handkerchief around his neck, a gold-tipped billy club in his hand. This he used all too effectively, breaking up riots by knocking off hats and, when the combatants stooped to pick them up, booting them to the ground and hitting them again and again, his staff gleaming as it whooshed through the air. His tactics seem brutal today, but he was widely admired in his time, and by the 1830s, his fame had even spread to Europe. One story had it that an American and an Englishman were watching a riot in London one day when the American said, "Where I come from one man would have put down this disturbance." The Englishman replied, "You must then, Sir, come from New York in the United States, since that is the only place in which there lives such a man."

*   *   *

The House of Refuge had been founded by elite reformers, many of them Quakers. Appalled by the deplorable treatment of inmates in the country's prisons, where children were housed with adults and often punished mercilessly regardless of the severity of their crime, they aimed to establish a new prison model, one based on rehabilitation rather than revenge. And in some ways, they succeeded. The refuge was an improvement over earlier institutions. In the 1830s and 1840s, Alexis de Tocqueville, Frances Trollope, and Charles Dickens all praised the House of Refuge, as did later social reformers Dorothea Dix and Jacob Riis.

Not surprisingly, though, given the era and unfettered authority of institutional superintendents, the House of Refuge was also a nightmarish, abusive place. The rules were many, and those who disobeyed them were punished with a diet of bread and water, solitary confinement, restraints, and lashings with the notorious "cat of nine tails," a whip made of catgut wound with wire.

The House of Refuge also had extraordinary control over its inmates' lives. The children were held under indefinite sentences and could be released only at the discretion of the managers. Some boys were bound out to sea captains and sent away for years without their parents' knowledge, and families who tried to retrieve their children from the refuge were usually turned down by the courts. The reformatory was considered a school rather than a penal institution, and its inmates had fewer rights than adults charged with crimes.

What did the extended Horn family, watching the goings-on of the refuge from across the street, make of all this? Were they heartened to see steps being taken to help the city's impoverished youth, or early

practitioners of NIMBY ("not in my back yard"), or critics of the institution's harsh practices, or against the idea of prison reform altogether? The
Horn and Mildeberger names do not appear on the lists of early donors to
the refuge, though the names of some of their neighbors do.

Whatever their outlook, the Horns would have realized that the House
of Refuge was a harbinger of things to come. New York was continuing its
rapid transformation into a booming port and financial center. The Erie
Canal had opened in 1825, connecting the city to Lake Erie and the interior of the country, and creating tremendous opportunities for trade. Thousands of small riverboats were bringing grains, flour, whiskey, and other
goods down into New York Harbor, where they were being transferred
onto oceangoing vessels bound for all parts of the globe. New grain
elevators, warehouses, emporiums, mercantile firms, and banks had
sprouted up, seemingly overnight, and with the economic boom had
come more people. New York's population had more than tripled since
the turn of the century, ballooning from 60,000 in 1800 to 203,000 in
1830. This huge influx had led to the need for more housing and institutions, including schools, hospitals, hotels, almshouses, prisons—and a
juvenile reformatory.

Equally telling, Randel's grid was creeping steadily north. Greenwich
Village was no longer an independent settlement, and segments of every
east–west street up to Twenty-third had been opened, though most of those
streets, as well as the north–south avenues, were still incomplete, sparsely
populated, and unpaved. The days of the old Bloomingdale Road with its
cozy community of Knickerbocker families were numbered. The section
of the road that ran between Twenty-third and Fifty-ninth streets would
be renamed Broadway by 1850, and Bloomingdale Road above Fifty-ninth
Street would be replaced by the Boulevard in 1868, to be incorporated
into Broadway in turn in 1899.

In 1839, the House of Refuge burned down, probably the work of some
of its inmates, and was rebuilt at the foot of East Twenty-third Street. Here
it remained until 1854, when it was moved again, to Randall's Island (named
after an early British farmer, not John Randel Jr.). In 1935, the institution
was closed for good, and the Society for the Reformation of Juvenile Delinquents dissolved.

Austin Reed was still a resident of the House of Refuge when it burned down, but in the following month, he began an apprenticeship with a farmer in Rockland County. He was contracted to work for over four years, until he turned twenty-one, but conditions were harsh and he left before a year was up. He made his way back to Rochester, where he worked in a hotel until he was arrested for stealing and sent to Auburn state prison for two years. It was the first of many incarcerations—Reed would spend most of the next twenty years in prison, primarily for theft. Hot-tempered and rebellious, he was whipped at least twenty-three times in one two-year period, yet still managed to write the first known African American prison memoir, as relevant today as it was then.

CHAPTER 5

From Pigs to Ostriches

It was the late 1840s, and young Gene Schermerhorn was running up the Sixth Avenue side of the Twenty-third Street block, whirling a lasso, chasing a pig. From behind him, below Twenty-third Street, rose the stench of the Sixth Avenue omnibus stables (an omnibus was a large urban stagecoach), where over five hundred horses were housed, while ahead stretched the wilds of upper Manhattan. Panting, he passed a half dozen small brick buildings with stores on the bottom, living quarters up top, and empty grassy lots. Other boys were also out on the avenue, flying kites, hitting balls, and playing marbles in a dirt ring four or five feet across. "Knuckle down," "fen dubs," "fen everything," shouted the boys, clutching their bags filled with migs, China Alleys, and agates, until a gang of boys from another street appeared and everyone grabbed their marbles and ran. No girls were out. They were all home, helping their mothers with household chores. Gene lost sight of his pig.

This glimpse of Twenty-third Street block life comes from Gene's memoir *Letters to Phil: Memories of a New York Boyhood, 1848–1856*. At the time, Sixth Avenue and other nearby streets, most carved into the land just a decade or two before, were rutted and unpaved. The majority of New Yorkers were still living below Eighth Street, with many of the wealthiest residing on Lafayette Place or St. John's Square (now the entrance to the Holland Tunnel).

Much of the rest of the Twenty-third Street block was even less developed than the Sixth Avenue side. Only a few red-brick buildings and a stable stood on Twenty-fourth Street, while Fifth Avenue was empty except for a busy "post tavern" teeming with stagecoach traffic. Along Twenty-third Street between Fifth and Sixth avenues beckoned several pretty wooden houses with vine-covered porches and balconies, and a lumberyard, while along Twenty-third west of Sixth stood just a few homes, including young Gene's, at No. 72. Truck gardens and open lots stretched between the isolated abodes and in the distance loomed two Gothic Revival buildings belonging to the General Theological Seminary, once part of an estate owned by Clement Clarke Moore, the noted classical scholar and author of "A Visit from Saint Nicholas." A devout Episcopalian, he had donated his former apple orchard (Ninth to Tenth avenues, Twentieth to Twenty-first streets) to the church in 1827.

Among those living on the Twenty-third Street block as Gene ran by were grocers, coachmen, carpenters, bricklayers, milliners, and blacksmiths—ordinary folk working ordinary jobs. Little did most of them suspect that a decade later, their neighborhood would be the epicenter of fashionable New York, with Twenty-third Street between Fifth and Sixth avenues coveted as one of the city's most desirable addresses. Lots on Fifth near Twenty-third that had sold for $500 or $600 in the late 1830s were selling for $10,000 or $12,000 in the late 1850s. Emblematic of the change would be a mansion built at 49-51 West Twenty-third Street, where the 1840s lumberyard stood, by young Gene's trendsetting and extremely wealthy relatives, Mr. and Mrs. William Colford Schermerhorn.

The Schermerhorns were one of the oldest and most respected Knickerbocker families in New York. Their ancestor Jacob Janse Schermerhorn had arrived in New Netherland circa 1637, to settle near Albany. Decades later, his descendant Peter Schermerhorn moved to New York City, where he catapulted the family into fortune by operating a fleet of ships and purchasing extensive real estate; Schermerhorn Row on Fulton Street in Manhattan and Schermerhorn Street in Brooklyn are named after him. By the mid-1800s, however, the Schermerhorns had splintered into different branches of varying economic means. Gene belonged to a quiet, retiring branch of the family that had moved to Twenty-third Street either for financial reasons or because they preferred the country life. The William Colford Schermerhorns would choose the street for entirely different reasons.

* * *

The laying out of Manhattan's streets as envisioned by the Commissioners' Plan had begun three decades before young Gene started chasing pigs, but progress had been very slow at first. Third and Eighth avenues were ordered opened for their entire lengths in the 1810s, even before Randel finished surveying, but by 1830 only parts of them had become avenue-wide dirt roads. Ninth Avenue was leveled and graded as far north as Twenty-eighth Street by 1830, and Sixth Avenue soon thereafter, but serious work on the side streets did not begin until the mid-1830s. There were many problems that had to be addressed—how would the streets be paid for? How would the landowners be compensated? Who would do the work?—and legal suits to settle.

Fifth Avenue was opened from Washington Square to Fourteenth Street in 1824, from Fourteenth to Twenty-first streets in 1830, from Twenty-first to Forty-second streets in 1837—two years before the House of Refuge burned down—and from Forty-second to Ninetieth streets in 1838. Hills and valleys, meadows and bogs, pools and brooks were filled in and made flat, and streams were forced underground. The days of trout fishing and duck hunting mid-island were over.

Fifth Avenue was designated as the dividing line between east and west Manhattan from the start, and quickly became the preferred address of the very rich, as it was laid out with a sixty-foot-wide roadway and twenty-foot-wide sidewalks made for promenading. Early property owners were allowed to encroach fifteen feet onto the sidewalks, and as the years went by, they took full advantage, erecting steep stoops with fanciful porticos and planting gardens of many colors. Not until 1908 was the roadway widened to accommodate more traffic.

The first man to build a house on Fifth Avenue was Henry Brevoort Jr., whose father, Henry Brevoort Sr., was eighty years old when the first part of the street was laid out. An irascible, tight-fisted, and stubborn old Dutchman, the elder Henry owned a farm that stretched between the future Fifth Avenue and the Bowery, Ninth and Eighteenth streets. He sold vegetables from his truck garden on the corner of today's Tenth Street and Fifth Avenue and imported rare birds, which he sold out of a room in his antiquated house. His personal pet was a bear, which he kept chained in a watermelon patch in his front yard, much to the distress of his neighbors.

Henry Jr. built an imposing Greek Revival mansion on the corner of Fifth Avenue and Ninth Street in 1834, while his father was still alive and probably fuming at his son's profligacy. The mansion held five bedrooms, nine servant rooms, a billiard room, a library, and multiple parlors. Newspaper editor William Cullen Bryant called it "a kind of palace in a Garden," and soon other well-heeled New Yorkers, including Margaret and Christopher Mildeberger, then still living in the old Horn farmhouse, were rushing to erect grand Fifth Avenue edifices of their own.

Henry Jr. loved to entertain and in 1840 sent out invitations for an extravagant masked ball, to which the Mildebergers may have been invited. Masked balls were then all the rage in Europe, but still unknown in New York, and the city was all aflutter with the news. Wrote Philip Hone, New York's former mayor, in his diary, "Nothing else is talked about; the ladies' heads are turned nearly off their shoulders; the whiskers of the dandies assume a more ferocious curl in anticipation of the effect they are to produce."

On the night of the ball, some five hundred socialites, business moguls, politicians, writers, artists, and foreign dignitaries in costume clip-clopped up to the Brevoort front door. Passing under an awning, they filed in: Joan of Arc, Queen Catherine of Aragon, the Lady of the Night of the Polar Star, William Penn, Cardinal Wolsey, a sorceress, a monk, a goldfinch, and a mysterious man in black, who had slipped in uninvited and was asked to leave. Also in attendance were Lalla Rookh and Feramorz, characters from the then-popular narrative poem "Lalla Rookh," by Thomas Moore. Matilda Barclay, the daughter of the British consul, was Lalla, and the dashing T. Pollock Burgwyn of South Carolina was Feramorz. The two were secret lovers, and when the ball was over, they were nowhere to be found. They had slipped out at four A.M. without changing costume and were married before breakfast. Their elopement caused a furor—and an indignant backlash. "As a result masked balls were made taboo," the

Evening Herald later reported, "and a fine of $1,000 was imposed on any one who should give one—unless the giver told on himself, in which event the fine was reduced one-half."

The ban on masked balls would remain in effect for over a decade. No socialite dared buck convention, until, that is, young Gene's powerful relative Mrs. William Colford Schermerhorn, née Ann Cottenet, came along.

*   *   *

From the northern edge of old Henry Brevoort Sr.'s farm, the new Fifth Avenue continued north through or past the property of Isaac Varian (Eighteenth to Twentieth streets), Gilbert Coutant (Twentieth to Twenty-first streets), and the Horn family (Twenty-first to Twenty-sixth streets). The opening of the avenue did not affect the farmland on the Twenty-third Street block, as it hugged its eastern edge, but it did cut right through the old Horn farmhouse. The Mildebergers were not as perturbed as they might have been, however, as they were now focused on building their new home on Fifth Avenue, a handsome four-story brownstone twenty-five feet south of Twenty-third Street. The couple petitioned the city to let their old farmhouse stand until it was absolutely necessary to move it, and the city agreed. The edifice stayed put, riders and stagecoaches flowing around it.

Life for those who had already moved onto Fifth Avenue was leisurely and serene. The men of the families breakfasted around nine A.M. before heading downtown to their offices and returned home for a midday break at about two P.M., when a long and relaxing dinner was served. They then went back to work, returning at eight P.M., in time for tea, a substantial meal in that era. Women spent mornings at home, caring for their children and overseeing the servants, and afternoons visiting neighbors and strolling in their gardens.

Some of the more adventurous women also ventured north to "Upper Fifth Avenue," above Eighteenth Street, to see what progress was being made at muddy Madison Square. The city had declared the square a public place and ordered its grounds sodded, its bogs drained, Cedar Creek forced underground, and the Boston Post Road, which still cut through the square, eliminated. All this took time, and in the interim, the newly organized Knickerbocker Base Ball club moved in. Started by a group of clerks and businessmen, the club played a version of an English children's game known as one-old-cat, which involved four bases laid out in a diamond shape and a "feeder" who tossed balls to a "striker" holding a bat. The club would draw up the first formal rules of the game in 1845 and move to Hoboken, New Jersey, the following year, to lose the first recorded game of baseball to the New York Nine, 23–1. By 1858, there would be twenty-five baseball clubs in Manhattan and seventy-one in Brooklyn; many sports historians today believe that New York City, not Cooperstown, New York, was the birthplace of baseball.

Traffic on the avenue increased rapidly—so rapidly that in 1839 the city ordered the Mildebergers to remove their family farmhouse. Resignedly, they complied, and the creaky yellow wooden house with its peaked roof and wide veranda was rolled a few hundred feet north and west to an irregularly shaped plot of land near the corner of Twenty-third Street and Fifth Avenue. Here it would remain, the first known permanent structure on the block and a city landmark of sorts, for fourteen years.

Who moved the old farmhouse is unknown, but chances are good it was Simeon Brown, an enterprising man who moved over nine hundred buildings in the 1820s and 1830s, when Manhattan's streets were being laid out. Most were made of wood and relatively easy to relocate—he usually jacked them up over their foundations and rolled them along on logs. But he also moved about four hundred buildings with brick fronts and forty others built entirely of brick by using a system of his own invention that involved levers, tallow grease, and logs laid at right angles to each other. When Brown moved his first brick building in 1827, he invited 150 guests to a party in the home while it was being moved. Not a single window cracked.

With their new Fifth Avenue mansion complete, the Mildebergers had no more use for the family farmhouse and promptly leased it in the early 1840s to William "Corporal" Thompson, who hung a pair of spiky antlers out front and turned it into Madison Cottage, the "post tavern" of young Gene's time. Here stopped riders carrying mail between New York and Boston and stagecoach drivers eager to change horses and eat a quick meal. Business was good, and soon the cottage became *the* stop for anyone heading in or out of the city, with one conveyance leaving for the downtown every four minutes. Travelers could also stay overnight, as long as they obeyed the rules: no more than five people to a bed, no boots on the bed, no dogs upstairs, and no beer in the kitchen. Organ grinders had to sleep in the washhouse, and razor grinders and tinkers were not allowed on the premises.

A few years later, Madison Cottage evolved yet further, into a boisterous roadhouse that was especially popular among the city's turfmen, or horse-racing devotees. Dressed in top hats and frock coats, they would stand on its veranda and raise a glass or two or three as before them raced hundreds of rattling carts with spindly wheels, pulled along by bony trotters, their ribcages visible through their flanks. Other men, also dressed in top hats and frock coats, sat on the carts' buckboards, snapping reins as they urged their steeds on at dangerous speeds. All ranks of life were there, from butcher boys to stockbrokers, but when it came to refreshment at Madison Cottage after the races, it was mostly turfmen of the "better sort" who lingered.

Recalled one habitué many years later: "This was the hostelry of Corporal Thompson, the last stopping place for codgers, old and young. Laverty, Winans, Niblo, the Costers, Hones, Whitneys, Schermerhorns, the genial Sol Kipp, Doctor Vaché, Ogden Hoffman, Nat Blunt, and scores more of *bon vivants*, hail fellows well met, would here end their ride for the day by 'smiling' with the worthy Corporal, and wash down any of their former improprieties with a sip of his *ne plus ultra*, which was always kept in reserve for a special nightcap. There was a special magnetism about the snug little bar-room, always trim as a lady's boudoir, which induced the desire to tarry awhile, as if that visit were destined to be the last; so it frequently happened that a jolly party was compelled to grope slowly homewards through the unlighted gloomy road which led to the city."

Behind Madison Cottage stretched a windswept lot where cattle fairs and other exhibitions were held, usually in the fall. The cattlemen would post their lists of animals for sale in the cottage before ambling out back to peruse the pedigreed beasts, standing patiently in pens, massive heads swaying, tails flicking. One year a mammoth ox weighing 4,209 pounds and standing over six feet tall with a girth of ten feet was on display. Another year, four Spanish jacks from the royal stables of Spain were for sale.

Well-bred women were a rarity at Madison Cottage at first, but as it aged, that apparently changed. A May 9, 1847, announcement in the *New York Herald* sounds as though it were written expressly for gentlewomen and their male companions: "MADISON COTTAGE—This beautiful place of resort opposite Madison Square, corner of Twenty-third Street and Broadway, is open for the season, and Palmer's omnibuses drive to the door. It is one of the most agreeable spots for an afternoon's lounge in the suburbs of our city. Go and see."

Some of Madison Cottage's last years were sad ones though. In 1849 a devastating cholera epidemic ravaged the city. Everyone who could flee the downtown did, with some coming to stay at Madison Cottage, where a freshly painted sign out front read K.K.K., short for "Corporal's Cholera Cure."

The epidemic had begun with the arrival of a packet ship carrying passengers who had been exposed to the disease in Europe, where it had already killed thousands. The ship was quarantined off Staten Island, but some of its passengers escaped in small boats to Manhattan. Cholera began breaking out in boardinghouses the following week and spread rapidly, especially among the city's tens of thousands of recent immigrants, packed tightly together in crumbling tenement houses. Businesses, theaters, hotels, and churches shut down, and the roads became clogged with carriages, wagons, horses, and pedestrians fleeing the city. Bodies lay in the streets for days, and when finally picked up, were rowed out to Randall's Island and dumped into open pits. Rats swam over daily to gnaw off their flesh.

Caused by a bacterium usually ingested by drinking contaminated water, cholera is most common in areas of overcrowding and poor sanitation—an apt description of mid-nineteenth century New York. The city was filthy, its streets buried under decades of refuse and manure.

Nonetheless, because most of the cholera deaths occurred in the tenements, many genteel New Yorkers believed the scourge to be the poor's fault. "Those people" drank and lived in filth. "They" were criminals and lechers and prostitutes and Catholics. Their despicable lifestyles had weakened their systems—or perhaps they were being punished by God. Morally upright people didn't die of cholera, or so it was widely assumed until some highly respected New Yorkers succumbed.

Those who took refuge from the epidemic in Madison Cottage must have found the atmosphere there excruciating. Cholera victims suffer from agonizing stomach cramps, vomiting, and diarrhea, and if not treated, often expire within hours; 90 percent of those stricken with the disease in the nineteenth century died. The guests at the cottage must have appeared outwardly healthy—otherwise, they probably wouldn't have been allowed in—but everyone must have been intently scrutinizing everyone else, on the alert for the slightest sign of nausea, unusual tiredness, excessive thirst, or the glassy-eyed look that often heralded the highly infectious disease.

Corporal Thompson's "cure" likely involved a combination of fresh air and mysterious elixirs. The medical profession was unregulated at the time, and quacks all over the city had their "secret" cholera remedies, including magical potions or drenching patients with water and wrapping them in wet towels. Yet the treatments prescribed by the bona fide doctors traveling from "cholera nest" to "cholera nest" weren't any better. The most common were administering doses of mercury chloride and bleeding the afflicted with leeches.

Looked at from one angle, the Corporal was one of the block's first con men, selling promises he couldn't deliver. Looked at from another, he was a bastion of strength, offering hope to a confused, frightened people in a dark, desperate time.

In the end, the 1849 epidemic took 5,071 lives, out of a population of 500,000. That proportion was similar to an earlier cholera epidemic in 1832, which took 3,515 people out of a population of 250,000. Two more disastrous cholera waves would sweep through New York in 1854 (2,509 deaths) and 1866 (1,137 deaths), but the final one of 1892 would kill only 120. By then, London physician John Snow had linked cholera to contaminated drinking water, and his findings had led to changes in the water and waste systems of London, New York, and other cities.

*　*　*

It is the evening of May 2, 1853. The cholera epidemic of 1849 is all but forgotten. Men in long jackets and silk hats, accompanied by women in flared skirts nipped at the waist, are milling about impatiently outside an oval brick arena, seven hundred feet in circumference, topped with a red-white-and-blue tent. From its turrets flutter dozens of flags.

It is opening night. Madison Cottage is gone. Franconi's Hippodrome has taken its place. The Mildebergers have sold their property on the Twenty-third Street block to John B. Monnot, only the third owner of this piece of land since the Europeans and Africans first arrived in Mannahatta.

The doors of the hippodrome open, and the crowd stampedes in, pushing and shoving, boots crushing toes. A mob of six thousand rushes to their seats and another three thousand find standing room. It is, according to one newspaper reporter, the largest crowd ever assembled under one roof in New York.

Thrumming with excitement, the audience tries but fails to settle down. Before them stretches a freshly raked racetrack forty feet wide, ornamental gardens and illuminated fountains in its center. The tent soars seventy feet over their heads. A thousand flickering gas lights punctuate the scene.

The show begins. Five beautiful women course around the track on powerful steeds, followed by three golden chariots speeding by so fast their wheels scarcely touch the ground. Next come a steeplechase and hurdle leaps, and a troupe of unbridled thoroughbreds, manes flashing as they thunder past. Ostriches race ostriches, "Bedouins" chase ostriches, monkeys ride ponies, humans fly on a golden trapeze, and seven dromedaries, four deer, a beautiful giraffe, and two elephants parade by, one of the elephants pausing for a moment to stand on its head. The show's impresario polkas and waltzes upon a dancing horse, and during a grand medieval pageant called the Field of the Cloth of Gold, kings and queens in lustrous velvet promenade as knights level lances and fight with sword and shield. A white horse feigns death and is dragged off to a flourish of trumpets.

The audience sighs with contentment. The wait has been worth it.

*   *   *

The New York press had started covering Franconi's Hippodrome months before it opened. There'd been story after story about the cost of the venture—$40,000 for the building (about $1.34 million today), $20,000 for a single chariot ($670,000), $32,000 for the horses ($1 million), $1,000 a day for the cumulative salaries of the one-hundred-plus performers ($34,000/day)—as well as breathless notices about the animals, some of "colossal dimensions," traveling in packet ships across the Atlantic.

After opening night, however, not all the press was so enamored. In the days that followed, the *New York Daily Times* complained about the "blacklegs, gamblers, rowdies, and the miscellanea of polite roguery and blackguardism" involved with the show, and opined that the "Hippodrome is badly conducted, and exercises an injurious influence on the public morals." The paper also slammed the arena for its "unusually liberal supply of groggeries," flagrant endorsement of betting, and "system of indiscriminate admission . . . attended with highly immoral results"—that is, prostitution. Little did the paper's staff know that what they were witnessing was just the beginning. In the coming half century, many more blacklegs, gamblers, and prostitutes would appear on the Twenty-third Street block.

Franconi's Hippodrome was not the first spectacular to arrive in New York. There had been exhibitions of wild animals as early as 1763, and Thomas Pool, an American equestrian, had performed feats of horsemanship on a hill near today's Chatham Square in 1786. Seven years later, Scotsman John Bill Ricketts had come to town, bringing with him the city's first bona fide circus—rope walkers, tumblers, pantomimes, and a clown—and in 1808 two Frenchmen opened the city's second circus at Broadway and Worth Street. Shows featuring circus-like acts such as troops of trained dogs, bullbaiting, and wild animal fights had also long been popular on the Bowery.

But Franconi's Hippodrome was unlike any of these earlier operations. Billing itself as offering the "Amusements of the Ancient Greeks and Romans," it was modeled after the great amphitheaters of Rome, the most famous of which was the Circus Maximus, in operation for more than one thousand years. Known for their chariot races, horse races, and gladiator combats, the ancient hippodromes were oval in shape and had no central stage. The word *hippodrome* comes from the Greek words *hippo*, meaning "horse," and *drome*, meaning "racetrack."

The man behind the Twenty-third Street extravaganza was said to be Henri Franconi, an equestrian from a well-known European circus family.

His grandfather, Antonio Franconi, was a Venetian nobleman who had been forced into exile in 1756 after killing an opponent in a duel. Landing in France, he had worked as a lion tamer in Lyon and at a circus in Paris run by Englishman Philip Astley, the father of the modern circus. When the French Revolution began, Astley fled Paris and Antonio took over his operation, which he renamed Amphithéâtre Franconi.

Everyone in 1850s America knew the name Franconi, and citizens poured out onto lower Broadway to catch a glimpse of the famous Henri when he first arrived, riding up and down on an ostrich to advertise his family's latest venture. But suspicions soon arose. Other Franconi Hippodromes were opening in Connecticut, Massachusetts, Ohio, Pennsylvania, and upstate New York, and puzzled readers wrote to newspaper editors inquiring how Franconi could be in so many places at once. Answered one sage editor: "We don't know. Possibly it is one of the peculiarities of hippodromes to be in two or three places in the same time." Another was more direct: "Vive la humbug," he wrote.

Then, after the public's initial excitement over the Twenty-third Street hippodrome wore off and the negative newspaper reviews appeared, whispers began. Some said that the *artistes* were mediocre, that the acts were "nothing more than a Bowery circus in disguise," that the ostriches were "overgrown Shanghais" (chickens) with no speed. Others said that the races were fixed, and the word *hippodroming*, meaning "sport-fixing," entered the nineteenth-century American lexicon. One of the female equestrians was dashed from a horse and made to ride in a chariot even though her arm was broken and she was bleeding profusely. More accidents ensued, followed by tragedy.

On the evening of Friday, June 24, 1853, less than two months after the hippodrome opened, dancing girl Miss Augusta Taylor (real name, Charlotte Gilfillan), age twenty-four and recently separated from her husband, walked from the dressing rooms to the tunnel through which the entertainers entered the arena. Crouching down, she began the miserable trek through the dank passageway, which was over one hundred feet long and only four and a half feet high and three and a half feet wide. It was lit by candles, and as she climbed the ladder at the tunnel's end, her scarf and her dress caught fire. Flames shot out as she emerged, screaming.

Two or three gentlemen jumped from the boxes and rushed to immerse her in an illuminated fountain, but most of the audience stayed put, unperturbed, assuming it was part of the show. The hippodrome's management also paid scant attention. Scarcely had the young woman been carried out, burnt and unable to breathe, when the band struck up a lively tune.

At the inquest following Miss Augusta's death two weeks later, it came out that the hippodrome was not owned by the fabled Franconi family after all. Henri was nothing but a straw man, put in place to attract crowds. The real owners were a syndicate of eight American businessmen. Chicanery, pure and simple.

The hippodrome continued to operate for two more years, but between the accidents and the deceptions, its luster had faded. Ticket sales slowed until the operation was near bankruptcy. The arena's final performance took place in November 1855. The structure was shuttered, and its animals and fixtures auctioned off. A Mr. E. M. Shields bought the white bear—said to be the only one in America—for $475 (about $14,300 today), cage included, and a Mr. Henry Butler bought a Bengal tiger "with huge paws, and a powerful inclination to lie down," for $225 ($6,800), two lions and a lioness for $375 ($11,200), and a zebra and a leopard for $285 ($8,600). One "indiscreet gentleman" purchased an elephant without considering that he had no place to keep it except a small, carpeted back parlor, and another paid $120 ($3,600) for the "ridiculous gratification of having, in his own right, a whole cageful of monkeys to joke, whenever so disposed." The fate of those animals could not have been good.

The final demolition of the hippodrome took place four months later. "Neighbors are not sorry," reported the *New York Daily Times* on March 14, 1856.

Two months later, ground was broken for the Fifth Avenue Hotel. A spectacular in its own right, it would transform the block—and the neighborhood.

CHAPTER 6

Eno's Folly

Amos Richards Eno gazed out the window of his home at 26 East Twenty-third Street at the massive structure across the way, a contented smile flitting over his handsome, leonine face. He was proving them wrong, as he had known he would. Just three years earlier, everyone had called his latest venture, the Fifth Avenue Hotel, fronting the entire east side of the Twenty-third Street block, along Fifth Avenue and Broadway, "Eno's Folly." It was way too far uptown, way too far away from everything, they had said, and was certain to fail. Why, where would its guests even come from? Cows and pigs were still wandering the side streets nearby, and the area was pockmarked with vacant fields and empty lots. True, chocolate-colored brownstones stood along Fifth Avenue as far north as Twenty-third Street, but they were mostly residential—no business prospects there. Eno had paid his critics no mind. He trusted his real estate instincts. They had already made him one of the richest men in the city, and now, here he was, about to become even richer. One year after opening on August 23, 1859, the Fifth Avenue Hotel was booked solid; the *New York Times* was calling it "the best specimen we can offer of the possibilities of hotel luxury." And in a few weeks, the Prince of Wales, the first British royal ever to visit the United States, was coming to stay at *his* hotel. Not bad for a simple country boy from Connecticut.

Then again, Amos Eno was anything but simple. The first of a string of self-made New England millionaires who would live or work on the block, he was born in Simsbury, Connecticut, in 1810, the descendant of a Huguenot family from Valenciennes, France, who had fled to England after the town fell to the Spaniards in the late sixteenth century. His forefather Jacques Henno had been captured during the battle, but escaped and was declared an outlaw, wanted dead or alive, a hefty price on his head.

The American branch of the family had settled in Windsor, Connecticut, in the mid-1600s, where they worked the land and prospered, becoming one of the area's largest landowners. Later descendants fought in the French and Indian Wars and the American Revolution, and changed the spelling of their last name to "Eno."

Amos Eno was made of the same sturdy, enterprising stuff. The third of four children born to Salmon and Mary (Richards) Eno, he moved to Hartford to clerk in a dry goods store when he was sixteen. He kept his eyes and ears open, and a few years later was back in Simsbury, opening a store at Hoskins Station, where the New Haven and Northampton Canal was being built. Canal workers crowded into his store daily, buying up goods as fast as he could stock them, and he made a solid profit, so solid that in 1831, fed up with the provincialism and "staid puritanical character" of his hometown, he moved to Lower Manhattan with his cousin John J. Phelps. The two youths had "small means, small credit, but big hopes" as they opened a tiny dry goods store on Exchange Place behind the old Merchants' Exchange.

Strangers in the city, the fresh-faced cousins were unprepared for the hostility they encountered. New York's mercantile system was heavily stacked against newcomers, and no one would endorse them or provide them with credit. They were forced to buy goods through auction sales with cash, payable in thirty days, a tricky business. But they persevered, and in less than a year Eno & Phelps became the largest auction buyers in the city, making handsome money.

Eno had only a primary school education but loved to read, and in the evenings, after exhausting days spent buying and selling, he taught himself about science and history, languages and literature. Later in life, he told a newspaper reporter that when he was young, there was always "an interrogation point at the end of my nose."

When Eno was twenty-five, he married seventeen-year-old Lucy Jane Phelps, also of Simsbury, whose father, Elisha Phelps, had served in the U.S. House of Representatives. The young couple set up housekeeping near the Battery at first, but soon, like many of their contemporaries, moved steadily farther uptown—to Fourth Street near Washington Square, to Greenwich Street in the West Village, to East Twenty-third Street on Madison Square, and finally, years after the Fifth Avenue Hotel opened, into a mansion they built at 233 Fifth Avenue at Twenty-seventh Street (now the Museum of Sex). Along the way they had nine children, one of whom died in infancy and another at age three, and Amos joined the city's most important social and civic clubs. He also began buying real estate and did so well at it that in 1857 he gave up the dry goods business altogether to concentrate on his new passion, at which he was almost always successful. Worth over $20 million in real estate holdings alone when he retired in 1894 (about $608 million today), he was one of the richest men Connecticut produced in the 1800s. He was also as rich or richer than many of New York City's oldest upper-crust families—the Joneses, the Schermerhorns, the Van Cortlandts, the Van Rensselaers—who nonetheless regarded him, an unpretentious man, known for his sharp wit and gruff manner, as an uncouth arriviste.

* * *

To their loss. From the 1860s through the 1890s, Eno's Folly would serve as New York's most important social, political, and cultural center. Politicians, industrialists, and financiers would meet there. Royalty and heads of state would sleep there. Actors, singers, writers, and artists would dine there. Debutantes and their beaus would marry there. Every president from Buchanan to McKinley stayed at the Fifth Avenue, as did Prince Napoleon, the Emperor Dom Pedro of Brazil, the Crown Prince of Siam, the Marquis of Lome, and Prince Agustín de Iturbide of Mexico. Edwin Booth, Jim Fisk, Cornelius Vanderbilt, William Cullen Bryant, Horace Greeley, Peter Cooper, Samuel Clemens (Mark Twain), Jenny Lind, Charlotte Cushman, and Madame Patti—all were regulars. President

Abraham Lincoln gave a speech from the hotel's balcony before going on to Cooper Union to deliver another, more famous speech that started him on the road to the American presidency. General Ulysses S. Grant always occupied rooms 43 and 44 when he was in town, and General George McClellan lived in the hotel near the end of the Civil War. Presidents James Garfield and Grover Cleveland held their first major receptions at the hotel, and Theodore Roosevelt was nominated for governor of New York, and later vice president of the United States, in its "Amen Corner," a Republican meeting spot. "No other single hotel in the world has ever entertained so many distinguished people as have been received at the Fifth-Avenue," reported *King's Handbook of New York City* in 1892. "[It] is a sort of clearing-house for the city, the Nation, and the world."

*   *   *

The hotel was an American invention. Before its appearance in the 1820s, travelers in both America and Europe stayed in taverns and inns where they usually shared beds and towels, slept on sheets that were washed once a week—if they were lucky—and ate greasy meals at sticky communal tables. Innkeepers crowded as many guests as possible into a handful of rooms, where they slept spoon style in extra-large trundle beds.

The first building constructed expressly as a hotel—a word adapted from the French *hôtel*, meaning "town mansion"—is believed to have been New York's City Hotel, opened at 123 Broadway, near Wall Street, in 1794. Regarded as immense at the time, it contained 137 guest rooms as well as a half dozen unusually light and airy public rooms. Here the city's social elite gathered for political meetings and banquets, or to dance the cotillion and minuet at weekly subscription events given by gentlemen in knee breeches and silk stockings, dress swords by their sides. Nonetheless, the City Hotel was little more than an overgrown inn, as it was plain, utilitarian, and all but devoid of luxury.

Then came the eye-popping Tremont Hotel, opened in Boston in 1829 by a group of wealthy investors. Featuring a towering portico, rotunda with a stained-glass ceiling—the world's first hotel lobby—a dining room that could seat two hundred, shops, offices, and 170 guest rooms, the hotel was an instant tourist attraction. People came from miles around to gape at its indoor plumbing (on the ground floor only, as no one made plumbing supplies to carry water to higher floors), gas lights (in the public rooms only, as unsophisticated guests might blow them out in their bedrooms and die of asphyxiation while sleeping), bellboys, locks on every guest room door, and free soap in every room. The *National Intelligencer* called the Tremont a "palace of the public," and the term caught on.

Suddenly, every city wanted what Boston had. America's great age of commerce had begun, and towns of all sizes hungered for their own extravagant hostelry to show off their importance to the world. The Astor House went up in New York City, the St. Charles in New Orleans, the American Hotel in Buffalo, the American House in Philadelphia, the Burnet in Cincinnati, and the Planters Hotel in St. Louis, to name but a few. In his 1862 travelogue, *North America*, Anthony Trollope wrote, "When the new hotel rises up in the wilderness, it is presumed that people will come there with the express object of inhabiting it. The hotel itself will create a population."

The new luxury hotels became a symbol of what America was all about. Fantastically large cities-within-cities, they seemed to reflect the vast potential of the continent itself and the lavishness of many Americans' dreams. With their elaborate facades and extravagant beauty, they celebrated capitalism and the apparent ability of the poor man to become rich. In Europe, luxury was reserved for the elite, but in America, luxury was for everyone—everyone who could pay, that is.

Europeans marveled at what the Americans had wrought. In 1861, British journalist George Augustus Sala wrote, "An American hotel is to an English hotel . . . what 'an elephant is to a periwinkle.'" And in 1907, Henry James, writing about a much later hotel, the Waldorf-Astoria, in *The American Scene*, wondered whether the hotel spirit "may not just *be* the American spirit most seeking and most finding itself."

Each nineteenth-century luxury hotel tried to outdo the one that had come before it. The more marble, mirrors, gilt, carved rosewood, fine linens, and engraved silverware, the better. New York's Astor House had been regarded as the utmost in luxury when it opened on the corner of Broadway and Vesey Street in 1836, but was viewed as outmoded just twenty years later. The city's midcentury hotel jewels were the Metropolitan (1852) at Prince and Broadway, and the St. Nicholas (1853) on Broadway between

Broome and Spring. The first hotel to cost over $1 million (about $34 million today), the St. Nicholas was so over the top that one English visitor professed to not leaving his shoes outside his room at night for fear they might be gilded. No hostelry could possibly outshine the St. Nicholas, or so it was thought until the Fifth Avenue Hotel came along.

*   *   *

Costing twice as much as the St. Nicholas, the Fifth Avenue was the largest hotel in the world when it opened, a title it kept for fifteen years. The edifice rose six stories, occupied sixteen lots, and could accommodate over eight hundred guests in its five-hundred-plus rooms. Designed by the architects Griffith Thomas and William Washburn, it boasted a restrained Italianate facade of imported white marble and over one hundred suites, each with its own parlor, bedroom with fireplace, dressing room, and private bathroom—the latter a startling innovation at the time.

The hotel had five entrances, with the main Fifth Avenue entrance leading to a lobby stretching 165 by 27 gilded, mirrored feet. The lobby's ceilings were hand painted, and its floor made of alternating red and white marble squares. Tapestry-covered couches and armchairs, carved rosewood tables, and gleaming brass spittoons filled the hall. A marble front desk dominated one side of the lobby, next to a wide staircase that swept up to the second floor, while gleaming corridors led to public and private parlors, reading rooms, a telegraph room, a barber shop, a flower shop, a cigar shop, a railway ticket office, a theater ticket office, a post office, a newspaper stand, and a stock and exchange telegram room. On the second floor presided more public and private parlors, the main dining room, a breakfast room, a ladies' tearoom, and a ladies' reception room, which could be reached directly from a downstairs ladies-only entrance. Four hundred servants stood at the ready to attend to a guest's every wish, while out front stretched a long line of carriages waiting to take visitors to their desired destinations.

The first guest to register at the Fifth Avenue Hotel on opening day was E. N. Bond, a New York merchant. He was assigned room 442 and liked it so much he occupied it every night for the next forty-three years. Nearly two hundred other guests also registered on that first day, and from then on, few of the hotel's five hundred rooms were ever vacant.

The Fifth Avenue Hotel was the first hotel to feature "vertical screw railways," or elevators, one for passengers and two for luggage and freight. Six years earlier, engineer Elisha Graves Otis had exhibited the world's first elevator at New York's Crystal Palace Exhibition, and in 1857, the first elevator had been installed at the E. V. Haughwout & Co. building on the corner of Broadway and Broome Street. The hotel's elevators differed from these earlier lifts, however. Designed by a different Otis, this one named Otis Tufts, an engineer from Boston, they were powered by steam engines and revolving screws that passed through the cars. Guests entered the passenger elevator at the ground "station," took a seat in an ornate "little parlor," and waited as the car noisily jolted its way up. The elevator had been installed with the ladies in mind, but soon proved to be equally popular with the gentlemen—and the hotel's management. Hitherto, a hotel's top floor rooms were considered the least desirable and were therefore offered at a discount. No longer.

Deep inside the hotel on the ground floor was a large barroom outfitted with two marble counters. Reigned over by a Mr. McKinley, who would work at the hotel for decades, the exclusively male preserve witnessed constant wheeling and dealing beneath clouds of fine-cut Cubano, Cobargo, and Concha cigar smoke. The bar could be reached directly from a discreet entrance on Twenty-third Street—the door of choice for those "conservative gentlemen" not eager to be seen by the general public—but porters were posted at vantage points along the way to fend off any except "gentlemen in first-rate condition."

The hotel's dining room, designed by Washburn in the "French fashion," was another wonder to behold, at least according to many of the breathless reporters of the day. Beneath its frescoed ceiling stood five hundred chairs and twenty communal tables, each laden with the finest porcelain dishes, burnished with gold. Corinthian columns filled the room, huge mirrors lined the walls, and at night, hundreds of gas lights flickered and multiplied in the mirrors like "living fairies." Effused one reporter: "Here assemble every night wealthy parents—brilliant sons—lovely daughters— happy lovers. The early poets, with all their power of imagination, never pictured—never conceived—such scenes. All who for the first time gaze on them, are bewildered—enchantment—enchantment—are the exclamations that escape from their lips."

The reporters paid far less, if any, attention to the waiters enabling the enchantment. Most were recent Irish or German immigrants who, when not serving or clearing tables, stood encircling the room's perimeter with their hands behind their backs or towels draped over their arms. They had arrived at the hotel at around five A.M., after trudging through dark silent streets to the hotel's grimy back door, and stood on their feet fourteen to fifteen hours a day. When not serving meals, they prepared food, washed dishes, stoked fires, polished silver, swept floors, cleaned windows, and much more.

The Fifth Avenue also had its critics. Shortly after it opened, *Harper's Weekly* proclaimed it pretentious and uncomfortable, the sort of place where guests were afraid of "staining or spoiling [the furniture] by sitting upon it," and reported that a guest with dirty boots could ruin a fifty-thousand-dollar carpet in a single evening. Similarly, author Junius Henri Browne later opined, "Ill-breeding never appears so ill as when it is heavily gilded; and the well-fed guests of the Fifth Avenue are often amused, and then disgusted, with the pretentious commonality they cannot escape."

When the Fifth Avenue first opened, its average room cost $2.50 a day, a rate that included four meals—breakfast, lunch, dinner, and tea. By 1887, five meals were included—breakfast, lunch, dinner, tea, and a late-night supper—for the price of $5 a day. At the hotel's height in the 1880s and 1890s, its profits were rumored to be $250,000 (about $6.5 million today) a year.

* * *

The success of the Fifth Avenue Hotel abruptly changed the character of the block and the neighborhood. What had formerly been a tranquil refuge from the crowded, dirty downtown morphed into a hive of activity. Empty lots and fields disappeared as commercial enterprises moved in, some rising next door to the residential buildings that had started flooding the area just a few years before. New York's population was growing at an astonishing rate—from 313,000 in 1840 to 814,000 in 1860—and the city was moving ever northward.

The opening of the hotel also marked the start of the heyday of the Twenty-third Street block. For almost fifty years, from the late 1850s through the turn of the century, it would stand at the epicenter of the great metropolis.

The first to follow Eno's hotel uptown were other luxury hotels, among them the Hoffman House (Twenty-fifth Street and Broadway), St. James (Twenty-sixth and Broadway), Albermarle Hotel (Twenty-fourth and Broadway), Hotel Brunswick (Twenty-sixth and Fifth), and Gilsey House (Twenty-ninth and Broadway). All opened within a dozen years of the Fifth Avenue, and each soon developed its own distinct clientele. The Fifth Avenue was known for its wealthy young couples, financiers, and Republican politicians; the Hoffman House for its European guests and Democratic politicians; the Albermarle for its foreigners of distinction; the Hotel Brunswick for its horsey set; and the Gilsey House for its very particular military men, congressmen, and industrialists.

Next came the theaters, previously clustered around Broadway south of Union Square and along the Bowery. First to open was the Fifth Avenue Opera House (1865), a minstrel hall in a small building adjoining the Fifth Avenue Hotel on the Twenty-fourth Street side; a few years later, it would morph into the Fifth Avenue Theatre, the neighborhood's first legitimate (i.e., nonburlesque) theater, dedicated to serious drama. The famed Shakespearean actor Edwin Booth erected Booth's Theatre on the southeast corner of Twenty-third Street and Sixth Avenue in 1869, and Bryant's Opera House, which later became Koster and Bial's Music Hall, in operation for twenty-four years, opened on the northwest corner of Twenty-third Street and Sixth Avenue the following year. Other theaters debuted farther north on Broadway in the 1870s, and by the 1880s, the area contained dozens of entertainment venues.

And then came the prostitutes, long associated with both the hotels and theaters. Well-established madams opened bordellos, discreet ladies of the night rented rooms, and not-so-discreet women of all ages began lingering on the streets, along with a host of other questionable types—card sharks, pickpockets, blackmailers, and petty thieves. "One is struck by the number of suspicious looking characters always lurking about," remarked one Fifth Avenue Hotel guest as early as 1861, though it wasn't until after the Civil War that the underworld infiltrated the neighborhood in earnest. Then, even as Fifth Avenue glittered ever more brilliantly,

Sixth Avenue between Twenty-third and Forty-second streets became the
city's most notorious drag—twenty straight blocks lined with brothel
after brothel, saloon after saloon, dance hall after dance hall, and gambling
den after gambling den.

The Fifth Avenue/Broadway side of the block was all about hope,
laughter, money, power, the ego. The Sixth Avenue side was about rage,
poverty, desperation, subjugation, the id.

* * *

Early critics aside, by the time the Fifth Avenue Hotel opened, directly
across from Madison Square Park, its location was one of its chief assets.
During the three years it had taken to build the hotel, the square had
metamorphosed from a muddy, underdeveloped tract into a fashionable
residential park and *the* place for promenading. "Every man of taste takes
a turn in or around Madison Square—the most admired part of the city,"
wrote one proud New Yorker in 1859. "Here he meets the Venuses that
sculptors will never equal . . . and before him will pass more of the real
beauty and wealth of the nation than in any other spot."

The first home on the square, built for metalwork industrialist James
Stokes, had gone up at 37 Madison Square East in 1851 and was soon
followed by other homes on the east, north, and south sides. Among the
residents on the north side, lined with a continuous row of brownstones
by the mid-1860s, were Dr. John E. Gray, a well-known specialist in
homeopathic medicine, and Frank Worth, a prominent banker. Amos Eno
moved his family to the south side of the square sometime between 1856
and 1858 for the express purpose of overseeing the building of his hotel.
Much later his daughter Mary would recall those years: "I had, of course, a
very gay winter . . . It was then the custom to make visits in the evenings,
and our home was the resort for many young men, so that frequently out
of season we used to send for our neighborhood girl friends and impromptu
dances often took place . . . We had many delightful families living on our
square and nearby, and we were very social."

In 1859, the same year the Fifth Avenue Hotel opened, ground was
broken for what would become the square's most splendid private residence.
Built for the flamboyant Leonard Jerome, "The King of Wall Street," a tall

man with a bristling walrus mustache, the French Second Empire mansion with white marble trim stood at the southeast corner of Madison Avenue and Twenty-sixth Street. Contained within was a vast white-and-gold ballroom with two fountains, one spouting champagne, the other cologne, and a private six-hundred-seat theater, where Jerome's young female protégées performed; he was a notorious womanizer. The king was most proud, however, of his three-story stable. Separated from his home by an empty lot, the $80,000 (about $2.5 million today) edifice sported black walnut paneling, wall-to-wall carpeting, and stained-glass windows—all greatly appreciated, no doubt, by his thoroughbreds. Jerome later became one of the co-founders of the American Jockey Club and several race-tracks, and his daughter Jennie became Lady Randolph Churchill, mother of British prime minister Winston Churchill.

Not all of Madison Square was gentrified, however. Directly across from the Jerome mansion teemed the New York and Harlem Railroad Depot, stretching between Twenty-sixth and Twenty-seventh streets, Madison and Park avenues. Opened in 1832, it was a combination passenger depot, freight shed, and horse barn. Here passengers boarded horse-drawn cars to travel up Park Avenue via an underground tunnel to Forty-second Street. The cars were then attached to steam-powered locomotives and driven farther north.

Madison Square Park itself was still a simple affair too. There were none of its later elegant, curved walkways and fountains, and no central lawn—those were added in 1870 by the landscape architect Ignatz Pilat. Rather, the park was a utilitarian rectangle, slightly curved at its south-western edge by the meeting of Fifth Avenue and Broadway. Divided into six blocks, it was crisscrossed by footpaths and sparsely planted with young trees.

Among those observing the comings and goings on the newly fashion-able square was William Allen Butler, a prominent lawyer. So intrigued was he by what he saw that he wrote a long satirical poem about it for *Harper's Weekly*, later published as a book that became a bestseller. Titled "Nothing to Wear," it was inspired by his five sisters, who would spend hours getting dressed for promenading in the park, and ended with a description of the sadder lives being lived just west of the square:

Miss Flora M'Flimsey, of Madison Square,
Has made three separate journeys to Paris,
And her father assures me, each time she was there,
That she and her friend Mrs. Harris . . .
Spent six consecutive weeks, without stopping,
In one continuous round of shopping . . .
For bonnets, mantillas, capes, collars, and shawls;
Dresses for breakfasts, and dinners, and balls;
Dresses to sit in, and stand in, and walk in;
Dresses to dance in, and flirt in, and talk in;
Dresses in which to do nothing at all;
Dresses for Winter, Spring, Summer and Fall . . .

O ladies, dear ladies, the next sunny day
Please trundle your hoops just out of Broadway . . .
To the alleys and lanes, where Misfortune and Guilt
Their children have gathered, their city have built;
Where Hunger and Vice, like twin beasts of prey,
Have hunted their victims to gloom and despair;
Raise the rich, dainty dress, and the fine broidered skirt,
Pick your delicate way through the dampness and dirt,
Grope through the dark dens, climb the rickety stair
To the garret, where wretches, the young and the old,
Half starved and half naked, lie crouched from the cold . . .
Then home to your wardrobes, and say, if you dare—
Spoiled children of fashion—you've nothing to wear!

*　　*　　*

October 11, 1860. The long-awaited day had finally arrived. The Prince of Wales, the future King Edward VII of Great Britain, was sailing into New York Harbor. A crowd of at least two hundred thousand—one fourth the city's population—thronged the sidewalks, jammed the rooftops, packed the windows, and clung to the lampposts and trees between the Battery and the Fifth Avenue Hotel, all waiting to catch a glimpse of the teenager. The former rebel colony was being recognized by the motherland at last.

The prince's visit almost hadn't happened, though, because his mother, Queen Victoria, had been adamantly opposed to the idea. She was repulsed by the thought of British royalty visiting the upstart nation, but had finally been worn down by Prince Albert and her foreign secretary, who had convinced her that the visit would help improve relations between the two countries. She was also glad to get her eldest son, the heir apparent, out of her sight for a while, as she was finding him and his appetite for wine, women, and cigars increasingly annoying.

By the time the prince arrived in New York, he had already visited Canada, various cities in the Midwest, Washington, D.C., and Philadelphia. But New York, now firmly established as the commercial and financial capital of the United States, was regarded as the most important stop on his tour. Twenty-one-gun salutes fired off as his steamer, the *Harriet Lane*, neared Manhattan, and tens of thousands of hats and handkerchiefs flew into the air. Waiting to meet the prince as he debarked in his scarlet coat and white-plumed hat was Mayor Fernando Wood and seven thousand militiamen, their bayonets winking in the sun.

The prince changed into military uniform to review the troops and then took a short ride to City Hall, where he reviewed more troops. Deafening drums rolled as company after company passed, officer after officer saluted, and hour after hour went by. For those packed tightly together on Broadway, the wait was interminable. When the prince finally climbed into a barouche pulled by six horses to head uptown, it was already five ten P.M., and more than a few onlookers, in "intense grief," had gone home. Those who remained cheered themselves hoarse, threw bouquets in front of the carriage, and nearly knocked it over several times in their frenzy to get a closer look at the prince.

By the time the entourage reached the Fifth Avenue Hotel, it was dark, and the crowd waiting outside caught only a glimpse of a slim figure as the prince entered the hotel. Waiting to greet him in the lobby were various hotel managers, dignitaries, and hundreds of eager onlookers. But the prince was exhausted. Wearily he climbed the wide staircase to the second story and made a brief appearance on the hotel's balcony to wave to the masses. Then he went to bed.

The entire south wing of the hotel had been transformed for his visit. All the best furniture had been moved into his suite, and on loan on the walls were magnificent works of art, including *The Great Fall, Niagara*, by Frederic Edwin Church, a portrait of George Washington by Rembrandt Peale, a religious painting by Peter Paul Rubens, and a miniature of Queen Victoria. The latter may or may not have been appreciated by the visitor.

The next day, the prince toured the Astor Library, the Cooper Institute, the Deaf and Dumb Asylum, the University, and Central Park. He was honored with a torchlight parade by the Fire Department, which he viewed from the hotel's balcony, and a breakfast at Mayor Wood's home outside town at Broadway and Seventy-seventh Street. But the highlight of his visit was to be a grand ball at the Academy of Music on Fourteenth Street, organized and largely paid for by a committee of four hundred wealthy society men. A dance floor had been built above the academy's concert floor, English and American flags hung from the walls, and tall Sévres vases were filled with roses. All the while, the ladies discussed what to wear. Mauve, magenta, and solferino (a purplish red) were the fashionable colors of the day.

On the night of the ball, the crush of people inside the academy was tremendous, petticoat pressing against petticoat, hooped skirt against hooped skirt, as everyone waited for the prince to arrive. Amos Eno was not there, but two of his sons were, along with Paran Stevens, the manager of the Fifth Avenue Hotel, and his tall, striking wife, Marietta. At ten thirty P.M. the prince appeared in full evening dress, and a band struck up "God Save the Queen." Some of the ladies climbed on chairs to get a better view. One of the Sévres vases fell. Someone handed the prince his dance card. Another vase fell. Then came a great crash.

The temporary dance floor had collapsed. No one was hurt, but the frightened crowd retreated, and the prince was whisked off to the supper room for a glass of champagne. Carpenters rushed in to repair the damage, and at midnight, the dancing finally began, with a *quadrille d'honneur*, followed by waltzes. The prince danced with Miss Fish, Miss Mason, Miss

Fanny Butler, and many others, while the less fortunate ladies pressed aggressively against him, hoping for their chance. The prince didn't seem to mind, but when the ball was over a few hours later, he was reportedly covered with black and blue marks, caused by the pinches and squeezes of those ladies who had hoped to get a piece of him.

The next day, some commentators lamented the collapse of the academy's floor and criticized their fellow Americans for ineptitude. But most New Yorkers regarded the ball as a grand success and took pride in the city's ability to take catastrophe in stride. Only one woman had fainted!

While staying at the Fifth Avenue Hotel, the prince heard a strange new word—*shampoo*—and decided he wanted to try it. Derived from the Hindi *cāmpo!*, meaning to push or squeeze, *shampoo* had entered the English language a century before, but up until 1860 had primarily meant "to knead the muscles," as during a Turkish bath. A popular hairdresser was called in to the hotel and quickly got to work. His Highness was reportedly enchanted by the results and vowed to continue the curious procedure at home.

Gardner Wetherbee, a clerk at the hotel, would later remember the prince's visit well: "He had the suite on the first floor 23rd Street side, and was pretty much bored, as a jolly youth of nineteen might well be, by the ceremony he was obliged to face from the time he set foot in New York. So great was his relief to escape to the privacy of his suite that he and his immediate companions engaged in an enthusiastic game of leap-frog in the corridor."

Rumor also had it that the prince slipped out of the hotel at night to see if the city's nightlife lived up to its reputation. If he had, he probably slid over to the Sixth Avenue side of the block, only one of the first of a long stream of male hotel guests to do so. The Fifth Avenue Hotel was perfectly situated on the edge between the light and the dark, the authorized and the unauthorized, with the two spheres often spilling over, diluting, and invigorating each other.

CHAPTER 7

War

It is eight A.M. on the fine spring morning of April 18, 1861, six months after the Prince of Wales's visit. A crowd of five thousand is packed tightly together in Madison Square Park, the luckier ones pressed up close to the entrance of the New York and Harlem Railroad Depot at the corner of Madison Avenue and Twenty-sixth Street. The Sixth Regiment, Massachusetts Militia, is arriving from Boston, en route to Washington, D.C.

The horse-drawn carriages pull in, wheels grinding, reins jangling. The crowd explodes. "Bay State boys!" "Boston boys!" "Bunker Hill boys!" come the thunderous roars. The Civil War has begun.

On hand to meet the troops as they clamber out is Alfred B. Darling, a manager of the Fifth Avenue Hotel. The dapper forty-year-old proudly escorts some of the companies across the park for breakfast at the hotel, while others fall in line and march down Broadway to the Metropolitan Hotel, the St. Nicholas Hotel, and the Astor House, where they will breakfast. Fervent crowds jam the sidewalks and rooftops along the route, shouting, cheering, whistling, and waving a river of flags. The Sixth Massachusetts is among the first military units to answer President Lincoln's call for troops after the capture of Fort Sumter, South Carolina, by the Confederate forces on April 13, 1861. It will also be the first unit to sustain casualties, in Baltimore, only a day after leaving New York.

At the Fifth Avenue Hotel, the boisterous young troops push through the front doors, stack their long, unwieldy muskets in piles in the lobby, and bound up the stairs to the sun-dappled dining room. As they burst in, the hotel's regular guests immediately stand up, leaving their breakfasts unfinished, and give the soldiers their seats. Then the fashionably dressed lady guests, many of whom have never done a day's work in their lives, serve the Massachusetts men breakfast.

*   *   *

Among those who witnessed the arrival of the Massachusetts troops in Madison Square Park that morning was the Wall Street lawyer and aristocrat George Templeton Strong. "Immense crowd; immense cheering," he wrote in his tidy, precise hand that night in a diary he had been keeping since he was fifteen. "God be praised for the unity of feeling here! It is beyond, very far beyond, anything I hoped for. If it only last, we are safe."

Strong had good reason to feel relieved about his fellow New Yorkers' response to the opening salvos of the war. New York was a deeply divided city, with strong ties to the South. For decades, its economy had been heavily reliant on the cotton trade; New York bankers and merchants provided Southern planters with the credit and supplies they needed to grow and sell their goods. As early as 1822, half the city's exports were related to cotton, and by 1860, New York was exporting millions of dollars' worth of the crop annually. Wealthy Southerners and their families, often traveling with slaves, were fixtures in the city's finest shops, restaurants, and hotels, including the Fifth Avenue, which was popular among the out-of-towners, as it was near the railroad depot. Two of the hotel's managers, Darling and Hiram Hitchcock, were also well known in the South, as they had run other luxury hotels there in the 1850s.

Nor had New York City supported Lincoln in the years leading up to the war. During the 1860 presidential campaign, the city's mostly Democratic businessmen and political leaders had campaigned vigorously against him, arguing that if he and the Republicans won the election, the dreaded negroes would be everywhere, overrunning stores and restaurants, stealing jobs from immigrants, taking up seats in crowded street- and railroad cars. New York had abolished slavery only thirty-three years before and was still rigidly segregated and stone-cold prejudiced. True, the city was home to some prominent abolitionists, including the newspaper editor Horace Greeley and the Reverend Henry Ward Beecher, but they were a minority presence. Two thirds of the city's voters had cast their ballots against Lincoln in the 1860 election.

The Illinois senator had won by a landslide upstate, however, and New York State went Republican, an outcome essential to Lincoln's winning the election. Many in the city were horrified, and that winter, New York's tall, handsome, stylish, and corrupt-to-the-bone Mayor Wood, speaking not entirely tongue in cheek, proposed that with the Southern states seceding, New York should secede, too, and become an independent free city so that it could remain friendly with both sides and continue profiting from the cotton trade.

But the Confederate takeover of Fort Sumter had changed everything. New Yorkers were outraged by the attack on their country—and ready to fight back. They believed in the Constitution, and the last thing they really wanted was for the United States to split apart. Besides, like most Northerners, many were expecting a short war that would quickly squash the rebellion and reestablish the status quo, including the use of slaves in the South.

Two days after the Massachusetts troops passed through New York, a massive crowd of one hundred thousand jammed into Union Square for a pro-Union rally. Flags and banners flapped everywhere, and dozens of notables spoke, among them Mayor Wood, who had made an about-face and proclaimed himself pro-war.

The next day, hordes of young and not-so-young men rushed to join volunteer regiments, many organized by ethnicity. Most of the men had little, if any, military training. Anyone who wanted could raise a company (one hundred men) and declare himself a captain, or a regiment (one thousand men) and declare himself a colonel. Tent camps were erected wherever space could be found. Madison Square Park was soon overflowing, and the Fifth Avenue Hotel teemed with a mix of fresh-faced, elated youths and experienced military men traveling in from all over the Northeast.

From then on, the hotel would serve as the city's ground zero for the Union cause and the Republican Party, which would establish its state headquarters in room 10 in 1869. President Lincoln frequented the hotel, often coming and going at night to avoid detection, as did Secretary of State William H. Seward, whose statue now stands in Madison Square Park. Wealthy Republicans congregated in the hotel's lounges and bars, and formed the Union League Club, which helped fund the Union Army and war-related service organizations such as the U.S. Sanitary Commission, forerunner of the American Red Cross. All this was conducted with the solid support of Amos Eno, who wrote checks to the Republican Party.

Traveling around the city on Sundays became impossible, as the volunteer soldiers took over the streets to the cheers of thousands. Dressed in uniforms sewn by mothers, wives, and girlfriends, they marched to uptown picnic grounds, where they spent the afternoons target shooting, drinking, singing, and daydreaming about their courage in battles yet to come.

By early May, nearly half of the 16,000 troops defending Washington, D.C., were from Manhattan and Brooklyn. New York State would provide more Union troops than any other state during the war—about 400,000, or 17 percent of the total number of troops, with 150,000 of those from New York City. The state would also have the most casualties, 53,000.

* * *

New York's economy went into a nosedive soon after the war started and the cotton trade dried up. But then the military contracts began pouring in—for ships, artillery, ambulances, uniforms, medicine, and more—and in a quick reversal of fortune, the city's businessmen and upper classes were thriving as never before. Before the war, New York had been home to a few dozen millionaires. Afterward, it would house several hundred, and throughout the tragic conflict, the newly rich—snidely dubbed the "shoddy aristocracy"—flitted eagerly about in the city's luxury department stores, restaurants, and hotels. Whatever the Fifth Avenue Hotel had lost in the way of Southern guests, it more than made up for in the way of the parvenus, who reveled in showing off their wealth as conspicuously as possible.

Gentlemen powdered their hair with silver and gold dust; women draped themselves in $1,000 (about $31,000 today) camel hair shawls. Old New York society was appalled.

* * *

Living at the Fifth Avenue Hotel the year after the war began were the great Shakespearean actor Edwin Booth and his wife, Mary Devlin, also a talented actor. Passionately in love, eyes following them wherever they went, Edwin was twenty-eight and Mary twenty-one. They had met five years earlier playing opposite each other in *Romeo and Juliet*.

Edwin was the son of the celebrated English thespian Junius Brutus Booth, who was as famous a Shakespearean actor in his day as Edwin was in his. An eccentric man, prone to bouts of deep depression, Junius Brutus was also an alcoholic, known for passing out in front of the curtain, streaking naked through public streets, and once walking all the way from Boston to Providence in his stocking feet and underwear. And so, when Edwin was thirteen, his mother pulled him out of school to tour the country with his father to keep the elder Booth in line. Edwin had an older brother, Junius Jr., and a younger one, John Wilkes, but neither had the temperament to deal with the older man, and Edwin did. He was quiet, patient, and devoted to his father, whom he adored. For seven years, Edwin served as Junius's keeper, a slight youth overseeing a burly man.

After a time, Edwin began acting alongside his father, taking on small roles at first, and then, one night when Junius refused to go on stage, taking his place as Richard III. The crowd was silent as the pale, graceful teenager, dark curls tumbling to his shoulders, appeared onstage, but by the end of the evening they were on their feet, clapping and cheering wildly. Edwin had a rich, sonorous voice and acted with a kind of realism not seen before. Other roles followed, and by 1862, in an age that revered actors, Edwin had accrued enough fame and fortune to rent an apartment at the opulent Fifth Avenue. Most late afternoons found him and Mary relaxing by their drawing-room fireplace, Edwin in a velvet smoking jacket lying on a bearskin rug and practicing his lines while Mary listened, prompted, and played her guitar. The young couple usually dined early at a small table in their suite, with Mary's greyhound, a gift from Edwin, at their feet, so that they could leave in time for the theater. Mary always accompanied Edwin and watched him perform from a stage box, her lips moving with his every word. "We were all in all to each other," she later said of that time.

Edwin must have thought then that his troubles were behind him, that the world was his for the taking, that one happy year would follow another. But on February 21, 1863, after less than three years of marriage and two years of war, Mary would die of pneumonia without him at her side. Like his father, he had taken to drink, and on the night of her death, he was too inebriated to heed the urgent summons of his friends.

*   *   *

It is the hot sultry Monday morning of July 13, 1863. The excitement, gaiety, and bravado of the early months of the war are gone. Tens of thousands of Union soldiers have been killed, and tens of thousands more are badly maimed. Wounded soldiers haunt the streets, along with war widows, orphans, and desperate Southern women, some of whom loiter on and around the Twenty-third Street block to practice the world's oldest profession. "The harlotry of the city is largely reinforced by Southern refugee women who were of good social standing at home, but find themselves here without means of support and forced to choose between starving and whoring," wrote George Templeton Strong.

The city's poor and working class are also suffering. Basic provisions are scarce, and prices for everything from flour and milk to beef and coal have skyrocketed by a third or more. The already profound gap between the rich and the poor has widened tenfold.

Making matters worse in the minds of many is the Emancipation Proclamation, issued by President Lincoln six months before. Especially resentful are the city's thousands of impoverished Irish immigrants, who make up 25 percent of its population. Living in miserable, subhuman conditions with no relief in sight, the immigrants fear that the proclamation will lead to more competition for their already scarce and underpaid jobs.

And now has come the final straw. Lincoln has issued the Enrollment Act of 1863 to fill the depleted ranks of Union soldiers. The drawing of names began two days earlier, without incident, but since then the mood in the city has turned ugly and tense. Especially insulting to the poor and working class is the fact that the wealthy can buy their way out of the draft for $300 (about $9,500 today)—the equivalent of the average worker's annual salary.

The drawing of names is to resume at ten thirty that morning at the draft office at Third Avenue and Forty-sixth Street, but already by seven A.M., hundreds of workers are streaming uptown, beating copper pans and closing shops and factories as they go. Coming to a halt outside the draft office, their numbers swell to the thousands. The handful of policemen guarding the building exchange nervous glances.

At ten thirty A.M. someone in the crowd fires a pistol into the air and others begin throwing stones. Windows splinter and crash. "Down with rich men!" "No draft!" come the roars as the mob thunders its way into the office to destroy the draft records. Outside, John U. Andrews, a Confederate sympathizer and fierce anti-abolitionist, further incites the raging crowd. The deadliest riot in U.S. history has begun. It will last four days.

Someone pours turpentine, and the mob burns the draft offices to the ground. Then they march to row houses nearby where they believe the draft officers live and burn those to the ground too.

Thousands of other citizens, women as well as men, flood the streets. Armed with sticks and stones, and crazed with frustration and rage, they attack and burn more homes, pull up railroad tracks, chop down telegraph poles, raid arsenals and armories, loot shops and bars, destroy the offices of the Republican press, and murder and mutilate policemen, soldiers, and civilians.

"Now for the Fifth-Avenue Hotel—there's where the Union Leaguers meet!" someone shouts, and part of the mob breaks off to head downtown. Word of the impending attack reaches the hotel, and the panicked staff rushes to slam close the shutters, barricade the halls with baggage, and warn the guests to keep away from the windows. A hundred muskets are distributed, and, according to one early historian, a chief clerk goes into the streets in hopes of finding soldiers to protect the hotel. None are in sight. He mixes with the mob gathering in Madison Square and, thinking quickly, circulates rumors that the Fifth Avenue is filled with soldiers eagerly waiting for an excuse to open fire. No one believes him at first, but then two Union generals who are staying at the hotel come out on the balcony, and upon seeing their uniforms, "the rioters went away without even throwing a brickbat," reports one observer.

By happenstance, William Stoddard, Lincoln's assistant private secretary, is in New York that day, taking what he thought would be a rejuvenating break from his duties in the capital. As he nears the Twenty-third Street block, he stops in shock at the sight of a "surging, swaying crowd" "whooping, yelling, blaspheming and howling, demoniacs such as no man imagined the city of New York to contain . . . There were women among them and half-grown boys . . . They carried guns, pistols, axes, hatchets, crowbars, pitchforks, knives, bludgeons . . . Those men lying so careless-wise on the sidewalks, in the gutters and on the roadway at Twenty-third Street were not drunk; they were dead."

An especially sickening attack comes at four P.M. "Burn the niggers' nest," screams the mob as it heads to the Colored Orphans Asylum, perched on a pretty hillock on Fifth Avenue between Forty-third and Forty-fourth streets. Built by Quaker abolitionists, the well-stocked, four-story Greek Revival building is a prominent symbol of some wealthy whites' benevolence toward African Americans and, by extension, a symbol of their neglect of impoverished Irish immigrants. All 237 children inside the asylum escape safely out the back with the help of staff. Moments later, the mob swarms over the institution, uprooting trees, ripping clothing, destroying toys, and burning the building to the ground.

Edwin Booth, who moved out of the Fifth Avenue Hotel after his wife's death, is now living at 28 East Nineteenth Street. Stricken with grief, he has vowed to give up acting, saying it has lost all meaning for him, and to never drink again. He will break the first vow, but keep the second. With him in his home is his brother John Wilkes, a passionate defender of the Southern cause; Edwin's friend Adam Badeau, recuperating from wounds suffered in battle; and an African American male nurse, there to care for Badeau. The brothers and their companions shudder as they hear the mob storm by under their windows, worried that they might be discovered.

Edwin is a well-known Lincoln supporter; Badeau is a Union soldier; the nurse is Black. John Wilkes is the only one among them who can safely leave the house to forage for food and news. The brothers argue heatedly about Lincoln, slavery, and the war.

Finally, federal troops are called in. Arriving on the third evening of the riots, they march down the city's smoldering, rubble-filled streets, firing muskets and howitzers loaded with grapeshot. Some of the marauders scatter. Others fight ferociously to the death.

The only perpetrator of the riots who will be tried in federal court is Andrews, the Confederate sympathizer who helped incite the mob at the Third Avenue draft office. When the police arrive at his home to arrest him, they find a startling scene. The fierce anti-abolitionist lawyer who constantly railed against the lazy, shifty "darkies" is in bed with an African American prostitute. He is taken to prison in shackles and tried in the winter of 1864. Convicted of treason, he will serve three years in the infamous upstate prison of Sing Sing.

*　*　*

It is October 27, 1864. Fifteen months have passed since the riots, and on the surface, all is calm. But underneath, resentments fester.

The 1864 presidential election is only ten days away. Running against President Lincoln is his former top officer in the field, General McClellan. Beloved by hundreds of thousands of soldiers for his style and verve, the vain, self-important "Little Napoleon" once commanded the mighty Army of the Potomac. But he was slow to act in battle, and Lincoln removed him from his post. Seething, McClellan left Washington and moved to New York, where he took up residence in the Fifth Avenue Hotel for six months before moving into a townhouse.

Eight young men traveling in pairs from Toronto arrive at the Hudson River railroad depot on the West Side. One is a tall, lanky twenty-four-year-old with a moustache, goatee, and steel blue eyes. He walks with a stoop. Another is a slight, clean-shaven twenty-four-year-old with delicate features. A third is a good-looking, bearded twenty-nine-year-old with a conspicuous limp.

The young men speak with Southern accents, but no one pays them any mind. The city is filled with thousands of Southerners—refugees, merchants, planters and their families, prisoners of war out on parole.

The tall man with the steel blue eyes registers at the St. Denis Hotel and then, without unpacking, heads to the Fifth Avenue, where he registers as "Mr. Nicks, Portville, Pa." His companions disperse to other hostelries, where they also register more than once. The men reconvene to meet with a prominent pro-South New Yorker, and afterward the tall man and the clean-shaven youth go sightseeing. They attend various theater performances, travel to Brooklyn to hear the Reverend Beecher preach, and circulate among society folk in the Fifth Avenue Hotel as General McClellan reviews a torchlight parade in his honor from the hotel balcony.

The next day, November 4, the eight men are astounded to hear that the squat, snarly Union general Benjamin Butler, better known as the "Beast" because of his harsh military tactics in New Orleans, has also checked into the Fifth Avenue Hotel (later, he will move across the street to the Hoffman House). He has come north from Virginia, bringing thousands of troops with him, to ensure that the 1864 presidential election goes smoothly. A Union double agent has uncovered a Confederate plot to disrupt the political process. The Beast establishes an armed perimeter around the city and sets up gunboats in the river.

The eight men fume with frustration. They are the would-be perpetrators of the Confederate plot. Their plan is to set small fires throughout the city on Election Day, thereby creating a diversion that will allow their New York sympathizers to take over government and police buildings, free Confederate prisoners, and raise a Confederate flag over the city. After the takeover, and a similar one also underway in Chicago, they hope to force the North to allow the South to secede in exchange for peace.

The plot is not as farfetched as it sounds. The city is filled with Copperheads, or Northerners who support the Southern cause, who long to return to the peaceful, prosperous prewar days of the cotton trade.

The plot's ringleader is the tall man with the steel blue eyes, Lieutenant Colonel Robert Martin of Kentucky, who walks with a stoop because of a bullet wound in his right lung. He has already taken part in other plots against the North and, while in Canada, explored the possibility of poisoning New York City's water supply—shades of rumored twenty-first-century terrorist plots to come. The Confederates dismissed the idea because they thought they couldn't procure enough poison without alerting suspicion.

Martin's second-in-command is the clean-shaven youth, Lieutenant John Headley, also of Kentucky, who will later write a book about his wartime experiences. A third man, the good-looking bearded one with the conspicuous limp, is Captain Robert Cobb Kennedy of Louisiana. Kicked out of West Point for poor deportment, poor grades, and drinking, Cobb enlisted in the Confederate Army days after Fort Sumter.

The eight men meet with their New York co-conspirators, most notably James McMaster, the prominent editor and publisher of the *Freeman's Journal and Catholic Register*. A large, commanding man with piercing eyes and a deep, rumbling voice, McMaster has assured the men that there are twenty thousand Copperheads at the ready with firearms to rise up and take over the city. But the arrival of Butler and his troops is bad news. McMaster convinces the men to postpone their plot, and they sit sullenly by as Lincoln is reelected—no thanks to New York City, which again votes against him two to one—and Chicago fails to burn. Then comes even worse news for the conspirators. General Sherman has burned Atlanta to the ground and is beginning his ruthless march to the sea. McMaster and other prominent New York Copperheads withdraw from the plot, believing the Southern cause doomed. Two of the eight men also back out, but Martin, Headley, Kennedy, and three others remain.

Martin assigns Headley the dangerous task of picking up the "Greek fire" that is essential for their operation. Already ordered from a chemist in Greenwich Village, the colorless fluid is a mixture of phosphorus and bisulfide of carbon. Supposedly, it will ignite spontaneously upon contact with air.

Slipping through the narrow Greenwich Village streets, Headley finds his way to the chemist's shop, housed in a dark basement off Washington Square. Inside he finds a burly old man, who wordlessly hands him a suitcase so heavy that Headley has to change hands every ten steps to carry it. He looks for a carriage, but none is in sight, and so boards a streetcar heading north. The car is packed with people, and as Headley heaves the suitcase inside, he notices a peculiar sulfurous odor. "There must be something dead in that valise," one passenger remarks.

Near Central Park, Headley climbs out and heads to a small cottage owned by a Southern woman refugee, where his companions are waiting. He opens the suitcase. One of the chemist's four-ounce vials has broken; apparently the Greek fire doesn't ignite spontaneously after all. Its stench clogs the air as the Confederates pack the remaining twelve dozen vials into cheap black carpetbags.

It is now Friday, November 25, 1864, the day after Thanksgiving. General Butler and his troops have withdrawn from the city, and the sidewalks are thronged with holiday crowds. Two thousand people fill the Winter Garden Theatre on Broadway near Third Street, where Edwin Booth and his brothers John Wilkes and Junius Jr. are appearing together for the first—and what will prove to be the last—time, in a production of *Julius Caesar*. Edwin is playing Brutus, Junius is playing Cassius, and John Wilkes is playing Mark Antony. Another twenty blocks south, a more raucous crowd has gathered in Barnum's American Museum, to gasp at "three mammoth fat girls weighing one ton," "three giants 24 feet tall," and "two dwarfs weighing 17 pounds each."

At about eight P.M. the Confederate agents set out. They have agreed to start fires in nineteen of the city's finest hotels, but to do so early enough in the evening so that no one will be seriously hurt. Each man has his assignments; Martin's are the St. James, Hoffman House, Belmont, St. Denis, and Fifth Avenue.

The conspirators enter their designated hostelries one by one, head to the guest rooms, pile bedding on mattresses, douse everything with Greek fire, and strike matches. Then they leave the rooms, locking the doors carefully behind them.

The first alarm goes off at eight forty-three P.M. at the St. James Hotel just north of the Fifth Avenue. Minutes later, a fire is discovered at the St. Nicholas Hotel and another at Barnum's Museum, where desperate people and animals burst into the street, and a seven-foot "giantess," hair flying, lurches down the stairs and into a nearby saloon. Next comes a fire at the LaFarge House adjoining the Winter Garden, causing panic in the theater until Edwin commands silence, saying there is nothing to worry about. The play goes on. More fires ignite at the Metropolitan, New England, Lovejoy's, Belmont, and French's, as well as on the docks. Fire engines, hose wagons, and ladder wagons careen through the streets, all pulled by brawny Irishmen who insist on hauling the vehicles themselves rather than hitching up their horses. They enjoy the competition.

It is not until two thirty A.M. that house detective Michael Perry opens the door of room 148 in the Fifth Avenue Hotel, to be met by a rush of smoke. "Mr. Nicks" has set fire to the room's bedding and flung cartridges soaked with turpentine all over the floor. He was careless, however, and left some of the vials corked.

And it is carelessness in general that dooms the terrorist plot to failure. All the hotel fires fizzle out or are discovered before they take hold, probably because the men failed to open the windows and the fires didn't have enough oxygen to burn. Property damage is minimal, no one is seriously injured or killed, and no one is incited to riot.

The next morning, the conspirators sit in a parlor of the Exchange Hotel on Greenwich Street, reading the newspapers and discussing their next move. A burly man enters. Martin freezes. The man is Sergeant John Young, head of the city's fledgling detective force. He has been going from hotel to hotel, warning people to be extra vigilant because of the fires. He collapses onto a banquette near Martin, spies his open paper, and says, "I'm looking for who did it, and I'll be damned if I don't get them." Martin stiffens, bracing himself for arrest. But then a patrolman enters and tells Young he is wanted back at headquarters. He leaves.

Also reading the papers that day, over breakfast on East Nineteenth Street, are Edwin and John Wilkes Booth. They argue vehemently about the plot, with John Wilkes shouting that it is justified payback for Sherman's destruction of Atlanta. A furious Edwin forbids his brother from ever speaking that way in his house again.

That evening, the Confederate agents board a sleeper en route to Albany and travel on to Toronto. Sergeant Young traces them there but is unable to arrest them. A month or so later, Martin and Headley slip back into the United States by walking across the frozen Detroit River at night and return safely to Kentucky, but Kennedy makes the fatal mistake of traveling to Detroit by train. Because of his conspicuous limp, he is recognized, arrested, and sent to New York Harbor's Fort Lafayette (later submerged by the building of the Verrazzano-Narrows Bridge). He appeals for help to McMaster and the other powerful Copperheads, but all disavow any knowledge of him, and he is hung on March 25, 1865, just weeks before the South surrenders and the war ends.

Martin is captured a few months after Kennedy, while trying to help the Confederate president Jefferson Davis escape near the end of the war. He is not recognized at first, but then makes his own fatal mistake by bragging about his role in the plot to his cellmate. The cellmate rats him out, and Martin is transferred to Fort Lafayette to await trial as a spy. But the war is over by then, and Martin, like many prisoners in both the North and the South, is freed.

Headley lives a long and peaceful life, serves as Kentucky's secretary of state in the 1890s, and writes his book, *Confederate Operations in Canada and New York*. Still a die-hard Confederate in 1906, he dedicates it to the memory of the "defenseless non-combatant people of the South" and "the persecuted people of the North."

John Wilkes Booth assassinates Abraham Lincoln on the evening of April 14, 1865, and is killed by a sergeant's bullet twelve days later. Edwin is devastated. He has lost his wife, his brother, his president, and his good name. He is physically and psychologically unable to return to the stage for eight months, and then only does so at the urging of close friends and supporters.

Three years later, Edwin opens Booth's Theatre on the southeast corner of Twenty-third Street and Sixth Avenue and takes up residence on the Twenty-third Street block once again—this time in an upscale boarding house at 14 West Twenty-fourth Street, where he lives until 1873. Also living in the house in the 1870s is the popular spiritualist and medium Charles H. Foster, best known for "skin writing," wherein spirits supposedly write messages on his arms or forehead, and "pellet reading," which involves delivering messages supposedly from the dead written on slips of paper. Booth believes deeply in Foster's powers; he visited the spiritualist often in the year after Mary's death in hopes of communicating with her and wasn't disappointed. Once Mary apparently wrote her initials in big red letters on the back of Foster's hand, and another time, Booth wrote to a friend, "in a deep trance [Foster] almost smothered me with caresses (he afterwards said 'twas as much as he could do to keep from kissing me all the time) and talked as Mary talked."

Booth takes solace in his séances with Foster, his work, and in an odd accident of fate: in early 1865 he rescued Lincoln's oldest son, Robert, from being crushed by a train at a crowded Jersey City railroad station. As Robert recalled years later in a letter to the editor of the *Century Magazine*, the "train began to move, and by the motion I was twisted off my feet, and had dropped somewhat, with feet downward, into the open space, and was personally helpless, when my coat collar was vigorously seized and I was quickly pulled up and out to a secure footing on the platform. Upon turning to thank my rescuer I saw it was Edwin Booth."

CHAPTER 8

Cracks in the Vault

During the last year of the Civil War, one Mrs. Electa M. Potter hung out a shingle at 386 Sixth Avenue, a small brick building on the west side of the block, much to the disgust and indignation of her neighbors. A small woman with bloated legs, recently recovered from a severe bout of rheumatism, she was a "physician"—code, in her case, for abortionist.

Abortionists were easy to find in the mid-1800s. They advertised in the daily papers and handed out handbills. "SURE CURE FOR LADIES IN TROUBLE. NO injurious medicines or instruments used," ran one ad. "Ladies cured at one interview with or without medicine $5 . . . sure and safe," ran another. "Monthly pills, to remove obstructions and irregularities, however produced," ran a third.

Technically speaking, abortion was illegal in New York. Three decades earlier, in 1828, the state had passed a criminal statute holding an abortionist liable if he or she performed an abortion after "quickening"—the moment when the fetus begins to move, usually around the fourth month. And in 1845, that statute was strengthened to apply to all pregnancies, no matter what the stage. The laws were primarily aimed at protecting women from dangerous quacks, however, not ending abortions, and law officials, the press, and the general public usually looked the other way as women of all classes found their way to the physicians' doorsteps. Experts estimated that the rate of abortions to live births in the city in the 1850s was a sky-high one to five or six.

The most famous abortionist of the era was Madame Restell, whose business was so successful that she built herself a luxurious brownstone on the northeast corner of Fifth Avenue and Fifty-second Street, bought a glittering carriage with prancing horses, and hired liveried coachmen to escort her everywhere she went. Allegedly trained as a midwife, she treated thousands of women, some with pills and others with surgical abortions, before being charged with murder after one of her patients died in 1840. The case launched a bitter debate, similar to those still being waged today, but Madame Restell was found not guilty due to a lack of evidence. Seven years later, however, she was arrested again, this time for second-degree murder in another case, and sentenced to a year in prison on Blackwell's Island (now Roosevelt Island). Afterward, she stopped offering surgical abortions and just provided pills, but the press and moral reformers, many at least as enraged by her wealth as by her business, hounded her, calling her "Madame Killer," the "wickedest woman in New York." "Why do they persecute me so? I have done nothing to harm anyone," she cried one day to one of her servants. In 1878, she committed suicide.

As a bit player in a booming industry, Electa Potter was no Madame Restell, and her activities would have gone largely unnoticed were it not for her alleged involvement in a then even more controversial practice: divorce. Despite its liberal reputation today, New York has historically been ultraconservative when it comes to marriage. It was the last state in the union to pass a no-fault divorce law, in 2010, and from 1787 to 1966, the only grounds for divorce in New York was adultery. Couples with money often went out of state to separate—to Indiana in the 1800s or Nevada in the 1900s—while other unhappy men and women tried to get out of their marriages by framing their spouse for adultery.

Improbably, Mrs. Potter, an uneducated working-class woman in poor health, was named as the "other woman" in a scandalous celebrity divorce case involving Mary Stevens Strong and Peter Strong soon after her move to 386 Sixth Avenue. Mary was a queen of society, the daughter of a wealthy, prominent banker who was the chairman of the Sons of the American Revolution. Peter was a lawyer and third cousin of George Templeton

Strong, the lawyer and diarist. The couple had apparently been happily married with three children for about seven years when Peter's brother Edward, who had recently lost his wife, came to live with them in 1860. With Peter often out of the house on business, and Edward always there during many lonely hours, Mary plunged into an affair with her brother-in-law. After it ended two years later, she felt full of remorse and confessed to her husband. They stopped living together. However, wishing to avoid publicity, he did not bring suit against her until 1865 when she took their youngest daughter to her family's Long Island home and never returned. Mary's lawyers then countersued with the eye-popping claim that Peter had also strayed: he had had an adulterous relationship with Mrs. Potter while helping her run her abortion practice out of her former boarding-house at 124 Waverly Place, a building that he owned.

The case took many months to come to trial, with the press pouncing on every salacious detail, and lasted five weeks. Dozens of witnesses, from family friends and servants to private detectives and neighbors, were called on to testify before a jammed open court. "No case before our court for many years has attracted greater attention," reported the *New York Times* on the trial's opening day, November 24, 1865. It was all but unheard of for members of high society to appear in court—and all but unheard of for the dirty secrets of the rich and powerful to be on full display before the general public. High society lived in a sealed vault, a rarefied world beyond the ken of most, and seemed to have nothing in common with ordinary folk. Until, that is, cracks in the vault appeared.

Today, the probable outcome of the Stevens-Strong trial seems obvious. Mary had confessed to, and did not deny, her adultery; Peter's case was rock solid. But at that time, things weren't so simple. Mary's lawyers argued that their client was deeply religious and physically frail and had sinned only because of her husband's neglect and her brother-in-law's powers of seduction—arguments that carried great weight in that era. Women were regarded as fragile and in need of protection, and even as Mary had "dishon-ored" herself and her family, Peter had been at fault for being away from home too much, not ensuring his wife's happiness, and failing to protect her from his brother, who was also at fault for not being strong enough to resist temptation.

To avoid unseemly attention, Mary never appeared in court, but her powerful father, an "elderly, quiet mannered gentleman," was there daily. Behind his daughter 100 percent, he testified that Peter Strong had been a harsh, cold husband. Mary's sister also testified, stating that Mary had suffered several miscarriages because of Peter's neglect and that he had physically threatened her upon learning of her affair.

To prove Peter guilty of adultery with Mrs. Potter, Mary's lawyers, backed by her father, brought forth various witnesses of questionable character. One swore that he had seen Peter enter 386 Sixth Avenue on numerous occasions, staying from an hour to an hour and a half each time. Another swore that she had once seen Peter in bed with Mrs. Potter— albeit with his clothes on—and had assumed that he was her husband.

As for Mrs. Potter's abortion practice, there was little doubt that it had once operated out of her former residence at 124 Waverly Place. More contentious was the allegation that a botched abortion there had led to the death of a Mrs. Elizabeth Adams on or about April 18, 1863. In the months before the divorce trial began, witnesses testified that they had seen Mrs. Adams die in Mrs. Potter's bed and that Peter had been a frequent visitor to the house during Mrs. Adams's stay there. Both were indicted on the charge of murder, but the charges were dropped well before the divorce trial, as too much time had passed since the death to prove anything.

Next the Stevens' lawyers came up with an even stranger allegation: they claimed that their client, believing that she was having a miscarriage, had been advised by her husband to visit Mrs. Potter to ask for her help. The so-called physician had then aborted a perfectly healthy child, the lawyers said, with the connivance of Peter, who was convinced the child wasn't his. For her part, Mrs. Potter denied ever meeting Mary and testified that Mary's brother, John Austin Stevens, had offered her a large sum of money if she would testify that she had indeed performed the abortion.

George Templeton Strong followed the trial of his cousin Peter with deep sorrow and smoldering anger. He did not blame Mary so much as he blamed her father and brother for concocting what he believed to be bilious lies. "I have meant to go into the Superior Court every day, but I have been unable to do it," he wrote in his diary. "The memory has always appeared to me of that beautiful bride of twelve years ago in her pearls and white lace, and I have been forced to run away from the court room in which that noble creature is being dragged through the mud by her vindictive, senseless father and brother."

In the end, the trial resulted in a hung jury. All the jurors found Mary guilty of adultery, but two believed that Peter had been guilty of adultery as well. Those two jurors were accused of having accepted bribes from the Stevens family, a charge they vehemently denied.

Soon thereafter, Peter was granted his divorce petition and given custody of the couple's children, and Mary returned to her parents' home. Mrs. Potter moved away from the Twenty-third Street block, but where she went immediately afterward is unclear. Her name and that of her husband, Vernon, a fruit vendor, disappeared from the New York City directories for three years. In 1868, however, a Vernon Potter in "produce" was listed as working on Vesey Street and living in New Jersey.

* * *

Among the many wealthy society families aghast at the Stevens scandal were those living right around the corner from Mrs. Potter, in mansions along the Twenty-third Street side of the block. Quiet, peaceful, and lined with trees, the street was one of the most desirable addresses in the city in the 1860s and a delight to walk along, especially on sunny mornings, when "nurses with infants in their arms, and children with hoops, go-carts and toys, monopolized the sidewalks; elegantly-attired ladies sauntered along; and splendid equipages stood before the stately mansions, while their mistresses paid calls within." No place could be farther away in spirit from the tawdry goings-on at 386 Sixth Avenue.

Near the center of the block lived one of its richest couples, Mr. and Mrs. William Colford Schermerhorn, who began building their mansion the same year the Fifth Avenue Hotel opened. Their relative Gene Schermerhorn and his family had left West Twenty-third Street by then, probably because it had become too expensive and crowded. Young Gene was grown now and would live his entire life outside society's circles, never joining any clubs or organizations, or even having a formal profession. In contrast, William Colford was a well-connected lawyer, clubman, and man about town. He served on the boards of the Metropolitan Museum of Art and American Museum of Natural History, and was a trustee of Columbia University, a position he would hold for forty-three years. He was also devoted to the opera and symphony, a practitioner of homeopathy, a believer in spiritualism, and a good friend of George Templeton Strong. The two had known each other since childhood and had studied law together.

Mrs. William Schermerhorn, the former Ann Elliott Huger Cottenet, was the daughter of a wealthy merchant and granddaughter of General Edward William Laight of the New York State militia. A woman of beauty and grace who knew how to get what she wanted, she was said to be the perfect hostess. "The guests of that most charming and gracious Mrs. William C. Schermerhorn must be themselves in fault if they fail to enjoy their sojourn in Twenty-Third Street. She had the most wonderful talent for making people feel comfortable," wrote Strong in his diary.

Most Knickerbockers, as the descendants of the early Dutch families were still known, had a reputation for being clannish, smug, modest, and thrifty. Not so the William Schermerhorns in their prime. Socialites of the first order, they had been living downtown on Lafayette Place until realizing one day that their home was too dark and cramped for the many glittering soirees, theatricals, and balls they loved to host, and too far away from the new center of fashionable New York. Purchasing the double lots of 49-51 West Twenty-third Street in 1859, they hired the architect Detlef Lienau to design them a grand townhouse in the "modern French" style, complete with a large arched doorway, Beaux Arts–inspired details, and rooms expressly designed for entertaining—a music room, an art gallery, and a deluxe ballroom, where they would introduce the "German cotillion" to New York. Before the Schermerhorns, aristocratic New Yorkers had been dancing sweaty polkas and schottisches, but now they were graciously bending and swaying in a refined two-hour-long dance made popular by the Empress Eugénie of France.

Ann was also the first of New York's society women to host private musicales featuring professional musicians and, unlike the other hostesses who followed her example, always encouraged the artists to mingle with her guests. She and William hosted theatricals, too, with William sometimes translating the plays from the French and family members and friends playing the roles. "The performance was perfect," wrote Strong after one such event. "Everything the Schermerhorns undertake is carried out to the utmost perfection of detail."

From their downtown home, the Schermerhorns brought with them their opulent Louis XV furniture, to which a tale was attached. Fourteen years after the infamous masked ball and elopement at the Brevoort mansion on Fifth Avenue, Ann Schermerhorn had had the audacity to host a masked ball. What did she care about propriety and the citywide ban? She was a leader, not a follower! Casting about for a theme for her party, her eyes alighted on her furniture. Of course. Her theme would be the court of Louis XV, and all six hundred of her guests would have to dress accordingly. The ladies were delighted, but the men were not. Being forced to wear silk stockings and satin breeches was bad enough, but they would also have to shave off their fashionable mustaches, bushy sideburns, and beards of all shapes and sizes; facial hair had been strictly forbidden at the court of Versailles. Appalled, the invited gentlemen sent a delegation to their hostess to appeal her demand, but she would not relent. Salvation only came when it was discovered that the musketeer guards at Versailles had been allowed to sport facial hair. On the night of the gala, a full battalion of musketeers showed up.

William and Ann had three children, Fanny, Sarah—nicknamed "Miss Chattie"—and Annie, aged fourteen, ten, and three, respectively, when the family moved to the block in 1860. As a society mother, Ann would have kept her girls under a governess's thumb when they were younger and on a short leash when they were older. During their teenage years, they likely spent their mornings playing music, painting and drawing, strolling in the neighborhood, and perhaps visiting the Society Library on University Place. After lunch would come a drive and tea, followed later by dinner and social engagements.

The girls would also have been taught hundreds of complicated social rules, including the proper way to eat strawberries (pick them up by their stems), how to dissuade a potential suitor or unwanted friend (gently and without drama), and how to arrange books in a ladies' library (by gender, unless the writers were married, in which case their books could be placed together). Red roses meant true love, yellow roses meant jealousy or disenchantment. Calling cards left when the family was out carried coded messages: if a card's top left corner was turned down, it meant a routine visit; if the top right, congratulations; if the bottom left, goodbye when leaving town; and if the bottom right, condolences. There were other lessons to be learned as well, though not from their mother: A young lady who wanted to meet a man carried her fan or raised parasol in her left hand. A lady who wanted a man to follow her held an open fan or closed parasol in her right hand.

The Schermerhorns undoubtedly employed a cadre of servants, perhaps numbering as many as a dozen. At the top of the hierarchy would have reigned a housekeeper, butler, and social secretary. Housekeepers were responsible for supervising the rest of the staff, overseeing purchases, and keeping track of family linens, a time-consuming task, as inventories usually included imported sheets, embroidered tablecloths, and lace-trimmed undergarments, some very valuable, which had to be logged in and out of a notebook every time they were washed. Butlers oversaw the wine cellar, kept track of the china and silver, and always remained impassive in the face of drama. Social secretaries maintained a family's social calendar, answered their mail, drew up their guest lists, and knew all the latest gossip.

Ann must also have had a personal maid, serving as her hairdresser, makeup artist, fashion stylist, and all-around assistant. This maid would have been the first person to see her in the morning and the last to see her at night and may have gone with her to social events in case of a wardrobe mishap. Many society hostesses of the day designated a room for their guests' personal maids to wait in while their mistresses ate and drank, flirted and danced, gossiped and sniped.

Other Schermerhorn servants likely included a cook, several maids, and a muscular, red-faced laundress working in the mansion's steamy basement, stirring vats of hot water, lifting piles of wet clothing, and rubbing out stains. She or a maid always removed decorations and trimmings from the ladies' fancy dresses before washing them and sewed them back on again after the dresses were hung out to dry and ironed. Different irons were used for different jobs: one was for sleeves only, another for ruffles.

Footmen would have been needed every time the family ventured out for a drive in an ornate carriage, housed with their horses in a nearby stable. Tall, brawny Norwegians and Swedes were regarded as best for the job, as their stature was impressive, but any young man with shapely calves to show off in white stockings and knee breeches would do. Mrs. Schermerhorn may also have required her footmen to whiten their hair. "Will you powder?" was a standard question for job applicants, and those who did powder were paid more.

In middle age, when the two eldest of his daughters were grown, William Schermerhorn would become a Patriarch, with the *P* writ large, meaning a member of the ultra-exclusive Society of Patriarchs. The organization was created in 1872 by Ward McAllister, the self-appointed arbiter of New York society, in the realization that with the explosive growth of capitalism, the flashy nouveau riche had become too powerful to be kept out of society any longer, and it was better to let some of the best in rather than wait for the worst to take over. Most of the society's core members were Knickerbockers like William, but carefully vetted parvenus were gradually invited to join the exclusive club.

Each Patriarch was required to give a periodic grand ball, to which he was allowed to invite four ladies and five gentlemen, and McAllister invited fifty other "approved" guests such as the upstarts Cornelius Vanderbilt or August Belmont. "The whole secret of the success of these Patriarch Balls lay in making them select; in making them the most brilliant balls of each winter; in making it extremely difficult to obtain an invitation to them, and . . . to make them the stepping-stone to the best New York society," McAllister later wrote in his book *Society as I Have Found It*.

McAllister himself was not an aristocrat, just the son of a prominent Savannah attorney who had married an heiress. However, he was a close friend of Mrs. Caroline Webster Schermerhorn Astor, William's cousin and the doyenne of old money New York. It was Mrs. Astor who approved the Patriarchs' guest lists and Mrs. Astor who allowed McAllister to become a social force. A plump, plain, yet formidable woman, just as status-obsessed as her pudgy, pompous sidekick, she reigned over society with an iron hand—while always keeping her distance. She did not dance. She did not dine out. She never gave interviews or let herself be photographed.

Even more coveted than an invitation to a Patriarch ball was an invitation to Mrs. Astor's New Year's ball, open to only four hundred of the city's foremost socialites, as that was the number who could reportedly fit in her ballroom. On the night of her ball, held on the second or third Monday of January from 1872 into the 1890s, her mansion would blaze with lights as her guests promenaded through three drawing rooms before reaching their hostess, sitting on a red velvet couch, a diamond tiara on her head, her full-length portrait behind her.

The founding of the Society of Patriarchs coincided with the beginning of the Gilded Age, a term coined in 1873 by Mark Twain and Charles Dudley Warner in their satirical novel of the same name and used to describe the excesses of the post–Civil War period. During the Gilded Age, which would last until the early 1900s, all was money, glitter, glamour, and the best of times, or so it seemed. Underneath, though, destructive forces were festering. Greed, corruption, and misery among the poor were out of control, to come more and more to the fore as the decades passed and more cracks in the vault appeared.

*   *   *

Living next door to the William Schermerhorns, at 45-47 West Twenty-third Street, in a mansion also designed by Detlef Lienau, was William's older brother Edmund. A passionate music and opera lover, Edmund had hosted many concerts as a young man in his previous home on Great Jones Street. After moving to Twenty-third Street in 1869, however, he didn't socialize much. Said to have been disappointed in love, he withdrew from society and lived a reclusive life, perhaps reading the society pages every day to see what his former beloved, Ruth Baylies—now Mrs. Maturin Livingston—was up to. Or perhaps he just strolled around the block to the Twenty-fourth Street side. As fate would have it, Ruth and Maturin had moved into 30 West Twenty-fourth Street, almost directly behind Edmund's home.

Edmund never finished his mansion on the inside and often neglected it on the outside. He had a few faithful servants, but his only visitors were family members and the singers and opera stars whom he invited to perform in his home, often for him alone. He had a second home in Newport, Rhode Island—the watering hole of the New York elite post–Civil War— where he summered every year, but he lived in as much isolation there as he did in New York. Designed by George Champlin Mason, the stunning Italianate villa, named Chepstow, is now a house museum open to the public.

A few doors down from the Schermerhorns lived the Arnolds and the Constables. Aaron Arnold, founder of the prestigious department store Arnold Constable & Company, had been one of the first of the ultra-wealthy to see the potential of the Twenty-third Street block, building a home there at Nos. 29-31 in 1853. Arnold had come to America in the 1830s and personified the American dream. His first store had been a tiny hole-in-the-wall at 91 Pine Street, but within a year, he had moved to a larger location, and soon thereafter, a larger one still. Business was so good that in the early 1840s, he took on a partner, James Constable, who later married his daughter and built a mansion on Twenty-third Street next door to his. Everyone who was anyone shopped at Arnold Constable & Company, which by 1860 occupied a five-floor "Marble House" filling an entire block on Canal Street.

Also living on the Twenty-third Street side of the block in the 1860s were the Van Bushkirks, Cuttings, Ludlows, Snyders, the Reverend Gillette, and two prominent dentists: Dr. Stephen Main, who built a four-story Italianate home and office for himself at No. 23, and Dr. John Gardner Ambler, owner of a graceful Venetian revival home at No. 25. Dr. Ambler was known as an expert maker of artificial teeth.

Yet more wealthy families lived on the south side of the street, directly across from the block. Preeminent among them were the Joneses, who owned the three-story brownstone at 14 West Twenty-third, where Edith Newbold Jones, the future Edith Wharton, was born on January 24, 1862. Edith spent most of her childhood in Europe, and her family left West Twenty-third Street in the 1870s.

Next door to the Joneses at No. 12 lived wealthy Jewish stockbroker Benjamin Nathan and his family, whose four-story brownstone was one of the most extravagant in the city when it was built in 1860. "Their home was lavish to excess . . . with every luxury and comfort money could procure," reported the *New York Times*.

The Nathans were members of a powerful Sephardic family whose ancestors had been among the first Jews to arrive in Manhattan. Benjamin was a vice president of the New York Stock Exchange, a generous philan-thropist who helped found Mt. Sinai Hospital, and a member of two exclu-sive clubs, the Union Club and Saint Nicholas Society, that normally didn't admit Jews. At the pinnacle of his career when he moved to West Twenty-third Street, he, like Edwin Booth a few years before him, must have been looking forward to many years of happiness to come. But fate again had other ideas.

*   *   *

Around six A.M. on the hot, humid morning of July 29, 1870, Patrick McGuvin, an employee of the Fifth Avenue Hotel, was hosing down the sidewalk on the hotel's Twenty-third Street side when he heard a blood-curdling scream—"Murder!" Looking up, he saw young Washington Nathan bursting out of his house, clad only in his undergarments. Patrick started toward him, then stopped. Washington appeared drunk. Perhaps his scream meant nothing. But a moment later, young Frederick Nathan also burst out screaming. He was wearing a nightshirt with two dark stains, and his socks were soaked to his ankles with the same dark substance—blood.

McGuvin and Patrolman John Mangum, on his beat nearby, ran to the Nathan mansion and followed the brothers inside. The body of their father lay sprawled in the doorway of his private office on the second floor. His skull had been split at least six times and his left hand was broken. Blood soaked the carpet and splattered the walls. The murder weapon, a two-foot-long carpenter's "dog," or iron bar with flattened ends, lay near the front door, and there were signs in the bathroom of bloody hands being washed. Patrolman Mangum hurried off to the Fifth Avenue Hotel to summon his superintendent by telegraph, and the hotel's doctor went to examine the body.

Aside from Washington and Frederick, no other family members were at their Twenty-third Street mansion at the time. A few months earlier, Benjamin had purchased a forty-five-acre country estate in Morristown, New Jersey, and the family was summering there. Benjamin and his two oldest sons had only traveled back to the city the day before to commemorate the one-year anniversary of the death of Benjamin's mother at the Shearith Israel synagogue on West Nineteenth Street.

According to their later testimony, Washington and Frederick had gone out separately on the night before the murder. Frederick had returned at about eleven fifteen and said goodnight to his father before going to bed.

Washington, delayed by a violent thunderstorm, had returned between midnight and one A.M. and, passing by his father's room, saw that he was sleeping.

News of the grisly crime spread fast, and mere hours after Benjamin's body was discovered, crowds flooded down West Twenty-third Street to gape at No. 12. Streetcars, private carriages, and carts pulled up as close to the building as they could, tying up traffic for hours, well into the night and throughout the following days.

At first, the murder seemed to be the result of a botched robbery. Benjamin's safe was open and empty, and the gold watch and diamond studs he'd been wearing the night before were missing. But all the doors of the house had been locked, with no evidence of tampering, and Patrolman Mangum, who'd tried the front door twice in the night while walking his beat, as was the wont of most policemen patrolling wealthy neighborhoods, had noticed nothing amiss. Even more puzzling, none of the four people who'd been in the house, including a housekeeper and her son, had heard a thing.

The housekeeper was quickly ruled out as the possible killer, but her son, William Kelly, underwent intense grilling. A pale young man of twenty-four, with sunken cheeks and hollow eyes, he was a former Union soldier who lived mostly on an $8 monthly pension (about $160 today) he received from the U.S. government. The Nathans used him to do odd jobs and let him sleep in a room in their attic. On the morning of the murder, he testified, he had gotten up at about five A.M., dressed, and started blackening the Nathan men's shoes, which they had left for him the night before. Then he heard the brothers' screams. The police considered William a prime suspect at first, but ultimately concluded that he was too slight to have murdered the robust victim.

Suspicion then fell on the younger son, Washington, a handsome but volatile twenty-two-year-old who was notorious for drinking, gambling, and whoring. He and his father had argued frequently over his "habits of life." But Washington would not immediately benefit from his father's death. Because of Washington's wastrel ways, Benjamin had stipulated that his son's share of his inheritance, about $75,000 (roughly $1.5 million today), be placed in a trust until the boy either turned twenty-five or married a lady of the Hebrew faith. Washington and his father also got along well when not arguing about the younger man's lifestyle.

The inquest focused as much on exonerating Washington as it did on finding the real killer. He gave a detailed account of his movements the night before, which included drinking at the Fifth Avenue and St. James hotels, and spending nearly three hours with a prostitute at a Fourteenth Street brothel. These activities had taken place before the murder, but did not seem to be the actions of a man contemplating killing his father. Washington was not indicted—perhaps because of interference by his uncle Albert Cardozo, a powerful figure of dubious character in Tammany Hall and a judge on the New York Supreme Court. (Cardozo was himself later implicated in a judicial corruption scandal and forced to resign his seat on the bench.)

Benjamin Nathan's murder was never solved, and the family moved out of their Twenty-third Street mansion. It remained empty for years, and suspicion dogged Washington for the rest of his days. He continued to live a dissolute lifestyle and in 1879, while visiting an actress at the Coleman House on Broadway at Twenty-seventh Street, was shot in the neck by another woman. He miraculously survived and afterward became more subdued. In 1881 he married the divorced daughter of an opera producer. The bride wore black. The couple moved to London and then Paris, where just weeks before his death, Washington gave an interview to the *Chicago Tribune*, saying, "No blood could ever be found on any of my clothes, yet people say that I killed him. My poor father! My poor father!" He died on July 25, 1892, after a walk alone on the beach. His obituary read: "He never seemed to find company, being always alone and unattended and wearing upon his face the expression of a man utterly desolate. His hair in his exile turned entirely white. He was forty-four years old."

CHAPTER 9

Hotel Living

Jubilee Jim loved his wife, Lucy, and had no intention of betraying her, at least not at first. They had married when he was nineteen and she fifteen. She was an orphan, raised in a seminary in Springfield, Massachusetts, and he had also lost his mother as a young child.

And yet, Jubilee Jim was so often on the road—during their seventeen years of marriage, he and Lucy never lived together for more than six months at a time—and he had a way with the ladies. Attractive as a young man, with auburn hair and bright blue eyes, he loved to flirt, flatter, cajole—and more. Lucy apparently knew and accepted that. For the last seven or eight years of their marriage, she lived a quiet, outwardly respectable life in Boston with her lady friend Fanny Harrod while her husband lived a wild, rollicking one at the Fifth Avenue Hotel, raising eyebrows, loving one of the most beautiful women in America, and causing financial panic.

"She is no hair-lifting beauty, my Lucy," Jim once told the actress Clara Morris during those high-flying years, "just a plump, wholesome, big-hearted, commonplace woman, such as a man meets once in a lifetime, say, and then gathers her into the first church he comes to, and seals her to himself."

Born on April Fools' Day 1835 in the tiny town of Pownal, Vermont, James "Jubilee Jim" Fisk was the son of an old-fashioned peddler and a loving stepmother. He left school at age thirteen to work with his father, and soon proved to be such a natural salesman that he was going out on his own. He bought his own wagon, which he painted red and yellow with JAMES FISK JUNIOR blazoned across the top, started dressing in striped trousers and a top hat, and developed such an amusing sales pitch that housewives flocked to purchase his wares. Buying out his father, he acquired more wagons, hired drivers, and began using the railroads to deliver goods until his territory extended farther than any New England peddler's ever had before—from southern Vermont and New Hampshire through most of Massachusetts and into eastern New York.

Jim got most of his stock from the Boston dry goods firm of Jordan, Marsh & Company, and in 1860, Eben Jordan, noticing the young man's phenomenal success, offered him a job as a wholesale dealer. Jim leapt at the chance, but proved to be a dismal failure. The professional buyers, eyes hard as stone, were not as easily swayed as housewives by his over-the-top style. He was on the verge of being let go when the Civil War began.

Smelling money, the young salesman said a hurried goodbye to Lucy and rushed down to Washington, D.C., where he rented a lavish suite at Willard's, the best hotel in town, and began courting army supply officers, plying them with fine cigars, food, and drink, all at Jordan's expense. It worked. The contracts came pouring in. Jim also smuggled cotton through Union lines. He became rich, and Jordan, richer.

As the war neared its end, Jim's profits began to ebb, and he shut down his Washington operation. With $65,000 in his pocket, a small fortune at the time (about $1 million today), he visited Lucy in Boston and moved into the Fifth Avenue Hotel to try his hand at being a broker. He opened a sumptuous office on Broad Street, directly across from the New York Stock Exchange, and there, on the street of neoclassical buildings, a web of telegraph lines darkening the sky, invited the gamblers in.

It was a crazy time to be in New York. With a population of over eight hundred thousand, the city was both the nation's leader in trade and commerce and a crowded, appalling town. Crime was rampant and corruption widespread. William "Boss" Tweed was in ascendance—he would

gain control of Tammany Hall, the city's Democratic machine, in 1868—
and graft, larceny, and fraud had infiltrated virtually every municipal institution. The streets were filthy, badly paved, and jammed from dawn to
dusk with thousands of horse-drawn streetcars, private carriages, wagons,
pushcarts, riders on horseback, pedestrians, and pigs, which were allowed
to roam freely until 1867. During rush hour, it could take an hour and a
half to get from the Fifth Avenue Hotel to Wall Street, amid a cacophony
of ear-piercing whistles, cursing drivers, and screaming, panicking horses.
The city was home to some one hundred thousand equines, depositing a
thousand tons of manure and three hundred thousand gallons of urine
daily, and about two hundred horses died in traffic accidents every day.
Their corpses were often allowed to putrefy curbside for days or even weeks,
along with waist-high piles of reeking manure.

It was an even crazier time to be on Wall Street. Thanks to the bull
market that had developed during the war, speculators were operating at
a feverish pitch. There weren't enough hours in the day to handle all the
business, and so, after hours, by common consent, the gamblers flocked to
the corridors and lobbies of the Fifth Avenue Hotel to continue bartering.
Ordinary guests looked at each other in confusion as men dressed in loud
suits and frilled shirtfronts shouted out coded messages from every side—
"Take 'em!" "A thousand more!" "Closed at a quarter!" Then a Mr. Gallagher opened Gallagher's Evening Exchange in a small building adjoining
the hotel on Twenty-fourth Street. Railroad stocks, gold, and petroleum
were traded there throughout the night.

Wrote one participant of those heady days: "The street became demoralized. Brokers apparently lived without sleep or rest or peace. They haunted
the day boards with pallid faces and a strange glitter of the eye. High-
strung, fevered in blood, craving excitement from the very exhaustion of
overwork, they carried in their faces a prophecy of evil"—evil that would
come in the form of irregularities, fortunes made and lost overnight, and
the deflation that followed the Civil War.

Among those who suffered that evil was Jubilee Jim, who lost his entire
fortune in a few months. Just as the techniques he had used with housewives hadn't worked with professional buyers, so the techniques he had
used in the Capitol didn't work in New York. Speculators were not army

supply officers. Ruined, he left the city for the comforting arms of plump, wholesome Lucy. But New York hadn't seen the last of him. The buoyant, flamboyant huckster would be back.

Gallagher's was shuttered by the downtown exchanges after less than two years of operation, but night trading continued at the Fifth Avenue Hotel for years. The building that had housed the exchange was then revamped, to reopen a year later as the Fifth Avenue Opera House, home to Christy's Minstrels, a popular blackface troupe from Buffalo, New York. Their shows would begin with a white-faced man in formal attire in the center of a semicircle flanked by two men in blackface wearing gaudy swallowtail coats and striped trousers. One of these men was Mr. Tambo, who played the tambourine, and the other, Mr. Bones, who rattled a pair of clappers. The show consisted of jokes, ballads, and comic songs and skits, most caricaturing the singing and dancing of slaves. Racist New York lapped it up. Solomon Pieters must have turned over in his grave.

*   *   *

Among the speculators skulking around Gallagher's and the Fifth Avenue Hotel in those postwar years was Daniel Drew, a crafty, unscrupulous, poorly educated, yet extremely powerful man then in his late sixties. Tall and gaunt, with deeply creased skin, a domed forehead, piercing eyes, and jet-black hair despite his age, he used a broken umbrella as a cane and a red bandanna as a handkerchief. He had started out in the cattle business some forty years before, selling cows out of the Bull's Head Tavern at Third Avenue and Twenty-sixth Street, and at an early age supposedly hit upon a surefire scheme for making money: Before selling his cattle, he gave them lots of salt. They gulped down water, and their weights and prices shot up. Hence the term *watered stock*.

That story is probably apocryphal, but the term is attributed to Drew, and there is no doubt that he was a master of manipulation and doubledealing. Born impoverished in upstate New York, he had moved to the city as a youth and by the 1860s was one of its foremost financiers, as well as a director of the Erie Railroad, whose stock he manipulated almost at will. One Wall Street ditty went: "Daniel says up—Erie goes up. / Daniel says down—Erie goes down. / Daniel says wiggle-waggle—it bobs both ways."

Drew was also a Bible-thumping Methodist who built churches and taught Sunday school without seeing the slightest conflict between his religious beliefs and the financial ruin he wrought upon others. "He who sells what isn't his'n, must pay it back or go to prison," he once said with a shrug.

Jim went to visit Drew one day after moving back to New York in early 1866, and the two must have hit it off, for Drew hired him as his agent to sell his failing Stonington Steamboat line. Jim negotiated a much better deal than Drew had expected, and soon the shrewd old financier was helping the younger man set up his second brokerage firm on Wall Street. Now learning all the finer, darker points of the trade from one of the best in the business, Jim adapted quickly and became a rich man once again. He built a magnificent four-story mansion for Lucy at 74 Chester Street in Boston and moved into the most fashionable suite the Fifth Avenue Hotel had to offer. The Gilded Age was about to begin, and he was in his element.

*   *   *

For Jim to set up housekeeping in a hotel rather than a townhouse or mansion was not unusual in post–Civil War New York. Apartment living had not yet arrived, and a lack of housing stock and enormous rents led many wealthy and moderately wealthy New Yorkers to take up residence in luxury hotels, while those of lesser means did the same in boarding-houses. A full-time resident could stay at a luxury hotel for as little as $20 to $40 a week (about $320 to $640 today), including four meals and house-keeping, as opposed to renting a house of comparable quality for at least twice that much, not including meals and housekeeping. Permanent residents accounted for an estimated half of hotel residents in 1860s New York.

Which is not to say that hotel living was cheap. When adding in such expenses as bar bills, cigar bills, and other luxury "incidentals," the price tag could become astronomical. One bachelor who lived at the Fifth Avenue Hotel for forty years, until it closed on April 4, 1908, boasted that between his meals, suite of rooms, bar bills, and other costs, he had spent $800,000 (about $23 million today) during his stay.

The Fifth Avenue Hotel was especially popular with young couples of means, who usually rented out its finest suites on the lower floors. The smaller suites and single rooms on the higher floors were usually rented by bachelors, some gainfully employed, others not. Women seldom stayed at the hotel or any hotel alone, as unescorted ladies were regarded with suspicion. As late as 1885, the *New York Tribune* commented that no woman traveling alone could find hotel accommodations unless she had a letter of introduction or telegraphed ahead.

The ground floor of the Fifth Avenue, like the ground floors of most luxury hotels in the 1800s, was a mostly male preserve. Here, in the lobby, reading rooms, and bars, men with silk hats under their arms and flowers in their lapels gathered to talk shop, brag about women and the pots of money they had made, smoke, curse, and spit. Recalled one critical English visitor, "Alighting from our cab at the Fifth Avenue Hotel, we found ourselves in a lofty entrance hall, with a tiled floor—the latter plentifully bedewed with tobacco juice; while the atmosphere was that of a mild Turkish bath, pervaded by a strong odour of cigars."

In contrast, the hotel's first floor was a refined, mostly female preserve, with women congregating in ornate parlor rooms to socialize, play musical instruments, and flirt with male visitors. Men were allowed in the ladies' parlors, but women were seldom allowed in the men's.

Down the hall from the ladies' parlors was the hotel's main dining room, regarded as one of the best restaurants in the city, but not *the* best. That accolade belonged to Delmonico's, where, most historians agree, fine dining in America had begun thirty years earlier. Originally located downtown on William Street, Delmonico's had moved to the corner of Fifth Avenue and Fourteenth Street in 1862, and would move to the corner of Fifth and Twenty-sixth Street at Madison Square in 1876. The restaurant's tone was decidedly French, but it also specialized in local produce and created such then-innovative dishes as Baked Alaska and lobster Newburg.

Heavily influenced by Delmonico's, the Fifth Avenue Hotel served many of the same French dishes. However, it also offered some decidedly American ones, such as baked beans and pork. Breakfast menus typically included as many as fifty-two dishes and dinner menus as many as seventy-five, served in up to ten courses. Most dinner menus began with two soups, followed by two fish dishes, a half dozen boiled dishes (ham, calf's head, leg of mutton), and a similar number of cold dishes (lamb, tongue, lobster salad). Then came the entrées, which varied daily, followed by a course of roasts and another of game. Finally came two sweet courses, the first offering pastries, pudding, and cakes, and the second, nuts, fruits, and ice cream.

Between its opening in 1859 and the end of 1865, the hotel served close to a thousand different entrée dishes, many of them variations on each other. Much wild and domestic fowl was offered, along with many meats, usually slow cooked and accompanied by sauces. Often on the menus, too, was macaroni baked with cheese and cream. As the story goes, macaroni had become wildly popular in America after Thomas Jefferson traveled to northern Italy in 1787, brought back a pasta machine, and served macaroni with Parmesan cheese at his home in Virginia.

Oysters were served raw, escalloped, fried, baked in their shells, roasted, and pickled, and made into soups, patties, and puddings. The bivalves, especially little necks, were de rigueur in nineteenth-century New York, even though by that time most of the area's once abundant natural oyster beds had been depleted and the oysters came from Chesapeake Bay.

Two especially extravagant dishes often on the hotel's menu were canvasback ducks and terrapin, a small edible turtle found in the coastal waters of the eastern United States. The best canvasbacks were said to come from Maryland, where they acquired a distinctive flavor from eating the wild celery growing in Chesapeake Bay. The terrapin were usually served baked or stewed. Soup made from giant turtles captured in the Caribbean was occasionally featured as well, usually accompanied by Madeira wine.

Other common dishes included calf's-head stew, pigeon pie, breaded cow tongue, chicken curry, mutton cutlets, salmon croquettes, and pig's feet à la vinaigrette. Appearing much more occasionally were roasted rabbit, stewed squirrel with claret sauce, and "robins larded en croustade."

In charge of buying food for the hotel for most of its existence was Elmer Darling, nephew of the hotel manager Alfred Darling, the man who had welcomed the Massachusetts troops at the railroad depot at the start of the Civil War. Up before dawn every morning, Elmer's first task was to ask Albert Thompson, the hotel's steward, how many guests were in the house. With a white beard reaching to his waist, Thompson was one of the hotel's best-known characters. He had started out driving stagecoaches in New Hampshire and then worked for a hotel in Boston before being "discovered" and brought to New York.

Headcount in hand, Elmer would climb into a hack waiting out front and drive downtown to Washington Market, a chaotic jumble of sheds, stalls, piers, and as many as two thousand carts and wagons south of Fourteenth Street on the far west side (now the Meatpacking District). Here he jostled with the buyers of other luxury hotels and restaurants, each vying to buy the best of the best, and bargained ferociously with the market's sellers. On an average day, he would purchase 140 dozen eggs, 170 pounds of butter, and 525 quarts of milk, along with heavy sacks of meat, fish, poultry, fruits, and vegetables, and at least 4,000 oysters. Depending on what was on the hotel's menu that day, he might also purchase buffalo tongue, prairie chicken, venison, hare, truffles, snipe, plover, woodcock, squab, quail, pheasant, grouse, blackfish, striped bass, sole, trout, salmon, crabs, mussels, lobster, mackerel, ray, and shad. The variety and bounty of the foodstuffs sold in Washington Market was astounding, far surpassing anything offered in markets today, with almost everything harvested locally.

Because refrigeration had not yet been developed on a large scale, much of the meat that Elmer purchased had arrived in Manhattan "on the hoof." Herded along in cattle drives, some from as far away as Ohio, the beasts were loaded onto barges to cross the Hudson. Manhattan's largest meat companies had their own docks leading directly to tunnels, which in turn led to slaughterhouses. The meat was kept in icehouses until it was sold. Meat inspectors patrolled.

Eggs presented another challenge to the nineteenth-century food vendors. By 1873, the city was importing a million eggs a day, and before the eggs reached the market, they had to be "candled." This involved holding the orbs over candles to determine their freshness; the light could reveal abnormalities such as blood or meat spots. And so, in the predawn hours before Elmer and the other buyers thronged into the market, dozens of men in baggy shirts and misshapen hats sat beside hills of eggs shipped in from upstate and meticulously held them over flames one by one.

*   *   *

By the time Jim Fisk moved into the Fifth Avenue Hotel for the second time, the hostelry's long corridors, lit by flickering gaslight alternating with shadow, were known as "flirtation galleries." Ladies in silks and satins sashayed along them, hoping to catch the eyes of discerning gentlemen, while the discerning gentlemen, dressed in striped trousers and embroidered vests, tipped their hats and flaunted their diamonds. Diamonds had only begun appearing in sizable numbers after the Civil War, when the great diamond reserves of South Africa were discovered, and were regarded as much more alluring than the semiprecious stones and cameos that had been in families for generations.

Guests interested in purchasing diamonds of their own could consult the hotel's front desk clerk, who was often a walking diamond display case, working on commission. Pretending to be an expert, he might agree to sell the diamonds he was wearing or else direct the inquirer to a diamond dealer.

First, though, a guest had to screw up the courage to approach the clerk—often an intimidating thought. Dressed in a Prince Albert coat, stovepipe hat, high collar, and lurid necktie, the typical clerk would ignore a guest for many minutes before deigning to look up, pointed mustache quivering. "Whenever I feel that I need taking down a peg or two, and that I am getting too big for my clothes, I have a never-failing remedy," wrote one commercial traveler of the era. "I merely step into a first-class hotel, and approach Mr. Diamond Pin, and ask: 'Is Mr. Smith stopping here?' The great man, after four or five minutes, lifts his eyes, he speaks. I am crushed."

English writer Anthony Trollope blamed the surliness of the American hotel clerk on democracy. The clerk's attitude arose, he asserted, "entirely from that want of courtesy which democratic institutions create. The man whom you address, has to make a battle against the state of subservience, presumed to be indicated by his position, and he does so by declaring his indifference to the person on whose wants he is paid to attend."

The democratic nature of the hotel was also reflected in the makeup of its guests. Bound together by wealth or the illusion thereof, some were of the elite, some were nouveau riche, and some were pretenders, not nearly as rich as they professed to be. For this third group, the luxury hotel, costing much less than a private home, offered a chance to live in an aspirational, fairy-tale world. The furnishings were of the finest quality, the staff polite and attentive, the lobbies filled with potential business associates and lovers, and the dining rooms extravagant theaters in which to see and be seen. Here in the "palaces of the public," the pretenders must have thought, they could finally live the lives they had always deserved.

As the historian Molly Berger writes in *Hotel Dreams*, many social commentators of the day were aghast at what was going on in the luxury hotels. The flirtation galleries, the diamonds, the ostentatious display of wealth that might or might not be real—all were repulsive. Everything seemed to be about consumption, fashion, and money. Nothing seemed to be about that old-fashioned but bedrock American value: the work ethic.

In addition, the critics fretted, hotel life was unraveling the very fabric of society. Without a household to run, women were forgetting how to cook, clean house, entertain guests, take care of their children, and attend to their husbands. Bachelors were drinking too much, gambling too much, whoring too much, and postponing for far too long their duty to marry and reproduce.

Even worse, the luxury hotels were allowing for a most unsavory mixing of classes. The hoi polloi were creeping in, rubbing shoulders with the wealthy. Especially worrisome to many upper-crust families was the possibility that an eligible daughter might fall in love with a traveling salesman, or "drummer," as they were then derogatively called. Commercial travelers made up as much as 75 percent of the Fifth Avenue Hotel's transient business in the 1860s.

Then there was the criminal element, which, despite management's best efforts, was seeping in too. Fashionably dressed prostitutes were strolling down the corridors, well-groomed pickpockets were dining next to grand dames, illiterate gamblers were exchanging witticisms with famous writers.

In short, the luxury hotels, emblematic of the emerging Gilded Age, were leading the country down a perilous path. America was in danger of losing its moral compass.

Only a few social commentators appeared to notice that the luxury hotels were also offering something extraordinary—freedom for middle- and upper-class wives and daughters. Though women could not rent hotel rooms on their own, these wives and daughters, living with their families in the hotels, were appearing in public alone and on their own terms for the first time. Whether parading through the dining hall in a fancy new dress, sharing tea with a new acquaintance, or simply sitting on a bench and people watching, they were going where they wanted, talking to whom they pleased, taking unheard-of chances. Men were losing control.

*   *   *

Among the shadier types frequenting the Fifth Avenue Hotel post–Civil War were "banco skins," men who set up illicit banco games in obscure back parlors or upper-floor guestrooms. The ultimate sucker game, banco could be played with either dice or cards. The card layout involved forty-three spaces, of which forty-two were numbered, with thirteen also carrying stars, and one, a blank. The unstarred numbers represented cash prizes, while those with stars allowed the player to draw again. Players would be allowed to win up to a certain amount, but would eventually be dealt a "conditional hand" that demanded they stake a sum equal to the amount owed them and draw again. Told that the only way they could lose was to hit on one of two spaces covered with a metal cap, or "banco," they invariably drew again and, of course, lost.

The skins found most of their marks among out-of-towners and favored wealthy merchants and farmers. The touts would send out an accomplice known as a "feeler" to hang around a hotel lobby, identify a likely mark, and research his background. The feeler then passed this information on to a "catcher," who struck up a friendship with the mark and invited him out for a night on the town. The entertainment ended in the wee hours with a banco game among "friends."

The banco gang that worked the Fifth Avenue Hotel was the largest operation of its kind in the country. At its helm was Charles P. Miller, "King of the Banco Men," whose headquarters was a nearby lamppost on the southwest corner of Broadway and Twenty-eighth Street, against which he leaned throughout the night. Born in Texas, he had begun riding the rails as a teenager, to land first in New Orleans, where he found a job in a gambling house, and then in New York, where he opened a notorious "skinning dive" downtown, developed a loyal group of henchmen, and cultivated friendships with influential politicians and policemen. He is thought to have accumulated several hundred thousand dollars in his lifetime, but spent much of it on an extravagant lifestyle and gambling habit. He was killed in 1881 by the owner of a saloon on West Twenty-ninth Street.

Also notorious was Chauncey Johnson, captured at the Fifth Avenue Hotel in 1870. "One of the oldest and cleverest sneaks in America," according to New York's then chief of detectives Thomas Byrnes, Johnson had begun his career in a traditional manner, by robbing banks, but soon moved on to more ingenious schemes until he had "stolen more money collectively than any man in his line." One of Johnson's schemes involved approaching a bank teller's window with a long steel wire shaped like a fishhook and snaring bundles of bills when the teller wasn't looking. Another involved entering the offices of a major company and waiting for its cashier to take off his office coat and go to lunch; Johnson would put on the abandoned coat and grab whatever cash he could find.

Loitering near the front desk of the Fifth Avenue Hotel one day, Johnson saw a guest approach a clerk with a valuable package. The clerk placed the package in the hotel safe, but didn't lock it, and as he and the other clerks were busy helping guests, Johnson brazenly went behind the counter and took the package. He started toward the door, but tripped over a wastebasket and fell, attracting attention. He was arrested and sentenced to ten years in Sing Sing. After his release, he was a broken-down old man.

*   *   *

Jubilee Jim mingled easily with both the hotel's criminal element and its nouveau riche, but not with its more elite clients, many of whom despised him. Now a rotund thirty-something with a florid complexion, pomaded hair, and handlebar mustache, he had become more aggressive, gregarious, flamboyant, and full of himself than ever. Always brimming over with energy, confidence, and bad jokes, he paraded about the hotel nightly, a beautiful young woman always on his arm.

Jim's professional life had evolved as well. Thanks to his mentor Daniel Drew, he was now not only a hugely successful stockbroker but also a member of the board of directors of the Erie Railroad, the company whose stock Drew frequently manipulated. Drew had invited Jim and another of his protégés, Jay Gould, to join the board in 1867, and although the two men had hardly known each other at first, they quickly became close friends.

On the surface, Gould was the opposite of Jim. Slight, quiet, brooding, and intense, he dressed in somber colors, said little, and socialized even less, preferring to spend evenings at home with his wife and children. Like Drew, he had grown up poor in upstate New York and had a sly, almost sinister air about him that made others uncomfortable.

One man so extroverted, the other so reserved, one seemingly pure ego writ large, the other something deeper, darker, shadows underneath— reflections of the block, the city, and the Gilded Age itself. Yet surfaces aside, Fisk and Gould were much alike. Both were financial wizards. Both were courageous speculators. And both were consumed by a ferocious, almost primal drive to succeed, no matter the cost. The ends more than justified the means.

At first, all was business as usual at the Erie Railroad after the two young men joined the board. But in early 1868, Cornelius Vanderbilt, by then in his seventies and the richest man in America, moved to wrest control of the company from Drew and his partners. Vanderbilt already controlled the New York Central, Long Island, and Harlem and Hudson railroad lines, but lusted after the Erie, as it made the lucrative run between New York and Buffalo, where it received goods transported from the Midwest. He began secretly buying up Erie stock in order to gain a majority share and, as a precautionary measure, prevailed on a friendly judge to issue an injunction preventing the railroad from issuing any more stock. Before long, though, Fisk, Drew, and Gould caught wind of the scheme and came up with one of their own: they would ignore the injunction. Gleefully sneaking down to the printing press in the Erie office basement at night, they inked rollers, aligned paper, and signed on dotted lines to produce millions of dollars' worth of crisp new stock certificates.

"If this printing press don't break down," chuckled Jim as they worked, "I'll be damned if I don't give the old hog all he wants of Erie."

And what the "the old hog," meaning Vanderbilt, wanted, he got. He kept on buying, driving the price ever higher.

In the end, the threesome's plot was discovered, and a judge authorized their arrest. But again the men were a step ahead. Shoving the Erie's ledger books and over $7 million (about $129 million today) into carpetbags, they fled to the Hudson River docks, intending to take a ferry to Jersey City, where they would be outside New York jurisdiction. Drew boarded the boat immediately, but Fisk and Gould, high on being outlaws, impulsively turned around and caught a cab to Delmonico's for a "farewell luncheon" with friends. They had just started eating when a sheriff appeared at the front door.

The financiers escaped out the back and raced to the docks. By now, it was dusk, and they could not afford to wait for a ferry. They hired a life-boat and two oarsmen to row them across the Hudson, which was crowded with craft of all sizes. As their tiny vessel left port, a thick fog rolled in and sights and sounds became muffled. The men lost all sense of direction, and their boat was careening wildly about when a ferry suddenly loomed up out of nowhere and nearly ran them over. They escaped just in time, only to see another ferry bearing down even faster. Frantically, they reached up, grabbed its guardrails, and were drawn so close to its paddle-wheel that they were nearly sucked under. Finally, though, they were hauled safely aboard.

Reunited with Drew in Jersey City, the three men settled into the Taylor Hotel and hired policemen and thugs for protection against any sudden raids by Vanderbilt. Jim also sent for his paramour, Josie Mansfield, to join him. Photographs of Josie portray a languorous woman with a placid face, but she must have had other charms, as many regarded her as the most beautiful woman of her day. "She was tall and shaped like a duchess. Her skin was as fair in fibre and hue as the lily itself . . . [Her] eyes were of a peculiar gray, and lambent like the phosphorescent streaks of light that follow the wake of a ship in mid-ocean," wrote one admirer.

Jim had met Josie at the Thirty-fourth Street home of Annie Wood, actress and madam, where he and a friend had gone to celebrate after winning $100 (about $2,000 today) in a faro game. Josie, who was nothing if not avaricious, had noticed Jim's expensive clothes and asked to be introduced. Jim was immediately smitten. The two began appearing together at the Fifth Avenue Hotel and elsewhere, and the financier began paying Josie's bills. He also moved her into a series of ever-more respectable boardinghouses, one just around the corner from the hotel at 18 West Twenty-fourth Street.

At the Taylor Hotel, days and then weeks slipped by. That didn't bother Jubilee Jim. With his usual insouciance, he was enjoying himself thoroughly, slinging down whiskeys, telling the story of his narrow escape again and again, and squeezing Josie. But Gould was unhappy, and Drew was miserable. Jim's flamboyance and Josie's presence were driving him mad, and he blamed the two younger men for all that had happened. Furtively he sent word to Vanderbilt, saying he wanted to make a deal. Then he snuck across the river to meet him. They came to terms and were about to seal their deal when Fisk and Gould heard about it, burst into Vanderbilt's home one morning when he was getting dressed, and negotiated different terms, including the appointment of Gould as the Erie's treasurer and president.

Once back in Manhattan, Gould's first act was to appoint Fisk controller. And soon thereafter, he invited "Boss" Tweed, now in control of Tammany Hall, to join the Erie board, likely nailing down the details in a smoke-filled bar at the Fifth Avenue Hotel. The hotel was just down the block from the Erie's new offices, and Tweed, like many other politicians of the day, was a hotel regular.

The "Erie War," as the press dubbed it, had reached its crescendo, but it wasn't over quite yet. Drew still owned millions of dollars' worth of Erie stock and, after years of manipulating the Street, just couldn't leave well enough alone. He began double-dealing again. Some of his moves felt like betrayal to Fisk and Gould, and six months after their settlement with Vanderbilt, they retaliated by devising a scheme that led to Drew's complete and utter financial ruin. According to Jim, testifying later in court, the old crook then pleaded with the younger men to lend him enough stock for a week for him to get on his feet again, but they remained unmoved. "[You] should be the last man that should whine over any position in which you may be placed in Erie," Jim said coldly.

Two hundred miles away in Boston, Lucy must have heard rumors of her husband's romantic and financial shenanigans, but likely paid them little mind. Jim visited her in Boston regularly, and she visited him at the Fifth Avenue Hotel occasionally as well, though never without giving him ample warning first. She knew better than that.

CHAPTER 10

Death Onstage and Off

Among "Jubilee Jim" Fisk's many fierce passions was the theater. When not busy wheeling and dealing, he loved nothing more than attending opening nights, hobnobbing with theater folk, and flirting with young actresses. He was a fixture at many of the city's theaters and, soon after moving to New York for the second time, bought the Twenty-fourth Street building adjoining the Fifth Avenue Hotel that had housed Gallagher's exchange and the Fifth Avenue Opera House and turned it into a new theater. Naming it Brougham's Theatre after its manager, John Brougham, he had high hopes for its future, but it failed to attract audiences and he shut it down after a year.

Jim and the theater were natural bedfellows. The former peddler was nothing if not dramatic, a larger-than-life character in his own action-filled play. Wrote a fellow broker after Jim's return to New York: "The blonde, bustling and rollicking James Fisk, Jr. . . . came bounding into the Wall street circus like a star-acrobat; fresh, exuberant, glittering with spangles, and turning double-summersaults, apparently as much for his amusement, as for that of a large circle of spectators. He was first, large, and always, a man of theatrical effects, of grand transformations, and blue fire. All the world was to him literally a stage."

Jim was hardly alone in his passion for the theater. Throughout the 1800s, there was nothing New Yorkers from all walks of life loved more than seeing a show. Minstrelsy, variety, vaudeville, Shakespeare, opera—all had their avid followers.

*   *   *

One day in early 1869, about a year after the Erie War ended, handsome, debonair Augustin Daly, he of dark curls and flashing eyes, strode into the resplendent new Erie Railroad corporate offices on the corner of Twenty-third Street and Eighth Avenue. Formerly home to Pike's Opera House, the building had been renovated from top to bottom just months before by Fisk and Gould. A dazzling affair, bursting with carved wood-work, stained glass, lavish wallpaper, and frescoes, the edifice featured a seven-story safe guaranteed to be inflammable, printing offices, and a private dining room, with dumbwaiter service on every floor. The press had dubbed the extravaganza "Castle Erie" and Jim, "the Prince of Erie."

The new company headquarters had been Jim's idea, of course. The Erie's old offices had been cramped and dull, not at all fitting for such high-powered executives as himself and Gould. Equally important, the new building contained not just office space but also the biggest stage in Manhattan; Jim was ready to try his hand at being an impresario once again. With twenty-six hundred seats, the venue could host much more extravagant shows than the old, still-shuttered Twenty-fourth Street theater—shows that would be much better suited to his temperament and to Josie's talents, should she be interested.

By this time, Jim had also moved out of the Fifth Avenue Hotel. He was living with Josie behind Castle Erie in a $40,000 (about $800,000 today) brownstone at 359 West Twenty-fourth Street. He had built himself a stable nearby, too, in which to house his many fine horses and chariots, and had arranged for the Erie to buy two ferries, which he named the *James Fisk* and *Jay Gould*. He hadn't forgotten his humble beginnings, however. Shortly after opening the new offices, he had invited the people of the neighborhood to stop by whenever they needed rent money or food or a bag of coal. Though living just a block or two west of opulent Fifth Avenue, most nearby residents were laborers, factory workers, shopkeepers, clerks, or prostitutes, barely scraping by.

Upon entering Castle Erie, Daly may have taken a look at the wondrously revamped Grand Opera House theater before climbing the stairs to Jim's office, where the great man sat behind a desk on a raised dais. His chair was said to be held together with nails of pure gold.

Nervous but determined, Daly presented his case. He wanted to lease Jim's old theater on West Twenty-fourth Street.

"What security can you give?" Jim barked out.

"None," Daly replied.

"Then you must pay six weeks' rent in advance. The rent is twenty-five thousand dollars a year."

Daly blanched at the astronomical sum and said he needed time to think it over. Now in his early thirties, he'd been fantasizing about managing a theater ever since he was a nine-year-old living in Norfolk, Virginia, when he'd seen his first play and begun putting on shows for the neighborhood kids in a woodshed.

That evening, he discussed the subject with his brother Joseph. It is "folly to stop and count the cost, much less the risk . . . If you pause to consider the chances of failure, you will never accomplish anything," he said, seemingly trying to convince himself as much as his brother.

The next day, Daly went back to Jim with a check. The magnate looked from it to him and back again, stupefied. "This is the first man with money I have ever seen in the theatrical business!"

A two-year lease was duly drawn up, and Jim handed Daly the keys. Then the exultant young manager strode a few blocks east to the small jewel box of a theater at 4 West Twenty-fourth Street that was now his. He unlocked the door and slipped inside, his heart beating so fast he could hardly breathe. Drinking in the cool, musty air, he walked through the darkened rows of seats, and "went upon the stage and felt as one who treads the deck of a ship as its master," he told Joseph that evening.

The analogy was apt. The brothers were the sons of a sea captain who had died when Augustin was three and Joseph one. They had been raised by their mother, who had moved the family from Virginia to New York while the boys were still young in the belief that they would find more opportunity there. Barely making ends meet, she had worked as a seamstress and sent her sons to receive a few years of rudimentary schooling in the city's new public education system. Meanwhile, Augustin had continued to put on plays, this time in the backyard of their tenement building on the Lower East Side.

As adolescents, the boys went to work as clerks and attended night school. Augustin joined some of the amateur theatrical clubs then popular in the city, but they were focused on acting, and he had no interest in acting, "due to a haunting desire to become familiar with management." He had no money to back him, however, and so turned to his second love, journalism. By age twenty-one, he was the chief drama critic for the *Sunday Courier* and over the next decade was also hired as a drama critic for the *Express, Sun, Citizen*, and *Times*, sometimes writing for three or four papers at the same time.

It was a powerful position. Thousands of readers devoured his columns daily. But Daly was frustrated. He wanted to be *in* the theater, not write about it. He wrote plays in his spare time and, in 1867, achieved huge success with *Under the Gaslight*, featuring the first—and later much imitated—scene of a hero tied to the railroad tracks being rescued by his sweetheart as a train bears down. Now earning real money for the first time in his life, Daly was finally able to pursue his dream.

At the time, most American theater managers were fixated on hiring star actors and producing stock plays imported from Europe. Daly wanted to do something entirely different. He wanted to develop an integrated company in which every actor played both major and minor roles, and produce realistic melodramas with American themes—Daly is credited as being the father of modern American drama. The ninety plays he wrote or adapted are melodramatic by today's standards, but were revolutionary at the time, and out of his companies came some of his era's finest actors, including Fanny Davenport, Sara Jewett, Ada Rehan, Maurice Barrymore (patriarch of the Barrymore family), Tyrone Power Sr. (father to the movie actor Tyrone Power), and Isadora Duncan. A superb, exacting

acting teacher, Daly imposed heavy fines on his actors when they showed up late or forgot lines, but he was always willing to give an unknown a chance.

Daly named his theater the Fifth Avenue Theatre, and though it was smaller than many other theaters in town, it soon surpassed them all in reputation, with discerning theatergoers declaring its productions the best in the city, on par with the finest plays in London. Carriages lit with gas lights thronged down West Twenty-fourth Street in the early evenings, to come to a stop outside the theater's white marble facade. Dignified coachmen opened doors, leather creaked, and glittering patrons in satins and silks stepped out, while flower girls, beggars, and pickpockets watched hungrily from the shadows.

After the show was over, many in the audience strolled around the corner to the Fifth Avenue Hotel to discuss what they'd seen over a late-night supper or glass of champagne. Others—men only—headed directly across the street to John Morrissey's gambling resort at 5 West Twenty-fourth Street. Here a formally attired Black porter opened the door to reveal a lush, alluring hideaway within. The front parlor, with its silver and gold plate, was reserved for dining, while the back room, with its shiny dome, was reserved for gambling. A roulette table spun in its center, gaming tables beckoned on all sides, and a sideboard laden with jewel-colored bottles hugged one wall. Technically speaking, gambling was illegal in the city, but the house, like many others, operated openly, as corrupt officials and politicians looked the other way.

At the time, the six-foot-tall, two-hundred-pound Morrissey—rings dazzling on his fingers, diamonds blazing on his chest—was New York's undisputed gambling king, the owner or part owner of at least sixteen gambling houses all over Manhattan. His two most renowned resorts, at 8 Barclay Street and 818 Broadway (both of which had existed before he bought them and would continue for decades after he sold them), earned him millions of dollars during the 1860s, while his West Twenty-fourth Street house reportedly earned him nearly $500,000 (about $10 million today).

* * *

Helping to catapult the Fifth Avenue Theatre into fame was Clara Morris, a pale young actress from Ohio whom Daly hired at the start of his second season. Born into poverty, she was the eldest daughter of a bigamous marriage and, after she and her mother fled from her father, spent much of her childhood terrified that he might find them again. Daly offered Morris, who was neither especially pretty nor charismatic, only a meager salary at first and failed to properly introduce her to the rest of the company, whose glances at her shabby clothes kept her in agony. But all that changed after Morris began playing Cora in *Article 47*, a drama set in Paris.

The play revolved around Georges Duhamel and his octoroon lover, Cora, whom he tried to murder. She survived the attempt, and he was sentenced to five years in prison and banished from the city. Eight years passed. Georges was now living incognito in Paris with a young wife, and Cora was running a fashionable gambling house. He entered one evening and she recognized him. She sent an incriminating letter to the police, but then, stricken by guilt, plunged into madness and died. The play ended with Georges finally free of the "fatal passion" of the "colored" woman. Somehow, though Cora was the one whose life was destroyed, she was the one at fault. The block's early Black history had been forgotten in more ways than one.

On opening night Morris strode onstage confident and calm. The first two acts passed slowly, but then came the scene in which Cora goes mad. Anyone who saw Morris in that part would never forget it, wrote theater historian George C. D. Odell years later: "the rocking figure, the staring eyes, the muttered ravings . . . that last frightful maniacal shriek." Even more dramatic was the finale. As the scene ended, Morris collapsed onstage, and Daly rushed to lift her from the floor. She had fallen to the ground so violently that her bracelets had cut her flesh, and she took her curtain calls with both wrists bleeding.

Jim Fisk must have been watching the show from the audience that evening. It was opening night, and the Fifth Avenue Theatre was still *his* theater. As landlord, he had the best box in the house, which he furnished with huge silver water pitchers, more for show than anything else.

Jim also had the right to enter the theater's green room at will, much to the annoyance of Daly and the discomfort of many of the actresses. Daly had warned Morris about the financier in no uncertain terms, and she had listened at first, fleeing the room whenever he entered. As her reputation grew, however, she gained confidence, and the two became friends—there is no evidence of anything more. Jim spoke to her about his childhood, his frustration with his "growing stoutness," and his wife. Wrote Morris in one of her memoirs, "When anyone praised some wife, he would look up and say: 'Wife—whose wife? What wife? Bring your wives along, I ain't afraid to measure my Lucy with 'em. For, look here, you mustn't judge Lucy by her James!'"

On the afternoon of New Year's Day 1873, the Fifth Avenue Theatre caught fire. Morris had just gone to her home a few blocks away after the matinee ended when her landlord, who spoke little English, burst in. "Le feu! Le feu! Le théâtre!" he cried over and over in French. Then she heard two horses and a fire engine hurtling down the street and understood. Rushing out into the snow without her boots, she ran sobbing toward the smoke and flames. Someone grabbed her hand. It was Daly, who also lived nearby. He led her across the street and together they watched their beloved theater burn, taking their youth with it.

Daly would lease another theater on Broadway and Twenty-eighth Street almost immediately thereafter, and later open Daly's Theatre on Broadway and Thirtieth Street, where he produced acclaimed shows for over twenty years. The first American stage director to be recognized in Europe, he also opened a Daly's Theatre in London.

Morris would be applauded as "the greatest emotional actress of the English-speaking stage" throughout the 1870s, but her overly dramatic style of acting went out of fashion and she slid into obscurity. Married in 1874 to a man who exploited her for the rest of her life, she suffered from numerous health issues and by her late twenties became a morphine addict, an all-too-common occurrence in her place and time. Morphine was then a newly discovered wonder drug, used to treat everything from headaches to more serious afflictions, and male doctors often prescribed it to female patients for menstrual cramps, "diseases of a nervous character," and even morning sickness. In the 1880s and 1890s, the typical morphine addict was a middle- or upper-class white woman.

The charred shell of the Fifth Avenue Theatre remained an eyesore on the block for four years, but was finally rebuilt and reopened in 1877 as the

Fifth Avenue Hall by Amos Eno and Phillips Phoenix, a wealthy society man. Phoenix had owned a two-story private stable at 6 West Twenty-fourth Street, next door to the theater, since about 1860, and now added a third story and converted it into the theater's offices and dressing rooms. Two years later, the venue was rebuilt again, by George Mallory and Marshall Mallory, for Steele MacKaye, a prominent playwright, actor, theater manager, and inventor who developed the movable "double stage," allowing for scene changes within one or two minutes rather than four or five. He renamed his place the Madison Square Theatre.

As renowned as Daly, MacKaye also introduced the country's first folding chairs, first electric footlights, and an early air-conditioning system that involved circulating air over blocks of ice. Wrote English novelist Mary Duffus Hardy, astounded after attending a performance there one torrid summer day, "Immediately on entering, we felt as though we had left the hot world to scorch and dry up outside, while we were enjoying a soft summer breeze within. Where did it come from? The house was crowded—there was not standing-room for a broomstick, but the air was as cool and refreshing as though it had blown over a bank of spring violets." The Madison Square Theatre, later Hoyt's Madison Square Theatre, or more simply Hoyt's Theatre, produced plays for almost thirty years.

* * *

For those living and working at the Fifth Avenue Hotel, the New Year's Day fire at the Fifth Avenue Theatre brought back vivid, terrifying memories. A much more tragic fire had blazed in the hotel less than a month earlier, on December 10, 1872.

The fire had broken out on the hotel's top floor on its Twenty-third Street side just before midnight, when many of the guests and employees were already in bed. Fire engines arrived quickly and began shooting streams of water as panicked guests rushed to pack their trunks, settle their bills, and leave. They need not have worried. All the guest floors were safe. It was the servants' quarters, housed in a "cockloft," or attic built above the main part of building, that was ablaze.

After the fire was extinguished, the firemen went to check the cockloft and were horrified to stumble over bodies on the floor. Bringing in lanterns, they found fifteen women charred beyond recognition in a twelve-foot-square room. Many lay on top of each other near the room's only window, which opened onto the roof but was covered with a thick wire mesh impossible to remove with bare hands. The spiral wooden staircase leading to the cockloft had also offered no escape, as it was where the fire had started, perhaps by one of the gas jets lighting its passageway. Most of the victims, like most of the employees at the hotel, were Irish immigrants, some as young as seventeen. One bereaved father could only recognize the remains of his daughter by a ring on her middle finger.

Ironically, a city ordinance requiring public buildings to have fire exits had been passed only a year before, but its specifications were vague and most hotel managers had ignored it. They didn't want ugly fire escapes marring their hotels' stately facades and irritating their guests, who preferred not to think about unpleasant matters.

Edith Wharton was ten years old at the time of the Fifth Avenue Hotel fire and may have witnessed it from her family's home across the street, as it serves as the opening scene of her novella *New Year's Day*. In her telling, a wealthy old New York family is watching the fire and making fun of the nouveau riche as they flood out into the street. Exclaims one family member: "Oh, my dear, look—here they all come! The New Year ladies! Low neck and short sleeves in broad daylight, every one of them! Oh, and the fat one with the paper roses in her hair . . . Look at them scuttling!" Then the family notices two of their peers, the married Mrs. Lizzie Hazeldean and the playboy bachelor Henry Prest, exiting the hotel together. An embarrassed silence ensues.

*   *   *

Three years earlier, in 1869, while Jim had been keeping busy with Josie Mansfield and his theater activities, Jay Gould had been laying the groundwork for another audacious money-making scheme that would have far greater consequences than the Erie War: He and Jim would corner the gold market. They would buy up as much gold as they possibly could to artificially inflate its price, hoard it for a time, and then sell it at a huge profit.

Gould's machinations had begun soon after the inauguration of President Ulysses S. Grant on March 4, 1869, with the financier befriending

Abel Rathbone Corbin, a lawyer and speculator who had married Grant's younger sister. The Corbins lived not far from the Fifth Avenue Hotel, at 37 West Twenty-seventh Street, where Gould arranged to be introduced to Grant. The two men met frequently thereafter, a relationship that would taint Grant's presidency for years.

That August, Gould and Fisk put their plot in motion, buying up gold and encouraging their cohorts to do the same. With the help of Corbin, Gould had convinced Grant to keep the government's gold off the market, and prices rose to astronomical levels, closing at $144½ on September 23. The following morning, gold leaped even higher, to $160, and President Grant, catching wind of what was going on, announced that the Treasury would sell a whopping $4 million of government gold the next day. Wall Street went into a panic. Within minutes, gold prices plummeted from $160 to $133 and the stock market plunged twenty points. Nearly a thousand investors went bankrupt, and fourteen brokerage houses and several banks went under. But Fisk and Gould had gotten out just in time and made a fortune, at least according to the press; some modern historians are not so sure. And Gould paid a different sort of price. As the originator of the scheme, he became loathed by the public, who regarded him as evil incarnate, "the Mephistopheles of Wall Street," until the end of his days.

Curiously, Jim escaped the brunt of the reprobation. Though generally disliked by the upper and professional classes for his greed and crass manner, he was beloved by ordinary citizens, who reveled in his high spirits and swashbuckling style. They had crowed when he and Gould had brought down Daniel Drew during the Erie War, and they crowed again when he survived Black Friday, as the gold crash of 1869 became known. Many saw in him the realization of all their get-rich-quick dreams. The roly-poly bon vivant rolled on . . .

. . . until one day when he made a fatal mistake, putting into play the first act of a drama as histrionic as any that appeared on Augustin Daly's stage. He brought home business associate Edward Stokes, a handsome young man with a glossy black mustache, manager of the Brooklyn Oil Refinery Company. Josie was introduced and sparks flew.

By mid-1870, the Jim-Josie love affair was over and the Edward-Josie affair was on. Jim moved out of their West Twenty-fourth Street brownstone, which he had purchased in Josie's name, and into simple rooms near Castle Erie. Still, he continued to give her money and wrote her one anguished, impassioned letter after another in hopes of winning her back. She paid no attention. Rather, she coldly asked him for a long-term settlement so that she could continue the lifestyle to which she had become accustomed. Stokes didn't have the money that Jim had.

Another six months passed. Jim gave up on Josie, but seethed with anger at Stokes, and on January 7, 1871, had him arrested on charges of embezzlement. The younger man had taken out $250,000 (about $5 million today) in corporate funds from the Brooklyn Oil Refinery. He spent an uncomfortable weekend in jail, but the following Monday, a judge released him, saying that since the company was not a corporation, Stokes had the right to remove funds. Stokes immediately sued Jim for malicious prosecution and accused him of fraud, threatening to use the letters that Jim had written to Josie as evidence. He then offered to return the letters to Jim for $15,000 (about $300,000 today), and Jim countersued for blackmail. The cases went to court.

The *New York Herald* was there, reporting on January 5, 1872:

> The exquisite Stokes was all glorious in a new Alexis overcoat of a dull cream colour. An elegant diamond ring gleamed on his finger, like a glowworm in a swamp; a cane swinging carelessly, to and fro, before his manly legs. Fisk himself came into court in a strange kind of blue naval uniform that fitted him wretchedly, with its double rows of brass buttons. A diamond pin shone out of his fat chest like the danger light on the Sandy Hook bar.
>
> Miss Mansfield, who has been known from Maine to Oregon for her connection with Mark Antony Fisk and Octavius Caesar Stokes, soon entered the court. She has a pearly white skin; full, red lips; heavy eyelashes, and dark, lustrous, and very large eyes, which, when directed at a judge, witness, or jury, have a quick and terrible effect . . . Sitting there, this superb woman was the

personification of proud disdain as she cast her fiery and repeated
glances of contempt at the agonized Fisk.

Despite the quick and terrible effect of Miss Mansfield's eyes, the judge
ruled in favor of Jim the following day. Angry and dejected, Stokes went
to lunch at Delmonico's, now on the corner of Fifth Avenue and Twenty-
sixth Street, with his lawyer to discuss their next move. While there, he
received more bad news. The grand jury had indicted him on the charge
of blackmail; an order was going out for his arrest.

Infuriated, Stokes strode out of the restaurant to the Hoffman House
on Broadway at Twenty-fifth Street, where he was living, and then to Castle
Erie to find Jim. The financier wasn't there. He had left to call on friends
at the Grand Central Hotel on Broadway near Third Street. Stokes hailed
a cab and arrived at the hotel before Jim.

Stokes entered through a private door and went up the stairs to the
parlor floor. About ten minutes later, Jim arrived and started up the same
stairs. Stokes, still dressed in his cream-colored Alexis coat, stepped out
from hiding.

"Come along," he was heard to mutter to himself. "I have got you now."

Jim looked up. "I saw Edward Stokes at the head of the stairs," he told
a coroner a few hours later. "As soon as I saw him I noticed he had something in his hand."

A shot rang out. Hit in the abdomen, Jim shouted, fell over backward,
and tumbled down the stairs, his shiny top hat bouncing before him. He
immediately scrambled to his feet and Stokes shot again, this time hitting
his left arm. Jim fell a second time, sliding to the bottom of the stairs, and
as he lay there, Stokes turned and walked down the hall, throwing his pistol
under a lounge chair in one of the empty parlors. Then he went down to
the hotel office and said that someone had been shot.

"Yes," said one the hall boys who had seen him at the top of the stairs,
"and you are the man who did it."

A doctor and the police arrived. Stokes was taken to the Tombs, the
prison in downtown Manhattan, where he was held without bail. Jim
walked up the stairs on his own accord and lay down on a sofa in one of
the private parlors. He didn't seem to be badly hurt at first, but then black

blood began soaking the sofa—his intestine had been perforated in four places. He asked for his wife, Lucy, and a lawyer.

A police coroner came in. "Do you believe that you are about to die from the injuries you have received?" he asked Jim.

"I feel that I am in a very critical condition," Jim said.

"Have you any hopes of recovery?"

"I hope so," Jim said, ever optimistic.

Gould arrived, and though normally not a man to reveal emotion, he broke down with deep, audible sobs. "I cannot sufficiently give expression to the extent I suffer over the catastrophe," he told a reporter the next morning.

Lucy arrived from Boston at six twenty A.M., but by then, Jim was comatose with morphine. He died at ten forty-five A.M., having left everything he had to her, except for three thousand dollars for his parents and a few small bequests to friends.

Newsboys rushed into the streets with hot-off-the-press editions, and people congregated everywhere, frantic to learn more. "The scene at the Fifth Avenue Hotel was simply indescribable," reported the *New York Herald*. "As soon as ever the news of the shooting reached the clubs the members adjourned to the hotel as to one common centre . . . and by half-past seven there was scarcely any standing room in the lower floor of the hotel." Rumors flew in all directions, and the Fifth Avenue being the Fifth Avenue, a hallway was converted into a lively stock market. "Erie is sure to go up now, anyway," grunted one broker in the heat of the trading, and he was right.

The next day Jim's body lay in state in the Grand Opera House at Castle Erie between eleven A.M. and two P.M.—not nearly enough time for the tens of thousands who wanted to pay their final respects. Wrote one reporter, trying to make sense of the tremendous outpouring of grief: "They remembered that he had once been a poor, toiling lad who had wrought his success out of hard, earnest effort; that his steps upwards, while decked with a gaudy semi-barbaric show, were marked by strong traces of liberality and generosity of spirit that threw for the time the faults of his nature in the shade."

At two P.M. Jim's body was loaded into a hearse, and the funeral procession left for the railroad depot at Madison Square. Jim was to be buried near his birthplace in Vermont, where his parents were waiting. The sidewalks along West Twenty-third Street were lined with people as far as the eye could see. The only person who wasn't watching was Josie Mansfield, who had stopped answering her door and appearing in public. Upon hearing the news of Jim's death, she had said, as cold-hearted as ever, "I wish it to be distinctly understood that I am in no way connected with the sad affair. I have only my reputation to maintain." She died a pauper in Paris on October 26, 1931.

CHAPTER II

Ladies of the Night

Lizzie Wagner, age thirteen, was born in New York of German parents. Her father worked in shops when he could find employment, and her mother took in washing. As the oldest of four children, Lizzie helped out by selling flowers at the corner of Twenty-third Street and Fifth Avenue. Then one day she fell in with "bad company who led her into disorderly ways." Out late one evening, she went to the baths, fell asleep on a stoop on the way home, and was arrested.

Maria Pracreadi, "alias Julia," age sixteen, was born in France of French and Italian parents. Her father, a street musician and street sweeper, was often unemployed, and her mother sold shawls. Julia also sold shawls and swept streets. One day a man paid her two cents for sweeping, and a policeman, observing the transaction, arrested her.

Fannie Conner, age twelve, was born in New York City of Irish parents. Her father was dead and her mother worked as a live-in servant at a saloon. Fannie had also worked as a live-in servant at various establishments and was arrested one evening at Birdsall's, a concert saloon at 89 West Twenty-eighth Street, where she was employed as a waiter girl.

Ann Barry, age sixteen, was born in Ireland. Her father was dead and her mother worked in a tobacco factory. Ann worked at feather making, earning three to four dollars (about forty-eight to sixty-four dollars today) a week, and when she left work, she would "walk the streets and do as she pleased." This worried her mother, and so she had Ann arrested.

Such were some of the stories of the young women arrested for suspected prostitution in the dozen years after the Civil War. Technically, prostitution wasn't against the law; prior to World War I, there were few statutes criminalizing sexual acts, but the sex trade was regarded as a threat to the social order, and any woman stepping even slightly outside accepted norms was regarded as fair game for the morals police.

In fact, throughout the 1800s, all a woman had to do to be suspected of prostitution was to be alone on the street after dark. One much-publicized case in point before the Civil War had been that of Matilda Wade, who had left her home on Clark Street at about eight P.M. one evening in 1855 to meet her husband at his workplace on Spring Street, only a few blocks away. Walking calmly toward Broadway, she was stopped by a policeman, who arrested her for vagrancy—the usual charge for suspected prostitution. She was then taken with nineteen other women to a precinct house, where she was booked. She was not allowed to send for her husband and was locked in a jail cell. The next morning, she was convicted, reprimanded for refusing to tell how many years she'd been in the business, subjected to a medical exam to determine if she had venereal disease, and sent to the Tombs. Her husband petitioned the court, but it would be five days before his wife was released.

Citizens had been outraged over the Matilda Wade case, and her arrest had been declared illegal. Nonetheless, the practice of arresting women on the street had continued at a ruthless pace. A girl child resting on a stoop after visiting the baths, a sixteen-year-old receiving money for sweeping a street, a young woman out to enjoy some fresh air after a hard day's work—all were suspect.

*　　*　　*

Prostitutes had been part of the Twenty-third Street block ever since the Horn family stopped farming there in the 1830s. Ladies of the night had lingered about the hippodrome throughout its short existence, and probably about Madison Cottage as well. They had loitered across Madison Square at the railway depot and popped up at the doors of the Fifth Avenue

Hotel as soon as it opened. The hotel had been in operation just over a year when four plainclothes policemen appeared one November evening to stroll up and down near its entrance. They were responding to the many complaints they'd received about the "abandoned women" lurking nightly near the hotel. Almost immediately, the men were approached by a succession of "bold and reckless" "depraved street walkers" and, before the night was over, had arrested fifteen prostitutes, all in their twenties. The women were taken to a jail cell, where they spent the night singing "obscene songs, all of low class," and were brought before a judge the following morning.

Similarly, on the Sixth Avenue side of the block the same year the hotel opened, men in long tailcoats, high-waisted trousers, and fancy cravats were tapping their ivory-tipped canes discreetly on the door of "quite a private resort" three doors off Twenty-fourth Street. Run by Mrs. J. Ann Malloy, the house was known to only a few men of high standing, and gents visiting the resort for the first time had to send up letters of recommendation or they wouldn't be allowed in to meet the "very pretty and warm-hearted lady boarders" within. Those who were admitted, however, could rest assured they would be "well accommodated," or so wrote "A Free Loveyer" in the 1859 *Directory to the Seraglios in New York, Philadelphia, Boston, and All the Principal Cities in the Union.*

These early ladies aside, prostitution in New York before the Civil War had been largely contained farther downtown: to the dock areas in Lower Manhattan in the eighteenth and early nineteenth centuries; to the West Side below Canal Street, the Bowery/Lower East Side, and Five Points (a notorious neighborhood in Lower Manhattan) starting in the 1820s; and to these same areas and SoHo in the 1850s. But with the breakdown of society during the war and the city's move northward, prostitutes had begun appearing everywhere. In an 1866 address at Cooper Union, the Methodist bishop Matthew Simpson complained that there were more prostitutes in the city than Methodists and, a short time later, estimated that New York contained 20,000 prostitutes. The police retorted that those figures were exaggerated: there were only 3,300 prostitutes, working at 621 brothels and 99 assignation houses, 747 waiter girls offering their services at 75 concert saloons, and, of course, some "other women."

The exact numbers were irrelevant. New York had become a city awash with sex. "Cruisers" paraded about day and night, in summer and winter, spring and fall, batting their eyelashes, twirling their parasols, fluttering their capes. They were on the benches of Madison Square Park in the afternoons, inside and outside the restaurants in the evenings, inside and outside the theaters at night, and, of course, inside and outside the hotels at all hours. "Impure women of the 'higher,' that is the more successful class . . . abound at the hotels," noted author James McCabe in 1872.

The Gentleman's Companion, published anonymously in 1870, listed fifty-seven brothels and houses of assignation in the West Twenties, and that was just the beginning. Boardinghouses, concert saloons, and neighborhood bars, all known for their ladies, stood on almost every block intersecting Broadway and Sixth Avenue above Twenty-third Street. The number of such establishments would increase even more in the ensuing decade, and by 1880, the neighborhood would become the most famous sex district in New York City history, with Sixth Avenue operating as its wildly beating, licentious soul.

*   *   *

From the early 1860s through the 1890s, especially large numbers of streetwalkers loitered near the corner of Twenty-fourth Street and Fifth Avenue/Broadway every evening between seven P.M. and nine P.M. and along Sixth Avenue north of Twenty-third Street from seven P.M. to midnight. Those on the Fifth Avenue/Broadway side tended to be young, well dressed, and pretty. They smiled discreetly at gentlemen as they passed and sometimes followed them for a few feet, but always maintained a "maidenly reserve that perplexes while it allures," according to one observer. In contrast, those on the Sixth Avenue side tended to be older, less pretty, and more flashily dressed and heavily rouged. Brazen and bold, "loud-voiced and foul-tongued," they did "not hesitate to accost men."

The difference between the ladies of the two sides was one of class and age. Many of the streetwalkers on Fifth Avenue/Broadway were occasional prostitutes, out to supplement the meager salaries they earned as shop girls, domestics, or factory workers. Some lived in the city, while others came in from Brooklyn, Hoboken, Jersey City, or Harlem, laughing together as they smoothed their hair or applied a bit of color to their cheeks or lips. A few had regular clients whom they met at predetermined spots, but most had to catch as catch can. Usually they rented rooms by the hour in houses of assignation, some well appointed and others bare boned, depending on the pocketbooks of their johns. Prostitution was a job the young women could work at after hours, on an ad hoc basis, to help feed their families or afford a few luxuries—a new dress, a theater ticket—never mind that the work was filled with dangers: venereal disease, police harassment, robbery, brutal attacks. The young women's hearts must have been racing every time they went out.

Most nineteenth-century writers, almost all male, believed that young women of this type were doomed to live lives of increasing degradation, losing first their good looks, then their dignity, then their health, and finally their lives. Modern scholars such as Christine Stansell and Marilynn Wood Hill have found, however, that although that was certainly the case for some, other women of the era, especially those of the working class, prostituted themselves for only a few years before moving on to marry, have children, work ordinary jobs, and live ordinary lives. For them, prostitution was just a phase, a wayward stepping-stone on the path to adulthood.

Life was much darker for the streetwalkers on Sixth Avenue, most of whom were over thirty and otherwise unemployed. For them, prostitution *was* an increasingly degrading profession, often leading to alcoholism and drug addiction, along with deep humiliation and physical attacks. Men—and younger women too—often laughed at the disheveled, unsteady older streetwalkers as they wove their way down the avenue, struggling desperately to hold on.

Most of the Sixth Avenue prostitutes worked out of low-class brothels or boardinghouses. Others conducted business openly on the street, especially after the arrival of the Sixth Avenue Elevated (El) train in 1879, which thrust the thoroughfare into darkness after sundown, with plenty of shadows in which to hide. Operating on massive steel tracks supported by iron pillars three stories high, the El greatly improved the avenue's traffic congestion, but its rails and pillars blocked the sunlight and its belching steam engines rained sparks and soot. During the day, Sixth Avenue was a bustling, noisy place, crowded with businesspeople and shoppers, but after dark, as the gas lamps flared out and the brilliantly illuminated trains screeched by with "green and red fiery eyes staring ahead and plunging into darkness," everything changed.

Streetwalkers on all sides of the block had to watch out for cops. Brothels could operate openly by paying exorbitant rents and bribes to policemen and politicians, but streetwalkers had no such protection.

*　　*　　*

By the early 1870s, foot traffic in the neighborhood had increased exponentially over just a decade before. A half dozen luxury hotels now studded the area, the Broadway theater district was developing, and the Ladies' Mile, a fashionable shopping district that had begun in 1862 with the building of A. T. Stewart's department store at Ninth Street and Broadway, was moving steadily northward. Arnold Constable & Company and Lord & Taylor had relocated to Broadway between Nineteenth and Twenty-first streets in 1869, and the enormous Stern Brothers would open at 110 West Twenty-third Street (where the Home Depot stands today) a decade later. Still other department stores, including Hugh O'Neill's, McCreery's, and Siegel-Cooper, would open along Sixth Avenue south of Twenty-third in the late 1880s and 1890s.

At first, real estate on the Twenty-third Street block was not much affected by the shift. The Fifth Avenue Hotel still occupied its east side; wealthy citizens still resided on its south; attractive red-brick boarding-houses stood along its north side; and older brick buildings, some with shops occupying their ground floors, lined its west. In the late 1860s and 1870s, the "Boarders and Lodgers Wanted" column of the *New York Herald* always contained numerous listings for appealing rooms available on the block, especially on its Twenty-fourth Street side. One 1866 listing for 50 West Twenty-fourth Street read: "Rooms for rent. New and handsome house, first-class families and gentlemen only." Another for 30 West Twenty-fourth Street read: "Rooms with first-class board. Dinner at 6 o'clock." And an 1874 ad for 14 West Twenty-fourth Street, the building in which Edwin Booth had lived, ran: "Handsomely furnished rooms to rent, for single gentlemen, en suite without board."

Living in these boardinghouses at the time were mostly working- and professional-class people of all types: lawyers, physicians, dentists, stockbrokers, liquor traders, sugar brokers, milliners, managers, artists, clerks, and merchants. Already interspersed among them, however, and a harbinger of things to come, may have been a few "ladies of questionable character," whose numbers would swell as the decades passed. "One is struck with the great number of handsome young widows who are to be found in [respectable boardinghouses]," wrote McCabe in 1872. "The majority of these women are adventuresses, and they make their living in a way they do not care to have known."

* * *

The 1870 Gentleman's Companion listed no brothels on the Twenty-third Street block—Mrs. J. Ann Malloy's quite private resort of the early 1860s was apparently gone by then. For the lascivious gents staying at the Fifth Avenue Hotel, however, there were plenty of other convenient options to choose from, many just a five- or ten-minute walk away. One of the closest was the stylish "Hotel de Wood," run by Mrs. Kate Woods at 105 West Twenty-fifth Street. "Furnished throughout with the most costly and newest improvements," the three-story brownstone was home to "three young ladies of rare personal attractions."

If the Hotel de Wood was too crowded or not to taste, a "sporting male," as men of certain nighttime habits were then known, could choose to visit one of four other houses on the same block, or head to one of thirteen addresses on West Twenty-sixth Street between Sixth and Seventh avenues. *The Gentleman's Companion*'s favorite spots here were No. 116, kept by the "fun-loving, agreeable" Sarah Wilbur; No. 129, featuring six gentle lady boarders "whose merry laughs resound throughout the entire palace"; and No. 133, "an abode of Venus" run by S. A. Sanchez. To be avoided was No. 127, a second-class house with reports of a bear being kept in the cellar.

Even busier was the West Twenty-seventh Street block between Sixth and Seventh avenues, which offered twenty-three houses of varying quality and so many prostitutes it was impossible to walk down it at night. One first-class choice here was No. 128, run by a dashing brunette who employed five lady boarders to "drive away the blues" and had a regular physician attached to it. Houses to stay away from included No. 105, where the land-lady and her servants were "as sour as her wine."

Most famous immediately after the Civil War, and a "must see" for male out-of-towners, was Sisters' Row, which took its name from a huge musical hit produced by Laura Keene in 1860. Located on West Twenty-fifth Street, the row had seven unmarked side-by-side brothels reportedly run by seven sisters. Rumor had it that they had come to New York from a small New England town to seek their fame and fortune, but had failed to find legiti-mate jobs. Refusing to return to staid New England, and realizing the money to be made in the sex trade, the sisters reinvented themselves as big-city madams.

The Seven Sisters were among the most expensive bordellos in the city, their ladies "cultured and pleasing companions, accomplished on the piano and guitar, and familiar with the charms and graces of correct sexual inter-course." On certain days of the month, no man was admitted unless he had an engraved invitation, wore evening dress, and carried a bouquet of flowers. On Christmas Eve, all the brothels' proceeds were donated to charity.

Another option for the sporting male just after the war was the beguiling Louvre, a concert saloon on the southwest corner of Broadway and Twenty-third Street, diagonally across from the Fifth Avenue Hotel. A type of entertainment venue that first appeared in New York in the 1850s, the concert saloons derived their name from the fact that they provided some sort of live entertainment, usually just a musician or two on piano and strings (making them the city's first modern nightclub, the precursor to the cabaret), along with their main attraction, the waiter girls. Dressed seductively, the women did not receive wages but worked on a percentage basis by encouraging their clients to buy expensive drinks for them. Sex did not usually occur on the premises, but overt solicitation did. Most concert saloons were cheap, dingy affairs, but the Louvre was an excep-tion, as ostentatious as its name, with massive columns, a vast drinking hall with a splashing fountain, and a lounge where only champagne was served. Patrons were encouraged to sing along as small bands played and waiter girls in low-cut bodices swirled.

Two decades later, the more adventurous of the Fifth Avenue Hotel guests could also head a bit farther west to the "African Tenderloin," also

known as "African Seventh" or "African Broadway." African Americans
began moving into the neighborhood in the 1880s, some coming from
Greenwich Village, where they had been forced out by white immigrant
groups, others newly arrived from the rural South. Most worked as wage
earners, some as skilled artisans and professionals, and a few in the flesh
trade. West Twenty-fifth and Twenty-seventh streets near Seventh Avenue
thronged with Black prostitutes, while at the intersection of West Twenty-
seventh Street and Seventh Avenue competed four saloons, all frequented
by ladies of the night. A brothel at 110 West Twenty-fifth Street, run by the
Cuban "negress" Mrs. Durand, was "one of the toughest and most iniqui-
tous" in the city, according to *Vices of a Big City*, a pamphlet published anonymously by the *New York Press*, while Mme. Fisher's parlor house at 110 West
Twenty-eighth Street was one of the most refined. A former slave, Fisher
had come to New York in 1869 and opened her first house on East Ninth
Street before a wealthy lawyer, "whose name [was] known all over New York
State," bought her the more luxurious Twenty-eighth Street establishment.

Mme. Fisher, Mrs. Kate Woods, Mrs. Malloy, and other madams of the
city's first-class houses wielded considerable financial and political power.
Excellent businesswomen, savvy to the machinations of the city and the
art of bribery, they knew how to handle both people and money, and how
to set up a sumptuous parlor house as finely appointed as any Fifth Avenue
mansion. Sofas covered with satin and brocade filled the rooms, oriental
rugs covered the floors, and crystal chandeliers hung from the ceilings.

Often a fixture at the houses was an elegant Black servant who carefully inspected each potential guest through a grill before opening the door
and escorting him into a parlor, where the madam introduced him to the
ladies of the house. A pianist, "the Professor," usually also African American, tickled the ivories while small talk was made and the guest bought
overpriced bottles of wine or champagne for everyone present. Then he and
his chosen lady retired to a room upstairs. Men who didn't know each other
were never admitted to the parlor at the same time.

Most of the parlor houses employed fewer than ten women, and sometimes only three or four, as their prices were so high, they had no need to
employ more. These ladies received room and board in exchange for a
weekly fee and were expected to maintain an air of respectability at all

times. Streetwalking was strictly forbidden. Clients were solicited by sending engraved invitations to important visitors staying at the luxury hotels, hotel arrivals being routinely announced in the newspapers.

*   *   *

Operating along with the brothels were the neighborhood's many illicit boardinghouses, which began appearing on the West Twenty-fourth Street side of the block sometime in the mid- to late 1880s. Perhaps because of the nearby screeching El, the street had stopped appealing to well-off bachelors and families by then and had slid from respectability into neglect and despair.

Unlike in the brothels, where madams and prostitutes worked together to please men, the ladies of the boardinghouses typically worked individually, with each renting her own separate room and recruiting her own customers. But the distinction between the brothels and the boardinghouses was not always so clear-cut. As at the brothels, the prostitutes at the boardinghouses often dined together and shared customers, with their housekeepers often functioning much like madams. Conversely, the madams often referred to their brothels as "boardinghouses" and charged their ladies rents to camouflage their operations.

Some of the seedier boardinghouses, as well as some of the seedier brothels, contained "panel rooms," so named because of movable panels cut into the walls. The rooms were usually sparsely furnished, with only a bed and single chair on which the client was forced to put his clothes, as there was no other spot. Then, while he was otherwise engaged, a "badger," also known as a "creeper," slid open the panel, crept into the room on hands and knees, and went through the man's pockets.

Not much is known today about the illicit boardinghouses on the block's Twenty-fourth Street side, but they appear to have been dismal places. An 1892 police raid on the street emptied out three "low-class" disorderly houses in a row: May Stacom's at No. 14 (Edwin Booth's former building), Caroline A. Hasting's at No. 16, and Nellie Harrison's at No. 18 (one of the buildings where Josie Mansfield lived before Jim Fisk bought her a townhouse). Some of the women joked when arrested, others wept, even as they claimed to have legitimate jobs as seamstresses, factory workers, and domestics. The women were locked up for the night and fined ten dollars each by a judge in the morning. "The landladies, however, may not get off so easily," reported the *New York Times*.

Con men were operating on the block then, too, and later raids also shut down Charley Walters's dusky gambling joint at 42 West Twenty-fourth. Big-player regulars Chappie Levy, Dink Davis, and Teddy Alexander all skulked away from the decrepit den as soon as the cops descended. Their days of chomping on Walters's free sandwiches and cigars—inducements to make them stay later and bet more—had ended.

* * *

On February 28, 1889, a thirteen-year-old girl named Gracie Irwin went missing. Her much-older cousin Miss Caroline P. Smyth of 314 West Eighty-fourth Street contacted the police. Gracie's parents had died a decade earlier while the family was still living in Dublin, and Gracie resided with Miss Caroline. She had two older brothers and an older sister, but they were grown and living on their own.

Two days later, one of Miss Caroline's neighbors received a telegram. It was from Gracie. She was staying at the St. Omer Hotel, 384 Sixth Avenue, on the west side of the Twenty-third Street block. A detective was promptly dispatched.

A far humbler affair than its cousin on Fifth Avenue, the five-story, eighty-room St. Omer had been built to appeal to the middle class. A March 1879 advertisement in the *New York Herald* for the new hotel read: "ALL COME AT ONCE—LADIES AND GENTLEMEN, to St. Omer Hotel and Restaurant, 6th av. and 23rd st. Popular Prices! Popular Prices!! Popular Prices!!!"

Sportsmen in town to compete at the first Madison Square Garden, by then occupying the former railroad depot at Madison Square, were regulars at the St. Omer at first. Most famous among them was Frank Hart. The nation's first celebrated African American athlete, probably born in Haiti, Hart was a superstar in pedestrianism—long-distance walking and running—then easily the most popular sport in America, far more popular than baseball. Thousands of fans flocked to sawdust-covered tracks all over the country to watch men walking and running for up to six days and nights, covering upward of five hundred miles. Professional pedestrians were the nation's highest-paid athletes, and their races immensely profitable. When Hart set a new world record by covering 565 miles in six days at the first Madison Square Garden on April 10, 1880, he collected $7,967.86 in gate money, $9,000 in entrance fees, $1,000 for breaking the record, and a reputed $3,600 for betting on himself, bringing his winnings to $21,567.86 (about $480,000 today). When companies began inserting trading cards into cigarette packs in 1880, Hart was one of the first athletes to be included.

Throughout his career, Hart suffered from much racial prejudice and endured countless epithets hurled at him trackside; some fellow athletes refused to shake his hand. Yet he also had legions of white fans whose eyes followed him around the sawdust tracks for hours and, after his record-breaking win, was the most lauded athlete of any color in the country. News of his victory headlined in papers coast to coast, and the *New York Sun* printed a full-length illustration of him, arms crossed, on its front page. *Plessy v. Ferguson*, the infamous 1896 Supreme Court case that upheld the constitutionality of segregation and in effect banned Black athletes from participating in white athletic competitions, was still a generation away.

Athletes aside, though, the St. Omer Hotel was mired in trouble from the start. During its first year of operation, its proprietor was indicted for receiving goods under false pretenses, and a hotel guest was arrested for forgery. Six years later, two private detectives attempted to entrap the wealthy businessman Charles B. Sears of Buffalo by hiring redheaded May Thatcher, a self-possessed "dissolute young woman," to lure him into a compromising position at the hotel. Their scheme failed, and the two detectives and Thatcher were arrested.

By the time Gracie Irwin went missing, the hotel had fallen into even more ill repute. The *Evening World* called it a "notorious Sixth avenue resort," outrageously protected under the moniker "hotel," and questioned how the authorities could tolerate its existence.

When the detective dispatched to pick up Gracie arrived at the St. Omer, he found her "comfortably installed" in a room. He took her uptown to the One Hundredth Street precinct station, where she told her story. She had met a middle-aged man named James Burgess, who worked at a coal yard, the previous December while selling tickets for a church fair. She had enjoyed talking to him, and they met again and again. He never behaved improperly toward her, but said that it was a shame she didn't have more enjoyment in her life and promised to take her away forever and get her a nice flat. She was entranced by the idea. He was always very kind and "at Auntie Caroline's it was not very pleasant," she said.

Gracie began visiting Burgess at the coal yard so often that his colleagues remarked on it. Sometimes she brought him flowers. Then one day Burgess told her that the flat was ready, and he would meet her that evening at the corner of Ninth Avenue and Ninety-first Street. She waited for him a long time, and when he finally arrived, they took the El down to Twenty-third Street. He sent her ahead to register alone at the hotel, where she used her real name, and followed a short time later, registering as E. D. Brown. The hotel staff later told the police that they had no idea the two were together, but even if that were the case, they must have known something was amiss, as no legitimate hotel would have allowed a thirteen-year-old girl to register on her own.

Burgess remained with Gracie a few hours and left before dawn, giving her two dollars and saying he would be back the next day to buy her long dresses and take her to the promised flat. He also left his contact information with the hotel clerks and told them to get in touch if she made any trouble.

After hearing Gracie's story, the police arrested Burgess, a burly forty-seven-year-old married man, and charged him with rape. He pleaded not guilty, claiming that the girl had made him go with her. His wife stood by him; he was innocent, she insisted. Gracie's brothers came forward and said that their sister had probably run off because their cousin Miss Caroline had mistreated her. She half starved the girl, worked her until midnight, and whipped her for the slightest offense, they said. Gracie was taken away for the night by the New York Society for the Prevention of Cruelty to Children. What happened to her after that is unknown, but it would not have been unusual for a girl of her background to have drifted from one misguided night into a lifetime of prostitution.

*　　*　　*

Seduction, followed by abandonment, was widely believed to be the major cause of prostitution throughout much of the 1800s. Writers told of innocent girls picked up on their way home from Sunday school, from factories, from parks, and of an elaborate system of "bankers, express-men, runners, and agents" assigned to receive them. The seducers were said to hang about theaters, churches, summer resorts, graduation ceremonies, and the best hotels, where, under the pretense of being strangers to New York, they got to know young lady visitors, drugged and deflowered them, and sold them into prostitution. "If a daughter is missing from New York, or from a radius of twenty miles around, the police know usually where to look," concluded Matthew Hale Smith in *Sunshine and Shadow in New York*, published in 1869.

At times, the demand for new upper-class girls was so high that madams sent agents to New England and the Middle Atlantic states to seduce more. Especially famous in this regard were Red Light Lizzie and Jane "the Grabber" Haskins, who had a squadron of good-looking men and empathetic women in their employ. The good-looking men were instructed to check into respectable hotels, attend church services, seek out susceptible well-bred young women, invite them for walks and téte-a-tetés, and convince them to elope to New York. The empathetic women were told to promise the girls well-paying, enjoyable jobs and rooms in respectable boardinghouses. So many young women disappeared in this fashion in the mid-1870s that police captain Charles McDonnell arrested Jane the Grabber and sent her to prison.

Smith wrote of two highly respected gentlemen who were accosted on Broadway one night by a girl who seemed younger than thirteen. She was thinly clad and in feeble health. Striking up a conversation, the men learned that she came from Vermont. Her father was a farmer and her family, well respected in the community. One day a young man from New York came to spend a winter near her home and began appearing at the singing school and meetings she attended. She fell in love, and he proposed marriage. They eloped to New York, where he abandoned her and she took to the streets. The two gentlemen offered to help the girl return to Vermont, but she refused, saying, "It is now too late. I could not endure the cold pity of my mother, or the scorn of my sisters, or the taunts of my former associates . . . To all who once loved me I am as one dead."

Similarly, James McCabe wrote of a young girl who answered an ad in the newspaper for a chambermaid. She went to the designated address, and there a lady gave her fine new silk clothes to try on. The girl was reluctant to do so at first, but she finally did, at which point the lady ordered her to join the other prostitutes in the house. She refused and was brutally treated. She tried to escape, but couldn't get away until four days later when she and another girl climbed over a fence in the backyard.

Such accounts may well have been true, but when Dr. William Sanger, the chief resident physician of the hospital on Blackwell's Island, studied prostitution in depth in an 1858 study—the first serious researcher to do so—he found that women became prostitutes for more complex, prosaic, and all-too-familiar-sounding reasons than had earlier been imagined. Of the two thousand women he interviewed, most of them brothel workers, only about one eighth cited seduction and abandonment as the cause of their prostitution. About one fourth cited "destitution"; another one fourth "inclination"; a tenth "drink and the desire to drink"; and others "bad company," "persuasion by others," "too idle to work," or the death or intemperance of a parent.

Sanger also found that nearly half of the women had once worked as domestic servants, and another fourth in manufacturing jobs, before turning to prostitution. Their wages had been abysmally low, with three quarters of the women earning less than $3 a week (about $100 today)—not enough to support themselves at a subsistence level, let alone children if they had them. Hours were long, sometimes fourteen hours a day, and the jobs, boring and degrading. In contrast, prostitutes at high-class parlor houses worked far shorter hours, had much more interesting lives, and could clear up to a $100 a week (about $3,350). Of course, most prostitutes earned far less than that; Sanger estimated that the average income of prostitutes of all classes was $10 a week.

Although Sanger's study came out a decade before the West Twenties became known for prostitution, many of his findings continued to apply in the second half of the 1800s, as impoverished immigrants continued to pour into the city and decent-paying jobs for women remained scarce. Prostitution was not a profession that most women turned to easily, but it was the best option many women had, and probably the reason why one fourth of those interviewed by Sanger cited "inclination" as the reason for their trade. In an era when a respectable young lady couldn't even leave her house without a chaperone, prostitution offered women a modicum of independence and a way to hold their own in a world that belonged almost exclusively to men.

None of the women Sanger interviewed were under fifteen, probably because most were brothel workers. He paid little attention to streetwalkers or children, even though pedophilia and child prostitution were widespread in the mid- to late 1800s. Recent immigrant families often sent their girls and boys out alone to peddle flowers, fruits, toothpicks, or socks, making them easy prey. "Give me a penny, mister? Give me a penny, mister?" the flower girls would cry from their posts outside the Fifth Avenue Hotel.

CHAPTER 12

At the End of the Nightstick

On September 30, 1876, a strapping Canadian American policeman strode into the aging Twenty-ninth Precinct Station House at 137-139 West Thirtieth Street, and for a moment, all activity stopped. Cops and civilians alike looked up from whatever they were doing to take measure of their new boss. And they were not disappointed. Alexander "Clubber" Williams was all the papers made him out to be: tall, muscular, long-necked, and bullet-headed, with an air of menace and the hint of a sneer about him.

Williams had been a member of the New York Police Department (NYPD) for only a dozen years, but already he was the city's most notorious cop, a nationally known figure whose brutal exploits were consistently covered—usually with admiration, occasionally with criticism—by the New York press. His famous dictum, "There is more law in the end of a policeman's nightstick than in a decision of the Supreme Court," was already part of city lore.

Williams probably looked back at his new colleagues and clients with a mixture of arrogance and gloating anticipation. In the 1870s, the Twenty-ninth Precinct was the most important post in the city, lying as it did at the epicenter of New York prestige and power. Williams had spent the first ten years of his police career in tough working-class neighborhoods downtown and upon hearing of his new assignment, reportedly said, "I have had chuck steak for a long time, and now I am going to eat tenderloin." He was referring not to the district's many pleasures of the flesh but to the increased opportunity for graft that would now come his way. Williams's offhand comment gained traction, and soon the district was dubbed "the Tenderloin." The term passed into more general usage, to be applied decades later to vice-ridden districts in other American cities, most notably San Francisco.

When Williams first arrived in the Twenty-ninth Precinct, the Tenderloin stretched roughly between West Twenty-third and West Thirty-fourth streets, Fifth and Seventh avenues. Later, as the city continued to move northward, so did the district. By the 1880s, it extended to the mid-Forties and Eighth Avenue, and by the 1890s, to Fifty-seventh Street and Tenth Avenue. During the Tenderloin's heyday in the 1880s and 1890s—years that largely coincided with Williams's reign—an estimated half of its buildings were devoted to some sort of decadent pursuit, setting the city's all-time high for vice in one saturated district. Amusements of all types, high and low, exclusive and seedy, could be found in abundance within one compact, easily navigable neighborhood.

New York's Tenderloin also had another nickname—"Satan's Circus," coined by the moral reformers who were operating in the West Twenties and Thirties shortly before Williams arrived. Although accustomed to dealing with criminal elements downtown, the reformers were horrified by what they encountered uptown, and one crusader denounced all of New York City as a "modern Gomorrah" for allowing such an abominable neighborhood to exist.

The Twenty-third Street block lay within the Twenty-ninth Precinct's jurisdiction, and it wasn't long before Williams became a fixture on the block, swinging his nightstick, tilting his hat, and greeting prominent residents, politicians, and businessmen by name. Everyone knew "Big Alec." "I'm so well known in this city that the car horses nod to me in the morning," he once said. With one foot on the bright side of the block and the other on the dark, he frequented the Fifth Avenue Hotel, watched over the vaults of the block's Second National and Garfield National banks, policed the many parades that swept along Fifth Avenue, and either arrested or shook down the block's shadier denizens.

* * *

Like so many other players on the block, Williams had come a long way from his humble beginnings. Born to farmers in Cape Breton, Nova Scotia, Canada, in 1839, he had immigrated to New York with his parents as a boy and became a naturalized U.S. citizen at age twenty-one. He apprenticed as a ship's carpenter for W. H. Webb & Co., a shipbuilding company on the East River, for a few years, and traveled extensively for the company, to Mexico, Japan, and other countries. During the Civil War, he worked as a contractor for the U.S. government in the Brooklyn Naval Yard.

Williams joined the NYPD in August 1866 and because of his impressive build was soon assigned to the dangerous post of Broadway and Houston Street, deep in the territory of a tough Irish street gang. Two days after his arrival, he reportedly picked a fight with two local gang members, knocked them unconscious with his club, and hurled them through the plate glass window of the Florence Saloon. When their fellow gang members arrived, he knocked them unconscious, too, and for the next four years, was said to average a fight a day. In 1871 he was promoted to sergeant and given the command of a mounted patrol, and in 1872 was made captain of the Twenty-first Precinct in the East Twenties, where he broke up the Gas House Gang, a notorious group of street thugs.

Sometime during this period, Williams earned the nickname "Clubber." The New York cops of that era carried nightclubs made of locust wood, an extremely hard material that could crack open skulls, and used them with impunity. The NYPD was only three decades old, and clubbings were generally viewed as an important way for the police to ensure respect and maintain public control in an era when hardened criminals and gang members roamed the streets. Serious injuries and death following clubbings were common, however, with 9 percent of victims dying after the encounter.

Williams was the undisputed king of clubbings, a reputation he savored. He used his stick at the slightest provocation and was lionized by his fellow cops and most of the press for his courage and effective policing. In 1878, the *New York Times* commended him for being "the most conspicuously efficient disciplinarian on the force," and in the 1880s, the *Evening World* ran a regular feature recounting the exciting adventures of "the great and only Alexander Williams."

All this praise puffed up the already arrogant captain even more, and he became yet more aggressive and violent. Three years after his appointment to the Tenderloin, he twice overstepped the bounds of acceptable police behavior by savagely clubbing ordinary citizens, once on the edge of Madison Square and once directly in front of the Fifth Avenue Hotel. Both times he was taken to police court.

The first assault took place during a six-day pedestrian race that had begun just after midnight on March 10, 1879, in the former New York and New Haven Railroad Depot, then known as Gilmore's Garden, but soon to be renamed (the first) Madison Square Garden. On the first night of the race, the gas-lit arena, thick with blue cigar smoke, was packed with over ten thousand shouting, wagering fans, while another five thousand were outside the gates, clamoring to buy tickets and be let in. But the ticket sellers couldn't work fast enough, and when the race went off at one A.M., the impatient mob broke down the gates, spilled into the lobby, and began climbing into the stands. Williams and his men, in charge of security, surged forward. The "sound of the heavy blows rained upon the defenseless heads and bodies of the unfortunates who happened to be in the front ranks was sickening," reported the *New York Times*.

No one pressed charges that day, but the next evening, the crowds at the arena were even larger, with a dense mass of people sitting in the balconies, in the aisles, and along the railing that ran around the track. A boisterous group had gathered outside at one of the athlete's tents, and hearing the noise, Williams waded toward it, wielding his club indiscriminately, striking one savage blow after another. Some onlookers in the stands booed and hissed at him, and Williams looked up, furious, to lock eyes with William Vincent Blake, a thirty-five-year-old pottery designer from Trenton, New Jersey.

Seconds later, according to Blake, Williams was in the stands, violently prodding him in the chest with his club. "Come out of here you ____ ____ sneak thief," he shouted. Blake stood up, and Williams clubbed him on the shoulder. Then Williams grabbed Blake's coat collar and pulled him to the edge of the balcony, forcing him to jump down into the arena. Williams jumped down after him. "If you will show me the way out, I will go out," Blake said. But Williams mercilessly kicked and shoved him toward the exit. Then he clubbed him again across the shoulder.

Blake pressed charges, and that April, Williams stood trial for "conduct unbecoming an officer" at police headquarters on Mulberry Street. Blake produced six witnesses, but Williams produced more than fifty, among them other cops and referees from the race. He was also represented by two influential lawyers who argued that excessive force had been necessary to prevent a riot. A few weeks later, Williams was exonerated—for neither the first nor the last time.

Seven months later, on October 30, 1879, Williams was on trial again, this time for clubbing slender, red-haired Charles Smith, age twenty-six, at a military parade in front of the Fifth Avenue Hotel. According to Smith, he had been standing peacefully in the crowd by the side of the avenue waiting for the parade to begin when Williams and one of his men, Officer Fleming, passed by, ordering everyone to get back. Then, without warning, Williams raised his club and struck Smith on the shoulder. "What did you strike me for? What have I done?" said Smith, to which Williams replied, "I'll show you!" and struck him two more times. Officer Fleming rushed up to also strike Smith, at which point he passed out. A bystander drove him to New York Hospital, and when he came to, he found himself soaked in blood, with Williams by his bedside. Looming menacingly, the captain made him promise not to press charges—a promise Smith said he agreed to only because he needed medical treatment and was "afraid he would not get away." Williams left, probably congratulating himself on successfully evading trouble, but later that day, the afternoon papers ran front-page stories about what had happened, and a score of witnesses came forward, vowing to testify on Smith's behalf.

Those witnesses made no difference. Williams produced other witnesses who swore he had done nothing more than tap Smith on the shoulder. The jury listened to three weeks of testimony and then adjourned. Seven minutes later, they were back with their verdict: not guilty. Nothing, it seemed, could touch the ferocious Clubber.

Dozens more complaints were lodged against Williams over the next decade, with many involving a potentially more consequential charge: corruption. The captain's official salary was $2,750, yet by 1894 he would accumulate a net worth of at least $350,000 (about $10.6 million today).

Blatant evidence of Williams's corruption was everywhere in the Twenty-ninth, yet he skirted the corruption charges as easily as he skirted those of excessive force. In 1879, the same year that he was taken to court twice for clubbings, two complaints were lodged against him for his failure to close gambling houses. Neither went anywhere, and a similar complaint filed a few years later met the same fate.

Then, in a highly publicized case in 1885, Williams was brought to trial by the police superintendent himself, George Walling. Walling's son Frank, a textile salesman, had been fleeced out of over $500 (about $13,500 today) in the Tenderloin's gambling dens and went to his father for help. Walling used plainclothes detectives to collect evidence and filed charges. To some, Williams's conviction seemed assured. But the police department was a deeply divided, politicized organization, and Williams had much support from other cops and influential politicians. He was also again represented by powerful lawyers, among them Elihu Root, the future secretary of state under Theodore Roosevelt. Declaring the trial a "persecution," these lawyers produced a dozen character witnesses, along with a petition praising Williams signed by four hundred prominent residents and businessmen of the Twenty-ninth, including G. P. Putnam's Sons, publishers with offices on the block; Leonard Jerome, the "King of Wall Street"; and Ward McAllister, the self-appointed arbiter of high society. The police commissioners exonerated Williams 3–1, with the police board president saying, "No officer of the law is to be held responsible for the actual and entire suppression of all crime or of any particular crime."

That wasn't the end of it either. Three months later, Captain Williams, standing proud in his dress uniform at the Lyric Theatre on Sixth Avenue just north of the block, was lavished with extravagant testimonials during a ceremony hosted by five hundred precinct businesspeople and residents. At the event's finale, the group presented him with a huge commemorative album so heavy two men could barely lift it. It was adorned with three hundred pennyweights of gold and twenty-one diamonds, a "memento of the quickening and unfailing gratitude of the people in the Twenty-Ninth Police Precinct to the dauntless champion of their peace, a stately pillar of the law's eternal throne." Later, it would come out that the album had been largely paid for by madams and gamblers.

Two weeks after the ceremony, Walling was forced to retire, and two years later, in 1887, Williams was promoted to inspector. A "reward long deserved," commented the *New York Times*.

By the end of Williams's NYPD career in 1894, over 350 formal complaints would be filed against him—at least 100 more than against any other cop—and he would be taken to court eighteen times. He was never found guilty, though he was removed from his captain's position and appointed superintendent of street cleaning for two years. Throughout it all, he remained unapologetic for his behavior and continued to defend the practice of clubbing even after it was outlawed in 1892. When Mayor William Jay Gaynor used Williams's nickname in a derogatory fashion in 1912, when Clubber was seventy-two years old, he shot back, "Just ask the Mayor if he can point to a single person I ever clubbed that did not deserve it. He can't name one and he knows it."

* * *

On the southwest corner of the Twenty-third Street block, just down the street from the mansions of the Schermerhorns and others, stood the grand, five-story French Second Empire New Masonic Temple, built for the enormous sum of $1.2 million (about $31 million today) two years before Williams's arrival in the district by the architect Napoleon LeBrun. At its entrance stood two Egyptian-style bronze pillars, while at its top shimmered an ornate roof trimmed with ironwork. The building's Sixth Avenue side abutted the St. Omer Hotel.

The temple served as the state headquarters of the Freemasons, a secret male fraternal organization whose New York membership numbered about 75,000 in 1870, and about 125,000 by 1900. Numerous lodges, as the groups into which the Masons are organized are known, met here, as did the overarching Grand Lodge of Free and Accepted Masons of the State of

New York. Many of the city's most prominent nineteenth-century citizens were members, including Theodore Roosevelt, Senator Thomas Collier Platt, Major General Leonard Wood—and Alexander "Clubber" Williams.

Freemasonry had originated in medieval Europe as a guild for stonemasons, but quickly evolved into a social organization open to men of all trades and professions, and was transported to America by the British. George Washington, Benjamin Franklin, and about ten other signers of the U.S. Constitution were members, and the Masons played an important part in the American Revolution. The organization was fiercely opposed to monarchies and embraced the ideals of the Enlightenment— liberty, equality, and independence.

Like all Masons then and now, Williams would have joined the organization at the lowest of its thirty-three degrees (ranks), the Entered Apprentice, on the recommendation of two sponsors. During the initiation ceremony, he would have walked into the lodge blindfolded, to signify that he was living in darkness, with his left breast exposed to show that he was a man and his left pant leg rolled up to prove that he was able-bodied. Three men would have ordered him to reveal the organization's secrets and, when he refused, commanded him to kneel in front of an altar and swear to that refusal and to his desire to be delivered into the light.

Like all Masonic chambers, the room would have been laid out on an east–west axis. The Masons believe that the east represents light and knowledge; it is at the eastern end of the room that the Master of the Lodge always sits, in a throne-like chair under the letter *G*, symbolic of Geometry and "God, the Grand Architect of the Universe." To join the Masons, a man must believe in a Supreme Being, though that Supreme Being can be of any religion. Religious tolerance is a central Masonic value.

(That open-mindedness does not extend to women, who are not allowed to join the Brotherhood. There have been only a handful of exceptions, including one Madame de Xaintrailles, who during the Napoleonic Wars enlisted in the army dressed as a man. The French Masons knew that she was a woman, but as she was a courageous soldier who had risen to the rank of captain they decided to accept her anyway—much to the disapproval of many Masons worldwide. Even today, MasonicDictionary.com opines: "But the members [of the committee who accepted the madame] were Frenchmen, they were excitable and they were gallant; and consequently, in a sudden and exalted fit of enthusiasm, which as Freemasons we cannot excuse, they unanimously determined to confer the First Degree . . . of regular and legitimate Freemasonry, on the brave woman who had so often exhibited every manly virtue.")

After Williams pledged to never reveal the Masons' secrets, the lodge's Worshipful Master would have pounded a gavel once. Then the other Masons in attendance would have clapped once and removed his blindfold, to signify the acceptance of another "Brother," as the Masons call each other, into the organization.

The Masons liken their Entered Apprentices to large, rough, uncut stones, who, as they pass through the lessons of the second and third degrees, Fellow Craft and Master Mason, are transformed into smooth building blocks. Told through allegory and story, the lessons revolve around self-improvement—how to be a better man, a better husband, a better citizen—lessons that Williams for one certainly didn't take to heart.

After reaching the degree of Master Mason, a Freemason can rise through thirty more degrees (though few go further than the third) or join different branches of the organization, such as the Knights Templar, of which Williams was a member. Open only to Christians, the Knights Templar identify with a medieval order of the same name composed of monks who took up arms to protect Christian pilgrims traveling to Jerusalem.

On the ground floor of the New Masonic Temple were commercial spaces that the Masons rented out as moneymakers for their many charities and education programs. Deeper inside stretched the Grand Lodge, which could accommodate one thousand people, and seven rooms in differing architectural styles—the Tuscan Room, Roman Doric Room, Egyptian Room. All could be rented out by the public, as opposed to the fifth floor, which was reserved for the Knights Templar and other high-ranking orders. At the center of that floor was an octagonal hall designed in the medieval French Gothic style, flanked by an armory containing three hundred closets where the Knights kept their boots, swords, iron-mesh hoods, and white aprons made of sheepskin—the latter a symbol of the stonecutters of yore. Before certain meetings, the men would gather here to pull off their ordinary clothes and put on the garb of an earlier, more heroic age, dreams of daring deeds sparkling in their heads.

Then, as now, no outsiders knew exactly what took place during the Masons' many ceremonies. Nor did they know the meaning of the many secret handshakes and symbols, including an all-seeing eye similar to the one on the one-dollar bill. This had led to much suspicion, with some justification. In Europe, the Masons were known for plotting against royal governments and for their opposition to the Catholic Church; Catholics who became Masons were excommunicated from 1738 until 1983. In the United States, the Anti-Masonic Party, America's first third party, was formed in the 1820s following the mysterious disappearance of William Morgan, a former or would-be Mason in the town of Batavia, New York, who had threatened to expose fraternal secrets. Charges were brought against various suspects, but after twenty-odd trials, no one was convicted of any crime, and many Americans, fueled by evangelist ministers who had long railed against the Masons, believed that the organization had gotten away with murder.

All that turmoil had gone quietly underground, however, by the time the New Masonic Temple opened on the Twenty-third Street block on June 2, 1875. Tens of thousands of New Yorkers lined the streets that day to watch twenty-five thousand strutting men, organized into twenty-six divisions, each with its own band, march by for the building's dedication ceremonies. Many of the men had traveled to the city on special trains, and the "sun shone brightly, yet not too hotly, on the moving masses of the brothers of the Mystic Tie." Banners and plumes waved, sword blades flashed, and the ladies, who had turned out "at exceptionally early hours in immense numbers," swooned.

Williams probably participated in the New Masonic Temple's opening ceremonies and may have been in the Grand Lodge one year later, on May 28, 1876, for the funeral of Baron Joseph Henry Louis Charles De Palm, an Austrian-born nobleman fated to become better known in death than in life. A member of the Theosophical Society, which advocated cremation, De Palm was the first person in the United States to be cremated—a highly controversial idea at the time, as many Christians, believing that a cremated body could not be resurrected, regarded it as a sin. His executor had arranged for the Baron's pre-cremation "pagan funeral," as the press dubbed it, to take place at the temple as a way to publicize the ideas of the Theosophical Society. Over two thousand people showed up, including Thomas Edison, Major General Abner Doubleday, and protestors carrying signs declaring cremation blasphemous. As soon as the eulogy began, the crowd angrily leapt to its feet, and several people were arrested.

Many other large public funerals took place at the New Masonic Temple over the next two decades, and the building also hosted innumerable public concerts, exhibitions, and lectures, the latter ranging in subject matter from the works of Ralph Waldo Emerson to women's suffrage to the evils of Catholicism. Organizations of all sizes rented out its rooms too; among them were the New-York State Horticultural Society, Manhattan Temperance Association, and National Association of Master Plumbers. No ordinary workers, these plumbers, but rather 170 titans of their trade, gathered from all parts of the county. Wrote one awestruck *New York Times* reporter: "One hundred and seventy massive gold-headed canes thumped a chorus on the stone steps of the Masonic Temple yesterday. One hundred and seventy solitaire diamonds, locomotive headlight size, lighted the hall of the second floor. One hundred and seventy heavy gold watch-chains glistened on the vests of 170 fine broadcloth suits and 170 rolls of greenbacks of the size of an overripe bologna sausage rested peacefully in 170 capacious pockets."

Williams policed some of these events and took part in others. He was there to discuss the funeral arrangements of his colleague Inspector Thomas Thorne in 1885, and there to be appointed the new master of the Polar Star Lodge, No. 245, in 1892. He may also have been among the Masons who laid the cornerstone for the Statue of Liberty—sculpted by a fellow Brother, Frédéric-Auguste Bartholdi, in France—in 1884, and among the Knights Templar who escorted nine thousand Masons, all dressed in black frock coats, white hats, white gloves, and white aprons, to the laying of the cornerstone for Cleopatra's Needle in Central Park in

1880. U.S. Navy lieutenant Henry Gorringe, another Brother, had been in charge of bringing the 220-ton ancient Egyptian obelisk from Alexandria to New York.

On December 1, 1883, the New Masonic temple was almost destroyed by fire, and although it was soon restored, it had lost its glamour. By the turn of the century, it was regarded as "an old hulk." It was demolished in 1911, to be replaced by today's Masonic Building, a modern nineteen-story office building. Today's Grand Lodge and other Masonic spaces are housed in a second building, Masonic Hall, on the Twenty-fourth Street side of the block.

*   *   *

From the New Masonic Temple, "the Czar of the Tenderloin," as Williams came to be known, could saunter across the street to make sure that all was in order at Koster & Bial's Music Hall on the northwest corner of Twenty-third Street and Sixth Avenue. A high-end yet debauched variety theater/vaudeville house, Koster & Bial's was a favorite haunt of wealthy young men, who liked to loll in its balcony boxes while drinking, smoking, and watching can-can shows. Late in the century, the hall was owned by Alfred Darling, one of the managers of the Fifth Avenue Hotel.

Continuing north from Koster & Bial's, Williams could next stop at some of the brothels in the West Twenties, their porches ablaze with light after the sun went down, or step into one of the dozens of lowbrow faro banks, chips rattling and roulette wheels churning, that operated along Sixth Avenue and Broadway. Or he could visit more upscale gaming establishments such as John Daly's at 39 West Twenty-ninth Street or Richard Canfield's at 22 West Twenty-sixth Street. Daly's drew scores of wealthy society male folk, paid the police a huge annual payout, and was especially popular among Columbia College students, who came to learn how to gamble, then considered a necessary manly skill. Canfield's was a more exclusive affair, known for its fine private art collection and private rooms reserved for those who wished to exceed house limits.

Along the way, Williams could also stop at some of the district's many dance halls, which in the early 1880s were beginning to replace brothels as centers for sexual entertainment. On West Twenty-seventh Street reigned the Cairo Dance Hall and Buckingham Palace; on West Twenty-ninth, the Bohemia Dance Hall; on West Thirtieth, Sailor's Hall; and on West Thirty-fifth, the Tivoli. Loud music pulsated through the air as carriages arrived at the teeming venues throughout the late afternoon and night.

More sedate on the outside but just as raucous within was the French Madame's on West Thirty-first Street off Sixth Avenue, which took its name from its proprietress, a fat bewhiskered Alsatian woman named Matilda Hermann. Often sitting on a high stool near the cashier's cage, she acted as her own bouncer, reputedly wielding a bludgeon and seizing obstreperous women by the hair and flinging them out into the street. Hermann billed her resort a restaurant, but it offered no food except black coffee and liquor, to be imbibed as a three-piece band accompanied ladies dancing the can-can in the nude for one dollar a show.

Then there was the Haymarket, by far the most popular venue in the Tenderloin, named after the infamous red-light district in London. A dazzling three-story palace at Sixth Avenue and Thirtieth Street, half-hidden beneath the El, it had opened in 1873 and would remain in business until 1913, making it one of the longest-lasting of all the precinct's hotspots. Everyone from criminals to blue bloods flocked to the Haymarket, along with throngs of out-of-towners staying at the Fifth Avenue Hotel or other nearby luxury establishments. The hall featured a huge dance floor, a lively band, peep shows, and private, balcony-level cubicles in which women danced the can-can and posed in sexually explicit "circuses." During the hall's peak years, its owners paid the police $250 a week (about $6,500 today) in protection money.

Like most dance halls and concert saloons, the Haymarket admitted women for free and men for twenty-five cents. During its first decade, it catered mostly to the sporting male; "respectable" women seldom set foot inside. By the time Williams took over the precinct in earnest, however, societal mores were changing and women were venturing in, always accompanied by appropriate males, of course. In the early part of the evening, married couples often stopped by the hall for a drink or dessert after a show. Sometimes they took a seat in one of the hall's intimate booths, sometimes they took a turn on the dance floor, while around them caroused revelers and "loose women" who sauntered about smoking, drinking, and freely soliciting men. Yet during these hours, the hall never became too lewd or out of control. Manager Big Bill saw to that. He would bar clients for life for using "vile and abusive language" and expel both those women who displayed too much skin and "degenerates," meaning male homosexuals, who would then sometimes retire to the gay Artistic Club abutting the Haymarket in back.

All this changed after midnight, by which time the respectable women and many of the respectable men had left. Then the noise level in the hall soared as fights broke out and the dance floor swayed with drunken patrons and their prostitute partners. Pickpockets roamed the hall. Diamond Jim Brady, a regular, always left his diamonds at home before stopping by for a visit.

Late in its career, the dance hall was the subject of an evocative painting, *The Haymarket*, by John French Sloan, one of the founders of the Ashcan school. Originally from Philadelphia, John and his wife, Anna "Dolly," moved to New York in 1904 to settle on West Twenty-third Street between Sixth and Seventh avenues. John had met Dolly, an occasional prostitute, at a Philadelphia brothel and had great sympathy for ladies of the night, as well as scorn for the double sexual standard. His painting depicts three women in frilly white dresses and enormous hats entering the hall under the judgmental eye of a pompous, pot-bellied, middle-aged man. A little girl and her mother are passing by, and the mother, laden down with laundry, appears to be upbraiding her daughter as the girl looks back at the women with curiosity and, perhaps, admiration.

Williams undoubtedly knew the Haymarket's managers well, but as precinct captain, he didn't personally collect payouts from them or any of the businesses operating in his district. He left that to his underlings, most notably his protégé Max Schmittberger, a burly German with huge hands who had worked as a baker before becoming a cop.

Williams also seldom exchanged words with the various prominent society men, politicians, and businessmen he passed during his strolls. An unspoken pact to ignore the activities of one's acquaintances in the Tenderloin prevailed.

The same did not apply to the women Williams encountered, especially if he saw them behaving in what he deemed a "suspicious manner." He encouraged his officers to do the same, which was why, on the evening of Saturday, August 30, 1881, Officer William Riely, under Williams's command, arrested neatly dressed Mrs. Mary Cole for disorderly conduct as she waited patiently for her husband outside a Sixth Avenue saloon. She was taken downtown to the Jefferson Market Police Court, where a justice commended Riely for the arrest and sentenced Mary to ten days in prison. Moments later, her husband, John, arrived and demanded to see Officer Riely. Fists flew, and John was promptly arrested and sent to prison along with his wife.

As Captain Williams's rounds on and just off Sixth Avenue drew to a close, he could take a swing farther west to see what was happening in the African Tenderloin. He might stick his head into a brothel to spit out a racist epithet or two, or wield his club with unusual force in one of the four saloons at the corner of Seventh Avenue and Twenty-seventh Street. He wouldn't have noticed that some of the city's finest musicians, including stride piano player Willie "the Lion" Smith, were playing there.

He also wouldn't have noticed the superb talent at the African Tenderloin's most renowned hotspot, Ike Hines's Professional Club, which catered to the Black elite. Originally located on Minetta Lane and Third Street in Greenwich Village, Hines's club moved to 122 West Twenty-seventh Street (and later other addresses) in the mid-1880s. The club seemed gloomy on the outside, but inside it was filled with music and laughter, "a vertical house of mirth . . . The brilliancy of the place, the display of diamond rings, scarf-pins, ear-rings, and breast-pins, the big rolls of money that were brought into evidence when drinks were paid for, and the air of gaiety that pervaded the place, all completely dazzled and dazed me," wrote James Weldon Johnson in his novel *The Autobiography of an Ex-Coloured Man*.

Appearing almost every night at Hines's club were parties of white society men out slumming and white musicians who came to listen and learn. Ragtime was in the offing; Scott Joplin would live nearby at 128 West Twenty-ninth Street early in the new century, and by 1910, West Twenty-eighth Street between Broadway and Sixth Avenue would be known as Tin Pan Alley because of all the popular music publishing firms located there.

Slumming whites were also regulars at the Douglass Club, better known as Edmond's, owned by the prizefighter Edmond Johnson on West

Twenty-eighth Street, one flight up from a stable. Among them were Stanford White and Harry Thaw, who would later play out a tragic drama that began on the Twenty-third Street block, and Alfred Gwynne Vander- bilt, who was also the club's vice president and one of two reasons why the Douglass was allowed to operate past curfew. The other was the protection money paid to Clubber Williams.

As the captain finished his rounds, he must have been filled with an enormous sense of self-satisfaction. He was greatly feared by one half of the city and highly respected by the other. He owned an estate in Cos Cob, Connecticut, whose deck alone was worth $39,000 (about $1.1 million today), a townhouse in Manhattan, a half dozen hefty bank accounts, and a yacht. He dined at Delmonico's, frequented the Fifth Avenue Hotel, was a member of the Knights Templar, and knew everyone who was anyone. The press covered his every move, including his sailing races and vacations in New England, as if he were royalty. He was sitting so very pretty. What could possibly go wrong?

CHAPTER 13

Is She a Lady or Is She Not?

Tongues had started wagging as soon as Mrs. Paran Stevens, née Marietta Reed, first stepped foot in New York in 1860, and for three decades, they never stopped. She *said* she was the daughter of a wealthy merchant in Lowell, Massachusetts, but everyone *knew* her father was nothing more than a common grocer. She *said* she had met her husband, the manager and lessee of the Fifth Avenue Hotel, in the home of a school friend in Boston, but everyone *knew* she had once worked as a chambermaid in one of his hotels and perhaps as a Lowell factory girl as well. Just look at the way she dressed—all those flamboyant boas and overly brocaded dresses. Just look at the way she decorated—all those overgrown vases and mediocre works of art. And, most of all, just listen to the way she talked—loudly, impatiently, and with too many pushy ideas and strident opinions. Her Sunday night musicales were a sacrilege, and the way she had ingratiated herself with the Prince of Wales when he was in town . . . Really, it was simply too much to bear!

In reality, Marietta Reed was who she said she was: the daughter of Ransom Reed, a respected, well-established Lowell merchant who had sent all seven of his children to the best of schools. Marietta had grown up in a bourgeois household and, as "one of the most beautiful belles of Lowell," had had plenty of suitors. She had met her husband, Paran Stevens, three decades her senior, in 1850 when she was just nineteen while visiting a friend who was also a friend of his daughter. A widower with a kind face, black curly hair, and long fuzzy sideburns, he managed the best luxury hotels in Boston. He was immediately charmed by the vivacious, beautiful young woman, and she was impressed by his courtly manners, success, and wealth. The two wed and settled in Boston, where they had two children, a daughter and a son, and Marietta tried, but failed, to fit into society. She was not welcomed by the city's older matrons, perhaps because of her youth, perhaps because of her outspoken nature.

In September 1858 Paran was approached by Amos Eno. The Fifth Avenue Hotel was almost finished, but Eno had run out of the ready cash he needed to complete it, and the New York banks were refusing to lend him money. The nation was in the middle of a recession, and he was carrying a huge amount of unimproved real estate. Stevens, by then one of best-known hotel men in the country, "the Napoleon of Hotel-Keepers," agreed to provide the necessary funds in return for a long-term lease of the Fifth Avenue at a nominal sum. Eno, who had never intended to manage the hotel, would continue as its owner, but Paran would handle its day-to-day operations, with the help of a management company, Hitchcock, Darling & Co.

Both men must have been pleased with the arrangement and with each other, as they had much in common. Like Eno, Paran was a self-made New Englander of great energy and vision. Born in Claremont, New Hampshire, on September 11, 1802, he was the son of a storekeeper and grandson of a stern, formidable justice of the peace. Growing up, he had watched as his father had introduced a few "luxuries," such as molasses and tea, to their small puritanical hometown. Some of Claremont's citizens, possibly including his own grandfather, had immediately denounced the move as "a piece of foolish extravagance that would certainly lead to no good," but the products must have sold well enough for the young Stevens to take note; luxury coupled with innovation became the hallmark of his hotels.

Stevens's father had also run an inn in Claremont, opened shortly before Paran was born, and after the patriarch's death, Paran and his three brothers took it over. Within a few years, though, Paran was running it completely on his own, and running it so well that when a new luxury hotel, the New

England Coffee House, opened in Boston, he was offered the job of manager. From there, he moved on to manage other hotels in Boston, the Northeast, and the South, including the Continental in Philadelphia and the Battle House in Mobile. By the time he took over the Fifth Avenue, he was simultaneously running a half dozen luxury hotels nationwide—in effect starting up the world's first hotel chain, and possibly the first chain of anything.

Stevens was not only a superb hotel manager but also an astute businessman, adroit at attracting and manipulating investors. Before him, hotels had been planned mostly by architects and investors. Stevens, however, took an active role in the design of his hotels, sometimes convincing leery financiers to commit to purchases they didn't really want to make and inventing the role of modern hotel developer in the process. The world's first hotel tycoon, he was the person responsible for introducing the Fifth Avenue Hotel's elevators and for its extravagant furnishings, which cost over thirteen million in today's dollars.

Upon moving to Manhattan, Paran and Marietta first lived in the Fifth Avenue Hotel and then settled into an elegant home at 244 Fifth Avenue, just a few blocks north of the hotel and across the street from the site of the future Eno family mansion at 233 Fifth Avenue. Here Marietta quickly set about hiring servants, furnishing her home, and settling her children, while also becoming involved in the hotel's operations. Lauded by one admirer for having a "man's mind," she refused to sit idly by while Paran made all the business decisions. It was apparently her idea to redecorate the hotel's south wing for the Prince of Wales's visit and to borrow old masters paintings for its walls. She also made sure that she and Paran were invited to the prince's ball at the Academy of Music, where she must have pushed and shoved her way through the crowds to talk, flirt, and perhaps dance with the young royal. Little did she know then that Bertie, as the prince was known to his friends, was to play a pivotal role in her and her daughter's lives.

It was apparently also Marietta's idea to introduce the hotel's innovative "late supper," served at ten P.M., and to open fashionable shops on its ground floor. The supper was wildly popular from the start, in part because the hotel guests were welcome to bring along friends not staying at the hotel at no extra charge. But the second idea was met with outrage; the wealthy families living on the block did not want commercial establishments marring their tony residential neighborhood. Marietta paid them no mind—what did she care about the opinions of others?—and within a few years, two of the hotel's shops, Knox Hats and Maillard Chocolates, became world-renowned. Knox Hats was celebrated for giving away new hats to visiting statesmen, including Abraham Lincoln, in return for their old ones. Maillard Chocolates, which operated a five-story factory just a block away on West Twenty-fourth Street, was adored for its ornate decor, luscious chocolate ice cream, frozen violets, and creamy chocolate candies. Especially popular among wealthy young men on Valentine's Day were its $500 hand-painted boxes of chocolates (about $10,000 today). Embedded in one of the candies was a diamond ring.

Marietta's main preoccupation, however, had nothing to do with the hotel. Extremely ambitious, she wanted nothing less than to be accepted by the highest echelons of old New York society. But how to go about it? How to fight the rumors that she knew were swirling around her and become a welcomed guest at the homes of the Schermerhorns, Joneses, and other moneyed Knickerbockers? How to wrangle an invitation to Mrs. Astor's celebrated New Year's ball?

Marietta's first step was to watch and listen, to be attuned to every nuance around her as she and Paran ran the hotel, attended concerts and the theater, and socialized in the less exalted circles of the nouveau riche. Soon she came up with a plan. She would establish weekly musicales— small, informal musical gatherings—in her parlor on Sunday evenings. At the time, Sunday evenings were sacrosanct, reserved for staying home, spending time with family, and perhaps prayer. Marietta had noticed, however, that many of the men she met were chafing at the tradition and guessed that they would jump at the chance to escape their stifling living rooms.

She was right. Men and a few women began appearing at her Sunday evening soirees. Most were nouveau riche, not Knickerbocker, but still . . .

Marietta was now in her prime, a tall, striking woman with an olive-hued complexion, heavily lidded eyes, and masses of nut-brown hair swept up high on her head. Brash and loud, with a keen sense of humor and magnetic personality, she must have seemed like a breath of fresh air to those accustomed to more sedate environments.

Frederick Martin, a society leader and early visitor at Marietta's, described her in his memoir *Things I Remember* as an "unassailable" hostess who always dressed in "exquisite taste." He admired her immensely yet was also concerned about her going too far. "You don't know what people say about your Sunday evenings, they call it Sabbath breaking," he said to her one night. To which she replied with imperial disdain, "Do they indeed? They say. *What* do they say? Then *let* them say it."

Other visitors were more overtly critical.

"Well, Mr. Travers. I was beginning to think you had quite forgotten me . . ." Marietta said to one such guest one evening.

"My dear lady, it is impossible for me to resist the magnetism of your charming society, although I know it only draws me back to cold tea, hot Apollinaris [sparkling water] and bad music," he replied.

Marietta didn't miss a beat. "Never mind those trifling drawbacks," she laughed. "I think you find ample compensation for them when you know that at my musicales you meet all the most charming and civil people of the day."

Marietta's earliest musicales featured her sister Fanny Reed, a talented singer, who would later spend most of her life in Paris, where she hosted musicales of her own, attended by everyone from European dukes to American debutantes. Fanny would also become friendly with the composer Franz Liszt, who once praised her when she was traveling in Italy, saying, "All Rome is talking of your voice, mademoiselle."

Few, if any, high-society women attended Marietta's soirees, however, and most continued to regard her with contempt. In *Diary of a Union Lady, 1861–1865*, well-born Maria Lydig Daly wrote of seeing Marietta and Fanny at a party in December 1864, where Fanny sang the then new "Battle Hymn of the Republic" by Julia Ward Howe, and sniffed, "Mrs. 'Fifth-Avenue Hotel' was there, of course, with her sister. I would rather dispense with the music than have to take Mrs. Stevens with it." Try though Marietta might, she couldn't break into society's inner circles. The moneyed Knickerbocker families continued to shun her, and she was never invited to Mrs. Astor's balls.

As the Civil War neared its end, Paran and Marietta built a summer home in Newport, Rhode Island, among the first New Yorkers to do so. Their "cottage," designed in a lavish "steamboat gothic" style, was centrally located on Bellevue Avenue, the town's most fashionable thoroughfare, and stood at the end of a long walk through gardens made brilliant with lanterns at night. Marietta must have hoped that in the more relaxed atmosphere of Newport, she would finally gain entrée into old money circles, but it was not to be. She was the wife of a hotelkeeper; it didn't matter how much money she and her husband had.

*   *   *

Despite their age difference, Paran and Marietta were well matched in personality and spirit. Both were ambitious, creative, opportunistic, and acutely business-savvy, sensing trends before they occurred. In the early 1870s the couple made headlines by commissioning Paran's friend, architect Richard Morris Hunt, to build the Stevens House, one of New York's first apartment buildings. As the eight-story red-brick edifice went up three blocks north of the Fifth Avenue Hotel, citizens were astonished. Reported the *New York Times*: "[Many people] strained their necks to get a glimpse of the top of the cardboard-looking fabric, and wondered how on earth it was going to stand. These huge top-heavy buildings, run up in a hurried manner . . . are scarcely strong enough to resist a puff of wind."

Yet even more astonishing was the building's intended use. The edifice contained eighteen luxurious suites, each the size of a private home, with a parlor, dining room, kitchen, pantry, bedrooms, dressing rooms, and bathrooms, along with servant quarters in the attic. Apartment living was a startling concept to Americans at the time and was regarded as very European and somewhat risqué—all those strangers rubbing shoulders in the halls!

Paran and Marietta designed the interior of the Stevens House together, adorning its walls with frescoes and black walnut woodwork, and were looking forward to opening day. But Paran died in May 1872, a few months before that day came, and what should have been a joyful celebration was a sorrowful one. The Stevens House also proved to be ahead of its time. New Yorkers were not yet ready for apartment living (though they would be a decade later), and by 1879 Marietta was forced to remodel the building into the Victoria Hotel, aimed at ultrawealthy tourists.

After Paran's death, Marietta must have felt adrift. The partner with whom she had schemed and brainstormed and helped build a fortune was no more. She had no real friends in New York and had failed to make inroads into high society. She was hardly ready to give up on her coveted dream, however, especially since she now had an asset of enormous value: her daughter, Minnie, a beautiful young woman of marriageable age.

Minnie had plenty of admirers in New York, and for a period Marietta shopped her around. But nothing came of it, and soon the two women left for Europe, where they would live for long periods over the next half dozen years. Unlike New York's high society, the European elite didn't care so much about where a person's money came from, at least as far as Americans were concerned. Americans weren't descended from old aristocratic families, so what difference did it make if they made their fortunes in real estate and banking (the Knickerbockers) or in hotels and stock speculation (the nouveau riche)? Money was money, and many of the European aristocrats, in desperate need of funds to maintain their aging family estates, were open to the idea of marrying American heiresses. Such a match was good for both sides, as the heiress gained a coveted title and the aristocrat ensured the survival of his ancestral home. Having a titled daughter would also bring Marietta a huge fringe benefit—it would force New York society to accept her. As she well remembered from the Prince of Wales's visit a decade before, Americans worshipped royalty.

Minnie was in complete agreement with her mother's plan. As tough, ambitious, and self-possessed as Marietta, she too was hungry for social position. She must also have been resentful of the constant slights and rejections she had seen her mother endure and burning to deliver old society its comeuppance.

The Stevenses settled first in Paris, where Minnie attended Madame Coulon's finishing school, along with two other nouveau riche American heiresses, Alva Smith and Consuelo Yznaga, on the hunt for titled husbands. Then it was on to London, where Marietta reestablished contact with the Prince of Wales, who remembered her from his stay at the Fifth Avenue Hotel. Taken by the charming, spirited Minnie, the prince began inviting her to his palace, where her great beauty and sparkling wit made her an instant favorite. Three lords began courting her, but none had great status, and Marietta felt that her daughter could do better. After all, Jennie Jerome, whose family had once lived on Madison Square, had married Lord Randolph Churchill a year or two before, and rumor had it that Consuelo Yznaga had become engaged to the Viscount George Montagu, heir to the duchy of Manchester.

A season or two of one magnificent social event after another went by. Minnie and Marietta were enjoying themselves thoroughly, but growing anxious. No proposal of great enough magnitude had arrived. Time was running out—debutantes were usually "out" for only a few seasons before marrying. They returned to Paris, to try their fortunes there with the help of Marietta's sister Fanny, whose soirees were now attracting the crème de la crème of Parisian society. Minnie caught the appreciative eye of the Duc de Guiche. But then Marietta made a rare mistake. She circulated rumors that Minnie's fortune was larger than it was. The duc's father found out, and the duc withdrew his attentions. The rumor mill on both sides of the Atlantic churned.

Back to London mother and daughter went. Minnie was now twenty-five, and though still a favorite of the Prince of Wales and his friends, could no longer afford to wait for a titled aristocrat to appear. She therefore accepted the proposal of Captain Arthur Paget, a good-looking, well-educated, and resourceful man from an elite and well-connected—but not titled—family; his father was a general and member of Parliament. Paget was also a good friend of the prince, who was delighted with the match. He sent Minnie a gold serpent bracelet inlaid with diamonds, rubies, and sapphires as a wedding gift.

The couple were married on July 27, 1878, at the fashionable St. Peter's Church in Eaton Square. The bride wore a magnificent gown of white satin trimmed with orange blossoms; six diamond stars sparkled in her hair. Lord Beresford was the best man, the Dean of Windsor performed the service, and the Prince of Wales, who seldom attended commoners' weddings, was there. Reported the *New York Times*: "The man or woman who, 15 years ago, should have predicted that the daughter of the late Paran Stevens would have been married under these conditions, and

The earliest known view of New Amsterdam, published in Holland in 1651. NEW YORK PUBLIC LIBRARY

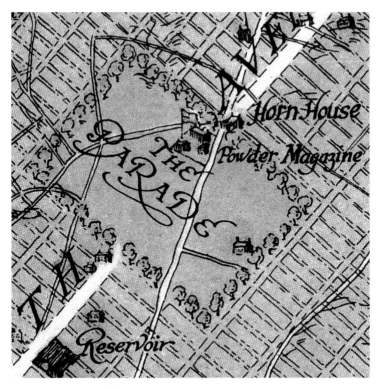

The Parade, as it was envisioned in 1811, from the cover of *Fifth Avenue, Old and New, 1824–1924* by Henry Collins Brown.

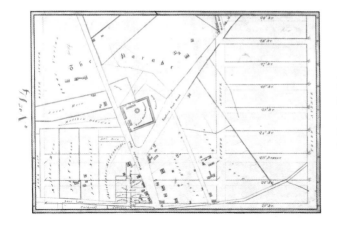

Detail from Randel's Farm Map
no. 14, 1819. CITY OF NEW YORK
AND OFFICE OF THE MANHATTAN
BOROUGH PRESIDENT/MUSEUM OF
THE CITY OF NEW YORK

Madison Cottage, 1850.
NEW YORK
PUBLIC LIBRARY

Franconi's
Hippodrome, 1853.
NEW YORK PUBLIC
LIBRARY

Amos Eno, 1897,
from *Notable New
Yorkers of 1896–1899*
by Moses King.

The Fifth Avenue Hotel in 1860, just after completion. © NEW YORK
PUBLIC LIBRARY

GRAND TORCH-LIGHT PARADE OF THE NEW YORK FIREMEN IN HONOR OF THE PRINCE OF WALES, PASSING THE FIFTH AVENUE HOTEL, OCTOBER 18, 1860.—[SEE PRECEDING PAGE.]

The 1860 Firemen's Parade for the Prince of Wales in front of the Fifth Avenue Hotel, from
Harper's Weekly. LIBRARY OF CONGRESS, PRINTS & PHOTOGRAPHS DIVISION

Dinner

BLUEPOINTS 30   COTUITS 30   CAPE CODS 30
LYNNHAVENS 35   MALPECQUES 40

SOUPS
Consommé Dandigné 40   Green Turtle 1 00 60   Bisque of Scallops 50 30
    Cream of Asparagus 50 30   Calf's Feet, English style 40 25

Boudins, Richelieu 1 00
Carciofini 40   Kieler Sprotten 30   Celery 50 30

FISH
Frostfish sauté, Meunière 65 40   Striped Bass, Anchovy sauce 85 50
  Crab Meat with Curry 1 00   Planked Bluefish 2 00 1 00
    Devilled Whitebait 60 40   Filets of Sole, St Nazaire 85 50
    Terrapin, Maryland 3 50   Kingfish, Soto Maior 85 50

ENTREES
(Cold) Mousse of Chicken, sur socle 1 00
Wellesley Farm Milk Pig, Cumberland sauce 1 25 75   Duck with Oranges 1 25
  Fillet of Hare, German style 1 00   Tournedos of Fillet, Bayard 1 50 80
    Chicken sauté, Archiduc 1 25   Sweetbreads, Royal 1 25
    Nonpareille of Lamb, Loie Fuller 1 00 60 Rice Birds, Paysanne 80

ROAST
Lamb 80 45   Capon 4 00 2 00   Mutton 60 35   Turkey 1 00 60

GAME
Red Head Duck 3 50   Venison 1 50   Partridge 2 50   Mallard Duck 2 00

SORBET CREME DE MENTHE 30

VEGETABLES
Potatoes, Chamounix 30 20 Broiled Fresh Mushrooms 1 00 Green Corn 60 40
  New Peas 60 40   Spinach with Cream 50 30   Artichokes 60
    Purée of Turnips 40 25   Rice Croquettes 40

SALADS
Escarole 50 30   Dixie 60 40   Tomato 50 30

CHEESE
Gervais 25   Pont l'Evêque 30 20   Edam 30 20

FRUIT
Cantaloupes 60 35   Sickel Pears 50 30   Hot House Grapes 75

DESSERT
Pineapple Pie 20   Coffee Soufflé Pudding 40 25   Rhubarb Pie 20
  Peach Timbale 40   Chartreuse aux pommes 40 Grape Tartlets 25 15
    Petits fours 25   Peach Short Cake 50   Cocoanut Soufflé 50

ICES
Pond Lilly glacée 50 Meringue Chantilly 30   Biscuit glacée, Bellevue 30
  Peach frappée 25   Café Parfait 25   Peach Ice Cream 25
    Turkish Coffee 20   French Coffee 15

APOLLINARIS 40 20   Wednesday, October 18, 1905   **JOHANNIS 40 20**

Half portions served in Fifth Avenue Restaurants and Cafés and to one person only.

A typical Fifth Avenue
Hotel dinner menu.
NEW YORK PUBLIC LIBRARY

STOCK GAMBLING AT "GALLAGHER'S EVENING EXCHANGE."—[SEE PAGE 299.]

Nighttime trading at Gallagher's Evening Exchange, from *Harper's Weekly*, 1864. NEW YORK PUBLIC LIBRARY

Edwin Booth in the 1860s.
NATIONAL PORTRAIT GALLERY,
SMITHSONIAN INSTITUTION

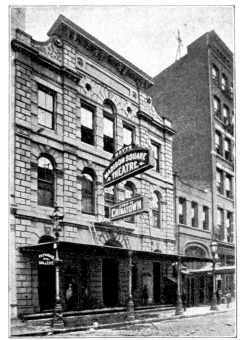

HOYT'S MADISON-SQUARE THEATRE, 24TH STREET, NEAR BROADWAY.

Hoyt's Madison-Square Theatre, from *King's Handbook of New York City* by Moses King, 1893.

Clara Morris, photograph by Napoleon Sarony, 1909. LIBRARY OF CONGRESS, PRINTS & PHOTOGRAPHS DIVISION

NEW-YORK *By* GAS-LICHT.
Hooking a Victim.

Ladies of the night in the mid-1800s, from *New York by Gas-Light and Other Urban Sketches* by George G. Foster. MUSEUM OF THE CITY OF NEW YORK

Frank Hart, ca. 1880. NATIONAL PORTRAIT GALLERY, SMITHSONIAN INSTITUTION

An electric "sun tower" in Madison Square, from *Harper's Weekly*, January 14, 1882.

NEW YORK CITY.—DEDICATION OF THE MASONIC TEMPLE AT THE CORNER OF TWENTY-THIRD STREET AND SIXTH AVENUE, JUNE 2D—HEAD OF THE PROCESSION PASSING THE TEMPLE.—See Page 210.

Dedication of the New Masonic Temple, 1875. NEW YORK PUBLIC LIBRARY

Dr. Parkhurst and "Sunbeam," from
*The Doctor and the Devil, or Midnight
Adventures of Dr. Parkhurst* by
Charles Gardner, 1894. COLLECTION
DEVELOPMENT DEPARTMENT, WIDENER
LIBRARY, HCL, HARVARD UNIVERSITY

THE DOCTOR AND HIS COMPANION IN DISGUISE.

Evelyn Nesbit, photograph by Rudolf Eickemeyer, 1903. LIBRARY OF CONGRESS, PRINTS & PHOTOGRAPHS DIVISION

Wide-angle view of Madison Square, with the Fifth Avenue Building on the edge of the park just right of the photo's center, ca. 1911–1914. NEW-YORK HISTORICAL SOCIETY

that his widow would, on the day of the wedding, receive a visit of congratulations from the Prince of Wales, would indeed have been deemed a visionary."

After the wedding, Minnie went into the marriage business. Her husband lacked the financial resources to give her the lavish lifestyle she craved, and with her access to royal circles, she could provide a highly remunerative service: introducing other nouveau riche American heiresses to near-destitute English aristocrats. Minnie also remained close to the prince, who spent much time at the Pagets' home and was the godfather of their firstborn child, Albert Edward.

Meanwhile, Marietta returned to New York, to ascend to what she had always deemed her rightful place in society. Though there were still some who would never fully accept her, she was now invited to most of New York's most prestigious events, had a box at the Academy of Music, and was a celebrated hostess whose Sunday evening musicales were immensely popular. Somewhere along the way, Sunday evenings had become just another night of the week.

In her novel *The Age of Innocence*, Edith Wharton fashioned her character Mrs. Lemuel Struthers after Marietta. Mrs. Struthers is a wealthy widow whose husband made a fortune in the shoe polish business, and rumor has it that she was once a model for one of his shoe polish advertisements. She wears bold feathers, combs her hair in the "Egyptian style," insists on knowing everyone who's anyone, and holds Sunday evening soirees that are initially shunned and then accepted.

"Oh, you know, everybody goes to Mrs. Struthers's now," remarks a character near the end of the book, causing Newland Archer, its central character, to reflect that it was thus "that New York managed its transitions: conspiring to ignore them till they were well over, and then, in all good faith, imagining that they had taken place in a preceding age . . . Once people had tasted of Mrs. Struthers's easy Sunday hospitality they were not likely to sit at home remembering that her champagne was transmuted Shoe-Polish."

Edith Wharton knew Marietta well because of Marietta's son, Harry Leyden. Six years younger than Minnie and three years older than Edith, Harry had studied at Oxford University for a period and was an attractive, popular young man who liked to organize social events at Newport. In the summer of 1880, Harry began courting Edith and visited her when she was on her European tour. He was with her when her father died in March 1882, and that August the two became engaged. Harry was said to be "desperately in love," and it seemed to be a happy match, but by the fall, they had already broken it off. Some of Edith Wharton's biographers have speculated that it was because of Marietta, who had doubtless been snubbed by Edith's mother in the past and may have harbored a grudge, or who may have hoped that Harry, like Minnie, would marry royalty. Edith's cousin Helen Rhinelander wrote in a letter to her brother Tom: "It is evidently Mrs S's fault, or rather she is the cause . . . I doubt Pussy [Edith] and H have changed in their feeling for one another, but that Mrs S is at the bottom of it all." Conversely, the breakup may have been due to the Jones family, many of whom found Marietta unbearable.

Town Topics: The Journal of Society had a different take on the matter altogether, opining that the split was due to "an alleged preponderance of intellectuality on the part of the intended bride. Miss Jones is an ambitious authoress and, it is said that, in the eyes of Mr Stevens, ambition is a grievous fault." How *Town Topics* came up with that speculation is suspect, however. The weekly periodical was run by Colonel William d'Alton Mann, who, after acquiring it in 1879 and changing its name from the *American Queen*, had added juicy society gossip to its mix of book reviews, fiction, sporting news, and financial advice. With his thick white hair, sparkling blue eyes, and cheerful demeanor, Mann looked like a generous, kindhearted grandfather, but he obtained many of his reports by bribing and blackmailing household staff, telegraph operators, hansom drivers, and the like to act as spies. His periodical became required reading among the wealthy, many of whom subscribed to it on the sly. When a story was especially scandalous, Mann would send a prepublication copy to the individual in question on the pretext of allowing them to correct any errors. That often led to a secret rendezvous at Delmonico's, where the accused would pay the publisher off to the tune of $10,000, $25,000, or more (about $270,000 and up today).

The end of Edith and Harry's engagement may also have come about because Marietta wanted to retain control over her son's inheritance for as long as possible; Paran's fortune was to go to Harry when he turned twenty-five or married, and he was twenty-three. Or the breakup might have occurred because she wanted to protect Edith. For Marietta, who could be generous at times, harbored a terrible secret. Her son had tuberculosis, then a long-lingering and often fatal disease. He would die two years later, in the summer of 1885, shortly after Edith's marriage to Teddy Wharton.

* * *

Marietta had inherited the bulk of Paran's approximately $4 million estate (about $86 million today), including $1 million in trust, $100,000 in cash, a sizable interest in the Fifth Avenue Hotel—which she would sell by the late 1870s—other sizable interests in several other hotels, and the couple's New York and Newport residences. However, Paran, well aware of his wife's impetuous nature, had designated her brother-in-law Charles Stevens and her son-in-law John Melcher, husband of his daughter from his first marriage, co-trustees of the estate, and no major financial transaction could be made without their approval.

Marietta was furious at the arrangement. As far as she was concerned, Paran's money was hers alone, and from 1872 on, she began fighting with her co-trustees constantly and vociferously, claiming in lawsuit after lawsuit that they were mishandling her estate and keeping funds from her. For over twenty years, the newspapers were full of stories about her suits, which she never won. MRS. PARAN STEVENS SUES AGAIN ran one tired-sounding headline.

Marietta didn't stop at just words and lawsuits either, as an October 4, 1887, *New York Times* article reported. Marietta had gone to Surrogate Court that morning to ask, once again, that Melcher and Stevens be removed as trustees of her estate for gross mismanagement. The reporter followed up by going to Melcher's home on West Twenty-first Street for a statement. A small man, not nearly as large as Marietta, Melcher hadn't heard of her latest move yet, but "fairly shuddered in his easy chair as he thought of her, and glanced nervously at the door—perhaps to see if it was chained," the reporter wrote. Melcher then said: "She has repeatedly assaulted me. Once she beat me over the head with an umbrella; once she struck me in the chest and broke every cigar in my vest pockets; at another time she seized an inkstand and was going to throw it at my head. Her language I will not attempt to repeat. She is a most dreadful woman when she is mad that I ever saw and she is very often [mad] I can tell you."

A few weeks later, Marietta appeared in court again, sweeping in with her customary flair, to argue her case. Reported the *Times*: "Mrs. Stevens is not an ordinary witness. Her presence yesterday was attested by a breeze of delicate perfume. She wore buff gloves and a wine-colored suit, with a Winter jacket and fur neckpiece. The outer wraps she removed and tossed aside, carelessly, as she entered, lifted a chair from a corner and dropped into it with an audible sigh." Marietta then pulled out a big bundle of papers, which she dramatically spread out around her, and as the hearing proceeded, kept interjecting, asking questions, and making running commentary. Her lawyers asked her to stop, but she paid them no mind and became more and more agitated. At one point she exclaimed, "The way I have been persecuted is most cruel"; at another, she lost her temper, shouted that she had been "tricked and duped shamefully," and started to cry. However, when "the session was ended Mrs. Stevens walked out smiling, and she laughed coquettishly with Mr. Zabriskie in the elevator."

Marietta also sued and was sued by others, including Richard Morris Hunt, the noted architect and friend of Paran who had designed the Stevens House. She refused to pay him his final $6,000 commission (about $157,000 today), claiming that he had never completed the apartment house according to the agreed-on designs and had used poor materials; he countersued for breach of contract. The court heard testimony for nine days and decided the case in five minutes, awarding Hunt $8,438 on January 18, 1878.

Then there was Miss Sallie Gibbons, who ran an art gallery at 1160 Broadway, just north of Twenty-seventh Street. Marietta owned the building, and something about the gallery must have irritated her because on February 27, 1884, she strode into the establishment and imperiously demanded that Sallie vacate the premises. Sallie refused, whereupon, according to her testimony in court, Marietta threatened and abused her. "I will spend my life to ruin you!" she allegedly shouted. Sallie sent for the police. Marietta sneered. "Do you know who I am? Do you know who I am?" She was very friendly with Captain Alexander "Clubber" Williams, she added. Nonetheless, when a patrolman arrived, he marched Marietta out. Sallie sued for ten thousand dollars and won the case, but the court awarded her only fifty dollars.

Next came Desire Schmitt, a French "chef of high degree," who sued Marietta for wrongful dismissal in 1891. He had been reluctant to work for her and only agreed to do so because she guaranteed him a year's worth of employment, he said. Yet after a short time, she started complaining over "trifles," and one evening abused him with shocking language, concluding with "Go! Leave this house at once and never darken its doors again." Marietta retorted that Desire was an ungrateful wretch. She had always treated him with great kindness and had only dismissed him because he drank so much wine that he became "a positive offense both to her sight and to her nostrils." Defiantly she declared, "You know I am a fighter, and I will fight this case if it costs $20,000."

Throughout these lawsuits, Marietta had continued to live in the home that she and Paran had established together at 244 Fifth Avenue. But having sold her financial interest in the Fifth Avenue Hotel and placed the Victoria Hotel in the hands of managers, there was little keeping her in the neighborhood, and in 1892, she moved into a cream-colored chateau at the northeast corner of Fifth Avenue and Fifty-seventh Street. The mansion and four neighboring ones had been built by Mary Mason Jones, Edith Wharton's corpulent and enormously wealthy great-aunt, in the late 1860s, when settled New York was still thirty blocks to the south and the area was filled with empty lots. Working with architect Robert Mook, she had designed the buildings in marble—an audacious choice in an era of look-alike brownstones. Citizens came north to gawk at what they dubbed "Marble Row."

In *The Age of Innocence*, Wharton fashioned her character Mrs. Manson Mingott after her great-aunt: "It was her habit to sit in a window of her sitting-room on the ground floor, as if watching calmly for life and fashion to flow northward to her solitary doors. She seemed in no hurry to have them come, for her patience was equaled by her confidence. She was sure that presently the hoardings, the quarries, the one-story saloons, the wooden green-houses in ragged gardens, and the rocks from which goats surveyed the scene, would vanish before the advance of residences as stately as her own—perhaps (for she was an impartial woman) even statelier."

Mrs. Manson Mingott was, of course, right. By the time Marietta moved into 1 East Fifty-seventh Street in 1892, stately residences, churches, clubs, and hotels lined Fifth Avenue as far north as Fifty-ninth Street, and freestanding mansions stood here and there as far north as Ninety-fourth Street. St. Patrick's Cathedral, between Fiftieth and Fifty-first streets, had been dedicated in 1879, and the first Plaza Hotel had opened on the west side of Grand Army Plaza at Fifty-ninth Street in 1890. Designed by McKim, Mead & White, it would be torn down in the early 1900s, to be replaced by today's Plaza Hotel, designed by Henry Hardenbergh.

Wharton's great-aunt had been known for her dazzling evening salons, balls, and dinner parties. On her guest lists had been many elite names—the Astors, the Goelets, the Van Rensselaers—but always conspicuously absent had been the name of Mrs. Paran Stevens. "There is one house that Mrs. Stevens will never enter," Mary Mason Jones had reportedly sniffed. "I am old enough to please myself, and I do not care to extend my sufficiently large circle of acquaintances." To which Marietta had reportedly replied that she would never set foot in Marble Row by invitation anyway.

Instead, she set foot in it as a resident. Mary died in her mansion at age ninety on May 29, 1891, and less than a year later, Marietta moved in. Such sweet revenge. She had the place completely redecorated, overfilling it with her trademark potted plants and mediocre works of art, and set about trying to outdo the social gatherings of her predecessor. In March 1893 she hosted a concert in her ballroom, played by all 60 members of the Boston Symphony Orchestra. A month later, she entertained the Spanish Duke and Duchess of Veragua (a territory in today's Panama) in an over-the-top reception attended by 150 members of high society.

Later that year, though, Marietta received some upsetting news. Her beloved Victoria Hotel, the building that she and Paran had designed together, was on the verge of bankruptcy. Once regarded as one of the most opulent and refined of all New York City hostelries, it was now seen as old-fashioned. Its vacancy rate was soaring, its new bookkeeper had absconded with $30,000 (about $870,000 today), and its management wasn't paying wages.

Two years later, the Victoria Hotel failed altogether. Marietta was heartbroken—and frantic. She had large financial interests as well as emotional ones tied up in the hotel. MRS. PARAN STEVENS PROSTRATED, ran an April 2, 1895, headline in the *New York Times*, above a story that read, "The butler refused to take cards or to give any information, except that Mrs. Stevens was suffering from a very severe cold." In truth, she had had a massive heart attack, apparently brought on by the news of the hotel's collapse.

Three days later, she was gone.

At a time when few newspapers ran obituaries for women, all the major New York papers ran one for Marietta, a testament to her hard-earned social status. Some of the obituaries noted her less-than-admirable characteristics, but others were extraordinarily effusive. *Harper's Weekly* called her a "remarkable female" and "very notable woman" who "not only got what she wanted, but she had an abundance of fun with it after she had made it hers . . . She had great courage, great energy, great force. She was very tough, very game, very able, very enterprising, exceedingly interesting, and they say, impulsive, generous, and kind . . . [New York] has lost its most brilliant ornament."

Equally high praise came from the society pages of the *New York Times* three days later: "When, as the wife of Paran Stevens, possessed of wealth, she knocked on the door of exclusive fashion, there was much rolling up of the eyes and much whispering within. Admittance was denied. Stories, creations of gossiping old women, were circulated . . . but undaunted, socially ambitious, she pursued her course until those who had rolled their eyes and spoken in whispers felt themselves honored to be invited to her house . . . Her drawing rooms in the last years of her eventful life [became] the centre for all that is commendable in social life."

Marietta had done it. In an era when women were expected to be soft-spoken, obedient, and demure, she had been pushy, opinionated, and often unpleasant, and gotten away with it. Both uncouth and courageous, egotistical and generous, ruthless and enterprising—in short, a complex modern woman embodying many attributes of her adopted city—she had waged a relentless war to live life on her own terms and, against all odds, had won.

CHAPTER 14

Betrayal

As the century entered its last two decades, Mr. and Mrs. William and Ann Schermerhorn were facing assault on all sides, their Twenty-third Street mansion encroached on from every direction by the worst elements of society. It was bad enough, the couple must have thought, that prostitutes and swindlers were living right around the corner on Sixth Avenue and Twenty-fourth Street, and that a brutal murder had been committed directly across the street while their daughters were growing up, but now unwashed tramps and beggars were always underfoot, crass businessmen were parading up and down *their block* as if they owned it, and—even worse—the children of wealthy neighbors whom they had known for decades were betraying them.

True, despite the degeneration of their block, it was the height of the Gilded Age, and money was pulsating through the city. The Ladies' Mile was teeming, enormous mansions were sprouting up as far north as the fabulous new Metropolitan Museum on Eighty-second Street, skyscrapers were poking the heavens, nouveau riche robber barons—John D. Rockefeller, Andrew Carnegie, and J. Pierpont Morgan—had become household names, and society's parties were more luxe and over-the-top than ever. Ladies shopping in Paris for the season came home with as many as three or four dozen magnificent gowns, an equal number of richly embroidered chemises, a half dozen extravagant cloaks, Russian sables, and hair nets of gold and silver, sometimes valued at a total of over $20,000 (about $575,000 today). Hosts gave out lavish party favors—gold snuff boxes, sapphire stock pins, antique ivory fans—and William's cousin Mrs. Caroline Webster Schermerhorn Astor was throwing ever-more splendiferous parties for the "Four Hundred," the number of people who reportedly could fit in her ballroom. "The Wealth concentrated in the hands of residents of New York is almost inconceivable," wrote Moses King in his 1892 *King's Handbook of New York City*.

Exciting scientific developments were happening too. Alexander Graham Bell had demonstrated his electric speaking telephone five blocks away at Chickering Hall in 1877, and other new inventions, including the phonograph, electric iron, fountain pen, and kinetoscope, were appearing. Best of all, in 1880, electric "arc lights," flaming out like white stars in the dark of night, had been erected on 20-foot-high cast-iron posts all along Broadway between Union and Madison squares, and 160-foot-high "sun towers" stood in Madison Square Park. Attached to the top of each tower was a circular carriage carrying six enormous electric lamps of six thousand candlepower each. Developed by Charles Francis Brush, a thirty-one-year-old engineer, the lights were so powerful they could be seen from the Orange Mountains fifteen miles away, but blinded passersby on the street.

Thomas Edison, Brush's foremost competitor, was working on rectifying that problem. He was developing an incandescent bulb that provided a softer light, and soon his bulbs would begin to appear along Broadway, too, at first mostly on theater marquees. Gradually, the old Tenderloin was being flooded with a wondrous white magic, turning the district from the shadowy haunt of undesirables and sporting males into an extravagant entertainment arena that appealed to both sexes. "Crowds throng the sidewalks; the lights of the omnibuses and carriages dart to and fro along the roadway like myriads of fire-flies; the great hotels, the theatres and restaurants, send out their blaze of gas-lamps, and are alive with visitors," wrote one observer in 1881. Ten years later, Broadway would be known as the "Great White Way," with out-of-towners at least as awestruck by its electric lighting as by its theater productions.

But step right outside their front door and what did the Schermerhorns see? Hideous-looking cripples, scruffy Italian organ grinders, beggars with minders hiding in the shadows, and tramps sticking out their grimy paws whenever a gentleperson passed. Countless mud-splattered omnibuses, creaking stages, overflowing wagons, and decrepit peddler's carts were constantly rattling by, pulled by nags ejecting gushing streams of urine and reeking mounds of manure. A man with St. Vitus' dance and a horrid, scarred visage bowed unctuously and leered at the ladies, scaring them half to death until they dug out a few coins. Another beggar, supposedly paralyzed from the waist down, pushed himself around in a four-wheeled wagon, while a third man with a shiny bald pate mewed piteously as he held out his cap. Raggedy children as young as six or seven dogged respectable citizens for blocks, hawking hairpins, matches, and a dozen other useless things. *Damn these street Arabs!* many a gentleman muttered under his breath.

And even Madison Square, that once delightful park for an afternoon stroll, had been transformed. It had become a place of spectacle, with boisterous crowds of ten thousand or more heading to Madison Square Garden for prizefights, bicycle races, circuses, and other low-class entertainments, and the park itself the site of constant political rallies and demonstrations. Even worse, the square was now seemingly filled with as many slovenly, shuffling, sniffling homeless men hitching up their pants, pulling tight their coats, as it was with gentlemen in gray top hats, gentlewomen in pretty skirts, and well-dressed couples sauntering arm in arm. The unwashed hordes had first appeared during the Panic of 1873, when thousands of businesses failed and tens of thousands lost their jobs. They then receded into the cityscape for two decades, only to come flooding back with a vengeance during the Panic of 1893, when sixteen thousand businesses failed, seventy thousand New Yorkers lost their jobs, and twenty thousand became homeless. Among the new unfortunates were many women, some quite elderly, who were now loitering outside the Fifth Avenue Hotel every afternoon cranking peculiar-looking handmade organs, lit by candles, that emitted faint sounds likened by one observer to half-smothered infants crying for help.

The Schermerhorns were not the enthusiastic socialites they once had been either. In their sixties and seventies in the 1880s and 1890s, they had put their youthful exuberance behind them and settled down into an old-fashioned Knickerbocker kind of life. They were still hosting their weekly musicales featuring first-rate talent and the occasional family dinner party, but William was no longer a Patriarch—the society was dying anyway—and the couple was not on Mrs. Astor's "Four Hundred" list in 1892. William was devoting much of his time to Columbia University affairs, while Ann was being described in the press as "a grand dame of the old school" and other similar phrases.

The Schermerhorns' three daughters were all grown now, too, and Fanny and Annie were married. On the surface, everyone in the family seemed to be happy and doing well, but there were undercurrents. The middle daughter, Sarah, was suffering from acute kidney disease, and, at William's insistence, all his daughters and their spouses were still living in the family's Twenty-third Street mansion. There were no grandchildren. Everything had changed.

*   *   *

During the 1880s and 1890s, the buying and selling on Twenty-third Street between Fifth and Sixth avenues never seemed to stop. Boot-black stands stood on the corners, and shops and offices had replaced many of the once numerous family homes. On the south side of the street, Stern Brothers had demolished three brownstones near Fifth Avenue in 1878 to erect its large department store, and Booth's Theatre at Sixth Avenue closed in 1883, to be replaced by James McCreery & Co. Dry Goods. On the north side, ground floors of former residences had been converted into shopfronts, and several new commercial buildings of five to eight stories had gone up. Seemingly overnight, the block's south side had morphed from being one of the most leisurely promenades in the city into a bustling mart of trade.

Furniture companies beckoned shoppers to both sides of the Schermerhorn mansion. To the family's east was D. S. Hess & Company, manufacturers of "artistic furniture," which had built a five-story neo-Grec building designed by architects D. & J. Jardine at 35-37 West Twenty-third Street in 1880. To the family's west at 61–65 West Twenty-third Street was Robert J. Horner & Co., operating out of a five-story building with a cast-iron facade designed by the prominent architect John B. Snook in 1885. The site had previously held a stone-fronted private residence, but now Horner was using his upper two stories as a factory—a factory? Here on Twenty-third Street?—and the lower ones as offices and showrooms. A shrewd businessman, he aimed his products at the middle and professional classes, not the wealthy, as had most earlier furniture makers, with great success. Horner was also the first to design his showrooms as if they were actual rooms in a house, still the selling model used by furniture stores today.

Yet another major furniture company, George C. Flint, moved to West Twenty-third Street in 1894, thereby turning the block into the city's fore-most furniture district. Flint's occupied a new eight-story neo-Renaissance building at 43-47 West Twenty-third Street designed by Henry Harden-bergh, who would later design the Plaza Hotel. The building extended through the block to West Twenty-fourth Street and was so large, marveled the *New York Times*, "that each piece on display stands by itself, and can be inspected from every side without delay or inconvenience."

Hess, Horner, and Flint were followed by yet more furniture compa-nies as the end of the century approached and passed, but the block's life as a furniture district would prove to be as short as its life as a posh resi-dential district. A fire at Horner's in 1904 and another at Flint's factory on West Twenty-ninth Street in 1906 hastened its demise. Horner's and Flint's merged to become Flint & Horner for a period, but by the 1910s, both would be gone from the block, replaced by wholesale china and glass firms, small clothing manufacturers, and toy companies.

* * *

Presumably even more disturbing than the furniture stores to the Schermer-horns' peace of mind was the Eden Musée, which had opened right next door to their mansion, at 55 West Twenty-third Street, on March 28, 1884. Stretching clear through the block to Twenty-fourth Street, the Eden was part wax museum, part music hall, and part tea garden, and was filled with lurid, lowbrow attractions—or so the upper crust grumbled. Never mind that the Eden held likenesses of Queen Victoria, President Chester Arthur, and dozens of other august figures; in its basement was a Chamber of Horrors packed with grisly instruments of torture, and in its music hall debuted such questionable acts as nine muscular Viennese lady fencers and the precocious six-year-old Master Walter Leon, who lisped as he gave lectures on topics such as "is marriage a failure?"

The exterior of the Eden was as déclassé as its interior. A hodgepodge of architectural styles, it was covered with carved sea nymphs, draped female figures, and excessive ornamentation. On its balustrade stood three-hundred-pound stone urns, one of which was knocked over during fierce winds six months after the museum opened, to fall on the head of a sixty-year-old lithographer who was instantly killed.

The Eden's founders had high aspirations. It was their intention, they said, to open a "Temple of Art," where one and all could educate and amuse themselves "without risk of coming into contact with anything or anybody that was vulgar or offensive." They wanted to distinguish their venture from the more sensationalist dime museums downtown and attract a more exclusive audience—that is, the country's rapidly growing middle class, a term that hadn't even existed until the 1850s or come into widespread usage until after the Civil War, with the creation of a vast number of new white-collar jobs. And the founders' pitch had worked. Well-dressed families and women on their way home from the Ladies' Mile flocked to the Eden in droves, happy to pay the twenty-five-cent admission fee. The museum was so popular that streetcars even stopped midblock as their conductors called out, "All out for the Musée!" pronounced "Moosie" by the hayseeds. The Schermerhorns must have shuddered.

Reporters proclaimed the Eden's waxworks a wonder to behold. Created from life models and pictures, their hair, eyebrows, and eyelashes were real and sewn on by hand, and they were bathed, repainted, and dressed in fresh clothes twice a year. In the museum's vestibule stood a wax pickpocket robbing a wax tourist, while deeper inside stretched three major exhibits: Americans Enlightening the World, The Rulers of the World, and People Talked About, each containing at least twenty wax figures. But it was the Chamber of Horrors that got the most ink. Here reigned such gruesome scenes as "Execution of a Burmese Criminal," "Beheading in Morocco," "The Hindu Woman's Sacrifice," and "Execution of Criminals by Electricity." All the museum's wax figures were created by one man, artist Constant Thys, who spent twenty-eight years at the Eden and died of a heart attack while working on a Christmas display.

Debuting at the Eden two years after it opened was its most popular attraction, a ten-foot-tall "automaton" with a full black beard named Ajeeb. He wore a white turban, white robe, and red cape, and held a hookah in his left hand. Ajeeb was a chess- and checkers-playing genius, thanks to a small man hidden inside his robes, who easily defeated all comers, including the actress Sarah Bernhardt, the New York Giants pitcher Christy Mathewson, and the short-story master O. Henry. The writer had a room at the Martz Hotel, 47 West Twenty-fourth Street, across from the block and often dropped by the Eden to challenge Ajeeb to a game, sometimes sending out for a pint of Irish whiskey, which he slipped under Ajeeb's robes from time to time to share with his opponent.

Even as O. Henry became a household name, no one in New York then or for years to come knew who the writer really was: William Sydney Porter, a former convict who had served time for embezzlement. Whether O. Henry really was a thief or just guilty of sloppy record keeping is unclear, but it was during the thirty-nine months he spent at the Ohio Penitentiary in Columbus that he began writing stories under the nom de plume "O. Henry," and during his years at the Martz Hotel that he began his tremendously successful career.

The Eden was run by a marketing genius, Richard Hollaman, who introduced the city to everything from its first orchid show to Japanese acrobats, Russian magicians, Spanish dancers, and a Hungarian orchestra that became immensely popular, with socialites hiring it to play at private balls at $1,000 a pop (about $29,000 today). But Hollaman's biggest contribution to entertainment history was his early embrace of film. In 1898, he produced a nineteen-minute film version of *The Passion Play of Oberammergau*, filmed on the rooftop of the Grand Central Palace hotel, that ran for nine months, making the Eden the first venue to feature motion pictures as part of its regular programming. The Eden was also Edison's first motion picture licensee.

Ironically, film brought about the end of the Eden. By the 1910s, the public was more interested in moving pictures than wax museums, and on

June 7, 1915, the "Moosie" filed for bankruptcy. Ajeeb and some of the Chamber of Horrors tableaux were sold to Coney Island, where they continued to attract crowds until 1928, when they were destroyed in a fire. The building that housed the Eden was demolished in 1916.

* * *

On West Twenty-third Street, east of the Eden Musée and D. S. Hess furniture store, stood yet another new commercial building, this one perhaps especially disheartening to the few remaining families on the block because it had been built by two of their own—Richard Arnold and his sister, Henrietta (Arnold) Constable, whose father had founded Arnold Constable & Company. The younger Arnolds had grown up on the block yet seemed to have little feeling for their old family home, as they razed it and four other brick buildings on adjoining lots in 1880, replacing them with a commercial building that stretched through to Twenty-fourth Street. Designed by architect William Schickel, the six-story neo-Grec edifice at Nos. 27-33 had two distinct matching sides, with retail spaces on the ground level, office and loft spaces up above, and passenger elevators in the front, middle, and rear.

Among the first tenants of the western side of the building, 31-33 West Twenty-third Street, was the Co-operative Dress Association, founded on the idea that consumers could save money by cutting out the middleman. For an annual fee of twenty-five dollars, members could buy their clothes directly from the co-op without worrying about retailers' markups. The association's president was Kate Field, one of America's first celebrity journalists and a singular figure in an era when women still lacked the right to vote. Intelligent, outspoken, and beautiful, she wrote for various prestigious newspapers, including the *Chicago Tribune* and the *New York Herald,* founded her own weekly publication in Washington, D.C., and was a close friend—and perhaps more—of Anthony Trollope. Her *New York Tribune* obituary in May 1896 described her as "one of the best-known women in America."

While the cooperative association may have aimed at offering less expensive clothing, its emporium was a luxe affair. On its second floor reigned a dress department that sold all the latest Parisian fashions, and on its fifth floor were an elegant reading room, reception room, directors' room, and lunchroom, where members could relax after shopping.

With its prime location and celebrity president, the co-op seemed destined for success, but ran into immediate trouble. During its first year of operation, its manager quit and a number of employees were laid off. Then, another six months later, it closed. Some blamed its failure on Field's exorbitant $10,000 salary (about $260,000 today), while she blamed it on "a lot of dirty little claimants, who had no bowels of compassion."

Meanwhile, the eastern side of the building, 27-29 West Twenty-third Street, began attracting publishing companies. Up until just a decade or so earlier, Boston, then the nation's intellectual and cultural capital, had been home to the country's foremost book companies, publishers of such early American writers as Emerson, Nathaniel Hawthorne, Henry Wadsworth Longfellow, and Henry David Thoreau. But with the flood of immigrants arriving in New York in the late 1800s, new publishers such as Alfred A. Knopf began publishing translations of contemporary foreign books that sold well. Older New York publishing firms took note, and by the 1910s, the city was the country's undisputed international book publishing center.

Among the first publishers to move to the block was G. P. Putnam's Sons, which took the ground floor of Nos. 27-29 for its bookstore and space upstairs for its offices, a lease it kept until 1911, when it moved uptown. The firm had been founded in 1838 by George Palmer Putnam, a former bookstore clerk who had published the revised works of his friend Washington Irving, along with Susan Warner's novel *The Wide, Wide World*, America's first bestseller, selling forty thousand copies in its first few months. Theodore Roosevelt wrote *The Winning of the West*, a four-volume account, at a desk in Putnam's offices in 1888, and the book was then edited, printed, bound, and sold out of 27-29 West Twenty-third Street. Putnam's was also the firm that had paved the way to modern book publishing after the Civil War by implementing a royalty system; before then, most American authors, like many self-published authors today, had published at their own expense.

Two more major publishing companies moved into the double-sided building in the late 1880s, to also remain on the block until the early 1910s:

E. P. Dutton & Co. (Nos. 31-33), which had relocated to New York from Boston, and Henry Holt & Co. (No. 29). They were followed by the Fine Art Publishing House, which opened a small gallery upstairs in 1892, and publisher G. W. Dillingham in 1894. Many other smaller, lesser-known publishers also had offices nearby. The 1892 *Trow's Business Directory of New York City* lists four more publishers on the north side of Twenty-third Street between Fifth and Sixth avenues, and ten more on the south side. In the 1890s, the original *Life* magazine, whose name was purchased in the 1930s by future media mogul Henry Luce, was published out of 28 West Twenty-third Street. The whole block was as vibrantly alive with words and ideas as it was with commerce.

*   *   *

Even as great changes were taking place on the Twenty-third Street side of the block, the Fifth Avenue Hotel remained stalwart, as important a center as ever, though it was hosting more businessmen and tourists and fewer socialites than in the past. The Republican Party was continuing to meet there, as it had since the Civil War. The Democrats of Tammany Hall controlled the city, but the Republicans controlled the state, and it was here that President Ulysses Grant had met with bankers during the financial Panic of 1873, and a Reverend Burchard denounced the Democrats as the party of "rum, Romanism, and rebellion"—a swipe at the city's Irish Catholics—during a pro-Republican rally for presidential candidate James Blaine in 1884. That speech, which Blaine did not denounce, is said to have cost him the election to Grover Cleveland, who eked out a narrow victory decided by the electoral college vote in New York State.

The Republicans maintained their state headquarters in the hotel's room 10, held their formal meetings in its Parlor D.R. (equipped at times with as many as seven telegraph wires with which to send and receive the latest news), and assembled informally at the "Amen Corner," a V-shaped bank of plush red settees formed where two broad corridors met toward the back of the hotel. The corner had been a gathering spot for Republican leaders since the 1860s, but it wasn't until the 1890s that it acquired its nickname, from the meetings held there by the Republican boss and U.S. senator Thomas Collier Platt, who lived at the hotel for over a quarter century.

Platt was a slight, pale, and physically unprepossessing man, yet he wielded enormous power, brokering deals and dispensing patronage "from Montauk Point to Buffalo," as he was prone to boast. He had the habit of holding party conferences at the bank of settees on Sundays, in what the press dubbed "Platt's Sunday School," and his sycophants chorused "Amen" to every pronouncement he made.

Among Platt's most influential moves was nominating Theodore Roosevelt for New York governor in 1898, thereby setting in motion his path to the U.S. presidency. Platt disliked Roosevelt personally, but the Republicans needed a strong gubernatorial candidate, and Roosevelt was their best bet. Roosevelt didn't much care for Platt either, but grudgingly agreed to go along with his policies, a promise he did not always keep.

Also living at the Fifth Avenue Hotel in the 1880s was another Republican power broker, U.S. senator Roscoe Conkling. A dandy who dressed in black cutaway coats, bright bow ties, high silk hats, and English gaiters buttoned over shiny pointed shoes, Conkling spent much time in the hotel's billiard room. He didn't play, but he liked to make bets on others' shots. He was also a passionate amateur boxer and one evening fought the muscular professional Frank Derraven in his suite, knocking over furniture and shattering lamps. When the bout was over, Derraven's nose was broken, Conkling was bleeding profusely, and the hotel's guests were scandalized.

Conkling took great pride in his well-toned physique and physical fitness—a pride that literally caused his fall. During the blizzard of March 12, 1888, when he was no longer living at the Fifth Avenue, but at the nearby Hoffman House, he left his Wall Street office for the New York Clubhouse on Madison Square. About eighteen inches of snow had fallen by then, yet a few hansoms were still on the street. He hailed one, but when its driver quoted the astronomical sum of $50 (about $1,300 today), Conkling rejected the ride. He was still a robust fifty-eight, after all, and there was no reason he couldn't walk the three miles. He trudged north, buffeted by winds that were knocking over streetlamps and freezing gas lines, and ever more snow; forty inches would fall within thirty-six hours. Three hours later, he reached Madison Square, but failed to recognize where he was. Snow was everywhere and the streets were deserted. Even the English sparrows that lived in the park were gone, having flown through an open door of the Fifth Avenue Hotel to roost in its lobby. Conkling wandered in circles, collapsing two hours later within sight of his club. He died three weeks later of an abscess in his brain that had developed due to his exposure to cold. His friends erected an eight-foot-tall bronze statue in his memory in the southeast corner of Madison Square Park, where it still stands today.

*   *   *

As stalwart as the old Fifth Avenue Hotel was in some respects, it could hardly be counted on to uphold traditional values. It had never been a Knickerbocker kind of place, and now, elite families like the Schermerhorns must have murmured, it was going from bad to worse. Just look at its ever-more déclassé guests and at the damages wrought by another member of the block's younger generation at the Second National Bank, headquartered inside the hotel.

The bank had been founded in the early 1860s by Amos Eno and nine other businessmen and was, like the hotel itself, an immediate success, so much so that its stockholders were repaid their original investment in a single dividend a few years after it opened. The bank was one of the first in the city to serve both commercial and individual customers, with many wealthy Madison Square patrons storing their valuables in its basement vaults.

The Second National had been influential in another way as well. One day while attending to a customer, teller Joseph Case noticed that many of the people waiting in line were women. That gave him an idea: Why not create a special parlor in the bank, complete with its own tellers and bookkeepers, that catered exclusively to women? He took his idea to the bank's directors, and they agreed. Soon, other banks were following suit.

So it was that by 1880 the Second National Bank was one of the most respected private banks in the city. Run by an able financier, it had paid regular dividends for thirteen years and always had plenty of cash on hand. But then Eno made a disastrous miscalculation. He named his seventh child and fourth son, John Chester Eno, president of the bank. A disarming man-about-town, John had spent several years working at the powerful banking firm of Morton, Bliss & Co. downtown and was already a Second National Bank director. He was still in his early thirties, though, and his appointment was opposed by many of the bank's other directors, who thought him too inexperienced for the job. Still, Amos was the principal stockholder and had the final say.

At first, all was business as usual under John's leadership, though a few of the bank's directors were concerned about his near-daily visits to his Wall Street brokers. Was he spending enough time managing the bank? they asked. Father and son assured them that he was.

The directors should have trusted their instincts. On a Sunday morning, May 11, 1884, John confessed to his father that he had embezzled nearly $4 million (about $107 million today) from the bank to cover his stock market investments. The Second National was broke.

Shaken and enraged, Amos, now seventy-three years old, convened an emergency family meeting, attended by his other children, their spouses, and William Walter Phelps, the son of his old Connecticut business partner, now a Republican U.S. congressman known for his fiscal acumen. All recognized that should the Second National Bank fail, it could have consequences extending far beyond the bank's depositors and directors. One week earlier, the brokerage giant Grant & Ward and the Marine National Bank had both collapsed. Word of another failure could send Wall Street into a panic and the country into depression.

On Tuesday, the press caught wind of the scandal and appeared at the Enos' doors, to be sent away with "no comment." That evening, the bank's board met and Amos agreed to pay almost all the $4 million debt out of his own fortune. To the waiting press, the board delivered a statement shortly after midnight: "The Board of Directors of the Second National Bank take pleasure in informing the public that whatever loss has been incurred has been made up; that its capital is intact, and the bank is prepared to meet its obligations on demand." No mention was made of the embezzlement.

The next morning, an angry crowd converged outside the bank and, as soon as it opened, surged to the tellers' windows, rapping frantically on the glass with their bank books. Patience, ordered the head cashier, payment would begin at ten A.M. Scowling, the crowd lined up, men on the right, women on the left, with lines extending far out along Twenty-third Street and Fifth Avenue. Keeping order was Captain Alexander "Clubber" Williams.

The bank stayed open two hours later than usual to accommodate everyone, and about five hundred withdrawals were made. More long lines formed the following day, and by Thursday, the crisis had passed.

On May 24 a warrant was issued for John Chester Eno's arrest, and three deputy marshals were dispatched to his home at 46 Park Avenue, near Thirty-sixth Street. Here they found other law officials and Pinkerton detectives already watching the house. All assured the marshals that John was inside, and they rang the front bell. Ladies in fine dress appeared. "Mr. Eno is not here and you can't have him," one of them said. The marshals replied that, nonetheless, they would have to search to house. "Search the house! Never!" screamed one of the ladies. The marshals hemmed and hawed, apologized and shrugged, but eventually paraded inside and searched the house from the basement to the roof. John was not there, they announced when they returned to the street, much to the astonishment and anger of those watching the house. The marshals left, and the detectives continued their watch.

At two A.M., Father Thomas Ducey of St. Leo's Roman Catholic Church pulled up to John Eno's door—his third visit in ten hours. He remained inside for an hour, then left. When asked if John was inside, he replied, "No, he is not there. I cannot tell you where he may be; I have not seen him for a day or two."

Father Ducey was a curious figure in the Madison Square neighborhood in the 1880s. A vigorous, confident, and charismatic man, he had convinced the cardinal a few years earlier that the area needed a new Catholic church—to be headed by himself, of course. St. Leo's went up on East Twenty-eighth Street near Fifth Avenue in 1880 and, soon after opening, became a place to see and be seen. Every Sunday, the wealthy thronged through its front doors to hear Ducey preach, usually on a social issue such as women's rights, on which he took radical, progressive stances. He also invited different speakers to address his congregation every week and gave

especially warm welcomes to socialites, actors, artists, and visiting
Europeans. His masses attracted people of all faiths, among them John
Chester Eno and his sister Antoinette, who were Protestant.

Also church regulars were the Delmonicos, owners of Delmonico's
restaurant. Father Ducey functioned as the family's chaplain and dined
frequently at their establishment—so frequently that his favorite biblical
text was said to be Matthew 11:9, "The Son of Man came eating and
drinking."

Nothing in Father Ducey's early years presaged his rise to such power.
Born in Ireland in 1843, he had come to New York with his widowed mother
at age five, just one more of the many thousands of Irish immigrants
escaping devastating famines. His mother found work as a housekeeper for
James Topham Brady, a wealthy lawyer and bachelor, but she passed away
a few years later.

Ducey, now an orphan, seemed destined for a life of poverty. Instead,
Brady, known as a great advocate for the poor and a crusader against corruption, adopted him. Brady had raised his six younger siblings after their
parents died and had a soft heart. He passed his radical values on to his
adopted son, along with a taste for luxury, and introduced him to many
influential citizens. Brady hoped that Thomas, too, would go into law, but
Thomas chose the church.

When Brady died in 1869, he left Ducey a small fortune, freeing him
to continue his adoptive father's progressive crusades. He was also posted
to the pulpit of St. Michael's Church on Ninth Avenue, where he established St. Michael's Club for young men. It is hard to read a description
of that club today without alarm bells going off: "Early in his priestly
career," reported the *Catholic News* in 1909, quoting Monsignor Michael
Lavelle, "Father Ducey developed a fondness for young men, for poor young
men and men of easier position, men, who by reason of their position in
the world are continually tempted by the snares of the world, and into this
field, the welfare of young men, Father Ducey threw himself with all his
zeal and energy."

On June 1, 1884, one week after Father Ducey's visit to 46 Park Avenue,
John Chester Eno was captured in Quebec on board the steamer *Vancouver*,
scheduled to depart for England the following morning. With him was

the good Father. His parishioners were shocked. What was he doing there? Did he mean to go to England with Eno? Commented the *New York Times*, "The Rev. Father Ducey, of St. Leo's Church, appears to have aided [Eno] in his flight and accompanied him to administer comfort and consolation in his exile . . . the priest probably played his part for a money consideration. It is a fine business for a minister of the church which professes to exercise a special rigor upon offenders against the criminal law."

U.S. law officials took Eno and Ducey to Montreal and brought them before a judge, only to have their efforts thwarted. Canada's extradition treaty covered murder, assault with intent to murder, piracy, arson, robbery, and forgery, but not embezzlement. Eno was let go, and Ducey returned to New York.

Soon thereafter, Eno was joined in Canada by his wife, children, and sister Antoinette, whom some thought had helped him steal from the bank. Nothing was ever proved, but Antoinette's husband, Charles Wood, was known to be an overenthusiastic speculator cast in the same mold as his brother-in-law. Ironically, the family settled down in Sillery, just outside the Old City of Quebec, which was named for a wealthy French diplomat who had become a priest and renounced all worldly goods.

Not a man to renounce much of anything, John Eno did quite well for himself financially in his new home. He became involved in the building and financing of the Canadian railroads and was made a director of the Great Northern Railway of Canada. Socially, though, things were difficult. "Neither [Eno] nor his wife is ever invited out, nor are they visited by society people," wrote the Montreal correspondent for the *New York Globe and Mail*.

In 1893, after nine years of living in exile, John Eno decided to return to the United States and face criminal charges. His father was in poor health by then and had retired to the old family home in Simsbury, Connecticut, where he spent his evenings studying Latin, Italian, and French, and translating Caesar, Dante, and Victor Hugo into English. He had never recovered from the shame that John had brought on the family and had written him out of his will.

With their father gone from the city, John, his sister Antoinette, and their families moved into Amos's New York residence at 233 Fifth Avenue and, according to one family historian, aggressively set about replacing his servants with their own. The rest of the Eno family was said to be appalled, but John and Antoinette reportedly ignored them.

Meanwhile, law officials were still attempting to bring John to justice. But nothing they did was effective. All charges against him were either quashed by judges on technicalities or dropped by prosecutors for mysterious reasons. In 1899, his freedom was fully restored.

Amos Eno died in his New York home on February 21, 1898. By then, he was rumored to be worth over $40 million (about $1.25 billion today), with real estate holdings that included some of the choicest parcels of land in the city. "Integrity, tenacity, and judgment, continued to be striking elements of Mr. Eno's character up to the time of his death," commented his *New York Times* obituary.

Funeral services were conducted at the Madison Square Presbyterian Church, on the southeast corner of Madison Avenue and Twenty-fourth Street, by the Reverend Charles H. Parkhurst. Although a generation younger than Eno, Parkhurst had been close to the older man and his eulogy was an emotional one: "I always found Mr. Eno a friend with whom I could counsel and from whom I could gather strength and courage . . . Those of us who knew him well knew that he stood as a bulwark of moral integrity, facing for years the buffeting of the natural forces of evil, moral crookedness, inconsistency and dishonesty."

There were no such glowing eulogies or obituaries for John Chester Eno, who died on February 28, 1914. An examination of his accounts showed that he had died much as he had lived—deeply in debt.

* * *

Through it all, the commerce and the scandals, the construction and the betrayals, William and Ann Schermerhorn stayed put in their old mansion on West Twenty-third Street, their daughters and sons-in-law beside them. Once at the vanguard of their social set, they were now its rear guard, the only ones of their peers still living on the block.

In 1891, William's older brother, the recluse Edmund, passed away at age seventy-five in his villa in Newport, where he had been living full time for the last six years. More isolated than ever, he had even stopped going to church, as he had taken umbrage over a sermon on the worship of money, believing it to be directed at him. He had all but abandoned his home on West Twenty-third Street by then too; it had "stood for years like a closed vault, which, indeed, it resembles more than a house," wrote one reporter.

William died on New Year's Day 1903 at the age of eighty-two, leaving behind an estate worth over $1.6 million (about $48 million today). Ann and her two older daughters, Fanny and Sarah, carried on at the family home, but her youngest daughter and her husband, finally freed from William's yoke, moved out. Ann was in her eighties now, yet still had some of her old spark: she was the first woman of her social set to take up riding in motor cars and could often be seen traveling around Newport in an automobile.

Less than a year after William died, the couple's daughter Sarah passed away at age fifty-three from kidney disease. Her mother was beside her when she died, in Bar Harbor, Maine, where they had been vacationing.

Ann passed away four years later, but held on to the old Schermerhorn home even in death, as she left an injunction in her will stipulating that the house be occupied as a residence until the last of the family died. Fanny and her husband were therefore forced to live there whenever they were in town, but they spent most of the year at their farm in East Greenwich, Rhode Island. Only after Fanny died a year later did the family finally abandon the mansion, by then regarded as "a relic of a past generation" and the only residence left on either side of Twenty-third Street between Fifth and Sixth avenues.

CHAPTER 15

Roundsmen of the Lord

He was big, he was bold, he was mutton-chopped. He had a thickset neck, Atlas shoulders, and calves of exceptional size. His legs were short and looked like tree trunks. He was Anthony Comstock, self-appointed roundsman, or police officer, of the Lord.

Comstock's personal mission was to eradicate vice in all its forms wherever it could be found, and on April 3, 1897, his indefatigable snuffling brought him to the bookshop of the G. W. Dillingham publishing company at 33 West Twenty-third Street. He entered the shop, dressed in his usual dark clothes that needed pressing, a stiffly starched white shirt, black bow tie, and large, heavy shoes that he'd purchased at Coward's, a shoe store that catered mostly to policemen and firemen and always had his size, thirteen, in stock. Under his clothes, the fifty-three-year-old wore red flannel underwear.

Nonchalantly, he perused the bookshop as if he had all the time in the world. But under his thick eyebrows, his truculent blue eyes were darting here and there, to alight with glee on *Mme. Tellier's Girls*, by Guy de Maupassant, a story about a French brothel keeper and her employees, newly translated into English by Edwin Ellis. He paid for the book and left the shop, only to return a moment later and ask to speak to a representative of the Dillingham company. Manager John C. Cook appeared. Comstock squared his shoulders.

You have published an "immoral book," he said, furrowing his brow. He then demanded to be given all copies of *Mme. Tellier's Girls* and the stereotype plates with which they had been printed.

Cook was flabbergasted. "This book contains, besides its title story, 'The Inheritance,' and 'Butter Ball,'" he said. "The last that I have named made the author famous in a day. These three stories are masterpieces already classical. If you doubt this, read Henry James, question William Dean Howells . . ."

"The work shocks me," Comstock retorted, drawing down his upper lip as he always did when he was angry. "I represent the average person. I do not comprehend your literary subtleties. These may have been a reason for this book in France; there is none here."

Cook tried to respond, but Comstock interrupted him, "You can understand that I did not come here to learn the art of literary criticism." Then, despite the fact that he had no warrant or legal paper of any kind, he and his deputy seized all the copies of *Mme. Tellier's Girls* they could find and marched self-righteously out the door. Cook protested weakly, but did nothing. Comstock was a powerful figure in late nineteenth-century New York.

The roundsman had begun the Lord's work over three decades earlier, at age eighteen, by breaking into a Connecticut saloon after hours and opening the spigots of its kegs, draining their contents onto the floor. He would end it at age seventy-one, after "over-doing in a purity convention." During his reign of terror disguised as piety, he destroyed an estimated 50 tons of books, 284,000 pounds of plates for printing "objectionable books," and nearly 4 million pictures. He also arrested, or had arrested, at least 3,600 people on charges of obscenity, abortion, and gambling.

The son of devout Congregationalists, Comstock had been born in New Canaan, Connecticut, in 1844. Devoted to his mother, who died when he was ten, he spent his boyhood working on the family farm, trapping animals, collecting postage stamps, and attending church. The Civil War began while he was still in high school, and he enlisted, to be shocked to the core by the "wicked" troops swearing, smoking, and drinking around him.

After the war ended, Comstock moved to New York with only $3.45 (about $70 today) in his pocket. He found a job as a porter in a dry goods store and rose quickly to the rank of shipping clerk and then salesman, earning $27 a week. He bought a house in Brooklyn, joined a Congregational church, and married sweet, self-effacing Margaret Hamilton, ten years his senior and the daughter of a Protestant elder. Small and emaciated, always dressed in black, Margaret rarely said a word and adored her husband.

In 1872 Comstock tried to get a circulating library shut down for offering "vile books" and organized police raids on porn shops and saloons that were failing to observe the Sabbath. His energetic campaigns came to the attention of leaders of the Young Men's Christian Association (YMCA), who were as concerned about vice as he, and together they founded the New York Society for the Suppression of Vice, a quasi-official body dedicated to policing public morality. At first, the society focused on censoring literature—with Comstock famously declaring, "Books are the feeders for brothels"—but soon expanded to organize raids on bordellos, concert saloons, dance halls, and gambling dens.

That still wasn't enough for the tireless young crusader. In 1873, he successfully lobbied Congress to pass what became known as the Comstock Law. The edict made it illegal to send by mail any material deemed "obscene, lewd, or lascivious" or related to abortion or contraception. To enforce it, Congress appointed Comstock as a special agent of the U.S. Post Office, an unpaid position that he joyfully embraced. His mission: to hunt down miscreants "as you hunt rats, without mercy," he said.

Much of the press and many politicians, along with churches and religious groups, applauded Comstock's work. Pornography, prostitution, and promiscuity in all its forms had been running rampant for too long, as far as much of the public was concerned.

One of the "highlights" of the crusader's career was the arrest of Madame Restell in 1878, when the abortionist was sixty-seven years old. Comstock called at her office one day, posing as a worried husband who could not support another child. Restell provided him with birth control pills, and he returned the next day with the police, who arrested her. Calmly, Restell put on her velvet cape and a hat with black ostrich plumes and called for her victoria. Then they drove downtown to the Jefferson Market Police Court, where she was arraigned. She posted bail and returned home. The weeks before her trial dragged on, with the press decrying the "wickedest woman in New York" daily, and in the wee hours of April 1, 1878, she lay down in her tub, filled it with water, and slit her throat from ear to ear. "A bloody ending to a bloody life," Comstock noted in his files, and bragged that Madame Restell was the fifteenth wicked soul he had driven to suicide. After that, he stopped counting, publicly at least, perhaps because someone had finally convinced him that it was unseemly to boast of such a thing.

Comstock was involved in at least one more suicide, however, some twenty years later. In 1902, Ida C. Craddock, an eccentric forty-five-year-old spinster originally from Philadelphia, was living in room 5 at 34 West Twenty-third Street, across the street from the now-aging Fifth Avenue Hotel. Calling herself the earthly wife of an angel, she had written a pamphlet, *The Wedding Night*, which offered advice for the newly married. How, as a spinster, she could possibly know about such things was a scandal in its own right, but when the pamphlet came to Comstock's attention, he was most outraged by her description of "the science of seduction." He had her arrested, tried, and convicted. She served three months in jail and was released, only to be arrested again a short time later for sending *The Wedding Night* through the mail. The pamphlet had been well reviewed by medical journals and offered much-needed instruction in that era of sexual ignorance, but at the trial a partisan judge described it as "indescribably obscene" and, incredibly, did not allow the jury to see it. They pronounced her guilty. The night before her sentencing, she slit her wrists and turned on the gas. Her suicide note read: "I am taking my life because a judge, at the instigation of Anthony Comstock, has declared me guilty of a crime I did not commit." Her note to her mother was prescient: "[The] world is not yet ready for all the beautiful things I have to teach it . . . Other people will take up my work."

Comstock was let go from the U.S. Post Office in 1906, by which time he had largely become a public joke, as he was attacking even such trivial things as bridge games and church raffles. Nonetheless, his reputation was still intact enough in 1915 for President Woodrow Wilson to appoint him the U.S. representative to the International Purity Congress at the San Francisco Exposition. While there, Comstock wore himself out rushing from one panel discussion to another and, a few days after returning home, died. The Comstock Law lived on, however, to become recodified and reenacted various times in the new century, even as the country became more tolerant. As late as the early 1960s, the U.S. Supreme Court upheld the Comstock Law in a case brought against a writer/editor couple who had published and circulated a magazine with homosexual content.

*   *   *

During the 1890s, a more thoughtful and complex reformer—and one who would have far more influence on the Twenty-third Street block—arrived on the scene: Reverend Charles H. Parkhurst of the Madison Square Presbyterian Church, the man who would later eulogize Amos Eno. The church stood directly across the park from the Fifth Avenue Hotel and was one of the wealthiest in the city, counting among its members many banking, political, professional, and merchant families. Attending the church along with the Enos were Senator Platt of the Amen Corner and the Roosevelts, who lived nearby on East Twenty-first Street. Teddy Roosevelt had been baptized at the church in 1860 and went to its Sunday school.

The opposite of Comstock in many ways, Parkhurst was slim and fit, scholarly and reserved, with long curly hair and round steel-rimmed glasses. Born in Framingham, Massachusetts, he had been a pastor in Lenox, Massachusetts, before being appointed to the Madison Square church. His sharp, penetrating mind had caught the attention of other church leaders. Nonetheless, he was neither a particularly prepossessing man nor a riveting speaker. One weekly magazine criticized his lecturing style as "somewhat strained" and his voice as "not very musical." He also had the disconcerting habit of seesawing back and forth from foot to foot as he spoke.

And so none of his congregants was quite prepared for the thunderous sermon their then fifty-year-old reverend delivered on Valentine's Day 1892. Sitting smugly in their habitual pews, doubtless silently criticizing their neighbors while congratulating themselves, they were rudely shaken alert by the sound of vehement, unsettling words pouring out of the pulpit.

Their city's politicians and policemen, Parkhurst roared, were nothing more than "polluted harpies that, under the pretense of governing this city, are feeding day and night on its quivery vitals. They are a lying, perjured, rum-soaked and libidinous lot . . . while we fight iniquity they shield or patronize it; while we try to convert criminals, they manufacture them."

Parkhurst's sermon, much of it published later that day in the *World*, caused a sensation. Though most New Yorkers were well aware of the city's many brothels, saloons, and other disreputable spots, they were shocked by his accusations of municipal corruption.

New York's Mayor Hugh Grant, his Tammany Hall colleagues, the police, and most of the press promptly denounced the reverend. The *New York Sun* demanded that he be driven from the pulpit and the city's district attorney ordered him to appear before a grand jury with proof of his charges. Parkhurst faltered. He had no proof. His sermon had been based on articles he had read and stories he had heard. He was laughed out of court, the jury rebuking him for character assassination.

Angered and embarrassed, Parkhurst decided to fight back. He knew he was right and would prove it, by going undercover and personally gathering the evidence he needed. He hired private detective Charles Gardner, a huge young man with a huge mustache, to take him on a tour of the city's raunchiest spots for six dollars a night, and enlisted John Langdon Erving, an earnest young congregant nicknamed "Sunbeam," to come along as a witness.

Gardner, who would later write *The Doctor and the Devil*, a book about their adventures, went to pick up Parkhurst and Erving on the appointed evening and "screamed almost with laughter." He had instructed the two men to dress like disreputable gentlemen, but Parkhurst was wearing a suit with trousers that "had the very aroma of the pulpit about them," and Erving looked like "a dandy dressed up in his last year's suit."

"I think we will do," Dr. Parkhurst said complacently as Gardner looked them over.

"Do!" Gardner shouted. "Good gracious, sir, clergyman stands out all over you!"

Gardner took the men to his apartment at 207 West Eighteenth Street, where he kept a wardrobe full of garments for his undercover missions. He gave Parkhurst a pair of loud black-and-white checked trousers, a dirty shirt, and a "double-breasted reefer jacket"; tied a piece of old red flannel shirt around his neck; and slicked back his long curls with a wet bar of laundry soap. He gave Erving a pair of rubber boots and some tattered clothes and tied another piece of the red flannel shirt around his neck.

The trio set out, taking the Third Avenue El down to Cherry Hill, then the name of the East River waterfront near the Brooklyn Bridge. Once a prosperous area where George Washington and John Hancock had lived, the neighborhood was now a garbage-choked slum inhabited by poor immigrants, prostitutes, and derelicts. The adventurers wandered first into a saloon known for its lively trade in stolen goods, and then into a dive where, wrote Gardner, "on each chair sat something that originally had been a woman." Later came a stop at a seedy dance hall where a two-hundred-pound hooker named Baby propositioned Parkhurst as he "sat in blissful ignorance sucking on [an] orange."

Over the next few days, the threesome continued their underground tour, visiting bars, concert saloons, opium dens, and houses of ill repute throughout the city. They entered "tight houses," so called because the young women therein wore nothing but revealing neck-to-toe tights, and "dead houses," where drunken men could crash for five or ten cents a night. They encountered cops imbibing free liquor while nonchalantly watching shady goings-on and met at least fifty streetwalkers within a few blocks of police headquarters at 300 Mulberry Street.

Especially mortifying to Parkhurst and Erving was their stop at the Golden Rule Pleasure Club on West Third Street in Greenwich Village, run by a tall, graceful, dark-haired woman named Scotch Ann. Wrote Gardner: "In each room sat a youth, whose face was painted, eye-brows blackened, and whose airs were those of a young girl. Each person talked in a high falsetto voice and called the others by women's names." Parkhurst was puzzled by the scene, and Gardner had to explain to him that the youths were men, at which point "The Doctor instantly turned on his heel and fled from the house at top speed."

Nonetheless, throughout their tour, Parkhurst remained relentless, drinking far more liquor than was his usual wont, hiding his shock as best he could, and sometimes staying out until dawn. The reverend was "a very hard man to satisfy," Gardner later reflected. "'Show me something worse' was his constant cry."

Parkhurst was especially interested in visiting brothels in the Tenderloin, as the district was just a few blocks from his church and probably the haunt of some of his parishioners. Agreeing, Gardner started leading the way to the French Madame's on West Thirty-first Street when he noticed plainclothes cops following them. Shaking them off, he instead led the party to Hattie Adams's brothel at 29-31 East Twenty-seventh Street, where they witnessed a "dance of nature" performed by five young women to the accompaniment of a blindfolded piano player. The women entered the room fully clothed, but gradually threw off everything except their garters and stockings and danced a provocative can-can that included playing leapfrog. They invited the men to join in, but only Gardner took up the challenge.

Two days later, Parkhurst, Gardner, and Erving sat down to fill out separate affidavits, writing down names, addresses, and details of all they had seen and heard. Four detectives previously hired by Gardner also stopped by to hand him a report listing 254 saloons where at least 2,438 customers, including many policemen, had been illegally drinking on the Sabbath.

That Sunday, March 13, the Reverend Parkhurst again delivered an impassioned anticorruption sermon. He had let his intentions be known beforehand, and his church was jammed, people overflowing onto its steps. Parkhurst began by saying that he was not going to speak as a Republican or Democrat, Protestant or Catholic, but simply as a man who believed in the Ten Commandments and the law of God. He then revealed how he had gone "down into the disgusting depths of this Tammany-debauched town," to find it "rotten with a rottenness that is unspeakable and indescribable, and a rottenness that would be absolutely impossible except by the connivance, not to say the purchased sympathy, of the men whose one obligation before God, men, and their own conscience, is to shield virtue and make vice difficult."

Parkhurst's second sermon rocked the city even more violently than the first. He was again called before a grand jury, but this time, his first-person report, backed up by two credible witnesses, received a serious hearing and led to indictments—though not of the police, whom the grand jury concluded were merely incompetent, not corrupt. Saloons operating illegally were shuttered or fined, and two madams were arrested, tried, convicted, and sentenced to the Blackwell's Island prison. Their trials were closely followed by the general public, who delighted in all the seamy details, and came up with a popular new ditty: "Dr. Parkhurst on the floor / Playing leapfrog with a whore / Tarara Boomde-ay / Tarara Boomde-ay."

* * *

Parkhurst's testimony led directly to the 1892 cleanup raids on the Twenty-fourth Street side of the block: it was on May 4, 1892, three months after his second sermon, that May Stacom's at No. 14, Caroline Hasting's at No. 16, and Nellie Harrison's at No. 18 were all targeted for the first time in their history, along with ten other of the "best-known disorderly houses" in the Twenty-ninth Precinct. Clampdowns continued throughout the city that year and the next as the police put on a show to convince the public of their goodwill. Mostly only small-time operators were arrested, however. The more powerful players were advised by the police to close shop and leave town, and even relatively minor madams such as Stacom were informed of the raids ahead of time. Neighbors testified that Stacom had witnessed the raid on her boardinghouse "from her private carriage on the opposite side of the street and nearly in front of her house."

All this catalyzed Mrs. Mary Sallade, a fifty-five-year-old divorcée living in a house that she owned at 53 West Twenty-fourth Street, across from the block, into taking matters into her own hands. Fed up with the police department's inaction and worried about the effect the disorderly houses were having on her property value and daughter, she began to collect evidence against her neighbors.

First up on her crusading agenda was Mrs. Annie Pond, who kept a house on the block directly across from hers. Sallade entered Pond's house in the summer of 1894 and saw enough to have Pond arrested and held on $500 bail (about $15,000 today) for operating a disorderly house.

Next came the Arlington Hotel, also on the block, at 54 West Twenty-fourth Street. (It would later move to the north side of West Twenty-fourth Street.) On August 7, 1894, Sallade went to Jefferson Market Court to ask for the arrest of the hotel's proprietor, Jacob Schneider. She had no concrete evidence against him, however, and the judge dismissed the case. Undaunted, Sallade told reporters that it didn't matter; she would get the evidence she needed with the help of her neighbors and "was not afraid that the police would make life unpleasant for her."

Three days later, on August 10, 1894, Sallade assembled a committee of businessmen and property owners living or working on West Twenty-fourth Street between Fifth and Sixth avenues to help her in her crusade. Among them were the architects Thorpe and Knowles of Nos. 19 and 21; the photographer Benjamin J. Falk and the booksellers Meyer Brothers of No. 13; the picture seller W. H. Ketchum of No. 19: the publishers Putnam's Sons of No. 8; and Dr. Kennedy of No. 35. The group voted to work independently of the police, pursue their complaint purely on business grounds, and send a letter to everyone on the block announcing a meeting to be held at the offices of Thorpe and Knowles the following Tuesday.

On the appointed day, about fifty residents and property owners turned up and were called on one by one to give three-minute speeches about the block's condition and what should be done about it. Many supported the idea of a cleanup crusade, but when it came time for Mrs. T. Cox of No. 50 to speak, she sprang to her feet, accused Sallade of being a publicity hound, and said that all her boarders had been driven away by the divorcée's actions. Sallade countered that she had frequently seen Cox's boarders lewdly displaying themselves in her windows, turning Cox apoplectic.

An attorney representing the owner of No. 18 also took issue with the crusade, saying that "the notoriety arising from Mrs. Sallade's campaign has completely ruined this block for residential purposes. Even if every shady person in the block cleaned out to-night, no respectable tenant could be induced to move in. It will only be available for business purposes here-after." The attorney's statement would prove to be prophetic, but not for the reasons he cited; by the 1910s, nearly every residential building on the block would be torn down and replaced by an office-and-loft building.

About two weeks after the meeting, Mrs. Sallade's name appeared in the papers again. She kept a donkey in her backyard (causing a neighbor to say that she, too, kept a disorderly house) and a restaurant owner on the block wanted to put it to work, as recompense for the falling off of his business since her crusade began. She agreed, and that Saturday a donkey was seen walking up and down West Twenty-fourth Street bearing the sign:

Mrs. Sallade's Donkey.
Belonging to Her His Character
is Above Reproach.
So is the character of
Blank's Restaurant.
Table D'Hote Dinner Only
40 cents.

Ultimately, Sallade's campaign failed. None of the disorderly houses on the block were permanently shut down, and although the case against the Arlington Hotel's manager was eventually taken to trial, it was dismissed.

* * *

Among the houses on the block that the police raided in the mid-1890s was Mrs. Annie Cummings's place at 40-42 West Twenty-fourth Street. She and her ladies of the night were duly arrested, but of more interest to the police was a young man who had been living there: Richard E. Young Jr. A warrant was out for his arrest. It had been issued by his grandmother Emeline Bushnell, who lived across the street at 15 West Twenty-fourth and feared for either her grandson's well-being or her own safety.

Richard Jr. was the son of Richard D. Young, a one-time millionaire perfumer who had lost his entire fortune in middle age. As a child, Richard Jr. had been surrounded by luxury, but as an adult, he was destitute—and addicted to drugs, a habit he had learned by smoking opium with the Chinese in San Francisco, according to his grandmother.

Richard Jr. may well have turned to drugs because of his father's precipitous loss, but there could also have been an entirely different reason altogether: mental illness, which ran in the family. His father had begun his career as the preeminent partner of a well-known perfume company, Young, Ladd & Coffin, and later founded his own firm, the R. D. Young Perfumery Co. Along the way, he married Emma Bushnell of an old New York family, with whom he had five children, and for many years, their lives seemed happy and stable. But then things began to go terribly wrong. In 1885 Emma filed for a separation, and three years later Richard Sr. declared he had gone "temporarily insane" due to business difficulties. He suffered from "melancholia" and was hospitalized three separate times. After his final release, he became convinced that Emma was committing adultery and hired thugs to shadow and harass her. He also attempted to shoot her. She filed for divorce, he countersued, and by the time it was over, Richard Sr. was a convicted criminal. "[His] recent troubles are a matter of profound regret to his many friends in this part of the world," lamented a perfume trade journal as the formerly highly respected businessman disappeared from public view.

Whatever Richard Jr.'s reason for turning to drugs, his use of them was not unusual in nineteenth-century New York. As far back as the 1840s, the diarist George Templeton Strong had noted, "opium chewing prevails here extensively, much more so than people think," and in 1869, the misogynist writer George Ellington declared that "women of all classes of society in New York use stimulants and narcotics to a greater or less extent." Hashish and arsenic were favorites before the Civil War, with women drawn to arsenic because it made them "look pale and interesting," but by the late 1860s, morphine, opium, and laudanum were more popular. The city's ladies of the night were especially partial to opium, with heartbreaking results. Following the 1890s raids, Manhattan's jails were filled with hundreds of prostitutes suffering withdrawal symptoms.

Richard Jr. could have purchased his narcotics cheaply and legally, without a prescription, at any drugstore near West Twenty-fourth Street or strolled a few blocks north to the opium dens of West Thirty-third Street. Two were housed at 142 West Thirty-third and another, run by a twenty-three-year-old woman, at 135 West Thirty-third. The street's most opulent resort at 138 West Thirty-third, frequented by society men and known for its luxe yen dows (pipe bowls), yen dongs (opium lamps), and embroidered banquettes, must have tempted Richard, but was probably beyond his means.

After the raid on Mrs. Cummings's house, the police took Richard Jr. to court, where a judge committed him to Bellevue Hospital for an "examination into his sanity." Then he, like his father before him, disappeared from public view. Mentally ill, a drug addict, or both—it hardly mattered. The 1890s were ill-equipped to deal with the mysteries of the human psyche.

*   *   *

Meanwhile, the political reverberations from Parkhurst's testimony were just beginning. On December 4, 1892, Tammany Hall retaliated against the reverend by arresting Charles Gardner, the detective who had led him on his tour, on the trumped-up charge of attempting to extort money from one Lillie Clifton, who ran a house of prostitution on West Fifty-third Street. At the trial, evidence was presented to prove Gardner's low character: he had once run an unsuccessful laundry and an unsuccessful cigar store, divorced his first wife (and perhaps tried to sell her into white slavery), and married a young girl in a ceremony performed not in a proper church but in the Statue of Liberty. Three other madams, a saloonkeeper, and the owner of a bowling alley then took the stand and testified that Gardner had extorted money from them as well.

Gardner was defended by John Goff, a member of Parkhurst's congregation, and William Travers Jerome, a young reformer. They argued that Gardner had been framed in order to discredit Parkhurst. The jury didn't buy it. They found Gardner guilty and sentenced him to two years of hard labor. Gardner appealed and, after spending eleven months in the Tombs, was exonerated. Lillie Clifton had confessed to the New York Supreme Court that she had accused Gardner because a police captain had put her up to it. But it was too late for Gardner. Broken and penniless, he moved to the West, where he was sucked into one drunken brawl after another.

Throughout it all, Parkhurst continued his campaign against vice and corruption. Recognizing the recent police raids for the sham they were, he began hammering away at the need for a state investigation. Some forty civic and religious groups joined him in his fight and finally, in January 1894, the Lexow Committee was appointed.

Headed by the Republican state senator Clarence Lexow, a small man with a high voice and a beard parted down the middle, the committee was charged with investigating the New York Police Department. Assisting them were their lead counsel John Goff, the reformer William Travers Jerome, Reverend Parkhurst, and a team of detectives. The men rounded up and aggressively interviewed 678 witnesses, to eventually compile 10,576 pages of evidence documenting citywide corruption.

One of the commission's main persons of interest was Alexander "Clubber" Williams, now an inspector. Though once again many of the Tenderloin's biggest operators had been spirited out of the city, dozens of smaller entrepreneurs came forward to testify against him. Neighborhood madams said that they had paid Williams $500 (about $15,000 today) for permission to open, followed by monthly payments of $25 to $50 ($750 to $1,500); pool room operators had paid him up to $300 ($9,000) monthly; policy shops, or numbers rackets, $15 ($450) monthly; and larger gambling operations, much more. Streetwalkers, too, had paid for protection, and thieves had routinely handed over a percentage of their gains to the police.

The most damaging testimony against Williams came from his former protégé Max Schmittberger, who had served under him in the Twenty-ninth Precinct for sixteen years. A huge, quiet man, Schmittberger meticulously detailed the payments that had been made to his boss by the district's hundreds of illegal resorts.

Finally, near the end of the hearings, Williams took the stand, dressed in an inspector's uniform with velvet cuffs, brass buttons, and much gold braid. His hair was neatly brushed, his mustache carefully curled, and on the bridge of his nose perched a pair of gold-rimmed glasses, through which he stared defiantly at the committee. He was fifty-five years old.

"I suppose, Captain Williams," lead counsel Goff said, "that there has been no man in the police department in the city of New York charged with so much corruption as you have?"

"I have not heard of it," Williams said.

"You have never heard of being charged with corruption?"

"Sometimes, yes."

"Oh, yes, occasionally. Why you have been charged with everything from taking a needle to an anchor," Goff said, and reminded the inspector that he had once been taken to police court for accepting a diamond ring from one madam, two cows from another, and a gold-topped cane, pistol, velvet vest, slippers, six handkerchiefs, and eighteen pairs of socks from a third.

Williams denied it. He also denied taking a large diamond cross from a "notorious woman in the Tenderloin" to give to his wife or a large diamond ring that he had been seen wearing daily until the hearings began. He had never heard the word *dive* before the committee lawyers used it and had never taken the "pigeons"—meaning under-the-table tips—that Delmonico's had sent regularly to the precinct house to ensure adequate protection during society events. He knew absolutely nothing about bribes or protection money and had no personal knowledge of any corruption anywhere in the department, though of course it could have occurred without his knowledge.

Goff then tackled the issue of Williams's suspicious wealth—an estate in Cos Cob, Connecticut, a townhouse in Manhattan, a half dozen hefty bank accounts totaling over $350,000 (about $10.6 million today), a yacht, and more.

"Are you prepared to swear you never received a dollar outside of your salary while you were captain of the Tenderloin?" Goff asked.

"I received money, but not from the Tenderloin, as you call it," Williams replied and then said that he had earned his wealth through stock returns and real estate investments he had made in Japan as a young man.

Goff produced a document from the Japanese consul saying that foreigners were not allowed to purchase property in Japan. Williams shrugged. "I was there," he said.

"You have become rich upon police corruption," Goff pressed.

"If I was rich, Mr. Goff," Williams said. "I wouldn't be here answering questions."

"You mean to say, that in the face of this mountain of evidence against you both as a neglectful man and as a corrupt man that you are yet in a position to say everyone has lied about you?"

"Yes, sir," the inspector said.

When Williams finished testifying on December 28, 1894, he was embraced by dozens of friends and supporters who shook his hand and congratulated him. In their minds, he had testified brilliantly and would be completely exonerated. They were right. No charges were filed against the inspector. However, five months later, he was forced to resign by the city's new reform police commissioner, Theodore Roosevelt.

"Inspector, you're a slick one," a friend said as Williams handed in his resignation.

"I always was," he replied with a self-satisfied laugh.

* * *

The Lexow Committee investigations led not only to the appointment of Teddy Roosevelt as police commissioner but also to the election of a reform mayor, William Strong, in 1894. A war against vice and corruption began, but it didn't last long. Three years later, Tammany politicians again swept the elections, causing wild celebration in the Tenderloin. "Well, well, reform has gone to hell!" crowds chanted as they blew horns and danced in the streets.

A more long-lasting outcome of the Lexow Committee was the Raines Law, passed by New York State in 1896. Among other things, the law imposed severe new restrictions on saloons, declaring it illegal to sell liquor by the drink on Sundays except with meals in hotels. But the law had the opposite of its desired effect. Any saloon that could quickly patched together ten rooms—thereby becoming a "hotel"—and started serving "sandwiches," some reportedly consisting of a rock between two slices of bread. Prostitutes could now move more easily than ever between saloons and hotels, and by the early twentieth century, the Raines Law hotel had replaced the brothel and boardinghouse as the city's leading institution of prostitution.

And so, the corruption continued . . . to reach a climax in July 1912, when small-time bookmaker Herman Rosenthal, better known as "Beansy," complained to the *New York World* that his gambling dens were being badly damaged by the greed of one Lieutenant Charles Becker and his associates. Two days after the story appeared, Rosenthal was gunned down outside the Hotel Metropole at 147 West Forty-third Street by a group of gangsters from the Lower East Side. Many believed that the gangsters had committed the murder at the behest of Lieutenant Becker. A public uproar ensued.

On July 29, Becker was arrested, to be tried and convicted of first-degree murder that fall (some modern scholars believe that he was wrongly convicted). Presiding as judge over the trial was the relentless John Goff. Becker went to the electric chair in Sing Sing on July 30, 1915—the first American police officer to be put to death for murder. At six feet tall and 215 pounds, he was the largest criminal ever to be executed and had to be shocked three times over nine excruciating minutes. His electrocution was described for many years afterward as "the clumsiest execution in the history of Sing Sing."

The Rosenthal-Becker affair coincided with the demise of the Tenderloin. By that time, men and women were socializing together with greater ease, prostitution had gone underground, and many Raines Law hotels, along with the old concert saloons and dance halls, were being replaced by office-and-loft buildings. A more modern epoch was about to begin. Before it did, though, the era had one more important chapter to play out, a chapter that had begun on the Twenty-third Street block just after the turn of the century.

CHAPTER 16

American Beauty*

One evening in 1901, a strikingly beautiful young woman rang the bell of a nondescript four-story building at 22 West Twenty-fourth Street. Next to her was the delivery entrance for the FAO Schwarz toy company, which occupied the building's ground floor, with its main entrance at 39-41 West Twenty-third Street. To her left blazed the lights of the Fifth Avenue Hotel, laughter splintering out of its dining room windows, and the magical tower of the second Madison Square Garden, sparkling against the night sky. To her right lurked the shadowy stoops and doorways of run-down boarding houses, men in misshapen jackets slinking in and out, and the back of the Eden Musée. A few well-dressed theatergoers may have been lingering outside the Madison Square Theatre at 4 West Twenty-fourth Street, but the show was over and most of the hansoms that had been waiting on the street earlier were gone, off to take their patrons home or to dinner at Rector's or one of the other magnificent new lobster palaces in Longacre Square (now Times Square).

The young woman, Evelyn Nesbit, waited patiently. Sixteen years old, and relatively new to the city, she had just come from the theater herself.

---

* The dialogue and description of many events in this chapter are as cited in Evelyn Nesbit's two memoirs and newspaper accounts of her court testimony.

She was a chorus girl in the hit show *Florodora* at the Casino Theatre—a huge step up from the demeaning department store jobs she and her mother had worked in Philadelphia and the modeling jobs she'd taken in New York after the death of her beloved father. A Pittsburgh lawyer, he had provided the family with a comfortable home, but life had been rough and precarious since his death eight years earlier.

The dingy door opened automatically—as if by magic, Evelyn marveled—to reveal a worn wooden staircase leading up to another door. It, too, opened as if by magic, and Stanford White, the noted architect, appeared, bathed in light. Tall and barrel-chested, with spiky red-gray hair and a big, bristling mustache, he had been quite handsome when he was young, but was forty-seven years old now and going soft around the middle and jowls. To Evelyn, he seemed appallingly large and terribly old.

"Hello!" he boomed out in his deep, resonant voice.

White had grown up in the city, the son of the essayist, critic, and scholar Richard Grant White. White Sr. had never made any money to speak of, but was close friends with many of the era's finest artists and architects, including John La Farge, Louis Comfort Tiffany, Calvert Vaux, and Frederick Olmsted. Those connections had helped Stanford land an apprenticeship with architect Henry Hobson Richardson, and six years later, he'd joined with Charles McKim and William Mead to form what by 1901 was the greatest architectural firm of the Gilded Age—McKim, Mead & White. Among their many Beaux Arts–inspired masterpieces were the Villard Houses on Madison Avenue, Pennsylvania Station (demolished in 1963) on Eighth Avenue, the First Bowery Savings Bank on the Bowery, Washington Arch in Washington Square Park, and the second Madison Square Garden in Madison Square Park, built on the site of the first Madison Square Garden/old railroad depot in 1890.

White's personal life was as dashing and dramatic as his designs. A man of enormous talents and appetites, prone to going without sleep for days when immersed in a project, he was not only an architect but also an accomplished furniture designer, collector of fine paintings and objets d'art, connoisseur of food and drink, tireless club man, patron of the theater, lavish host, loyal friend, and insatiable lover of young women, despite being simultaneously devoted to his wife and son. Ostentatious, egotistical, selfish, and self-indulgent, yet also generous, gentle, charming, and great fun, he seemed to embody both the glamour and the tragedy of the Gilded Age.

"Where are the rest of the people?" Evelyn asked when she reached the top of the stairs.

"Isn't it too bad?" White said. "They have turned us down."

Evelyn felt terribly disappointed. She had been looking forward to another lively evening with Stanny, as White had asked her to call him, and his glittering circle of friends. "Had I better go home?" she asked nervously.

"No, we'll have a party all to ourselves," White said, smiling apologetically. He was an old hand at manipulating young women.

He ushered her into the dining room, hung with floor-to-ceiling red velvet curtains and dimly lit by concealed lights, then a startling innovation. Overstuffed divans laden with oriental cushions hugged walls crowded with medieval tapestries and fine paintings. To one side was an antique Italian dining table set for four.

At the sight of the table, Evelyn hesitated again. Being Stanny's only guest seemed wrong to her. Still, she was starving and happy not to go back to her empty hotel room. She shared it with her mother, but Mrs. Nesbit was in Pittsburgh now and had asked White, whom she had met on numerous occasions and trusted, to look after her daughter while she was gone. Both mother and daughter regarded the architect as a kindly uncle, a role he had taken great care to cultivate, buying Evelyn a piano, arranging for her brother to attend a military academy, and even paying a dentist to fix her teeth.

While Evelyn ate, White did most of the talking. He told her about a meeting he'd had with Thomas Edison, to whom he promised to introduce her one day, and gave her a present, a cast-iron toy bank with the figures of William Tell and his son on top. Delighted, she clapped her hands and asked for a glass of champagne, which she had tasted for the first time at Stanny's just a few months before. He gave it to her and then, to her surprise, allowed her to sneak another. Usually, he allowed her only one glass, saying that nice girls didn't drink more.

When Evelyn was finished eating, she stood up and reached for the flowing red cape that White had given her. She was ready to go home.

"Stay," he pleaded in a soft, alluring voice that she was too young and inexperienced to interpret. She felt flattered by his attention and safe in his company. He took the cape from her shoulders. "There's a lot in this house you have never seen, and it will amuse you."

Evelyn's curiosity was piqued. Stanny was so full of surprises. On her very first visit to West Twenty-fourth Street, with a singer from *Florodora*, he'd taken the two young women to his apartment's top floor, also hung with floor-to-ceiling curtains and lit by concealed lights. Only one object had stood out in the darkness: a gorgeous red velvet swing, set high in the room near a tin ceiling. At White's invitation, Evelyn had hoisted herself up onto the swing and allowed him to push her, again and again, as she tried to pierce a Japanese parasol at the other end of the room with her foot. Each time she succeeded, Stanny clapped and shouted, beaming with pleasure, and replaced the torn parasol with another.

Perhaps he had other equally amusing games in other upstairs rooms, she thought.

White led the teenager up a tiny flight of stairs she had never noticed before and into a small back room filled with more medieval tapestries and fine paintings. A collection of dramatically lit antiques was displayed, while to one side stretched a voluptuous moss-green couch. But what impressed Evelyn the most were the room's mirrors, covering every inch of the ceiling, walls, and floor. She twirled about, thrilled to see her reflection at every turn, and had another glass of champagne, laughing at the way the bubbles tickled her nose.

White pushed aside one of the tapestry hangings to reveal an even smaller room, this one deep purple and holding an enormous four-poster bed. Mirrors shone darkly in the bed's headboard and the dome of its canopy, while all around its top were tiny hidden electric lights. One touch of a button and the lights glowed amber; another touch and they glowed rose; a third touch and they glowed blue. Evelyn was mesmerized. The lights reminded her of scenes in fairy tales, of nymphs' palaces under the sea.

Feeling light-headed, she sat down tentatively on the bed, and White poured her another glass of champagne. It tasted bitter, she complained after a sip, but White encouraged her to drink up and she did. A minute went by and then, as Evelyn described it years later, "There began a buzzing and a drumming, a persistent thump—thump—thumping in my ears. I felt dizzy and sick, and the objects in the room became blurred and indistinct . . . The sound of his voice came to me as of one speaking from a great distance—Then all went black."

Evelyn may have been drugged—a possibility she later dismissed—or she may just have had too much to drink too fast. Either way, the result was the same. She awoke to find herself lying on the enormous bed with only "an abbreviated pink undergarment" covering her breasts, White naked beside her. Her mind fuzzy, she didn't immediately understand what had happened, but instinctively knew that "it was horrible—horrible" and screamed.

"For God's sake, don't," White said. He quickly threw on a red satin robe and gave her a purple-and-yellow kimono. Then she noticed a red streak on her inner thigh and began to cry.

"Don't cry, Kittens," he said, leaning over her. "Don't. Please don't. It's all over. Now you belong to me."

He took her on his knee, tousled her hair, kissed and tried to soothe her, but she couldn't stop trembling. Dressing hastily, she returned to her hotel room, where, unable to sleep, she stayed awake all night, staring out the window. She felt empty and confused. No one had prepared her for sex. "I went . . . that night a child with no knowledge of the big and stunning facts of life," she later said. And Stanny . . . who was he? She had trusted him, but he had betrayed her; "He was a strange being to me; an aspect of life [had been] revealed in a flash and chang[ed] all my perspectives."

When White came to see her the next day, he found her still sitting by the window of her hotel room. Kneeling at her feet, he kissed the hem of her dressing gown and begged for forgiveness. She remained motionless and silent, cramped and shivering.

"Why won't you look at me, child?" he asked.

"Because I can't."

He caressed her, telling her not to worry, that everyone did such things, all his friends, and all their mutual acquaintances. Everyone was bad, he said, everybody was evil.

"Everyone?" she asked, glancing at him despite herself.

"Yes," he said, smiling, and began to rattle off names and tell stories. Then he said that even though everyone did such things, no one ever talked about it. Talking about it was an unforgivable sin and she must keep silent. "A girl must never talk; she must just keep things locked up in her bosom and confide in nobody," he said.

Too young and vulnerable to question anyone in authority, let alone a powerful figure like Stanford White, Evelyn sat still, "dazed and bewildered as all the fair fabrics of [her] faith crumbled in the dust." Stanny was so much older and wiser and more experienced than she, what he said must be true, she thought. She was too overcome with embarrassment and shame to even consider saying anything anyway; the #MeToo movement was still over a century away.

Evelyn was also accustomed to obeying and being exploited by men. She had been supporting her family by posing as a model for meager fees for years. Her delicate, dark beauty, so different from the voluptuous blond bombshells of the day, had entranced the artists who'd met her, from the painter Frederick Stuart Church to the illustrator Charles Dana Gibson, and her photographs had appeared in all the New York City papers. For most of her life, men had been instructing her how to pose, how to move, when to speak.

Over the next few days, Evelyn played the scene of her rape over and over in her mind. She didn't hate Stanny or feel repulsed by him. She just felt numb. She had already lost her father, her home, and her childhood, and now she had lost her trust in the one man whom she'd thought embodied all that was good in the world.

With no one to talk to, least of all her mother, who was remote and seemingly unable to cope with the world, Evelyn then deliberately decided to accept what had happened and move on. Stanny might be a monster, but he was a kind monster, "a benevolent vampire," who offered her companionship, luxury, and an entrée into wondrous worlds. Despite what he had done to her, and without anyone to tell her otherwise, she regarded him as thoughtful and kind. Decades later, she would write: "Stanford White was a great man. That is how I see him after all these years. That he did me a wrong, that from certain moral standards he was perverse and decadent, does not blind my judgment . . . My remembrance of him is a sad but appreciative one."

During the months that followed, Evelyn continued to see White frequently. Sometimes she visited him at his West Twenty-fourth Street love nest, where he made her laugh so hard her ribs hurt and talked to her about books, music, and art—she loved to read and had once dreamed of going to Vassar. Then they might have sex on a lion-skin rug that lay before a roaring fire or ascend the tiny stairs to the mirrored room and four-poster bed. Afterward, Evelyn, still naked or nearly so, would climb onto the red velvet swing and soar through the air, shadows licking her limbs as White watched from below.

Other times Evelyn would visit White in his apartment atop Madison Square Garden, a dazzling, joyful terra-cotta affair with pedestrian arcades below and a soaring Moorish tower above. Much more elegant and refined than the first Madison Square Garden, it included a main arena that could seat fourteen thousand, theater, concert hall, restaurants, shops, and rooftop garden where audiences could eat and drink while watching shows. The tower led to an observation platform 289 feet above ground and heart-stopping views of the city. Higher still was a two-person perch, and above that, *Diana*, a gilded thirteen-foot-high weathervane of the goddess of the hunt designed by the sculptor Augustus Saint-Gaudens, one of White's closest friends. Illuminated by more than one thousand incandescent lightbulbs at night, Diana was naked—an outrage! protested many.

When Evelyn arrived at White's tower apartment, she usually found it filled with people milling about sumptuous rooms furnished with the architect's trademarks: Tiffany sconces, gilt mirrors, velvet couches, paintings, tapestries, and oriental rugs. The actors Ethel and Lionel Barrymore might be there, or the singer-actress Lillian Russell and her paramour Diamond Jim Brady, or the photographer Rudolf Eickemeyer, who at White's direction had taken a suggestive and widely circulated picture of

Evelyn reclining in a kimono on a bearskin rug. White's apartment was the meeting place of the cultural avant-garde.

Gradually, though, complications arose between Evelyn and Stanny. To her great shock, Evelyn discovered that the architect had other young women friends on whom he lavished attention and was, in his way, loyal to his wife and son, whom he often visited on Long Island or stayed with at the White mansion on Gramercy Park when they were in town.

She started entertaining other suitors, including Harry Thaw, a wealthy thirty-one-year-old playboy whose father had made a fortune in the Pittsburgh coal and railroad business. Thin-lipped and bespectacled, Thaw had been expelled from three universities, but with a monthly allowance of $8,000 (about $250,000 today), saw no need to pursue his education further or join the family business. He preferred to spend his time drinking and playing cards, visiting houses of prostitution, and traveling to Europe. He was also prone to severe temper tantrums, insomnia, fits of incoherent babbling, and violent sadistic acts that his mother hushed up by bribing his victims with money.

Evelyn knew little of Thaw's darker side when he began courting her in 1902, after watching her perform more than forty times in her new role in *The Wild Rose*. He sent her flowers and love letters every day, and though she disliked him at first, she grew to regard him as a friend. He was always thoughtful and courteous, and after a few months, he invited her and her mother on a luxurious, all-expenses-paid trip to Europe. They accepted.

Thaw was on his best behavior at first. In London he arranged for Evelyn and her mother to stay in one hotel while he stayed in another, for propriety's sake. But then one afternoon while the ladies were having tea at Harrods, he reportedly lured a bellboy into his room, dragged him into the bathroom, made him undress in the bathtub, and beat him with a riding whip. Thaw denied these charges, but after a doctor and lawyer were called in, he paid $5,000 (about $156,000 today) to "square the matter."

Unaware of the details of the incident, Evelyn believed Thaw when he told her that it had been greatly exaggerated, and the party traveled onward, adhering to a grueling nonstop itinerary that Thaw insisted on. Evelyn and her mother began to quarrel until finally Mrs. Nesbit decided to go home.

Thaw and Evelyn then proceeded to Paris, where Thaw entered her suite one evening and asked her to marry him.

He had already proposed to her several times before, but she had always successfully sidestepped the question. This time, though, she later wrote, "there was no fending him off with excuses, with reasons or with explanation as to why marriage was not desirable." Gripping the arms of her chair until her knuckles turned white, she could feel herself being dragged "down and down into a dark rabbit hole."

"I must know the truth," Thaw said, thumping his fist on the back of her chair. He began pacing around the room and babbling under his breath.

Feeling frightened and very alone in a foreign city where she knew no one, Evelyn whispered, "I cannot marry you."

"Why not?"

"Because—" She started shaking.

Thaw placed his hands on her shoulders and stared straight into her eyes. "Is it because of Stanford White?" he asked. Like many in their circle, he had long suspected her involvement with the architect, whom he had despised for years for reasons that predated Evelyn. He suspected White of blackballing him from New York's elite clubs and was probably jealous of his success, both professional and sexual.

After years of keeping silent, Evelyn finally lost her resolve and told Thaw everything. He listened nervously as she talked, his body tense, his face twisted in disgust, and when she described the rape, he pawed at his cheeks and sobbed hysterically, astonishing her with his excessive emotion.

"The beast! The filthy beast!" he shouted. "A sixteen-year-old girl! Damn him, damn him, damn him to hell!"

Evelyn tried to calm him down, but he wouldn't listen and pressed her to tell him every last detail she could remember. As she spoke, he stroked her hand in sympathy, saying that he didn't care what had happened, it wasn't her fault, he loved her still.

The couple continued their travels, touring France, Holland, and Germany, with Thaw treating Evelyn with respect and courtesy. They kept separate rooms, but were without a chaperone—considered improper at the time.

One day they came to the Schloss Katzenstein in Austria, a grim, isolated Gothic castle perched on a steep slope overlooking a valley. Thaw had rented it for their exclusive use for three weeks. They spent their first week relaxing, taking walks in the woods, and dining in an exquisite rose garden, tended to by only a caretaker and his wife.

Then one night, Thaw dismissed the caretaker and his wife early. Tired after a long day, Evelyn went to bed right after dinner and fell into a deep sleep. About fifteen minutes later, the lock in her door turned, a shaft of light shot across the room, and a seething, naked, glassy-eyed Thaw leapt in. He slashed her across the legs with a riding crop, ripped off her night-gown, whipped and punched her, and threw her on her back and raped her. When he was done, he screamed and shouted at her about sin, inde-cency, and White, left the room, and locked the door. Sobbing, she remained upright, not wanting her blood to dry against the sheets, and wondering—incredibly—if this was the punishment she deserved for having had sex with White.

Five minutes later, Thaw was back, dressed in his pajamas. Evelyn braced herself, but he was composed and sympathetic, and carried a glass of brandy in his hand.

"Drink this," he said.

"Why, why have you done this awful thing to me?" she wept.

"I *had* to do it."

"But why? Why?"

"You are too impudent. You are entirely too impudent! I had to punish you."

Evelyn remained Thaw's prisoner for the next two weeks, but when they left the castle, he acted as if nothing had happened. Sunny and energetic, he barely seemed to remember what he had done, and they resumed their travels. Not until weeks later did they finally return to New York. White welcomed Evelyn back warmly, but was distracted and consumed with work and financial worries. His generosity and profligate habits had plunged him deeply into debt, and he had recently lost $300,000 (about $9,300,000 today) in the stock market. His health was also in decline. He was suffering from constant colds, bladder infections, and bowel trouble, which would later develop into incipient tuberculosis, degeneration of the liver, and Bright's disease. Evelyn realized once and for all that they could have no future together.

Months passed, with Evelyn changing addresses frequently to hide from Thaw. Inevitably, though, his private detectives found her, and he began showing up at her door, seemingly contrite and sane. He bombarded her with notes, telegrams, and flowers, and begged for her forgiveness, saying that, overwhelmed by his hatred of White, he had had a temporary fit and it would never happen again. A year went by until finally, worn down by Thaw's pleading and worried about money, Evelyn gave in. Harry could be sweet, she told herself. The two were wed on April 5, 1905. Thaw's forbidding mother disapproved of the marriage, but agreed to it after Evelyn promised to give up the theater and never ever talk about her past.

The newlyweds moved into the Thaw family mansion in Pittsburgh, a dour place dominated by the older Mrs. Thaw. Evelyn's gay life of attending the theater, dining out, and meeting interesting people was over, replaced by a dull round of church events, family dinners, and trite conversations. Thaw took on the role of pious son and husband. Evelyn grew increasingly unhappy.

* * *

Fourteen months after their wedding, on June 25, 1906, Evelyn and Thaw were back in New York, stopping for a few days before a planned trip to Europe. It was an extraordinarily hot day, and Evelyn had already taken two cold baths before dressing to go out in the evening. They were going to dinner and a show—what show, she didn't know. Thaw always made all the arrangements.

Slipping into a white summer satin gown with thirty pearl buttons down the back, she went to meet her husband at a nearby bar. He was wearing a black tuxedo, white straw boater, and long black overcoat—incongruous in the heat. Two of his male friends joined them, and they traveled downtown to Café Martin, housed in the former Delmonico's on the edge of Madison Square. Directly across from them towered Madison Square

Garden, the sight of which must have sent a wave of sadness through Evelyn, still only twenty-one years old.

"What play are we seeing?" she asked her husband when they had finished eating. *Mamzelle Champagne*, he replied. Evelyn blanched. *Mamzelle Champagne* was a new musical opening that night in the garden's rooftop theater. Usually, Thaw refused to set foot in any building even remotely connected with White. She felt light-headed with the heat, the wine from the meal, and a sense of foreboding.

The foursome crossed the square, rode the elevator up to the rooftop theater, and took seats at their table, halfway to the back. Above them sparkled the illuminated tower with *Diana* revolving on top.

The show started and limped along—it was not going to be a hit. An impatient audience began to stir, whisper, and cough. Thaw, still dressed in his long overcoat, twitched and fiddled, and kept getting up from their table.

Near the end of the show, at around eleven P.M., White came in and headed to his usual spot near the stage. He had planned to be in Philadelphia that evening, but had stayed in New York to have dinner with his son. Evelyn looked around for Thaw, but he was nowhere in sight, and when he did reappear, she wasn't sure if he had seen White or not.

Onstage, the chorus girls started singing "I Challenge You to Love," about two men dueling over the love of a woman. Evelyn glanced nervously at her husband, who suddenly stood up again, looking pale and distraught. She suggested they leave. Their friends agreed—the show was awful—and they headed toward the elevator. Halfway there, Evelyn noticed that Thaw was no longer with them. Another song, "I Could Love a Million Girls," began. She stood on her toes, scanning the crowd, but couldn't see her husband anywhere.

A shot rang out. Evelyn froze and opened her mouth in a silent scream. In her mind's eye she saw everything: Harry in his long black coat pulling out a pistol, Stanny bleeding profusely and slipping to the floor. Two more shots rang out. The music faltered and stopped.

Thaw raised his pistol triumphantly in the air and emptied its unused shells. He had stood less than two feet away from White and pumped three bullets into him, two into his head. Stanford White, age fifty-two, was dead.

A fireman attending the show nervously approached Thaw and asked him to surrender his weapon. He did so with an air of relief and was escorted to the elevator. "Oh, Harry, what have you done?" Evelyn cried as he walked by. He smiled, kissed her on the cheek, and replied, "It's all right, dear. I probably saved your life."

The policeman took Thaw to the Twenty-ninth precinct house in the old Tenderloin, and from there he was transferred downtown to the Tombs. A newspaper photograph taken of him a week or so later showed him sitting in his cell at a cloth-covered table, dining on a catered meal from Delmonico's. In the background was a brass bed. No ordinary accommodations for a millionaire such as he! He showed no remorse and claimed to hear the heavenly voices of young girls calling to him, approving of his deed. He also believed that he would be acquitted. "No jury will convict me of any crime when they hear the truth," he said. "I killed White because he ruined my wife. I am not crazy."

That outlook may seem delusional today, but was not so in the early 1900s, when many believed that a husband could legitimately kill a man who "dishonored" his wife, then often regarded as the property of her husband. Thaw was receiving hundreds of letters daily applauding him for the murder, while White was being vilified by the press, labeled everything from a "fiend" to "a sybarite of debauchery." A headline in *Vanity Fair* on July 13, 1906, read: STANFORD WHITE, VOLUPTUARY AND PERVERT, DIES THE DEATH OF A DOG.

Thaw's first lawyer, Lewis Delafield, argued adamantly with his client: the only way he could avoid the electric chair, he told Thaw, was if he pleaded insanity. Thaw refused, labeled Delafield a traitor for even suggesting such a thing, and fired him. His mother then hired a team of twelve alienists (psychiatrists), at the cost of $500,000 (about $15 million today), to prove that her son had been seized with a "brainstorm" (in effect, a brief bout of temporary insanity). That new term soon morphed into another new one, "dementia Americana," meaning a supposed form of temporary insanity that comes over a man when he believes that his home or family has been violated.

Thaw's trial began on January 23, 1907, and lasted three months, with thousands of spectators milling around the courthouse every day. Some even erected makeshift tents in the streets where they slept at night so as not to miss a single moment.

Shortly after the trial began, the Thaw family hired a new attorney, Delphin Delmas of San Francisco, famous for having never lost a case. With the insanity plea off the table, Delmas's plan was to paint such a dark picture of Stanford White that the jury would forgive Thaw for the murder. The best witness for the defense would therefore be the woman he'd deflowered, Evelyn Nesbit.

When Evelyn heard the plan, she felt sick to her stomach at the thought of bearing witness against White. But Delmas kept at her. The only way she could save her husband from the electric chair, he said, was if she took the stand and described everything that had happened in clear, convincing detail.

"Everything . . ." she whispered as she took in what he was saying. "But it is an unthinkable thing that I must stand up in open court and tell . . ."

"Nothing less will serve. Your husband's life is in the balance. After all, what does it matter?"

What does it matter? What does it matter? Evelyn thought, trembling, as she stared out the window of the hotel room where she was staying during the trial. To stand up in court and tell the world the secrets that she'd kept hidden for years?

Delmas waited, his hand in his vest pocket. Nearby sat Mrs. Thaw, dressed entirely in black.

Evelyn felt she had no choice. She didn't want Harry to die.

Throughout the trial, Evelyn appeared in court every day, dressed in subdued colors. The first time she took the stand, in a plain navy-blue suit with a white Peter Pan collar and a broad-brimmed hat, a palpable silence fell over the court, followed by a murmur as she removed her veil and revealed her still almost childlike beauty. On the inside, she was panicking, but on the outside, she appeared collected and spoke in a simple, unaffected manner about her relationship with White—the dinner parties, the champagne, the red velvet swing, the sex. She had promised herself she wouldn't cry, but broke down halfway through—"I can't go on! I can't! I can't!" she cried. A doctor rushed up with restoratives, the courtroom windows were opened, and Evelyn continued. She left the witness box deathly pale, barely able to stand, as Thaw bawled and thrashed to and fro in his chair.

On another day, during cross-examination, District Attorney William Jerome—the same man who had aided Reverend Parkhurst during his investigations—asked Evelyn if she knew that having sex with a married man was wrong. She admitted that she did and that she bore some "hostility against [White]" for certain things he had done. But then she added that except for having "a strong personality," White "had been a very grand man. He was very good to me, and very kind." Tears flowed down her face as she spoke. Some onlookers gasped in surprise.

Later in life, Evelyn would say: "The world didn't see what I remembered best, myself on the stand trying to save a husband I didn't love from going to the chair for killing a man I did love."

The trial resulted in a hung jury: seven jurors voted guilty, and five, not guilty by reason of insanity. Outraged, Thaw flew into a fit of crying and rage.

A second trial began a year later. Much less sensational, it lasted less than a month. The verdict this time: not guilty by reason of insanity. Thaw was sentenced to incarceration for life at the Matteawan State Hospital for the Criminally Insane in Fishkill, New York, where his great wealth again allowed him to live in comfort. In comfort, but not free. He escaped to Canada in 1913, probably with the help of his mother, and three years later, was arrested in California for horsewhipping and sexually assaulting a nineteen-year-old male student. Found not guilty by reason of insanity again, he was committed to a tighter security hospital near Philadelphia, where he remained until 1924, when he was released, probably again thanks to his mother. He purchased a home in rural Virginia, where he made friends with his neighbors, joined the volunteer fire department, and became widely regarded as an eccentric but harmless man. He died of a heart attack on February 22, 1947, at age seventy-six.

* * *

The Thaw family lavished Evelyn with praise throughout both trials—she was their "brave little Nesbit," their "most courageous girl"—and paid her basic expenses. Afterward, though, they cut her off completely. Cruel and vindictive, they saw her as little more than an insect who had invaded their plush, insulated world. She deserved to be crushed.

Evelyn went to visit Thaw often at the Matteawan State Hospital at first. "I was sorry for him, and pity retains love even as it creates it," she wrote. But he could still be brutal toward her and finally she gave up. They divorced in 1915.

Her reputation ruined, Evelyn went back to work as a performer and dancer, landing mostly minor roles. She had a son, Russell, whom she claimed was Thaw's, conceived during a conjugal visit at the hospital. He denied it. She married again, to the dancer Jack Clifford, who was good to Russell, but the White-Thaw scandal weighed heavily on their marriage and they divorced. She descended into drug and alcohol abuse and tried to commit suicide several times, once by swallowing Lysol. The press gleefully reported her many missteps—drunken brawls, arrests, evictions, unpaid bills, suspected abortions—and a largely unsympathetic public devoured every word. Thaw came to see her on various occasions, and there was some talk of them getting back together, but it never happened, and when he died, he left her only $10,000 out of his $1 million (about $12 million today) estate, the same amount he left a coffee shop waitress he barely knew.

Several times, Evelyn tried to pull herself together by opening her own business. In 1921 she set up a one-hundred-seat tearoom on West Fifty-second street, just off Broadway, marked by a sign that read EVELYN NESBIT's SPECIALTY SHOP. On the menu was deep-dish apple pie that she baked herself. Later, she established Club Nesbit in Atlantic City. Both ventures failed. In a still puritanical age, most people regarded her as nothing more than a curiosity and cautionary tale about what happened to "wayward" girls. She was branded an outcast, indelibly sullied by the events of her youth, no matter that predatory males had been their root cause.

Finally, when Evelyn was in her sixties, her life took a turn for the better. She moved to California to be near her son, now a pilot, and grandchildren, and took a job teaching ceramics and sculpture at a community college; she was an artist of some talent. Times changed, and in 1954, she was hired as a consultant for the movie *The Girl in the Red Velvet Swing*, starring Joan Collins and Ray Milland, for which she was paid $50,000 (about $486,000 today). The film treated her character sympathetically, and she enjoyed a rare spate of favorable publicity. She died in California on January 17, 1967, at age eighty-two.

* * *

The Thaw-Nesbit-White case scandalized and titillated the nation. It had all the elements of a dime-store novel: a talented architect, a beautiful woman, a wealthy maniac, rape, sex, fame, murder. Yet from today's perspective, the whole affair seems not so much scandalous as tragic.

Like others connected with the Twenty-third Street block, Stanford White and Harry Thaw were one thing on the outside, something else within. As beguiling as the Fifth Avenue Hotel itself, White was so immensely talented, dynamic, and gregarious that few suspected he had a darker side. Thaw couldn't hide his id as well, but when it was under control, he, too, seemed like the most gentlemanly of gentlemen.

Evelyn was a young, naive girl caught between two powerful men who preyed on her beauty and poverty in an era when women had few options. Only sixteen years old when she met White, she had no one to talk to or advise her as the wealthy men swooped in, showering her with gifts and promising her the stars.

* * *

The contents of the White mansion on Gramercy Park went up for auction on April 5, 1907, with everything except the mantelpieces for sale. White's family had to settle his immense debts. Society treated the ghoulish occasion as a grand event and poured in to survey the pickings: carved Italian furniture, Renaissance pillars, Chinese vases, Flemish tapestries, a Venetian chest, an early German harp, leopard-skin rugs, Mongolian tiger rugs, an Apache Indian flute, and much, much more. The Whitneys, the Goelets, Mrs. Cooper Hewitt, Mr. David Belasco, and representatives from the Metropolitan Museum of Art were all there, the women wearing hats two feet in diameter, their feathers tickling noses. The house auction lasted two days and was followed by a second auction, this one focused exclusively on White's hundreds of paintings, many by the likes of William

Chase, Albert Ryder, Childe Hassam, and Gustave Courbet. What happened to the contents of White's West Twenty-fourth Street hideaway is unclear, but it seems likely that its fine paintings, tapestries, and objets d'art were included in the sales. The red velvet swing disappeared.

*   *   *

One year after the Stanford White murder, the Fifth Avenue Hotel closed, a victim of changing times and Manhattan's relentless move uptown. On that parting day, April 4, 1908, the Amen Corner hosted its last meeting, patrons spent a reported $7,000 (about $199,000 today) in drinks at the bar, and throngs of men and women who had once stayed at the hotel came to visit it one last time. "All day long and far into the night its wide, spacious main corridor was literally black with people," reported the *New York Times*. Among them were an elderly woman and a middle-aged man, who asked to see Room 363. The man had been born in that room—the first, but not the last, child born in the hotel. Just before midnight, newspapermen and politicians gathered to sing "We're Here Because," and then the lights went out. The throng of mourners moved out the door, leaving empty corridors behind.

Four days later, the hotel's furnishings and fittings were auctioned off. Most of the two thousand bidders were women, and most were far less aristocratic—and much fatter—than those who had attended White's auctions, if the *New York Times* reporter is to be believed: "'Fat?' said one of the auctioneer's men, who had to push through the crowd now and then, 'If half of those women weigh 100, they weigh 250.'" The women followed the auctioneer about from room to room, snatching up beds, nightstands, dressers, and sofas, while the male shoppers were most interested in the barroom's chairs and accoutrements. The ball atop the hotel's flagpole was sold, as was the front office's thermometer, purchased by the ex-mayor of Norwich, Connecticut, for seven dollars. "I want it as a souvenir of the hot and the cold times I had here in this old hotel for past thirty years," he said.

One item that was not auctioned off, to the disappointment of many, was a small supply of brandy, vintage 1799, which the hotel proprietor Elmer Darling, the man once in charge of buying food for the kitchens, had decided to keep for himself. The brandy had been originally laid "in the wood" at the Revere House in Boston and brought to the hotel by Paran Stevens.

Shortly thereafter, the Fifth Avenue Hotel was demolished, to be replaced by the still-standing neoclassical Fifth Avenue Building, now known as 200 Fifth Avenue. Designed by Robert Maynicke and Julius Franke for the Eno family, who still owned the property, it would rise fourteen stories, span over two hundred feet on each side, be devoted entirely to offices, and go up with breathtaking speed, opening for business just thirteen months after demolition began. The "wrecking of the old hotel will be handled without respect for old traditions and without much regard for salvage," reported the *New York Times* on April 12, 1908.

The twentieth century had begun.

CHAPTER 17

Modern Times

Among the many real estate properties that Amos Eno had left to his heirs when he died in 1898 was the northern section of a triangular slice of land just south of Twenty-third Street, where Fifth Avenue crosses Broadway. Some New Yorkers referred to the triangular slice as the "cowcatcher," perhaps because cows had meandered there during the days when Madison Square was used for grazing, or because its shape resembled that of the iron piece at the front of locomotives designed to catch stray steer. Others called it the "flatiron" because of its resemblance to the appliance used to press clothes.

Eno had purchased the 3,200-square-foot property in 1857, just before buying the Fifth Avenue Hotel site, for $25,000 (about $750,000 today), filled it with four three-story buildings, and leased them out to various concerns, reaping enormous profits. Among his tenants over the years were a combination chiropodist and manicurist shop called "the Fountain of Youth," a hosiery shop, a photographer's studio, a dentist offering "painless treatment," and the Erie Railroad ticket office. The southern and larger section of the triangle belonged to the Hickson Fields family, who, at the time of Eno's death, was leasing it to the Cumberland, a seven-story apartment building.

The Cumberland's huge exposed northern wall faced Madison Square and companies rented it for advertisements, which were visible for blocks around: Benson's Porous Plaster, Spencer's Steel Pens, Sapolio's Tonic. Especially spectacular was a giant electric sign erected in 1892 that blinked six lines in succession in letters three to six feet tall: SWEPT BY OCEAN BREEZES / ORIENTAL HOTEL / MANHATTAN HOTEL / SOUSAS BAND / PAINS FIREWORKS / HAGENBECK. The first of its kind in the city, the sign became a sightseeing attraction, forerunner of the Times Square signs yet to come.

Noticing the success of the Cumberland's advertising, Eno erected a screen of his own atop the Erie Railroad ticket office and rented it out for "magic lantern" (early slide projector) and stereopticon shows. The entertainments featured a mix of scenic pictures interspersed with ads and drew large crowds, who often lingered in Madison Square after their workdays were done. The *New York Times* and *New York Herald* took note and began using the screen for news bulletins that ran from early evening until midnight. On election nights in the 1890s, tens of thousands of spectators gathered in Madison Square to await the election returns, flashed across the screen, while Republican Party officials did the same from the Fifth Avenue Hotel and Democratic Party officials watched from the Hoffman House at Twenty-fourth Street and Broadway.

Eno's screen made him even richer than he already was. From the 1870s on, offers to buy his oddly shaped lot came pouring in, but he always turned them down. His triangle would be worth more than a million dollars before he died, he predicted, and he wasn't far off the mark.

* * *

After Eno's death, his heirs liquidated all his properties to settle his estate. His youngest son, William Phelps Eno, bought his father's triangular lot for $690,000 (about $21 million today), to sell it three weeks later to Samuel Newhouse, the "copper king," for $801,000 ($25 million). In 1901 the lot was sold again, along with the lower portion of the triangle still owned by the Hickson Fields family, to the Fuller Company for a total of $1,515,000 ($47 million today), and the building of the first skyscraper north of Union Square began.

The architects were Daniel Burnham, famed worldwide for designing the dazzling 1893 Chicago World's Columbian Exposition, and Frederick Dinkelberg, who had already executed at least one skyscraper in southern Manhattan. Dinkelberg worked for Burnham's firm, and it was he who was the primary designer of what soon became known as the Flatiron Building.

The edifice was to be unlike anything anyone had ever seen before: a narrow, V-shaped, twenty-story steel skeleton sheathed with terra-cotta brick and topped with an ornate cornice. The steel skeleton would allow for the walls at the base of the building to be no thicker than the walls at the top, and the terra-cotta was intricately designed with classical and Beaux Arts motifs. Terra-cotta was fireproof and lighter and cheaper than masonry, making it a perfect building material for skyscrapers.

Before construction could begin, however, all tenants of the block had to be gone. And therein lay a problem. One occupant of the Cumberland, Colonel Winfield Scott Proskey of the National Guard, refused to leave until his lease ran out. The Fuller Company turned off his gas and water, but he shrugged, bought a small gas tank, and hauled his water up in buckets through his window. The company demolished the building's staircase, but he bought a ladder. He was offered $5,000 (about $156,000 today), but he said he was not interested in money. "This is a question of personal *honah*," he said in his native Florida drawl. Weeks passed with no solution in sight as papers across the country carried the story of the plucky David holding out against the big business Goliath. Then lawyers discovered that the colonel had filed for bankruptcy three months before. He owed creditors nearly $20,000 ($623,000). His lease was purchased for an undisclosed sum, and he moved across the street to the Fifth Avenue Hotel, by then in its final stage, where he would live for the next two years. The construction of the Flatiron could finally begin.

Late in the following month, June 1901, a brutal heat wave descended on the city. New Yorkers flooded into Madison Square Park, seeking relief. But the benches that had once stood beneath its shady trees had been moved out into the sun. In their place beckoned elegant cane-bottomed rocking chairs, which cost five cents to sit on. The chairs had been introduced into the park the previous April by Oscar Spate, an Englishman, with the blessing of the city's park commissioner. Paying for park chairs was customary in London and Paris, Spate had told the commissioner, and could help prevent derelicts from lounging about in the park all day.

That July 1 Abraham Cohen, a student at the nearby College for Dentistry, collapsed onto one of the chairs, drenched in sweat. It was one of the hottest days yet; sixty-six people would die of the heat before the day was over. A park attendant appeared and asked Cohen for five cents. Cohen refused to pay and was arrested. The newspapers picked up the story, and the public exploded with fury. Since when were park chairs reserved for the well-to-do? Dozens upon dozens of people headed to Madison Square, deliberately sat down on the chairs, and refused to pay or move, saying it was a free country. Then on July 6 a huge mob of men and boys attacked a new attendant named Thomas Tully as he tried to collect the five-cent fee. "Lynch him! Kill him!" they cried as they punched him and hit him with brickbats. Panting and bleeding, Tully ran across the park and into the Fifth Avenue Hotel, the mob at his heels. The head porter saw him coming and, with the help of two assistants, slammed the lobby doors shut as soon as he had passed safely inside.

Five days later, the city's park commissioner called a press conference. He was canceling Spate's contract. That afternoon and evening, thousands of people gathered in Madison Square Park to celebrate with speeches, music, and fireworks.

*   *   *

The building of the Flatiron started in earnest in January 1902, to proceed at a mind-boggling pace. With its steel beams already precut and predrilled, the frame went up at the rate of a floor a week, generating enormous excitement. People traveling by in streetcars craned their necks to catch a glimpse of the rising skeleton, while pedestrians milled about in front of the Fifth Avenue Hotel, gawking at each new development. The old hostelry now seemed hopelessly dark and outmoded; it was the new Flatiron that seemed to embody the light, optimism, and commercial spirit that had always infused the Fifth Avenue side of the block.

At 307 feet and 22 stories high, the Flatiron was built in the shape of a right triangle, with the right angle at the corner of Fifth Avenue and

Twenty-second Street. The building's two longest sides met in a curved acute angle just south of Twenty-third Street, where an odd, one-story glass protrusion popularly known as the cowcatcher was later built. The edifice looked different from every angle. From the north, it appeared angular and bold; from the east, flat and two-dimensional; from close up, classical and commanding in its terra-cotta designs.

After the Flatiron opened for business, some decried it—"A stingy piece of pie," reported the *New York Tribune*—but many loved it, and it quickly became a symbol of the new skyscraper era. Wrote Alfred Stieglitz, who immortalized the Flatiron in a series of photographs in 1903: "It looked, from where I stood, as if it were moving toward me like the bow of a monster ocean steamer, a picture of the new America which was in the making."

* * *

Six years after the Flatiron was completed, the Fifth Avenue Building replaced the Fifth Avenue Hotel. At the insistence of the Eno family, the new edifice was built in the shape of the old and retained some of its elements. The architects Maynicke & Franke reconstructed the hotel's broad marble corridors, included an interior court with skylights, and designed an Oak Room bar with paneling taken from the hotel. In addition, the firm commissioned a new version of the hotel's old sidewalk clock. Mounted on a fluted Ionic column fifteen feet tall, the gilded cast-iron masterpiece still stands—an ornate architectural gem listed on the National Register of Historic Places. "Fifth Avenue Building" read the words inside its large, round face, marked around its edges with Roman numerals.

Among the first to move into the Fifth Avenue Building were, appropriately enough, stock exchange firms: Miller & Co.; Newburger, Henderson & Loeb; Edey, Field & Sloan. Menswear companies such as John A. Salve & Sons (gloves) and Hanan & Son (shoes) also moved in, along with Bausch & Lomb Optical, M. Guggenheim (jewelry importers), E. Greenfield & Sons (chocolates), Aetna Life Insurance, and New England Mutual Life Insurance, one of whose agents went mysteriously missing on the afternoon of May 28, 1914. He had gone out to lunch at one P.M. as usual and stopped by a Madison Avenue hat store, where he bought a cap and left behind the Panama hat he was wearing, asking that it be mailed to his home. The hat arrived, but he did not, and was apparently never heard from again.

The building also attracted numerous organizations that reflected the concerns of the new century. Among them were the Cloak, Suit and Skirt Manufacturers' Protective Association, a group of factory owners formed to counteract the growing power of the garment union; the Citizens' Municipal Committee, devoted to improving the lives of the poor and working class; Big Brothers, the forerunner of today's Big Brothers Big Sisters; the Aldine Club, a group of publishers and editors; the Society of Friends of Music; the New York Baseball Club; and the House of Childhood, which published a fifty-two-page booklet describing a new teaching method recently developed by the Italian educator Dr. Maria Montessori. Her first Casa dei Bambini had opened in Italy in 1907 and its innovative ideas spread quickly; by 1916, there were over one hundred Montessori schools in the United States.

The next twentieth-century addition to Madison Square was the astonishing fifty-story Met Tower, which shot skyward on the square's east side in 1909. Part of a two-block complex between Madison and Park avenues, Twenty-third and Twenty-fourth streets, to be built over three decades by the Metropolitan Life Insurance Company, the edifice was the world's tallest building for four years, until it overtaken by the Woolworth Building downtown. Designed in the Renaissance style by Napoleon LeBrun, it featured a monumental four-faced clock and octagonal lantern that flashed on the hours.

In 1919 the Met Life complex also devoured Reverend Parkhurst's Madison Square Presbyterian Church, beloved by many for its gold mosaic dome and stained-glass windows by Tiffany. Designed by Stanford White and considered one of his finest buildings, the church had stood for only thirteen years.

White's Madison Square Garden still dominated the north side of the park, but its days, too, were numbered. It would be torn down in 1925, to be replaced by the thirty-four-story New York Life Insurance Building, topped with a gilded six-story roof. The skyscraper was designed by Cass

Gilbert, who had once worked in White's offices and who tried, but failed, to salvage some of the old garden's architectural elements.

* * *

A New York City was also in the making. The City of Greater New York had been created on January 1, 1898, consolidating Manhattan, Brooklyn, Queens, the Bronx, and Staten Island into one metropolis and instantly increasing New York's population from 2 million to 3.4 million. The city's first true subway line, run by the Interborough Rapid Transit Company between City Hall and the Bronx, opened on October 27, 1904, to tremendous excitement, with thousands of people gathering at the stations in hopes of securing a ride; the Brooklyn Rapid Transit Company opened a Broadway line with a stop on the block's southeast corner in 1917. By 1937 New York would have seven hundred miles of subway track handling 4.2 million passengers a day.

The old arc lights that had once illuminated Broadway between Union and Madison squares were gone. The area was now lit by milky globes of electric light mounted on pretty cast-iron lampposts. Thomas Edison had introduced grid electricity to the city on September 4, 1882, when he flipped a switch on a power station on Pearl Street in lower Manhattan. Within a year, over five hundred wealthy New York families had electricity in their homes, and by the early 1910s, most major businesses, theaters, restaurants, and hotels, including those on the Twenty-third Street block, had electricity too.

Horseless carriages and double-decker buses had also arrived, further clogging the neighborhood's already congested streets. Madison Square Garden had been the site of the nation's first auto show in 1900, featuring 160 different vehicles, some equipped with "internal explosion" engines, and Madison Square was now *the* place for showing off one's latest toy. The new contraptions vied with the old long yellow cable cars and horse-drawn vehicles of every description. The noise was overwhelming: grinding engines, clanking horseshoes, grating wagon wheels, and the insistent whine of the underground power lines that pulled the cable cars. Accidents were frequent.

The crossing of Broadway and Fifth Avenue at Twenty-third Street in front of the block was an especially harrowing spot. During the late 1800s, the intersection had been somewhat controlled by a gigantic policeman wearing white gloves, who with "a little rattan stick directed horse-drawn traffic, in the manner of a bandmaster conducting a symphony," according to one observer. But with the arrival of horseless carriages, a bandmaster was no longer enough. Thick columns of two-way traffic clogged Broadway, Fifth Avenue, and Twenty-third Street; impatient drivers refused to stick to their sides of the road; and there were no pedestrian crosswalks or safety islands.

Enter William Phelps Eno, Amos Eno's youngest son and the man who had first purchased the Flatiron lot. He had been acutely aware of traffic flow ever since he was nine years old, when he and his mother were caught for hours in a snarl of vehicles. He once said, "That very first traffic jam (many years before the motorcar came into use) will always remain in my memory. There were only about a dozen horses and carriages involved, and all that was needed was a little order to keep the traffic moving. Yet nobody knew exactly what to do; neither the drivers nor the police knew anything about the control of traffic."

One day in 1900, after missing the opening of a Metropolitan Opera performance because of a traffic jam, William had had enough. He wrote a piece about the need for traffic control for *Rider and Driver* magazine. The article created a stir and led to him drawing up New York's first road traffic regulations, enacted in 1903, and the first "Rules of the Road," adopted by New York in 1909 and by London and Paris soon thereafter. Dubbed "the Father of Traffic Safety," William also instituted such then unheard-of innovations as one-way streets, traffic lights, pedestrian cross-walks, and passing on the right; helped popularize stop signs, taxi stands, and pedestrian safety islands; and designed Columbus Circle in New York City and the traffic circle around the Arc de Triomphe in Paris. Thanks to him, the chaos at the Fifth Avenue, Broadway, Twenty-third Street junction was gradually brought under control.

* * *

The new Madison Square edifices and technological developments dramatically changed the character of Madison Square Park. Where once wealthy young women in the latest Parisian fashions had roamed, now roared rivers of clerks and factory workers, pouring across the park in the early mornings and late afternoons with a purposefulness unknown in the nineteenth century. The first of the laborers began appearing around six A.M. and then again around five P.M.—a small trickle that turned into a stream that turned into a torrent.

Watching them rush by were the hungry and the homeless. Times might have changed, but the presence of the poor had not. Still park regulars, they often gathered by the Worth Monument, a granite obelisk that stood on its own triangular island on the park's west side in honor of General William Jenkins Worth, a leader during the Mexican–American War (1846–48). Near the monument was a fountain where the homeless bathed and where they waited for free coffee, delivered every morning by a local newspaper; artist John Sloan captured the haunting scene in his 1905 painting *The Coffee Line*. The poor also gathered at the corner of Twenty-sixth Street and Broadway across from the monument after dark in hopes of securing a bed for the night. Theodore Dreiser describes the dispiriting ritual in *Sister Carrie*: "On every hand curious figures were moving— watchers and peepers . . . They were peevish, crusty, silent, eying nothing in particular and moving their feet . . . Hats were all dropping . . . Trousers were all warped." Those who arrived first would be led downtown by a chaplain who would help them procure shelter for the night in one of the missions on the Bowery. Those who arrived later would sleep on the streets.

*   *   *

As the twentieth century had arrived on the Fifth Avenue side of the block, so it had also arrived on its Twenty-third and Twenty-fourth street sides. By the 1910s, almost all the block's two- and three-story buildings were gone, replaced by tall office-and-loft edifices. Ranging from six to twelve stories, they offered freight elevators, mail chutes, automatic sprinkler systems, and floors with high ceilings and open layouts—all designed to appeal to companies, not individuals or families. Many were built in a neo-Renaissance or neo-Grec style, and some stretched clear through the block, with their main entrances on Twenty-third Street and their service entrances on Twenty-fourth Street. Most are still standing today.

The block was now considered part of a wholesale commercial district that extended from West Fourteenth Street to the West Thirties. In a mere half century, West Twenty-third Street between Fifth and Sixth avenues had morphed from housing New York's wealthiest families into a fashionable retail district into a bustling commercial zone, while West Twenty-fourth Street had lost its boardinghouses, legitimate and otherwise. Most of the Ladies' Mile was also gone. B. Altman's and Macy's, formerly on Broadway around Twentieth Street, had moved uptown around Herald Square; Stern Brothers and McCreery's, formerly on the south side of West Twenty-third, had closed for good. Even the Eden Musée was no more. TWENTY-THIRD STREET'S BUSY RETAIL BLOCK DESTINED FOR GREAT WHOLESALE CENTRE, read a March 1, 1914, headline in the *New York Times*, above an article reporting that the block, "which for years was one of the busiest and most popular shopping centres in New York, has been virtually deserted in so far as its former commercial interests are concerned."

Liberally sprinkled in among the block's new wholesale tenants were small clothing manufacturers, especially shirtwaist (blouse) and corset makers. The garment industry had started migrating into the area with the development of the Ladies' Mile—manufacturers needed to be close to the stores they furnished—and stayed thereafter. They set up small factories south of Twenty-third Street at first, but by the 1910s were operating along both sides of Fifth Avenue as far north as Thirty-fourth Street. An April 1915 census counted 491 garment factories employing 51,476 workers in the area around Madison Square.

New York is about nothing if it's not about change.

* * *

An observer walking west on Twenty-third Street from Fifth Avenue in the 1910s would have passed one wholesale- and manufacturing-oriented building after another, starting with one of the oldest: the six-story edifice at 27-33 West Twenty-third Street erected by the department-store heirs Richard Arnold and Henrietta Constable in 1880–81. Once the home of book publishers and the Co-operative Dress Association, it now housed shirtwaist, underwear, and upholstery goods companies. Next door at 35-37 West Twenty-third Street was the five-story building designed in 1880 by

D. & J. Jardine for the furniture company D. S. Hess, now housing various china-and-glass wholesalers.

Near the center of the block, at 43-47 West Twenty-third Street, and extending through to 24-28 West Twenty-fourth, stood the eight-story edifice built by Henry Hardenbergh in 1893–94. The building occupied the former site of Edmund Schermerhorn's mansion and five other small brick buildings.

William and Ann Schermerhorn's mansion at 49-51 West Twenty-third Street had finally been torn down and replaced by a twelve-story modern French building designed by Schwartz & Gross in 1911–12. On its ground floor were large showrooms and, up above, loft spaces leased to shirtwaist manufacturer Charles Iger and china-and-glass company L. Bernardaud. Next door, on the site of the former Eden Musée at 53-57 West Twenty-third Street, back entrance 34-38 West Twenty-fourth, was another twelve-story commercial edifice, erected in 1916–17 by steel construction expert William Harvey Birkmire. At 61-65 West Twenty-third stood the seven-story building with the cast-iron facade designed in 1886 by architect John B. Snook.

At the corner of Twenty-third Street and Sixth Avenue reigned the nineteen-story Masonic Building, erected on the site of the former Masonic Temple in 1913. Designed by Brother Harry Knowles, the handsome edifice, sheathed in limestone, brick, and terra-cotta, served as a sort of Sixth Avenue counterpart to the Fifth Avenue Building. Housed in its many offices were dozens of companies, organizations, and professionals, while on its ground floor was the Excelsior Savings Bank; their leases helped support the Freemasons and their philanthropic programs. Connected to the building in back, but fronting West Twenty-fourth Street, was Masonic Hall, also designed by Brother Knowles and nineteen stories tall, where the Masons' mystic ceremonies now took place.

Elsewhere on West Twenty-fourth Street stood a six-story Schickel & Ditmars building that had replaced three smaller buildings at Nos. 14-18 in 1903–4; a twelve-story Browne & Almiroty edifice that had replaced two smaller buildings at Nos. 30-32 in 1910–11; and a ten-story Philip Goerlitz edifice built at Nos. 40-44 in 1905–6. Early tenants at these addresses included more shirtwaist merchants, embroiderers, apparel companies, and outerwear merchants.

Only a handful of pre–Civil War buildings still occupied the block. Among them was 6 West Twenty-fourth Street, still owned by Phillips Phoenix, who had first used the edifice as a stable and later converted it into offices and dressing rooms for the Madison Square Theatre. Now in his seventies, Phoenix had transformed the three-story building yet again, this time into a restaurant with an apartment on the top floor. Designed with an Arts and Crafts facade by Maynicke & Franke, the same firm that designed the Fifth Avenue Building, the unusual building still stands and still houses a restaurant.

Also still standing, and surviving to this day, were two four-story homes on West Twenty-third Street built in the 1860s for prominent dentists. Dr. Stephen Main's Italianate dwelling at 23 West Twenty-third Street was now a combination residential and commercial building, as was Dr. John Gardner Ambler's Venetian Revival home at 25 West Twenty-third.

* * *

Working in the block's shirtwaist factories were mostly Jewish and Italian immigrant women, many of them teenagers. Their days were long—a sixty-five-hour workweek was the norm—and wages and working conditions, abysmal. Finally, on November 22, 1909, Clara Lemlich, a twenty-three-year-old employee of the Louis Leiserson company at 26 West Seventeenth Street, had had enough. While attending a garment union meeting, dominated by the union's male leaders, she stood up and demanded the floor. Speaking in Yiddish, she said, "I am a working girl, one of those who are on strike against intolerable conditions. I am tired of listening to speakers . . . I offer a resolution that a general strike be declared—now." The next day, about twenty thousand women walked out of hundreds of shirtwaist factories all over the city, very likely including the block. More joined them the following day, in a strike that lasted eleven weeks. It was the largest strike by women ever held in the United States, and though they won only some of their demands, their uprising led to the "Great Revolt" by the mostly male coat and suit makers the following year, which in turn helped spread unionization throughout the garment industry.

Three years later, on February 11, 1913, two thousand "white goods" (undergarments) women workers marched from union offices on East Fourteenth Street to the Wilbur Dyer undermuslin factory in the block's Masonic Building. Carrying pickets, humming labor songs, and walking arm in arm, they passed through a line of policemen assembled all along West Twenty-third Street between Fifth and Sixth avenues. Company agents came out and tried to remove them. Fighting broke out, and Miss Rose Krause was arrested for slapping a policeman in the face. As she was led away to a nearby police station, a throng of picketers followed, shouting out their support and encouragement.

Also supporting the rights of factory workers was the American Museum of Safety, which opened on the block at 18 West Twenty-fourth Street on May 4, 1915, with exhibits on "the value of safety" in the factory, on the street, and in the home. On display were "gruesome exhibits" on occupational diseases, showcases on nutrition and the ill effects of alcohol, and a layout showing what needed to be done to protect workers from the dangers of moving machinery.

The museum would not remain on the block for long, however, and neither would the garment factories. The area's high-end retailers and wealthy residents along Fifth Avenue were complaining. It was impossible to go out at lunchtime for all the unwashed masses crowding the streets! Banding together into the Fifth Avenue Association, the residents and retailers embarked on an intense lobbying campaign and through the adroit use of zoning laws managed to move the garment industry out of the Fifth Avenue/Madison Square area by the late 1920s. A new Garment Center District was established farther north and west, between Twenty-fourth and Forty-second streets, Sixth and Ninth avenues—the former home of the original Tenderloin.

* * *

On Good Friday 1917 came a turning point for both the nation and New York City: the United States entered World War I. Before the war, the

United States had been a secondary power. Afterward, it emerged a global leader, with New York challenging London as the center of the world.

The city's role in the war had started before the country even entered the conflict, with J. P. Morgan and other financiers supporting the Allies by offering large loans. Afterward, Governors Island was transformed into a critical supply base, while New York Harbor served as the main embarkation point for troop and cargo ships headed to Europe. One in ten soldiers were from New York.

Liberty Loan Bonds were floated to help fund the war, and to help sell the bonds, a temporary Liberty Bank, draped in red, white, and blue, was set up in Madison Square Park. Cheering crowds marched in Liberty Loan parades down Fifth Avenue to the square's "Altar of Liberty" as bystanders roared and the flags of the twenty-two Allied nations waved. (Eighteen months later, even larger crowds would assemble to welcome the returning troops home as they passed under a magnificent temporary Arch of Victory spanning Fifth Avenue just north of the block; to this day, the city's Veterans Day Parade begins at Twenty-third Street and Fifth Avenue.)

The Fifth Avenue Building was transformed, too, morphing into the city's hub for war relief organizations. First to arrive were the Committee of Mercy and the British-American War Relief Committee, both run by women. The Committee of Mercy helped destitute European war widows and bought soup carts for the Belgium Army. Pulled by ponies through the trenches, the carts were essential to the war effort, according to the *New York Tribune*, as they provided soldiers with a boiled hot-pot soup of meat, vegetables, and broth.

More relief organizations followed, including the National Allied Relief Committee, Fatherless Children of France Committee, Russian War Relief Committee, and International Reconstruction League, an umbrella organization that on July 9, 1916, called on all Americans to take part in a "self-denial week" to help raise money for war-ravaged Europe. That same year, a young French war hero organized an exhibit of French books at the offices of the newly formed Federation of Alliance Française, also in the building. The Alliance Française is now one of the largest and most respected French-American cultural organizations in the United States.

Occupying the edifice, too, was the Boy Scouts of America (BSA), which played what today seems like an astonishingly active role in World War I. Modeled after the Boy Scout Association established by Sir Robert Baden-Powell in Britain in 1908, the U.S. organization was founded in a small room in a New York City YMCA in 1910. One year later, it moved into the Fifth Avenue Building, with only seven employees. Already, though, it was garnering much attention, as Teddy Roosevelt and John D. Rockefeller were honoring Baden-Powell at a dinner at the Waldorf-Astoria that same day.

In the spring of 1917 the BSA organized three "patriotic back-to-the-soil" conferences, with the aim of teaching its scouts how to set up two million gardens across the United States to increase the country's food supply. The conference instructors also taught the boys how to patrol the coasts, cook for refugees, and administer first aid, and trained them for work at the Red Cross. Those over eighteen could then join the Red Cross and go to the front.

Three months after the conferences, the BSA set out on fundraising missions for the war effort, to sell a total of $300 million worth of Liberty Loan Bonds by the war's end. Furthermore, when the war department was in dire need of black walnut for construction work but was told that finding such wood would be almost impossible, the BSA sent its troops out into the forest. They returned with more than twenty-nine million feet of the needed lumber.

*   *   *

On the muggy summer day of July 28, 1917, any BSA employee not out scouring the forests or raising money for Liberty Loans could have looked out the windows of the Fifth Avenue Building at a startling sight. Marching down Fifth Avenue was an eerily silent but determined crowd. All that could be heard were the soft thuds of their feet, the muffled beats of their drums, and the stifled sobs of onlookers. Women and children were in front, dressed in white. Men were in back, dressed in dark colors. And leading them was a troop of African American Boy Scouts, a reminder that the BSA, like many others associated with the block, was not exactly what it professed to be.

Organized by the nascent National Association for the Advancement of Colored People (NAACP), the all–African American protest march had started at Fifty-ninth Street at one P.M. Numbering about ten thousand, the protestors carried banners reading MOTHER, DO LYNCHERS GO TO HEAVEN?, MR. PRESIDENT, YOUR HANDS ARE FULL OF BLOOD, and WE ARE MALIGNED AS LAZY AND MURDERED WHEN WE WORK. A group of boys held a sign that read WE ARE FIFTEEN YEARS OLD; ONE OF OUR AGE WAS ROASTED ALIVE. The marchers were protesting the wave of racial violence then sweeping the country: the lynching of black men in Waco, Texas, and Memphis, Tennessee, cheered on by thousands of whites; the vicious decimation of East St. Louis following race riots that left up to two hundred African Americans dead and six thousand homeless. They were protesting Jim Crow, segregation, white supremacy, and American hypocrisy. They were protesting President Woodrow Wilson, who had campaigned on a pro-civil-rights platform, but failed to deliver, and entered the country into war on the promise of bringing a democracy to Europe that did not exist at home.

The boy scouts leading the march belonged to one of dozens of African American troops formed soon after the BSA's founding. Not allowed to join most white troops, they formed their own.

Throughout the Silent Protest Parade, as it became known, the demonstrators said not a word, to devastating effect. Predating the 1968 March on Washington by 51 years and the 2020 Black Lives Matter demonstrations by 103 years, it was the first protest of its kind in New York and only the second time that African Americans had publicly demonstrated for civil rights.

The Silent Protest Parade ended at Madison Square Park, where a crowd erupted in cheers. But the marchers were not allowed to enter the park. Instead, they were directed down the West Twenty-fourth Street side of the block. Few, if any, among them knew that the land they walked along had once belonged to a freed Black slave and his family.

CHAPTER 18

On the West Side

On the sultry afternoon of July 24, 1915, the Sixth Avenue Elevated screeched into the Twenty-third Street station on the west side of the block and shuddered to a halt. A young woman climbed aboard, taking a seat in the center of a car beside a tall, heavyset German with a bristling black mustache and dimpled chin. He was absorbed in a book. On the seat beside him sat a fat briefcase.

World War I was underway in Europe by then, and the ocean liner RMS *Lusitania* had been sunk by the Germans just ten weeks before, killing over one thousand innocent civilians, including over one hundred Americans. But the United States was still a neutral country. The flurry of World War I activity on the Fifth Avenue side of the block was still two years away.

At the Fiftieth Street station, the German, a lawyer named Heinrich Friedrich Albert, suddenly shot to his feet. The train had stopped and was about to move on; he had to get out. Shouting to the guard to wait, he raced out the door and had just reached the platform when the young woman called to him, saying he had forgotten his briefcase. "No, it's mine," another man said and grabbed it. The man then sprinted out the front door as Albert was trying in vain to push his way back into the train through the rear. The train pulled out of the station, leaving both men on the platform. The second man, a U.S. Secret Service agent, covered the briefcase with his coat, leaned nonchalantly against a wall, and pretended to light a cigarette. Albert looked frantically around and then, not seeing the brief-case or suspecting the agent, raced down the stairs to the street. *Why, oh why hadn't he sprung for a cab?*

Albert was a German spy, in charge of a $40 million (about $523 million today) propaganda and sabotage ring aimed at furthering German inter-ests and preventing American munitions from reaching Britain and France. The Secret Service had suspected him for months. The contents of his briefcase would prove their suspicions correct. Some of his papers revealed that the Germans had created false-front companies that kept American munition producers too busy with their orders to fill the genuine orders from Britain and France. Other papers unveiled a German plot to tie up all American sources of toluol, a key ingredient of TNT.

* * *

The Sixth Avenue El, keeper of secrets large and small, defined the west side of the Twenty-third Street block for six decades. From the year it opened in 1878 until it was razed in 1939, its hulking carapace crouched over all aspects of life there. During the day, it was impossible to escape its clat-tering cars, shrieking brakes, and constant stream of passengers surging to and from its platforms on its "new and improved style of moving stairway[s]," or escalators. During the night, it was impossible to escape its flickering shadows and whispers of underground life. By the 1910s, many of the avenue's once omnipresent streetwalkers and con men were gone, thanks to the uptown movement of the Tenderloin, but illicit behavior on its sidewalks continued.

One such incident occurred on the night of January 19, 1921, when George Watt of Brooklyn met a girl under the El at the corner of Twenty-third Street and Sixth Avenue. She asked him to escort her home, but when they reached her doorway, a man named Paddy suddenly appeared—presumably by design. "I've been looking for you for some time," he said. "You're the bird who has been forcing his attentions on my wife." Paddy then punched George and stole his gold watch and stickpin.

The Sixth Avenue El operated on four double-track lines, running seventy cars per hour from five A.M. to midnight at two- to three-minute intervals. The line began at Rector Street and ended at 53rd Street, where it connected with the Ninth Avenue El, which continued to 155th Street, and carried more than two hundred thousand passengers per day, according to the Interborough Rapid Transit Company.

Unlike the Third Avenue El on the east side of town, whose passengers were predominantly working class, the Sixth Avenue El serviced mostly the middle class—shoppers on their way to the new Herald Square shopping center at Thirty-fourth Street, which had replaced the Ladies' Mile, and office workers on their way to work in midtown or downtown. The line's stations, topped with fanciful cast-iron pavilions, had been designed by the landscape artist J. F. Cropsey to resemble cottages and contained heated waiting rooms.

Nonetheless, the Sixth Avenue El, like all the city's elevated railroads, was loud, dirty, slow, and prone to all the same problems that plague mass transit today: overcrowding, theft, sexual harassment, drunken brawls, hateful epithets, accidental deaths, suicides, and, according to one *New York Times* reader, "the spitting crime," which was especially egregious when committed by "the man who looks like a gentleman, but acts like a beast." On more than one occasion, the line's platforms were so packed that a would-be passenger was pushed into the path of an oncoming train. On another particularly gruesome occasion, body parts of a stricken woman fell from the tracks above onto the sidewalk below, causing several passersby to faint.

Standing in the El's shadows in the middle of the block, at 384 Sixth Avenue, was the former St. Omer Hotel, still operating as a rundown haven of despair, albeit under an ever-revolving roster of names. It was the Medallion Hotel in the 1910s, the New England Hotel in the 1920s, the Hotel Huntington in the early 1930s, and the St. Denis Hotel (not to be confused with the more famous and much more refined St. Denis Hotel at Broadway and Eleventh Street) in the late 1930s; it would keep the latter moniker through the early 1970s. Sixth Avenue would be renumbered in 1929— No. 384 became No. 724—as the thoroughfare was extended to Canal Street for the building of a subway tunnel beneath it, but life in the old hotel would remain mired in the 1800s for most of the twentieth century.

On March 25, 1934, a clerk at the former St. Omer, by then the Huntington, would receive a phone call from an unidentified man suggesting that the clerk go to a second-floor room to see how a woman there "was feeling now." The clerk did as suggested, to find a slender brunette lying dead, apparently the victim of strangulation. She and a man had checked into the hotel at ten P.M. the evening before, registering as "Mr. and Mrs. Pinto." The man had left in the morning, but the woman had not. She was wearing a brown sports skirt, brown shirtwaist, and brown sports shoes. She had no identification on her.

On December 6, 1943, twenty-six-year-old Sylvia Goldfarb would marry thirty-three-year-old Rocco Arena and move into his furnished room in the former Huntington Hotel, by then the St. Denis. Sixteen months later, he was arrested and indicted for the first-degree murder of William Sorrels, a merchant seaman found dead in a telephone booth in a tavern at 156 Canal Street. Sylvia was arrested, too, but not for murder. She was charged with bigamy. Her first husband and ten-year-old child were living on Second Avenue. In her defense she said that it wasn't her fault, she loved both men. Her first husband took her back.

*   *   *

After World War I ended and the Prohibition era began, the former St. Omer Hotel also likely served as the site of a speakeasy or other illegal drinking spot. Hidden bars ranging from underground dives to high-class hideaways sprouted up all over the city in the 1920s, often appearing or disappearing overnight. Some estimated that Manhattan held more than five thousand illegal speakeasies at the height of the era, while the New York Police Department at one point estimated the city's number of drinking spots to be as high as thirty-five thousand.

If the old hotel did house a speakeasy, it was no doubt a low-class establishment, probably serving twenty-five-cent glasses of beer and fifty-cent glasses of "smoke," meaning cheap liquor. Its "gin" was likely made of industrial alcohol mixed with glycerin and oil of juniper, while its "Scotch" was likely made of grain alcohol colored with prune juice or creosote. To add insult to injury, these concoctions would have cost two to ten times as much as they had pre-Prohibition.

Informal bars may also have arisen in some of the block's office-and-loft buildings. Employees there may have gathered in back rooms to indulge in a cocktail or two after their workday was done—a common practice at the time. With most of the block's residents gone, however, and the area's former hotels and theaters relocated farther uptown, the block was no longer a center for nightlife. Revelers were heading elsewhere—to the exuberant jazz clubs of Harlem, the upscale speakeasies of Midtown, the fancy townhouses of the Upper East Side, or the over-the-top bars of Wall Street where one might be met by "white-coated fellows . . . flinging the shakers up and down lustily to the tune of rattling ice."

For despite Prohibition, 1920s New York was booming in every conceivable way. Its population had soared to seven million; "sky-climbing buildings" were rising everywhere from Lower Manhattan to a new Park Avenue rebuilt from railyards; Broadway was shining brighter than "a hundred Eiffel towers, a thousand Rue Pigalle"; and gigantic Midtown shops were overflowing with lavish displays of gold and furs. The Harlem Renaissance was exploding with the voices of Langston Hughes, Zora Neale Hurston, and many others. Shockingly modern women in flapper dresses were out jitterbugging until dawn while also moving into professions most had never considered before. New York had become a city of dreams, a magical metropolis, where anything and everything seemed possible.

But not on the block. The block remained quiet. It had been left behind.

*   *   *

Taking up one half of the Sixth Avenue side of the block was the side wall of the Masonic Building, main entrance 71 West Twenty-third Street. Among its many tenants in the 1920s were lawyers, accountants, apparel companies, religious organizations, and a branch of the iconic Fuller Brush Company, known nationwide for its army of clean-cut door-to-door salesmen. Before being hired, every "Fuller Brush Man," a phrase coined by the *Saturday Evening Post* in 1921, had to sign a pledge to be courteous, kind, sincere, and helpful, and every sales call started with a gift to the housewife. It was a new sales technique focusing on the client rather than the product, and it turned its founder, Alfred Fuller, from a poor man— the eleventh of twelve children born to a Nova Scotia farmer—into a millionaire.

Tenants such as the Fuller company provided the Masons with a steady income stream up until the early 1930s. But then the Great Depression hit, and slowly but inexorably the entire city ground to a halt. One of every three New Yorkers lost their jobs, half the city's manufacturing plants closed, and roughly 1.6 million out of the city's population of 6.9 million went on the relief rolls. Tenants vacated the Masonic Building in droves, and it began operating at a loss. Especially devastating was the departure of one of its largest tenants, the Erie Railroad, Jim Fisk's old firm, which moved out of the seven floors it had occupied for nine years.

The unemployed and the homeless roamed the streets, some dressed as if still going to work, others giving up all pretense as they carried all their belongings in so-called Hoover bags (paper bags), slept under Hoover blankets (old newspapers), and lived in Hoovervilles (shantytowns set up in parks and empty lots). Lines of silent, impassive faces waited in breadlines that stretched for blocks. Children whose parents were unable to feed them were sent to live in institutions or foster care.

New York needed to reinvent itself—and astonishingly, it did, though it took over a decade for it to regain its financial footing. Under the leadership of New York mayor Fiorello LaGuardia and U.S. president Franklin Delano Roosevelt, the city established enormous work-relief programs that created the infrastructure of modern New York, generating tens of thousands of jobs in the process. Projects ranged from the development of La Guardia Airport and the Long Island Expressway to the restoration of the Central Park Zoo and the construction of 255 city playgrounds.

Funding for the programs came primarily from FDR's Works Progress Administration (WPA), part of his New Deal package. Most of the WPA jobs were in construction and engineering, but the administration also created white-collar jobs, and in 1936 three of these white-collar WPA programs—the Federal Education Program, Federal Music Project, and Federal Theatre Project—opened branch offices in the Masonic Building. The Federal Education Program had the largest footprint, as it ran a Guidance Service center in the building that provided free counseling and training for the unemployed, but it was the Federal Theatre Project that had the largest, and most controversial, presence.

*   *   *

Headquartered in Washington, D.C., the Federal Theatre Project was directed by an extraordinary woman, Hallie Flanagan. An unlikely choice for the position, she came from an academic background (much to the annoyance of the Broadway theater establishment, who had hoped to install one of their own in the job) and had little administrative experience. She was best known as the founder and director of the Vassar Experimental Theatre and as the first woman to receive a Guggenheim Fellowship, in 1926. The grant had allowed her to spend fourteen months in Europe and Russia, where she studied new forms of theater and met many of the greatest playwrights of her day, including Luigi Pirandello, Konstantin Stanislavsky, and Vsevolod Meyerhold. She was most impressed with what she saw in Russia—its workers theaters and experimental productions were the most vital in the world, she wrote in 1929. The statement went largely unnoticed at the time, but set off alarm bells in the late 1930s, as a fear of communism, then growing in influence in the wake of the Depression, began sweeping the country.

Flanagan was one of the first of many witnesses subpoenaed to appear before the House Un-American Activities Committee (HUAC), established in Washington, D.C., on May 26, 1938. The committee's purpose was to investigate anyone it suspected of harboring communist ties; before it was finished in 1975, it would destroy the careers and lives of hundreds of Americans.

Flanagan's hearing began on the wintry morning of December 6, 1938. Great chandeliers hung from a high ceiling above two long tables shaped like a T, a witness chair at one end, the committee chairman Martin Dies at the other. Barely five feet tall, Flanagan was dressed demurely in a plain dark dress, brightly colored scarf, and hat. Nonetheless, within minutes of taking the stand, she flummoxed the rangy, cigar-chomping Dies, a Democrat from Texas. Recorded in the congressional hearings is this spunky exchange:

THE CHAIRMAN: Now, will you just tell us briefly the duties of your position?
MRS. FLANAGAN: Yes, Congressman Dies. Since August 29, 1935, I have been concerned with combating un-American inactivity.
THE CHAIRMAN: No. We will get to that in a minute.
MRS. FLANAGAN: Please listen. I said I am combating un-American inactivity.
THE CHAIRMAN: Inactivity?

MRS. FLANAGAN: I refer to the inactivity of professional men and women; people who, at that time when I took office, were on the relief rolls; and it was my job to expend the appropriation laid aside by congressional vote for the relief of the unemployed as it related to the field of the theater.

Though the congressional papers do not record it, Chairman Dies must have been momentarily at a loss for words—for what would prove to be only the first time that morning.

* * *

By the time Flanagan appeared before HUAC, she had been directing the Federal Theatre Project for almost four years, to resounding success. Deeply committed to producing dynamic, challenging drama for audiences of all income and education levels, she had established five regional theater centers across the country; employed up to fifteen thousand people at peak periods, including such rising stars as Joseph Cotten, Arthur Miller, Clifford Odets, and Elia Kazan; and brought some sixty-four thousand performances of twelve hundred plays to thirty million spectators in forty states. Less than 35 percent of those plays had charged even a nominal admission. Many who attended had never seen live theater before.

Among the project's most impressive achievements was the Living Newspaper, a series of productions that dramatized current events. Based on a similar series that Flanagan had witnessed in Russia, the plays usually had progressive, left-wing themes—a huge black mark against her as far as HUAC (fervently anti-FDR and his New Deal programs) was concerned. *Triple-A Plowed Under* attacked the U.S. Supreme Court for killing an aid agency for farmers. *Power* advocated public control of energy companies. Even more alarming to the conservative congressmen, the plays attracted huge, enthusiastic audiences. *One-Third of a Nation*, inspired by FDR's famous description of Depression-era America—"one-third of a nation ill-housed, ill-clad, ill-nourished"—played in New York City for ten months to a total audience of about 220,000 and on stages nationwide 7,600 times.

Under Flanagan's direction, too, a suspect Negro Theatre Project had been established in cities throughout the United States, with the most famous headquartered at the Lafayette Theatre in Harlem; it promoted racial equality—a "cardinal keystone of Communism," a Democratic senator from North Carolina commented. The Lafayette had presented more than thirty plays, including a now-legendary production of *Macbeth* featuring an all–African American cast directed by Orson Welles. Then an unknown twenty-year-old, Welles set Shakespeare's play on a mythical island suggestive of Haiti, and when word of the production got out, it generated enormous excitement. Seventh Avenue had to be closed for ten blocks on either side of the Lafayette on opening night.

But HUAC wasn't interested in any of this. They were interested only in the fact that Flanagan had many—too many—Russian friends. During the hearing, she was grilled on her trip to Russia and various articles she had written, especially one published in *Theatre Arts Monthly* seven years before. In it, she had described a meeting of workers theaters in New York as having a "certain Marlowesque madness." To which Representative Joseph Starnes of Alabama, the committee's chief inquisitor, responded, "You are quoting from this Marlowe. Is he a Communist?"

The room rocked with laughter, but Flanagan did not laugh. The jobs of eight thousand theater professionals, three thousand of them in New York City, hung in the balance. "I am sorry," she said. "I was quoting from Christopher Marlowe."

"Tell us who Marlowe is, so we can get the proper reference, because that is all we want to do," Starnes said.

"Put in the record that he was the greatest dramatist in the period of Shakespeare, immediately preceding Shakespeare," Flanagan replied.

The hearing adjourned soon thereafter. Flanagan had testified for only four hours, but the congressmen did not call her back. Having previously interviewed a disgruntled New York stage manager who testified that "the set-up of the whole Arts is nothing more or less but a fence to sow the seeds of communism," and an even more disgruntled secretary who testified that Flanagan "had been known as far back as 1927 for her communist sympathy," they had already made up their minds. Though not a single committee member had ever attended a Federal Theatre production, they were convinced of its subversive activities.

On January 3, 1939, the committee concluded that a "rather large number of the employees on the Federal Theatre Project are either members of the Communist party or a sympathetic with the Communist Party." Five months later, on June 30, 1939, Congress terminated the project's funding.

The next day, the Federal Theatre Project's offices in the Masonic Building shut down. Reported the *New York Times*: "Only a watchman answered the phone yesterday at the project's old New York Headquarters at 71 West Twenty-Third Street."

Shortly after closing the Federal Theatre Project, Congress moved aggressively to shrink all WPA programs. Unemployment was still sky-high, but Hitler had invaded Austria and parts of Czechoslovakia, and funds were needed to build up the U.S. military. Two years later, the Japanese attacked Pearl Harbor and the United States entered World War II, sending the country's factories into full production mode. A national relief program was no longer needed. The WPA was shut down completely in December 1942.

* * *

Meanwhile, throughout all the comings and goings of the Masonic Building's tenants, the Freemasons were conducting their mystic ceremonies in a separate building, Masonic Hall at 46 West Twenty-fourth Street. The hall had been built in 1908, five years before the Masonic Building, and the two edifices were connected in back, with their hallways and some of their rooms leading into each other.

The Masonic Building was handsome, but the Masonic Hall was magnificent. Its outside glistened, a Beaux Arts facade accented with "one of the finest examples of decorative brickwork in New York," commented the *Real Estate Record and Buyers' Guide*. Its inside glittered, with rooms and halls bursting with gilded ceilings, gold leaf trim, mosaic panels, and stained glass.

On the building's third and fourth floors stretched its centerpiece, the twelve-hundred-seat Grand Lodge Room, used for the statewide Masonic convention held every May, and leased out for concerts, lectures, funerals, and other special events the rest of the year. The acoustics in the room were so good that the New York Philharmonic would later use it as a rehearsal space.

A dozen smaller lodge rooms, each two stories and capable of holding 150 people, filled the upper floors. As in the old Masonic Temple, these rooms were sumptuously designed according to period—Egyptian, Renaissance, Tudor, Gothic, Colonial—and laid out on an east–west axis.

Then, as now, the lodge rooms had no windows—the better to keep secrets in—and each contained an altar, organ, three tall candles, and two "ashlars," the cinderblock-sized pieces of stone, one unfinished, the other cut and polished, that represent the passage of a Mason from Apprentice to Master. Each room also held two columns topped with globes, and scattered about were various Masonic symbols, including the builder's trowel and the architect's triangle.

Among the fifty-odd lodges that met, and continue to meet, in the Masonic Hall was St. Cecile No. 568, named after the patron saint of musicians and the only lodge allowed to convene during the daytime, as it is composed of actors, musicians, magicians, and other performers who work at night. Louis B. Mayer was "raised"—meaning initiated—into the lodge in Masonic Hall in 1914, two years before moving to Los Angeles to form his own production company and later co-found Metro-Goldwyn-Mayer (MGM). Jazz orchestra leader Paul Whiteman was raised into New York's St. Cecile's in 1922, and magician Harry Houdini, in 1923.

Like his fifth cousin Theodore Roosevelt before him, Franklin Delano Roosevelt was a Mason, and all New York City ground to a halt on February 17, 1933, when the then president-elect arrived in town to raise his son Elliott to the degree of Master Mason. As a Knight Templar, FDR himself officiated at the ceremony, wearing the traditional Mason apron made of lambskin. Twelve motorcycle policemen, all Masons, served as a special guard as he entered and exited the room.

Yet more U.S. presidents would join the Freemasons after FDR, among them Harry Truman, Lyndon Johnson, and Gerald Ford, bringing the total number of U.S. presidents who were Masons to at least fifteen. From its earliest days on, the organization served as a sort-of informal conduit to the halls of power, a path by which middle-class and upper-middle-class men could meet successful professionals in other fields, form potentially lucrative business associations, and generally expand their spheres of influence—one of the reasons why the fraternal order, open by invitation only, has long been viewed with suspicion.

*   *   *

After World War II began, the Masons turned the entire second floor of the Masonic Building into a Servicemen's Center, equipped with a seventy-five-bed dormitory, recreation room, and other services for soldiers on their way to and from the war. One of eleven such locations established by the organization throughout the state, it was used by about 140,000 men, some Masons, others not. As during World War I, New York Harbor had again become a major embarkation point for ships heading for Europe, with over 850,000 New Yorkers joining the armed services, more than from any other American city.

The block may have inadvertently contributed to the war effort in another way as well. The Sixth Avenue El had been razed in 1939, replaced by the Sixth Avenue subway, and its twenty thousand tons of steel sold to a dealer on the West Coast. Rumor had it that the dealer had in turn sold the steel to the Japanese, who had melted it down for the bombs dropped on Pearl Harbor. Wrote E. E. Cummings in his 1944 poem "plato told":

> plato told
>
> him:he couldn't
> believe it(jesus
>
> told him;he
> wouldn't believe it)lao
>
> tsze
>
> certainly told
> him,and general
> (yes

mam)
sherman;
and even
(believe it
or

not)you
told him:i told
him;we told him
(he didn't believe it,no

sir)it took
a nipponized bit of
the old sixth

avenue
el;in the top of his head:to tell

him

*   *   *

In the early 1980s the Grand Lodge of Free and Accepted Masons of the
State of New York would purchase the former St. Omer's Hotel and four
other small eyesore buildings on Sixth Avenue and Twenty-fourth Street
that stood beside and between their two impressive edifices. The buildings
were torn down in 1983 and replaced by a parking lot that still exists today.
Then, as now, the Masons owned the entire Sixth Avenue side of the block.
All physical vestiges of the former St. Omer and Sixth Avenue El were
gone, but their shadows still seemed to linger in the deserted, windswept
lot at night, reminders of secrets past.

CHAPTER 19

Toys, Toys, Toys!

Morris and Rose Michtom were Russian immigrants who owned a tiny store in Brooklyn that sold candy and other small items, including hand-made dolls that Rose sewed at night. One day in 1902 Morris saw a political cartoon depicting President Theodore Roosevelt, an avid big game hunter, refusing to kill an adorable trapped bear. The cartoon garnered national attention, and Morris asked Rose if she could make a few toy bears like the one in the cartoon. She obliged, and her $1.50 "Teddy's bears" sold quickly—so quickly that in early 1903, with the help of a wholesale firm, the Michtoms founded the Ideal Toy & Novelty Company. Decades later, Ideal would have a showroom in the Fifth Avenue Building, where the company would display other bestsellers: the "drink-and-wet" doll Betsy Wetsy (1934), the fortune-telling Magic 8 Ball (1950s), the game Kerplunk (1967), and the Rubik's Cube (1980).

As a teenager living on New York's Lower East Side in the late 1890s, Joshua Lionel Cowen invented a toy train powered by electricity. As a young man, he dropped out of college—three times—took a job in a dry cell battery manufacturing firm and then an electric lamp company before leaving to found his own firm, the Lionel Manufacturing Company, which made "electric novelties." Still, he continued to tinker with toy trains and one day pitched a toy store owner with an unusual idea: the owner could fill one of Cowen's trains with his merchandise and display it in a window as an "animated advertisement." The toy owner agreed to give it a try. But when Cowen returned the next morning, the train was gone. Disappointed, he rushed inside, to find the owner waiting for him. The train, not his merchandise, had attracted attention and sold immediately. Could Cowen make more like it? A year later, Lionel Manufacturing was producing electric trains, and by 1910, Cowen was a wealthy man. Today, a plaque in 200 Fifth Avenue, as the Fifth Avenue Building is now known, honors him and others who "have given 'boys' of all ages much happiness over the years with a circle of track and a tinplate engine."

Young A. C. Gilbert was a Yale man with a degree in medicine and a champion track-and-field athlete with an Olympic gold medal. He seemed headed toward a successful career in medicine, perhaps as a team physician. But A. C. had a secret, one well known to all his friends. He loved magic much more than he loved medicine or sports, and one afternoon in 1909, took his father to a small factory near the Yale campus to show him a trick he had invented. *Look!* he excitedly told his father, *I can turn an empty vase into a bunch of flowers! And I have dozens more tricks just like it!* His confused father nodded; he would always support his son. After graduation, A. C. began commuting to New York to sell his magic wherever he could. Nearing Manhattan one afternoon on the train, he noticed men building towers out of steel lattices. Soon thereafter, the Erector Set was born. The A. C. Gilbert Company opened a showroom in the Fifth Avenue Building in the early 1920s and took up the entire building at 1 West Twenty-fifth Street, just north of the block, in 1941. Named the Gilbert Hall of Science, it featured elaborate train layouts and building exhibits that attracted children of all ages.

Richard James was a mechanical engineer working in a shipyard in Philadelphia during World War II. One day he was experimenting with torsion springs—springs that work by twisting—and accidentally knocked one off his desk. Much to his surprise, it bounced and then bounced again, almost as if it were walking. Intrigued, he took it home to show his wife, Betty, who named it "Slinky." A year later, the couple formed James Industries, had four hundred springs made, and hawked them from store to store. No one was interested. Finally, Gimbels of Philadelphia placed an order. The springs sold out in less than ninety minutes. Elated, the

Jameses took their toy to the 1946 Toy Fair in the Fifth Avenue Building and by 1950 had sold more than one hundred million Slinkys. It was all a fairy tale come true, until a thunderbolt struck: Richard walked out to join a religious cult in Bolivia, leaving Betty and their six children behind and taking most of the company's money with him. Shaken but not defeated, Betty gritted her teeth and negotiated several strategic moves that saved the company. The Slinky Dog, later featured in the movie *Toy Story* and its sequels, debuted at the Toy Fair in the Fifth Avenue Building in 1962.

In 1945 friends Elliot Handler and Harold Matson started selling picture frames out of their garage; they named their new company Mattel. As a sideline, they used the frames' scraps to make doll furniture, and when the furniture began selling better than the frames, they switched to making toys. But it was Elliot's wife, Ruth, who catapulted the company into fame and fortune. One day, or so the story goes, she noticed their daughter, Barbara, making her own dolls by cutting out pictures of young women in magazines, dressing them up in clothes also cut from magazines, and pretending they were adults. Inspired, Ruth created a doll with an adult body—and a near-impossible figure—and named it Barbie, after their daughter. The doll debuted at the 1959 Toy Fair in the Fifth Avenue Building. Two years later, the Handlers introduced a boy doll named after their son, Ken.

*   *   *

For much of the twentieth century, the Fifth Avenue Building served as mecca for the toy industry. Ives Manufacturing Company, an early electric toy train maker, may have been the first to move in in 1914, followed a year later by E. C. Schoonmaker, a doll company. By the early 1920s, close to twenty toy firms had operations in the building, a number that would double in the 1930s. In 1926 the building began hosting exhibits for the annual Toy Fair, and in 1949 the Toy Industry Association, the industry's foremost trade group, moved in. Hundreds more toy companies followed, and in the 1960s, the building began renting exclusively to the toy industry. It also acquired an official new name: the Toy Center. Still, there wasn't enough room for all who wanted in, and the center expanded across Twenty-fourth Street into 1107 Broadway, constructing a ninth-floor sky bridge between the two buildings in 1968. By 1981, the Toy Center South and

North contained more than six hundred toy businesses spread over a million square feet, while the Toy Fair, held every February, reigned as the industry's foremost event. During the gargantuan extravaganza, which was strictly off limits to children and the general public, thousands of buyers from toy stores all over the world flooded onto the block to purchase most of their merchandise for the year. On the site where stockbrokers in loud suits had once roamed picking up tips and shouting out bets, toy buyers now converged to peruse the industry's latest products and place bets of their own on what would be the next hot thing—Hula Hoops, Pet Rocks, Cabbage Patch Kids, Tickle Me Elmos, anyone?

*   *   *

Many of the toys introduced in the Fifth Avenue Building had been invented by recent immigrants, or the children of recent immigrants, often Jewish, who went on to become multimillionaires—twentieth-century versions of the New England Protestants once connected with the block. The Michtoms were Jews from Russia, Joshua Lionel Cowen was the grandson of Jews from eastern Europe, and Ruth Handler's parents were Jews from Poland. Antonio Pasin, the inventor of the Radio Flyer wagon, another iconic American toy showcased in the building, had arrived in the United States in 1914 as a penniless sixteen-year-old from Italy. The toy giant Hasbro, originally named Hassenfeld Brothers, had been founded by three Polish Jewish immigrants in Rhode Island in 1926 as a scrap textile firm before making toys. Leslie Berger, founder of Cardinal Industries, creator of games and puzzles, fled Hungary at age nineteen to escape the Nazis.

And it had been another Jewish immigrant, Frederick August Otto Schwarz, who had been the first to bring toys to the block, many decades before the Toy Center was established. From 1897 to 1911, his dazzling store had occupied the entire seven-story building at 39-41 West Twenty-third Street, its back entrance abutting the staircase to Stanford White's love nest.

The company had begun with one Henry Schwarz, the son of a highly regarded jeweler and goldsmith, who had emigrated from Germany just before the Civil War. Settling in Baltimore, he opened a toy store that soon became the most celebrated in the city, and around 1870 his brothers sailed from Germany to join him. Gustave Schwarz opened a toy store in Philadelphia, Richard Schwarz opened one in Boston, and Frederick August Otto Schwarz opened one in New York. F.A.O.'s first shop, the Schwarz Toy Bazaar, stood at 765 Broadway, but moved to 42 East Fourteenth Street in 1880 and to West Twenty-third Street in 1897. By then, F.A.O.'s son Henry was largely running the business, already described by the *New York Times* as "the largest dealer in toys in this city," while Father Schwarz, as he was fondly known by his employees, "putter[ed] around the store in a black skullcap, his long brown beard flowing elegantly among the toys."

Henry, F.A.O., and other members of the Schwarz firms traveled to Germany every year to purchase most of their merchandise. Few toys were being made in the United States at the time, and as everyone knew, the best toys came from Germany, especially Nuremberg, where toymaker guilds had been operating since the fifteenth century. Expert craftsmen, working with wood from the Black Forest, land of myths and fairy tales, specialized in carved and painted toys, while large German factories produced high-quality dolls, mechanical toys, and construction sets. The Schwarz men also made regular stops in Switzerland, France, and England, and in London one year came across a wooden perambulator. Modern baby carriages were then unknown in America, and the Schwarzes had a large shipment sent to their store, where they became a perennial bestseller.

FAO Schwarz was also known for its unique methods of promotion. It was one of the first companies in the United States to establish a mail-order business, sending out gift catalogs as early as 1876, and apparently the first to feature a live Santa Claus at Christmastime. Ladies in its workroom made papier-mâché eggs filled with toys for Easter and giant-sized Jack Horner pies, stuffed with gifts under a paper crust, for the winter holidays.

Two years after the Fifth Avenue Building opened, FAO Schwarz outgrew its West Twenty-third Street home and moved off the block, to settle first at 31 Fifth Avenue in 1911 and then at 745 Fifth Avenue, across from the Plaza Hotel, in 1931. Here it became a popular tourist attraction, legendary for its elaborate floor displays and exclusive, imaginative toys.

Four years after FAO left the block, another toy firm, the Strobel & Wilken company, moved in, opening up at 61-65 West Twenty-third Street.

Founded in Cincinnati in 1849, it had started out as a leather goods manufacturer, but around the time of the Civil War began importing toys, especially dolls with bisque (porcelain) heads. Next came the Meccano
Company, 71 West Twenty-fourth Street, which made miniature machines
such as telegraph sets that actually worked, and Morimura Brothers, 53-57
West Twenty-third Street, a Japanese import house that supplied more
bisque-head dolls, Nanking cotton-body dolls, toy tea sets, and wooden
toys.

*   *   *

These early toy companies aside, it was World War I that was the making
of the American toy industry—and the Toy Center. Because of the war,
European imports had all but disappeared, and anyone who wanted to buy
toys had to buy U.S.-made. Between 1910 and 1920, toy production in the
United States increased by 500 percent, and after the war ended, protective tariffs allowed American toy firms to multiply and thrive.

A key figure behind the boom was A. C. Gilbert, the inventor of the
Erector Set. As chairman of the newly formed Toy Manufacturers of
the U.S.A., forerunner of today's Toy Industry Association, then headquartered in the Flatiron Building, Gilbert traveled to Washington, D.C., to
meet with the secretary of the navy in October 1918. The Council of
National Defense had asked toy manufacturers to stop producing toys
and start producing goods essential for the war. But Gilbert argued that
toys themselves were essential for the war, as they were crucial for morale
and "exert[ed] the sort of influences that go to form right ideals and solid
American character." To prove his point, he unwrapped boxes of toys he
had brought with him. Moments later, national defense officials were on
the floor, playing and building. Toy manufacturing continued; the press
dubbed Gilbert "the man who saved Christmas."

Even the Great Depression of the 1930s failed to put a dent in the
industry. At the height of the misery in 1933, over fifteen million Americans were out of work, but toy companies flourished. With no money to
spend on entertainment or travel, families stayed home and played games,
especially board games. It was during the 1930s that Monopoly, the most
successful board game of all time, was born. Fisher-Price Toys, established

just after the 1929 stock market crash by Herman Fisher and Irving Price in East Aurora, New York, was selling more than two million toys seven years later. And when the Shirley Temple doll was introduced by the Ideal Toy company in 1934, under the close supervision of Shirley's mother, who made sure the doll had fifty-two perfect ringlets just like her daughter, doting parents stood in long lines to buy her.

The Toy Fair flourished as well. New York's first toy fair had taken place in 1903, with ten salesmen setting up exhibits in Lower Manhattan in hopes of catching toy buyers on their way to and from Europe. By the mid-1920s, however, the fair was a well-established New York event, held largely in Midtown hotels, where the toy manufacturers rented rooms, covered furniture with sheets, and spread their wares on top. The Fifth Avenue Building became one of several official Toy Fair hosts in 1934.

The Toy Fair was cancelled in 1945, due to World War II, but afterward, as the U.S. economy boomed, birth rates soared, and New York, now home to more than forty thousand factories and the world's biggest port, prospered as never before, its importance grew to dizzying new heights. Each Toy Fair was exponentially bigger than the one that had come before it, attracting buyers from all over the world. The 1948 fair boasted a record 100,000 toys on display in 800 exhibits, and the 1949 fair featured 130,000 toys in 1,200 exhibits. The 1953 fair involved sales of $450 million, and the 1961 fair, sales of $885 million.

* * *

As important as the Toy Center was to the toy industry, however, it contributed next to nothing to life on the block for most of the year. Only a few companies had working offices in the buildings—most just leased vast showrooms for tens of thousands of dollars annually that they left unused for eleven months out of the year. Not until the Toy Fair approached every February did the center wake up, with armies of workers descending to polish its floors, refurbish its metal work, and repaint its corridors. On fair days, heat for the buildings would be switched on at five thirty A.M., but switched off at nine A.M., as the buyers themselves provided the heat, jostling down the corridors, crowding into the elevators, and squeezing through the exhibits, happy to be together and meet old friends again.

The Toy Fair was a delirious party, an over-the-top carnival, a cozy schmooze fest for adults trying to predict what kids would want for Christmas that year. *What was unique? What would sell? What would attract both kids and their parents?* the buyers asked themselves as they roamed and explored, but seldom touched. Most of the toys on display were prototypes.

*   *   *

It is the mid-1960s. Toy buyers, exhibitors, manufacturers, and reporters are milling about outside the Toy Center, catching up on news and gossip before entering the Toy Fair. An armored truck pulls up. Armored guards step out, following by a short, slight man with boxes handcuffed to his wrists. Marvin Glass, "the King of Toys," has arrived.

According to writer Bill Paxton in his book *A World Without Reality*, Glass grew up in Chicago, the son of Louis Goldberg, a salesman, and Ruth Glass, and the grandson of impoverished Jewish immigrants from Russia and Ukraine. He was his parents' only child and, writes Paxton, when he was six or seven or eight, survived the unimaginable: his mother tried to kill him. One time by trying to throw him out the window, another time by turning on the gas and leaving the house. She was subsequently committed to an institution, and Marvin was sent to live with his aunt and uncle. There he made his first toys—a military tank big enough to sit in, a submarine that shot toy bullets.

Another of the block's great pretenders, Glass never talked about his past, pieced together by Paxton through dozens of interviews with his colleagues, family, and friends, but said he was from Evanston, Illinois, the Chicago suburb where he lived as an adult. According to Paxton, he changed his surname from Goldberg to Glass to obscure his Jewish origins and, though he claimed to be a graduate of the University of Chicago, likely spent his youth working with his father in the bootleg industry.

Glass's troubled past was probably the making of his genius—and his eccentricity, egocentricity, paranoia, generosity, and charm. He founded the country's first toy design studio, Marvin Glass & Associates, in Chicago in 1941, with the aim of developing prototypes to sell to manufacturers, and over the next forty years, his firm produced some five hundred mind-blowing, megahit games and toys. Among them were Mouse Trap, Operation, Ants in the Pants, and Simon. Glass was married five times, twice to the same woman, surrounded himself with Playboy bunnies, read four or five books a week, smoked constantly, never drank, and never seemed to sleep or eat, though he employed two chefs. More a salesman than an inventor, he was nonetheless the spark behind many creations and acquired some two hundred patents for his studio, including one for gigantic glasses that he named Super Specs. As the story goes, he was at a party where he was talking to a boring man wearing spectacles. The more the man talked, the more boring he became, and the bigger the spectacles grew.

Glass's first big break came at the 1948 Toy Fair in the Fifth Avenue Building. He and inventor Eddy Goldfarb had traveled there to showcase two new toys: the egg-laying Busy Biddy, a pocket-size chicken that laid white marble eggs, and Merry-Go-Sip, a domed plastic cup with a little merry-go-round inside that spun when a child drank from the cup through a straw. Both were instant sensations, despite—or perhaps because of—the fact that Glass tried to boost sales by handing out pictures of two nude women drinking from the cup.

Following that success, the Glass studio produced one wildly inventive hit after another, many first showcased at the Toy Center. Mouse Trap, inspired by artist Rube Goldberg's work, was introduced at the 1963 Toy Fair, and Operation, at the 1965 Toy Fair. Mouse Trap was the industry's first truly three-dimensional board game, a complicated affair with twenty-two plastic parts; it sold 1.2 million copies its first year.

The Glass studio was headquartered in a fortress-like building on North La Salle Street in Chicago. Paranoid that people were spying on him, the King of Toys had its windows papered over, double walls installed, and closed-circuit TVs set up. Toys in development were stored in vaults over-night, guards patrolled round the clock, employees were bonded and sworn to secrecy, and locks were changed frequently. Whenever Glass traveled with his prototypes, he kept them in boxes handcuffed to his wrists.

A good friend of Hugh Hefner, Glass hosted frequent late-night parties in his home in Evanston, an old carriage house that he had transformed into a "playboy pad." "Distaff guests frolic in Glass's huge ceramic-tile tub as his Jacuzzi whirlpool whips up bubbles. An elegant drink dispenser is close at hand," reported *Playboy* in May 1970, while also detailing Glass's elaborate hi-fi system, grottos, sauna, and extensive art collection with works by Pablo Picasso, Salvador Dalí, Marc Chagall, and Frederic Remington.

Glass was not a resident of the block and visited it only periodically. But it was the Toy Center and its annual Toy Fair that catapulted him into stardom; his studio was the toy industry's preeminent design firm for forty years. In a strange way, too, Glass seemed to be channeling the excessive, compulsive, workaholic, sexaholic spirit of some of the block's former denizens.

* * *

The Toy Center would continue to host the Toy Fair until the early 2000s, with an ever-increasing number of buyers attending every year. As earlier in the century, each Toy Fair was more extravagant than the one before it, as toy manufacturers went all out, hiring hundreds of actors to put on costumes—Smurfs, Care Bears, Wonder Womans, Power Rangers—and present imaginative shows to attract the buyers to their wares.

Yet in many ways, the center's best years were the 1960s and 1970s. One of its biggest tenants, Mattel Toys, moved out in the early 1970s, and in the mid-1980s, Hasbro and Coleco did the same. All three companies had grown to enormous size and needed more space and more contiguous floors than the Toy Center could provide.

Changes in the toy industry also affected the center. Electronics and video games entered the market, altering the way toys were developed and sold. Each product seemed to have a shelf life shorter than the one before it, and advertising on TV became crucial to a toy's success—as crucial as a good showing at the Toy Fair. Next, mergers and acquisitions hit the industry hard, with Mattel and Hasbro buying up many of their competitors, including Milton Bradley (Hasbro), Playskool (Hasbro), Fisher-Price (Mattel), and Tyco Toys (Mattel), and some of the frisson went out of the fair.

Finally, there came a devastating blow: the Toy Center was sold. Owned by the Wien and Malkin family since 1951, when they had purchased it from the Eno family, the Toy Center South/Fifth Avenue Building was acquired in 2005 by the Chetrit Group for $355 million. Two years later, it was sold again, to the L&L Holding Company for $480 million, while the Toy Center North/1107 Broadway went to Tessler Developments for $235 million. Neither firm had any interest in continuing the toy tradition. The Fifth Avenue Building would be converted into a modern office building and 1107 Broadway into luxury condominiums.

The Toy Center's final fair was held in February 2007, and the last of its toy tenants moved out the following summer. Its sky bridge was demolished in 2013. Today, the Toy Fair is held in the Jacob K. Javits Convention Center at Thirty-fourth Street and Eleventh Avenue.

CHAPTER 20

Dark Days

Around midnight on June 27, 1981, Gus Loges, sixty-five, and Willie Townsend, fifty-eight, were asleep on park benches in Madison Square Park. It was a cloudy night, with temperatures in the sixties, and the sidewalks were all but empty. Then suddenly and without warning, a stocky man in dark clothing crept up from out of the shadows and slashed both sleeping men in turn with a knife. Mr. Loges was cut on the right side of the neck, Mr. Townsend on the left.

The two were the fourth and fifth victims of eight men attacked by the slasher that night. None were fatally injured—all were in stable condition by the following morning—but the attacks were emblematic of two characteristics of New York City street life in the 1970s and early to mid-1980s: homelessness and crime.

Both had come about largely because of forces put into motion after World War II. White flight to the suburbs, a resultant decline in the tax base, the replacement of old neighborhoods with housing projects, and the enormous loss of manufacturing jobs—declining by 50 percent between 1950 and 1976—coupled with a nationwide recession and social unrest had shattered the city. One crisis had followed another—riots in Harlem and Bedford-Stuyvesant in 1964, a transit workers' strike in 1966, a sanitation workers' strike in 1968—and fear and decay stalked the metropolis. The Bronx was burning, garbage was festering, graffiti was smothering subway cars. Then came catastrophe: the 1975 fiscal crisis. New York had borrowed too much money. The banks were refusing to lend it any more. Desperate, the city applied to the U.S. government and President Gerald Ford for federal aid. To no avail. FORD TO CITY: DROP DEAD, ran the famous *Daily News* headline of October 30, 1975.

Ford reversed himself six weeks later, and the federal government agreed to guarantee the city's loans. The city implemented strict austerity measures and in 1981, ahead of schedule, succeeded in balancing its budget. But the twin scourges of homelessness and crime continued, affecting neighborhoods all over Manhattan and, in the middle of the island, none more so than the blocks around Madison Square.

*   *   *

At the heart of the homelessness problem was a lack of affordable housing and an influx of thousands of people with mental health conditions onto the city's streets. Between 1965 and 1979, more than fifty thousand patients were released from the state's psychiatric hospitals, due largely to the development of new drugs and changing public attitudes toward mental institutions. During the same period, the city's single-room occupancy hotels (SROs), which had traditionally provided low-income people with shelter, disappeared. In 1960, there were about 129,000 SRO units in the city; by 1978, there were only 25,000, a number that would fall yet further throughout the 1980s and 1990s. Driving the shift were changes in property tax policies and, more consequentially as the years passed, gentrification. The children of the white middle-class families that had moved out of the city post–World War II were moving back in, a stream that would swell to a tidal wave by the end of the century. SROs, along with run-down apartment buildings and abandoned warehouses, were being renovated into upscale apartments and condominiums. Once marginal neighborhoods were becoming chic.

With their homes literally pulled out from under them, the poor and formerly institutionalized had nowhere to go. Whereas earlier in the century, most of New York's homeless had been older white men, now thousands of people of all ages and races were on the streets. Especially heartbreaking was the rise in the number of homeless families, many also suffering from cuts in the city and federal welfare rolls.

To help address the problem, the city established so-called welfare hotels, meant to provide temporary housing for the displaced families until more permanent solutions could be found. Only a few such havens had existed prior to 1960, but in the 1970s the city was home to forty welfare hotels sheltering one thousand families, and by 1987 it was spending $150 million annually to house over five thousand homeless families in fifty-five welfare hotels—many near Madison Square Park.

Among the first of these 1970s hostelries was none other than the former St. Omer's Hotel on the block's west side, now known as the St. Denis and in its last incarnation before the Masons' wrecking ball. The welfare hotels garnered exorbitant fees for housing the homeless, with rents for a single room as high as $3,000 a month ($20,000 today), leading many greedy hoteliers to invite the homeless in. But in the St. Denis's case, the cash cow didn't last long. The hotel was removed from the city's list of welfare hotels in 1972, as it failed to meet even the required low standards for such housing; it "was found to be an undesirable place for welfare [recipients] to inhabit," a city spokesman said. Nonetheless, the hotel's owner-manager, Nathan Posner, found a way to claim that welfare recipients still lived in the St. Denis and in August 1973 was arrested for illegally cashing more than $6,000 (about $32,000 today) in public assistance checks.

Other, longer-lasting welfare hotels were just north of Madison Square Park. The closest were the Prince George, Latham, and Madison hotels, all on East Twenty-seventh and Twenty-eighth streets between Fifth and Madison avenues. By 1986, these three buildings were housing 600 families with 1,500 children, while they and four other welfare hotels between East Twenty-seventh Street and West Thirty-second Street held 1,090 families with 2,500 children—or one fourth of all the families being sheltered by the city.

The hotels were no places for children or parents. Typically, their halls were lit by bare bulbs, if at all; toilets and drains did not work; roaches skittered across floors and walls; stairwells reeked of urine and marijuana; and fights and break-ins were constants. Children stared blankly at television screens for hours on end. Parents slept with knives under their pillows.

Madison Square Park offered little respite for the families either. Neglected by the city, its patchy lawns turned to mud in the rain and dust in dry weather. Today's playground did not exist, benches were broken or missing, and fountains ran dry. Homeless individuals such as Mr. Loges and Mr. Townsend slept in the park by night, while drug dealers and petty criminals frequented it by day. Poverty, unemployment, and a crack and heroin epidemic had led to a crime wave; the New York Police Department had declared 1980 the worst year of crime in the city ever. Streetwise New Yorkers took off their jewelry before boarding the subways, held their purses and wallets tight when on the street, and sometimes asked their taxicab drivers to wait until they were safely inside their buildings before driving off. Madison Square was generally safe during the day, but the families always had to be on guard.

The Twenty-third Street block was too far away from the hotels' vortex to be directly affected by them, but their nearby location was another blow to its already diminished appeal. Trucks thundered down its Twenty-third Street side day and night, its Toy Center stood sullen and soulless most of the year, and its office buildings shut up tight at five P.M., taking all signs of life with them. As earlier in the century, the block was not a destination—just a place to walk through on the way to somewhere else. On Sixth Avenue three blocks south of Twenty-third Street pulsated the Limelight, one of the era's hottest and most controversial nightclubs, housed in a former church, while farther west flourished other discos, the experimental Squat Theatre, and the Rawhide leather bar, a gay outpost on Eighth Avenue and Twenty-first Street where, according to one observer, "pants were optional."

Most of the Madison Square–area welfare hotels would be shuttered by 1990, as the homeless families were moved elsewhere. But it would take over a decade for the square to fully recover from its deprivations and enter a new era. The northern end of Madison Square Park was partially revived in 1988 when asphalt paths were replaced and a playground added, but the park was not completely revitalized until 2001.

* * *

In 1985, during the height of the neighborhood's homelessness problem, the bad-boy celebrity photographer Robert Mapplethorpe moved onto the block. Few people took much notice, but even those who did had no idea that his move was a harbinger of things to come. Like Madison Square, the block would soon reach the end of one historical cycle and enter another. Advertising agencies, publishing houses, and restaurants were starting to move to Fifth Avenue and Broadway south of Twenty-third Street, and real estate brokers hoping to entice others to do the same had started referring to the neighborhood by a catchy new name: the "Flatiron District."

Born in 1946, Robert Mapplethorpe had been raised in a middle-class, Roman Catholic family in the suburb of Floral Park, Long Island. He loved art from an early age and spent endless hours coloring, sketching, and making jewelry—no matter that jewelry making was then considered a girl's craft. He went to a public school and reveled in being an altar boy, as it allowed him to enter shadowy realms filled with secrets. He was fascinated by Catholicism's rituals and by its emphasis on the battle between good and evil, light and dark, a battle that would play out in his own life.

When Mapplethorpe was twenty-one years old and studying art at the Pratt Institute in Brooklyn, he met Patti Smith, the poet, artist, and future rock and roll star. Instant soulmates, the two became lovers, staying up late into the night sketching, dreaming about their futures, and sharing stories of their childhoods. "We used to laugh at our small selves, saying that I was a bad girl trying to be good and that he was a good boy trying to be bad," Smith writes in her award-winning memoir *Just Kids*. "Through the years these roles would reverse, then reverse again, until we came to accept our dual natures."

Two years after they met, Mapplethorpe and Smith moved into the Chelsea Hotel at 222 West Twenty-third Street between Seventh and Eighth avenues, two blocks west of the photographer's future loft. The couple must have passed by the block many times, perhaps stopping to shelter in one of its doorways during a rainstorm, but probably never eating at one of its luncheonettes frequented by office workers. Desperately poor, they slept together in a single bed, cooked on a hotplate, washed their clothes in a sink, and worked obsessively on their art in the cheapest room the Chelsea had to offer.

As the Flatiron Building had seemed to embody the spirit of the Fifth Avenue side of the block in the early 1900s, so the Chelsea Hotel seemed to embody the spirit of its Sixth Avenue side in the mid- to late 1900s. For although the red-brick Beaux Arts edifice with its fanciful black balconies was best known as a haven for artists, it was also the haunt of more marginal types much like those who had once roamed the Tenderloin. Here, on the one hand, Thomas Wolfe wrote *You Can't Go Home Again* (1940); William S. Burroughs wrote *Naked Lunch* (1959); Bob Dylan kept an apartment from 1961 to 1964; Arthur Miller lived from 1962 to 1968; Andy Warhol filmed *Chelsea Girls* (1966); Joni Mitchell lived with Leonard Cohen, inspiring her to write "Chelsea Morning" (1968); Janis Joplin met up with Leonard Cohen, inspiring him to write "Chelsea Morning No. 2" (1968); and Arthur C. Clarke wrote the screenplay for *2001: A Space Odyssey* (1968). But here, too, on the other hand, roamed junkies, prostitutes, and pimps. Usually arriving as soon as the sun set, they frequented the hotel's first-floor SRO rooms as their counterparts had once frequented the Sixth Avenue side of the block.

"Junkies would break the lock [of the SRO rooms] and go in and shoot up all the time," Ed Hamilton, a former hotel resident and author of *Legends of the Chelsea Hotel*, told *Vanity Fair* in 2013. "And the prostitutes . . . the way it works is that three or four of them rent a room and they take turns with their johns, a john every half an hour."

* * *

In 1972 Robert Mapplethorpe received an intriguing phone call. "Is this the shy pornographer?" the voice on the other end asked. Speaking was Sam Wagstaff, the influential art curator and collector, fifty years old to Mapplethorpe's twenty-five. Wagstaff had seen a photograph of Mapplethorpe at a friend's house and asked for his phone number. The two men met that same day and became lovers.

Soon thereafter, Mapplethorpe took Wagstaff to a photo exhibit at the Metropolitan Museum of Art, where Wagstaff had a revelation: photography was an art form. Hitherto, photography had been widely regarded as nothing more than a mechanical process—photos were documents, not art. From then on, Wagstaff helped turn that viewpoint around by scouring flea markets and auctions, buying up photographs by such early masters as Julia Margaret Cameron, Gustave Le Gray, and Nadar, and convincing gallery owners and museum curators to exhibit them.

Wagstaff and Mapplethorpe ended their physical affair in 1976, but remained close. And when Wagstaff sold his photography collection in 1984, by then one of the largest and most valuable in the world, to the J. Paul Getty Museum in Los Angeles, he bought Mapplethorpe a loft on the block at 35 West Twenty-third Street. Originally home to the D. S. Hess furniture company, the four-story building had been converted into apartments with one unit per each of the upper floors and a commercial space below. Mapplethorpe's loft was on the top floor and cost a then-startling $500,000 ($1.2 million today). Today, the apartment units in 35 West Twenty-third Street are valued in the neighborhood of $5 million.

* * *

Mapplethorpe was far from the first celebrity photographer to live or work near Madison Square. Photography had been integral to the area long before his birth and would continue to be so for decades after his death.

The first major photographer to arrive on the square had been William Kurtz, who in 1874 set up an imposing studio and gallery at 6 East Twenty-third Street, a few doors west of Amos Eno's former home at 26 East Twenty-third Street and diagonally across from the block. A German immigrant who had begun his career as a lithographer and drawing teacher, Kurtz was a master of "cabinet photography," a new larger-format technique that allowed for more subtle work than had previously been possible. As a formally trained artist, Kurtz knew exactly how to work with light and dark, and customers flocked to pose for his "Rembrandt-style" portraits.

Moving into a studio at 256 Fifth Avenue near Twenty-eighth Street around 1885 was Napoleon Sarony, another highly acclaimed portrait photographer of his day. His 1888 photograph of the Union Army general

William T. Sherman was used as a model for the engraving of the first Sherman postage stamp, and one of his portraits of Oscar Wilde became the subject of a U.S. Supreme Court case that led to the extension of copyright protection to photography.

Renting space on the ground floor of Marietta Stevens's beloved Victoria Hotel on Twenty-seventh Street from the early 1880s through about 1900 was the celebrated photo dealer Charles Ritzmann. Born in Austria, he had originally traded in "Guns, Revolvers, Rifles, Fishing Tackle, and Sporting Goods," but after his move to Madison Square began selling celebrity photographs. In time, his gallery contained virtually every available image of every notable personage of the Gilded Age, from Samuel Clemens (Mark Twain) to Lily Langtry, in numbers far exceeding those of any other public source. Ritzmann was not a photographer himself, yet issued hundreds of photos, many appropriated without permission from other photographers, under his brand name.

Then there was the famed duo Edward Steichen and Albert Stieglitz, whose iconic pictures of the Flatiron Building are widely reproduced on posters and greeting cards to this day. The two were close friends, and in 1905 Steichen urged Stieglitz to open a gallery across from his apartment at 291 Fifth Avenue at Thirtieth Street. Stieglitz did so, and his "Little Galleries of the Photo-Secession," more popularly known simply as "291," went on to exhibit not just photographs by such names as Gertrude Käsebier and Clarence White but early masterpieces of avant-garde art. It was in the three tiny rooms of 291 that Americans first saw the work of Henri Matisse, Auguste Rodin, Pablo Picasso, Paul Cézanne, and many others.

Another wave of photographers arrived in the neighborhood in the 1960s. Taking over the inexpensive lofts that had been abandoned by clothing manufacturers after the demise of the Ladies' Mile, they set up studios and film labs on the blocks between about Seventh and Park avenues, Eighteenth and Twenty-fifth streets. A newsletter covering the goings-on of the new photo district was then established. Started up by a photographer's assistant hoping to find more work, *Photo District News* was free at first, but later morphed into an award-winning, subscription-based publication that is still regarded as required reading by professional photographers today.

Among the most influential of the 1960s photo pioneers was Baldev Duggal, who had arrived in New York from a small village in India in 1957 with just two hundred dollars in his pocket. The son of an insurance manager who had been imprisoned for peaceful resistance to British rule, he had a dream: he wanted to make more money than then U.S. president Dwight Eisenhower ($100,000 at the time; about $930,000 today). He lived in a YMCA at first and saved up enough money to take a single course at Columbia University. Given his dream, a course in business or finance would have made the most sense, but instead he chose a class in color theory. He had fallen in love with photography as a boy, thanks to his grandfather, who had given him a Kodak Brownie camera, the great equalizer that had taken photography out of the hands of the professionals and wealthy and put it into the hands of ordinary people.

From that start, Duggal moved on to establish a small film-processing business, using the bathtub in his apartment to develop film. His enterprise grew quickly, and in the early 1960s, he opened a laboratory at 9 West Twentieth Street, a twelve-story building that he later bought. A decade later, he developed a "dip and dunk" machine that automated film processing, previously done primarily by hand, and in the 1980s invested presciently in the then-new markets of digital imaging. By the time Mapplethorpe moved to the block, Duggal was a foremost name in the film and graphics business, and was indeed making more than President Eisenhower had.

Duggal's relationship to the block would also prove to be more than tangential, for in 1999 he would move his corporate headquarters into No. 29 of 27-33 West Twenty-third Street, the building that had once housed publishing companies, and open Duggal Visual Solutions on its ground floor. Into this huge, well-lit, state-of-the-art expanse would flock photographers and creative directors from all over the country. Every major museum in New York City had something produced by Duggal in its collection, and its work hung in offices all over the world.

Complementing Duggal's was the Aperture Foundation, publisher of the prestigious photography magazine *Aperture* and photography books. Founded in 1952 by Minor White, Dorothea Lange, and Ansel Adams, among others, the foundation moved its headquarters into a brownstone at 20 East Twenty-third Street in 1985, the same year Mapplethorpe arrived on the block. That winter *Aperture* published the first of many articles about him, and four years later opened the Burden Gallery, devoted to photography, on its lower floors.

For photography to be connected with the Twenty-third Street block seemed more than apt. Photography is all about light and shadow, brightness and darkness, presentation and obfuscation, the capturing of reality and the distortion of it.

* * *

By the time Mapplethorpe took up residence at No. 35, he was at the height of his career. Revered by some, reviled by others, he had had more than forty solo gallery exhibits and been the topic of countless articles and discussions. The subjects of his elegant, refined, and highly stylized black-and-white compositions had run the gamut from celebrities to flowers, but he was best known for his jaw-dropping, homoerotic pictures of naked and semi-naked men, many engaged in S&M: a naked white man hanging upside down, a chain around his neck, another man gripping his balls; a Black man in a polyester suit, his cock hanging out, his head cropped off; a self-portrait of the photographer in leather chaps, the thick bullwhip of a devil's tail hanging out his rectum. The blunt eroticism of his work had sent shockwaves through a country that still regarded homosexuality as deviant behavior and triggered a national debate about art and obscenity. To which Mapplethorpe had at one point responded: "I'm looking for the unexpected. I'm looking for things I've never seen before . . . I was in a position to take those pictures. I felt an obligation to do them."

Mapplethorpe decorated his new home with the best of the best: Stickley and Biedermeier furniture, black leather chairs, silk taffeta pillows, rare Gustavsberg vases, and expensive religious and occult objects arranged in small altars. On one wall hung a silkscreen portrait of him by Andy Warhol. Everything about the place, photographed by *House & Garden* in 1988, spelled perfection and control.

In 1986 a Whitney Museum curator commissioned Mapplethorpe to take photographs for a new book. Titled *Fifty New York Artists: A Critical Selection of Painters and Sculptors Working in New York*, it was to include portraits of such subjects as Louise Nevelson, Willem de Kooning, Jasper Johns, and Keith Haring. Mapplethorpe photographed some of the artists in his loft, and as the well-known men and women filed in and out of No. 35, many passersby on the block probably had no idea who they were. As a predominantly commercial thoroughfare, West Twenty-third Street was home to ordinary businesses run by ordinary businesspeople who paid little attention to the art world. Next door to Mapplethorpe's building in 27-33 West Twenty-third Street were the lofts and offices of Commonwealth Toy & Novelty, Belt Components, Sino-American Furniture, and Joe-Ann Company, maker of elastic goods. No. 25 held the 23rd Street Delicatessen; No. 49, Foto Cell; No. 61, Seido Karate, which remained on the block until 2019; and No. 63, Luigi's Pizza.

Also on the block, and reflecting a vastly different lifestyle than that of Mapplethorpe and friends, was Castro Convertible. The iconic, wholesome company had moved into 43 West Twenty-third Street in 1983 and chiseled its name in stone on the facade (still visible today). Like many of the Toy Center companies, Castro had been founded by an immigrant, Bernard Castro, who had arrived penniless in New York from Sicily in 1919. His first store had been just one of many small interior decorating shops in the city, but during the Depression, inspiration hit—he would make sofas that opened into beds. The idea earned him many millions and turned his daughter Bernadette into a celebrity; at age four, she began starring in Castro television commercials, demonstrating how even a small child could open a sofa bed.

At night in the mid-1980s, after the offices had closed and the businesspeople had gone home, the block went still, its streets shrouded in darkness, streetlights casting shadows. Only a few windows were illuminated, and all the ground-floor shops were shut. Up above, though, on the top floor of No. 35, a light was always on. Mapplethorpe was working, always working, or socializing with friends. In October 1986 he had been diagnosed with AIDS, the scourge that swept through New York's gay community in the 1980s and 1990s, and he knew his time was limited.

Wrote his lover Jack Walls in a poem for the Visual AIDS Last Address Tribute Walk many years later:

Robert and I lived here at 35 West 23rd street in the late 1980's.
Those years were very difficult years.
I was a heroin addict back then.
Robert was dying from AIDS . . .
These were very very dark times for me and for those who lived
through them with me.
For it seemed as if the whole world was dying.
All my friends,
friends of friends
friends of friends of friends of friends.
Some of these people I'd never even met,
but in death we were all friends,
we felt one another's pain.
These were dark times, and everyone was dying . . .

*   *   *

In July 1988 the Whitney Museum of American Art presented Mapplethorpe's first major solo museum show. The photographer had dropped to a skeletal 113 pounds by then and was sick all the time, yet on opening night, there he was, dressed in a stylish purple satin dinner jacket, white tuxedo shirt, and black velvet shoes monogrammed with his initials. A couch had been set up for him in one of the galleries, and here he held court as a crowd of sixteen hundred swirled around him. The paparazzi jockeyed for position and lightbulbs flashed.

The exhibit received rave reviews, and after the show, prices for Mapplethorpe's photographs skyrocketed. He luxuriated in all the attention and, astonishingly, returned to work, photographing in his loft from an adjustable chair with wheels, a nurse hovering in the background. He was certain that a cure for AIDS would be found in time to save him.

It was in that spirit that Mapplethorpe hosted what would prove to be his final extravagant act, held on the block on November 4, 1988. The event began in the early evening and lasted far into the night, as limousine after limousine pulled up to 35 West Twenty-third Street, celebrities piled out, and passersby stopped short—a scene reminiscent of the days when aristocrats arrived at the Madison Square Theatre, commoners watching from the shadows. It was Robert's forty-second birthday, and he had invited 250 people to help him celebrate, Death be damned. Among them were the actors Susan Sarandon, Sigourney Weaver, and Gregory Hines, all of whom he had photographed; the Earl of Warwick, the Prince and Princess Michael of Greece, the gallery owner Mary Boone; and numerous men in black leather. The guests brought gifts and helped themselves to beluga caviar as tuxedoed waiters circulated with flutes of champagne. A birthday cake appeared, and everyone sang "Happy Birthday." Robert made a silent wish and blew out the candles.

Four months later, on March 9, 1989, he was dead.

CHAPTER 21

Time Awaits

For three long years, from 2007 to 2010, the east side of the block seemed to slumber, perhaps in mourning for its lost toys, perhaps exhausted by all it had seen and heard. Time had washed in and out, in and out, seemingly more through the east side of the block than any other part. Lives and buildings fleeting by, retreating into the past, leaving only faint imprints behind.

Inside the old Fifth Avenue Building, however, men and women were hard at work. The edifice, now renamed 200 Fifth Avenue, was undergoing a $135 million renovation. L&L Holding Company, a real estate investment firm, had purchased the former Toy Center in 2007 and hired Studios Architecture to turn it into a modern office building—a challenge, as the building, along with almost the entire block and much of the area between Fifteenth and Twenty-third streets, Park Avenue South and Sixth Avenue, had been designated part of the Ladies' Mile Historic District in 1989 and was thus protected from major architectural change. The building's former bronze entranceway was being replaced by glass, its limestone-vaulted ceiling refurbished, and an abandoned space on its ground floor restored into an outdoor courtyard. New mechanical systems that used sustainable refrigerants were also being installed, along with a rainwater-capturing system on the roof and a Green-e sourced core electricity system, all of which helped the building earn LEED Gold certification for its environmental considerations, a first for a landmarked building.

L&L Holding was in the right place at the right time. Madison Square Park had been completely restored to its former glory in 2001, with its lawns and flower beds replanted, its paths repaved, and new entrance gateways, lighting, and a reflecting pool added. That same year, the restaurateur Danny Meyer had set up a hot dog stand just outside the park, run out of the kitchen of his nearby Eleven Madison restaurant, and three years later, the stand morphed into the first Shake Shack. Young professionals had replaced most of the down and out, and the buildings surrounding Madison Square, largely ignored by real estate companies for decades, were suddenly hot and getting hotter.

First to sign a lease with L&L, in 2007, even before 200 Fifth Avenue reopened, was the Grey Group, one of the world's largest advertising and media firms. Founded in 1916, Grey leased six floors and set about relocating from its longtime home at 777 Third Avenue. The move was a shock to many of its twelve hundred employees. Grey's old offices had occupied twenty-six floors; now the company had only six. Before, almost everyone had their own office; now there were only three in the entire firm. Like many other companies in the 2000s, the ad agency had adopted an open layout plan in hopes of fostering collaboration and shaking off its stodgy, traditional image.

About a year later another traditional, and in this case legendary, firm signed on: Tiffany & Co., which leased four and a half floors of office space. Eighty years older than Grey, Tiffany had been founded by a Yankee cut in the same mold as Amos Eno—Charles Lewis Tiffany, from the northeastern Connecticut town of Killingly. Tiffany's father had operated a cotton mill and general store and put Charles in charge of the store when he turned fifteen. Charles traveled often to New York on buying trips and in 1837, at age twenty-five, opened a shop of his own with neighbor John Young at 259 Broadway, across from City Hall.

Tiffany & Young sold stationery and "fancy goods" such as costume jewelry and parasols, as well as walking sticks, buggy whips, and cuspidors. Unlike virtually every other store at the time, it marked its merchandise with price tags, and all purchases had to be paid for in full with cash. No haggling. No credit. No exceptions.

From there, the firm moved on to selling jewelry, clocks, and porcelain imported from Europe, and soon began making jewelry of its own. Tiffany's designs differed from those of the Old World. They were simpler, and often drawn from shapes found in nature. These appealed to American women more than Europe's fussy Victorian designs, and by the 1860s, Tiffany's was one of the leading jewelry stores in the country. President Lincoln bought jewelry for Mary Todd at the store, and during the Civil War, Tiffany's supplied the Union Army with finely honed swords and surgical instruments.

Tiffany's moved to Union Square in 1870, where it remained until 1906, when it moved to Fifth Avenue, settling first at Thirty-seventh Street and then at its current flagship location on Fifty-seventh Street. Everyone who was anyone shopped at Tiffany's from the Gilded Age on, including the Vanderbilts, Astors, and Whitneys. Less respectable folk shopped there too. Diamond Jim Brady had Tiffany's make a solid gold chamber pot for Lillian Russell, an eye peering up from its floor. In 1885 the company redesigned the Great Seal of the United States and, in 1919, revised the Medal of Honor at the request of the U.S. Department of the Navy.

Then the world changed, as it has the habit of doing. Tiffany's was sold to Avon Products in 1978, went public in 1987, and in the early 1990s introduced merchandise aimed at the middle class, even while continuing to offer its high-ticket items.

Eighteen months after Tiffany's signed on, 200 Fifth Avenue reached 100 percent occupancy. Most of its ground floor was rented to an Italian food emporium, Eataly, while Lego, the Danish maker of interlocking plastic blocks, leased the huge retail space at the corner of Twenty-third and Fifth, once the site of Eno's Second National Bank. Toys had returned to the block, along with an eight-foot-tall Lego model of the Statue of Liberty's arm, honoring the actual Statue of Liberty arm that had stood in Madison Square Park from 1876 to 1882 as part of a fundraising effort for the statue's completion. Other, smaller stores, including Marimekko, a Finnish textile and clothing store, also moved in.

Next came a tenant unlike any other the edifice had housed before. In 2013 Tiffany's subleased its eighth floor to BuzzFeed, the online media company, then best known for its listicles, online quizzes, and quirky videos; the company's serious news operation was still in its infancy. BuzzFeed was to the future what Tiffany's was to the past, the brazen to the polite, the bold to the refined. Assistants on hoverboards zoomed around delivering packages to staffers in hoodies glued to double-monitor computers, a machine dispensed free frozen yogurt treats, and stuffed animals, coloring books, and games stood at the ready for those employees in need of distraction.

A major player in a new era, BuzzFeed was only one of hundreds of new media, high-tech, and other related start-up companies that had sprung up in the city, and especially the Flatiron District, around the turn of the twentieth century. The dot-com companies had started the wave in the 1990s as the internet took hold, and after that bubble burst in 2001–2, other tech innovators gradually took their place, bringing dramatic change to New York's economy. By 2016, New York State had the third-largest tech sector in the nation, with the city accounting for over 80 percent of the jobs. Between 2007 and 2017, the Flatiron District, dubbed "Silicon Alley," witnessed a 104 percent jump in jobs in the information sector and a 48 percent jump in jobs in the professional, scientific, and technical services sector.

BuzzFeed's tenancy on the block was brief, however. Four years after it moved in, its sublease with Tiffany expired, and it left 200 Fifth to sign one of the biggest leases between Thirty-fourth and Canal streets: six splashy floors of 225 Park Avenue South at Eighteenth Street.

*   *   *

Meanwhile, on the west side of block, a different kind of new economy innovator had been quietly in operation since 1999. Housed in the 1906 office-and-loft building at 40-44 West Twenty-fourth Street, 42 West 24 was an open office space offering short-term desks and work areas for individuals and teams that could be booked and canceled on short notice. Said to be the first such setup in the country, 42 West 24 was the precursor of the modern co-working environment later made popular by WeWork and others. Run by a software company, 42 West 24 placed no emphasis on community—a crucial part of co-working, which is all about networking and collaboration, sharing office amenities and equipment—but was still an important development. For the first time, entrepreneurs and start-up companies had a professional office space in which to work and grow. 42 West 24 is still in business today, offering clients flexible desk arrangements, private offices, conference rooms, and lounges in a low-carbon-footprint environment that includes chairs made of recycled Coca-Cola bottles.

* * *

For most of the twenty-first century, the block was also home to a more old-fashioned incubator of ideas: Touro College. The school had first opened its doors on West Forty-fourth Street in 1971 to a class of thirty-five men, but moved its main campus to 27-33 West Twenty-third Street in 1991, to flourish there with thousands of students, men and women, until 2018.

The school had been founded by Rabbi Bernard Lander, who had seemed as demented to some in his time as Eno had in his. A distinguished scholar who had grown up in an Orthodox family in Manhattan, Lander quit his prestigious position as dean at Yeshiva University at age fifty-three to embark on a project that would have daunted even a far younger person. He wanted to establish what many of his friends and associates privately called "Lander's Lunacy," a college that would teach both Jewish and secular subjects and serve a wide range of students, from Jewish scholars to recent immigrants of all faiths to others historically underserved by higher education.

Lander's Lunacy took far longer to get off the ground than Eno's Folly had, but when it did, it was equally successful. Contained within its Twenty-third Street campus was a School of General Studies, the Touro College Men's Division, and several graduate programs, including schools of social work, health sciences, and education. In the early 2000s, the School of General Studies merged with the school's New Immigrant Division to become the New York School of Career and Applied Sciences, one of its most popular programs, and Touro expanded into 43 West Twenty-third Street next door and 50 West Twenty-third Street across the street.

The rabbi's offices were in Nos. 27-33, and here the Orthodox rabbi and academic sociologist who specialized in the study of poverty and juvenile delinquency continued to serve as Touro's president until his death in 2010 at age ninety-four. By that time, Touro had a student body of over seventeen thousand men and women studying in twenty-nine locations around the world, including a school of Jewish studies in Moscow; colleges of osteopathic medicine in Harlem, California, and Nevada; a professional training school for Hasidic men and another for Hasidic women in Brooklyn; and branches in Paris, Berlin, and Israel. Dreams on the block, container of multitudes, came in all shapes and sizes.

*   *   *

Major change had also come to the Masonic Hall at 46 West Twenty-fourth Street. Between 1986 and 1996 the magnificent edifice had undergone a $15 million renovation, headed by Peruvian designer Felix Chavez of Fine Art Decorating, and when it was done, the press and public were invited in. Say what? astonished reporters asked. Was this the same secret society that had shunned the public eye for so long? Apparently so. The Masons were tired of the suspicion surrounding their organization and eager—some said desperate—to attract new members. There were about 85,000 Masons in New York State in 1996, compared with the all-time peak of 346,000 in 1930. Today, there are about 34,000 Masons in New York State, out of 1,076,000 nationwide, and the Masonic Hall continues to welcome outsiders in. Free tours of the building are offered six days a week.

*   *   *

To the right of the main entrance of 200 Fifth Avenue are two much smaller doors, one discreetly marked with the words CUCINA & MERCATO and the other with FINE ITALIAN FOODS. The small signs belie the splendor behind them: Eataly!, not just a food hall, but a "food temple," as its promoters like to call it. Part fancy grocery store, part sit-down restaurants, and part "food experiences," the enterprise includes a paninoteca, rosticceria, gelateria, espresso counter, cookbook store, and culinary education center.

Eataly opened its doors on August 1, 2010, and instantly the crowds came pouring in, buzzing through the market to alight upon one section or another. To one side was a glistening array of fishes fanned out across mounds of ice; to another, freshly baked focaccia bread and hand-rolled mozzarella. Over there was a savory pizza coming out of a wood-burning oven brought over from Italy, and in that corner beckoned an aisle of olive oil bottles, molten jewels upon a shelf.

Eataly was modeled after a food market of the same name founded in Turin, Italy, in 2007 by consumer electronics businessman Oscar Farinetti. Housed in a converted vermouth factory, the Turin market was an overnight hit, attracting over 2.5 million visitors a year, making it ripe for export.

Farinetti established the Flatiron Eataly with three partners: chef, restaurateur, and TV personality Lidia Bastianich; her son, restaurateur Joe Bastianich; and mega chef and mega TV personality Mario Batali. All three were at 200 Fifth on opening day, as was Mayor Michael Bloomberg, who praised the emporium for creating three hundred new jobs.

The Bastianiches and Batali were old friends. They had met seventeen years earlier, when Batali was the chef at his acclaimed Pó restaurant in the West Village, Lidia was running her renowned Felidia restaurant on the Upper East Side, and she and Joe had just launched Becco in the Theater District. Not long after meeting, the trio formed a partnership, the Batali & Bastianich Hospitality Group, and in 1998 opened Babbo, which shot to restaurant stardom thanks to glowing reviews and a Michelin star. More premier restaurants followed.

During their years together, all three partners had also become television personalities, with Lidia leading the way. She first appeared on *Julia Child: Cooking With Master Chefs* in 1993 and was such a natural that by 1998, she had her own show, *Lidia's Italian Kitchen*, on public television. Other shows came next, along with best-selling cookbooks. Viewers loved her no-nonsense style and classic Italian dishes.

They also loved her personal story. Lidia had begun learning the art of Italian cooking from her grandmother while growing up on the Istrian peninsula in what was then Yugoslavia (now Croatia). But the communist dictator Marshal Tito came to power, and as his regime tightened its control over the peninsula—forbidding the speaking of Italian and practice of Christianity—Lidia and her family fled. They landed in Trieste, Italy, where they spent two years in a refugee camp, partially housed in a former

Nazi concentration camp. Lidia, then eleven, helped out in her school by cooking in the kitchen.

In 1958 the family received visas to enter the United States and flew to New York, to settle in Queens. Lidia worked in restaurants to help her family make ends meet and at age sixteen met her future husband Felix Bastianich, a fellow Istrian immigrant. They wed in 1966 and opened their first restaurant in Queens five years later. Lidia worked as the restaurant's hostess at first, but soon became its chef. Her cooking drew crowds, and she and Felix opened a second restaurant, which drew even larger crowds. (She and Felix divorced in 1998, and Felix passed away in 2010.)

Joe Bastianich began working in his parents' restaurants as soon as he was old enough to help set the tables and joined the family business a year or two after graduating from college. Later, he coauthored books on Italian wine and served as a judge on the American *MasterChef* series and its Italian version, *MasterChef Italia*.

So the Bastianiches had acquired some measure of fame by the time Eataly opened on the block. It was nothing, however, compared with the fame of Mario Batali.

Gargantuan in size and spirit, Batali was America's super chef, super TV personality, and super success story. Born in Seattle, he had arrived in New York in 1992, at age thirty-one, with a duffel bag, a guitar, and a decade's worth of restaurant experience under his belt. He found a low-rent venue in which to set up his first restaurant, Pó, borrowed money from family and friends, and went to work. He had no liquor license, no air conditioning, limited cash with which to buy ingredients, and only thirteen tables, plus two out on the sidewalk in good weather. Nonetheless, the critics raved about the "pure Italianness" of his food.

From there, Batali moved on to ever-ascending heights, forming the partnership with the Bastianiches, opening more acclaimed restaurants, starring in his own cooking shows, and appearing as one of the original chefs on *Iron Chef America*. Audiences all over the country tuned in to watch the gregarious, heavyset, and often sweaty chef, thinning red hair pulled back in a ponytail, dressed in shorts and orange Crocs, cook up magic in the kitchen.

Batali owned only a minority interest in Eataly, but to the many foodies who poured into the emporium and its clones in the years after it opened, he embodied all that the place was about. His many products, including sauces, pastas, olive oils, vinegars, and books, all emblazoned with his beaming face, crowded its shelves, and its website promoted his products: "Find the best of Italy selected for you by Mario Batali . . . Only at Eataly.com!"

But in December 2017, it all came crashing down. The #MeToo movement had begun, and Eater, the food and restaurant news website, reported that four women had come forward to accuse Batali of inappropriate touching. More stories then followed, each worse than the one before.

No one working in the food industry was surprised. Dominated by powerful men, the restaurant world had always been rampant with callous, carnal, predatory behavior—and unabashedly so. Until the #MeToo movement, women working in the restaurant business were expected to put up and shut up, especially if they had career ambitions.

Thirteen months later, in March 2019, the Bastianich family formally ended their twenty-year partnership with the celebrity chef, and five months after that, Batali sold his minority interest in Eataly. The shelves of the food emporium were now packed not with Mario's face but with Lidia's.

*   *   *

The success of Eataly reflected a sea change that had swept through the neighborhoods surrounding Madison Square—and much of Manhattan—beginning in the late 1980s and escalating in the 2000s. High-end chain retailers such as Armani, Club Monaco, and Kenneth Cole had moved to Fifth Avenue just south of the square. The abandoned Ladies' Mile stores on Sixth Avenue and Broadway had been magnificently restored, to house big-box chain retailers on the ground floor and gleaming, high-ceilinged condos up above. Former photography studios had been converted into luxury residences for the upper middle class. The Chelsea Hotel had closed and the Limelight nightclub, Rawhide leather bar, and other underground gathering spots were no more. Gourmet food shops and expensive restaurants glittered everywhere, and the sidewalks were filled with young and not-so-young professionals glued to their cellphones. Robert Mapplethorpe wouldn't have recognized the place.

The change had largely come about because of New York's oldest raison d'être: money. Careerists employed in the financial, high-tech, other new economy, and real estate industries were bursting with it; an ever-growing number of well-heeled tourists—increasing 20 percent citywide between 2013 and 2019—were profligately spending it; international billionaires buying up pieds-à-terre and shell companies laundering money through real estate were heavily investing it, helping send rents and other consumer prices sky-high. The city's population had also increased by over a million people since 1980, leading to an explosion of what Jeremiah Moss, author of *Vanishing New York: How a Great City Lost Its Soul*, calls "hyper-gentrification." Manhattan, home to 65 billionaires and 380,000 million-aires by 2019—making it the wealthiest city in the world—was morphing from an island of diverse socioeconomic populations into a sanitized suburbia that only the rich could afford. Overall, the city's poverty rates remained intractable, at about 19 percent, but few of those 3.4 million poor frequented mid-Manhattan.

In many ways, the overflowing wealth had returned Madison Square and its environs to their nineteenth-century splendor. The park was clean and lovely, the site of frequent concerts and art exhibits, and its surrounding streets were safe. An inviting public space, Flatiron Public Plazas, was operating directly in front of 200 Fifth Avenue. Filled with movable tables and chairs, big shade umbrellas, and planters filled with flowers in the spring, summer, and fall, it hosted free programs and special events, including summertime tech and fitness classes, and a weekly history walking tour.

Hotels had moved back into the Flatiron District, too, with the number of hotel rooms in the area increasing almost 94 percent between 2011 and 2018. Closest to the block were the NoMad Hotel on Broadway between Twenty-seventh and Twenty-eighth streets, the Broadway Plaza Hotel at Broadway and Twenty-seventh Street, the Flatiron Hotel at Broadway and Twenty-sixth Street, and the Hotel Henri, a small boutique hotel across from the block on the north side of Twenty-fourth Street between Fifth and Sixth avenues.

Instrumental in bringing about many of the improvements was the Flatiron/23rd Street Partnership, formed in 2006 by property owners, businesses, residents, and others interested in revitalizing the area. One of the city's seventy-odd Business Improvement Districts, the association had hired a "Clean Team" that serviced the neighborhood seven days a week, collecting trash, removing graffiti, and more, and partnered with Urban Pathways, a nonprofit housing and support organization, to provide services to the few homeless still in the district—about a dozen individuals in all, some appearing on a chronic basis, others only periodically. The Flatiron/23rd Street Partnership was funded largely by an assessment fee levied on the commercial property within its district.

But with all the improvements had also come loss. The neighborhood's unique character had faded beneath its newly scrubbed facade, and, for all its amenities, the area had little of its nineteenth-century magic, early twentieth-century commercial energy, or late twentieth-century semi-outlaw feel. Whereas in the 1800s and 1900s, the district's businesses had been distinctive enterprises, many family owned, some devoted to photography and art, now many were bland lookalikes of corporate chains. Whereas in the 1800s and 1900s, the neighborhood had been composed of many distinctive peoples, now most everyone seemed the same.

The explosion of online retailing had also contributed to the blandness encroaching on the neighborhood and the city. Reported vacant retail square footage in Manhattan doubled between 2007 and 2017, from 2.1 million square feet to about 4.3 million, due largely to competition from the internet. By the late 2010s, most of the block's ground-floor commercial spaces held not retail shops but service providers such as health centers, restaurants, and banks. Duggal shuttered its magnificent photo retail shop at 29 West Twenty-third Street in 2018, to open a smaller store on the second floor of 43 West Twenty-fourth Street, across from the block, and launch ShopDuggal.com. No. 25 West Twenty-third Street housed a quick-service Indian kitchen; No. 35, an urgent care clinic; Nos. 49-51, a fitness training center; and No. 69, an Irish pub. No. 67, the only one-story building on the block, contained a deli, as it had for decades, and the ground floor of the Masonic Building, No. 71, held a Chase bank. No. 44 West Twenty-fourth Street held a furniture rental firm; No. 30, a taco eatery; and No. 6, the Arts and Crafts building once owned by Phillips Phoenix, a New Orleans–inspired restaurant. The one thriving store on the block, aside from those connected with Eataly, was P.C. Richard & Sons, an appliance megastore at 53 West Twenty-third, the former site of the Eden Musée.

The diversity of the city could now best be seen not on the block's streets but in its office buildings, full of dozens of companies involved in dozens of industries, including health care, media, advertising, design, law, insurance, technology, and finance. Notable tenants in the Masonic Building included New York City Audubon, a branch of the national organization; the Postgraduate Center for Mental Health; Mohawk Industries; Brightpoint Health; and the NYC Seminar and Conference Center. *Publishers Weekly* and *Fader Magazine*, a music and lifestyle publication, were also here, continuing the block's publishing tradition. A-CAP, a risk and services provider for the insurance industry, leased office space at 49-51 West Twenty-third Street, and VST Enterprises, a cybertechnology firm, housed its U.S. headquarters at 43 West Twenty-third Street. Unique Threading, an eyebrow beauty bar, occupied the second floor of 25 West Twenty-third. Edrington Americas, the American arm of the Scottish spirits company known for its single malts, had offices in No. 27, Touro College's former home; the school had moved out of the building and off the block in 2018, due in part to rising rents. Among the tenants in the former Castro Building at 43 West Twenty-third was the new-economy Rise New York, a co-working space created by financial giant Barclays, and the old-economy Spectrum, an internet, cable, and phone service provider.

* * *

In December 2017 construction began on the first new building to go up on the block in decades: 39-41 West Twenty-third Street/20-22 West Twenty-fourth Street. The project had been many years in the making. Anbau Enterprises had acquired the lots (once the site of the FAO Schwarz toy store on the south side and Stanford White's hideaway and the store's

back entrance on the north) six years earlier, but drawing up a suitable
architectural plan for them had been challenging. Since the block was part
of the Ladies' Mile Historic District, nothing could be built on it without
the approval of the Landmarks Preservation Commission. In addition, the
lots, like most lots on the block, were zoned for commercial use only, and
the developers were intent on erecting a residential building. To do so, a
special permit was required.

In the end, architects COOKFOX designed two connected residential
buildings, one twenty-two stories tall (on the Twenty-third Street side) and
the other ten stories tall (on the Twenty-fourth Street side). Together they
held forty-four luxury condos, four affordable rentals, retail spaces, a garage,
a children's playroom, and a fitness center. Some of the most expensive
condos were duplexes, some had terraces, and the prestigious upper floors
offered views of Madison Square Park. The condos were well on their way
to completion in early 2020 when life on the block abruptly stopped.

*   *   *

In February 2020 the future of the block had seemed inevitable. Along with
the rest of the city, it would only become more suburbanized, more soulless, more corporate. More high-end chains would arrive, more wealthy
residents would move in, and more of its once multitudinous identity would
disappear. Where were the block's former contradictions? Where were its
mysteries and secrets? Is all seemed gone for good.

But then in March, without warning to all but a vigilant few, came
catastrophe. It began with the sirens, wailing, wailing, day and night, in
homes and offices, in streets and parks, as the coronavirus crept in, slowly
at first and then roaring with the rage of a furious giant suddenly roused
from sleep. Offices, restaurants, and nonessential businesses closed. People
vanished from streets. Body bags proliferated. By the end of the month,
average daily foot traffic through the Flatiron Public Plazas in front of 200
Fifth Avenue had plummeted by 75 percent. Everyone was working from
home. Everyone was afraid to go out.

Months passed and summer approached. The wails of the sirens grew
less frequent and some things revived. People reappeared, sheathed in
masks and socially distanced, walking in Madison Square Park, dining at

sidewalk tables outside Eataly, shopping at P.C. Richard a few customers at a time. But as elsewhere in the city, the block's offices remained shuttered, and a few closed for good, as did the New Orleans–inspired restaurant at 6 West Twenty-fourth Street.

Following the death of George Floyd, a Black man killed in Minneapolis on May 25 by a white police officer kneeling on his neck for nine and a half murderous minutes, Black Lives Matter protests began. The city's first demonstration was small, with a group of about one hundred marching from Union Square to City Hall, but almost immediately, pent-up anger and frustration over racial injustice exploded throughout all of New York's communities, and hundreds of marches and demonstrations formed everywhere. Some protestors gathered in Madison Square Park, carrying signs that read WE CAN'T BREATHE, SAY THEIR NAMES, and NO JUSTICE, NO PEACE, while others marched or bicycled down Fifth Avenue or across West Twenty-third Street, past the block, echoes of the Silent Protest Parade a century before. Ground-floor business nailed plywood over their windows to protect against the handful of looters who had joined the overwhelmingly peaceful crowds.

In July an encampment of homeless people appeared on Sixth Avenue between Twenty-third and Twenty-fourth streets, across from the side of the block that never seemed able to escape its past. Mostly men, they set up makeshift homes of cardboard boxes and shopping carts. Why they appeared at that site and where they came from is unclear. The shelters had been closed because of the pandemic, but their clients had been moved to hotels—a welcome change for many. The encampment may have arisen because of the closing of the subways at night to allow for cleaning during the pandemic; under normal circumstances, the subways are open 24/7, providing a round-the-clock haven for those homeless individuals who prefer living on the streets to staying in shelters. Complaints about the encampment from area businessowners and residents began and escalated until, in September, the city cleared it away and the homeless moved elsewhere.

Fall came and the block settled in for the long haul, with most of its offices still closed, most of its residents still working from home, and most of its ground-floor businesses still only partially reopened. Nonetheless, the number of pedestrians passing daily through the Flatiron Public Plazas rose by an average 33 percent during the last months of the year as the city mustered on. Not until the summer of 2021 would a semblance of normalcy return.

*   *   *

What had seemed inevitable in early 2020 was no more. The only certainty was uncertainty. A return to the block's former contradictions seemed likely—or not. Some were predicting a continuation of New York City's pandemic-induced decline, an erosion of its tax base, and a new surge in homelessness and crime; others foresaw a postpandemic boom, triggering an avalanche of glitz and glamour. Would businesses on the block close? Restaurants shutter? Or would new upmarket tenants move in, more shiny money arrive? "The past and present wilt—I have fill'd them, emptied them. And proceed to fill my next fold of the future . . . not a bit tamed," wrote Walt Whitman, and so it is with the block and the city. Time awaits. Change awaits. Unpredictable. Unfathomable.

ACKNOWLEDGMENTS

First and foremost, I would like to thank Kenneth Jackson, Jacques Barzun Professor Emeritus of History at Columbia University, whose wonderful courses on New York City and urban history first inspired me to write this book. A thousand thanks, too, to my three outstanding editors at Bloomsbury: Nancy Miller, for believing in, and helping me find a focus for, this book; Daniel Loedel, for his many thoughtful edits and insightful ideas on how to reframe parts of my manuscript; and Elizabeth Ellis, for raising interesting points that I hadn't considered before. I am also indebted to the librarians of the New York Public Library and New-York Historical Society for helping me locate critical materials in their vast collections; Kenneth Cobb and the staff of the New York City Municipal Archives for directing me toward the block's earliest historical records; Miriam Berman for her expertise on Madison Square; my agent, Neeti Madan of Sterling Lord Literistic, for her unfailing support; my production editor, Barbara Darko, copy edtior, Paul Dragosh, proofreader, Katherine R. Kiger, and indexer, Harvey Lee Gable, for their careful reading of my manuscript; and everyone at Bloomsbury for shepherding this book through the publishing process.

IMAGE PLATE CREDITS

Page 1, top: The Miriam and Ira D. Wallach Division of Art, Prints and Photographs: Picture Collection, The New York Public Library. "Nieuw Nederlandt." New York Public Library Digital Collections. Accessed August 30, 2021. https://digitalcollections.nypl.org/items/510d47e1-2bb7-a3d9-e040-e00a18064a99.

Page 1, bottom: Brown, Henry Collins. Cover of *Fifth Avenue, Old and New, 1824–1924*. New York: Fifth Avenue Association, ca. 1924.

Page 2, top: City of New York and Office of the Manhattan Borough President/Museum of the City of New York.

Page 2, center: The Miriam and Ira D. Wallach Division of Art, Prints and Photographs: Picture Collection, The New York Public Library. "Madison Cottage, at Broadway and 5th Avenue, N.Y.C., 1850." New York Public Library Digital Collections. Accessed August 30, 2021. https://digitalcollections.nypl.org/items/510d47e0-d6cf-a3d9-e040-e00a18064a99.

Page 2, bottom: The Miriam and Ira D. Wallach Division of Art, Prints and Photographs: Print Collection, The New York Public Library. "M. Franconi's Hippodrome (N.E. Broadway & 23 St.) 1853." New York Public Library Digital Collections. Accessed October 5, 2021. https://digitalcollections.nypl.org/items/5e66b3e9-27cf-d471-e040-e00a180654d7.

Page 3, top left: "Manhattan: 5th Avenue—23rd Street." Irma and Paul Milstein Division of United States History, Local History and Genealogy, The New York Public Library. © NYPL.

Page 3, top right: King, Moses. "Amos Richards Eno." *Notable New Yorkers of 1896–1899: A Companion Volume to* King's Handbook of New York City. New York: Moses King, 1899. Reprinted from *Madison Square: The Park and Its Celebrated Landmarks* by Miriam Berman. Salt Lake City: Gibbs Smith, 2001.

Page 3, bottom: Library of Congress, Prints & Photographs Division, LC-USZ 62-132411.

Page 4, top: Rare Book Division, The New York Public Library. "DAILY MENU, DINNER [held by] [FIFTH AVENUE HOTEL?] [at] 'NEW YORK, NY'

(HOTEL)." The New York Public Library Digital Collections. 1905. https://digitalcollections.nypl.org/items/510d47db-74be-a3d9-e040-e00a18064a99.

Page 4, bottom: The Miriam and Ira D. Wallach Division of Art, Prints and Photographs: Picture Collection, The New York Public Library. "Stock gambling at 'Gallagher's Evening Exchange.'" New York Public Library Digital Collections. Accessed August 30, 2021. https://digitalcollections.nypl.org/items/510d47e1-0598-a3d9-e040-e00a18064a99.

Page 5, top: National Portrait Gallery, Smithsonian Institution.

Page 5, bottom left: King, Moses, ed. "Hoyt's Madison-Square Theatre, 24th Street, Near Broadway." *King's Handbook of New York City: An Outline History and Description of the American Metropolis*. New York: Moses King, 1893.

Page 5, bottom right: Library of Congress, Prints & Photographs Division, LC-B2- 745-7.

Page 6, top: Foster, George G. "Hooking a Victim." *New York by Gas-Light and Other Urban Sketches*. New York: Lithograph and publication by Serrell & Perkins, ca. 1850. Museum of the City of New York.

Page 6, bottom left: National Portrait Gallery, Smithsonian Institution.

Page 6, bottom right: Graham, Charles."The Electric Light in Madison Square, New York." *Harper's Weekly*, January 14, 1882. Reprinted from *Madison Square: The Park and Its Celebrated Landmarks* by Miriam Berman. Salt Lake City: Gibbs Smith, 2001.

Page 7, top: The Miriam and Ira D. Wallach Division of Art, Prints and Photographs: Picture Collection, The New York Public Library. "New York City—dedication of the masonic temple at the corner of Twenty-third Street and Sixth Aveune, June 2nd—head of the procession passing the temple." The New York Public Library Digital Collections. 1875. https://digitalcollections.nypl.org/items/510d47e0-dae1-a3d9-e040-e00a18064a99.

Page 7, bottom: Gardner, Charles. "The Doctor and His Companion in Disguise." *The Doctor and the Devil, or Midnight Adventures of Dr. Parkhurst*. New York: Gardner & Co., 1894. Collection Development Department. Widener Library. HCL. Harvard University. Accessed October 7, 2021. https://nrs.harvard.edu/urn-3:FHCL:876768.

Page 8, top: Library of Congress, Prints & Photographs Division, LC-DIG-ppmsca-12056.

Page 8, bottom: New-York Historical Society.

NOTES

I am deeply indebted to the many scholars whose work I relied on in writing this book. Many are mentioned in the notes and bibliography below, but two especially invaluable resources that I referred to again and again were *Gotham: A History of New York City to 1898*, by Edwin Burrows and Mike Wallace, and *Madison Square: The Park and Its Celebrated Landmarks*, by Miriam Berman. *Gotham* was my go-to source for general background information on New York City history; *Madison Square* was my go-to source for background information about the history of Madison Square and its surroundings.

For historical information on the block's buildings, including the names of their architects and early tenants, I was extremely lucky to have the New York City Landmarks Designation Commission's *Ladies' Mile Historic District, Designation Report* at my disposal. I am also especially indebted to Henry Hoff for his article "A Colonial Black Family in New York and New Jersey: Pieter Santomee and His Descendants"; Philip Field Horne for his unpublished paper "The Horne Family of Bloomingdale Road"; and Tom Miller, whose wonderful blog, *Daytonian in New York*, often provided me with jumping-off points for further research.

CHAPTER 1: IN THE LAND OF THE REAL PEOPLE

4   "It is a great fight": Daniel Denton, *A Brief Description of New York* (1670), quoted in Edwin Burrows and Mike Wallace, *Gotham*, 9.

5   "An extraordinary and spectacular event": Adriaen van der Donck, *A Description of New Netherland*, 21–22.

5   abundance of ecological communities: Eric Sanderson, *Mannahatta*, 10.

5   "men can scarcely go through them": Nicolas van Wassenaer, *Historisch Verhael* (1624–1630), quoted in J. Franklin Jameson, *Narratives of New Netherland, 1609–1664*, 71.

5   "with fish, both large and small": Jasper Danckaerts, *Journal of Jasper Danckaerts*, 36.

5   "foxes in abundance": David de Vries, *Korte Historiael Ende Journaels Aenteyckeninge* (1655), quoted in Jameson, *Narratives of New Netherland*, 220–21.

7 "useful in treating lunatics": Van der Donck, 116.

7 "called Manhattes": I. N. Phelps Stokes, *The Iconography of New York*, vol. 1, 6.

7 5,295 beaver pelts sent to Europe: Russell Shorto, *The Island at the Center of the World*, 44–45.

8 "High and Mighty Lords": "Peter Schagen Letter," New Netherland Institute, https://www.newnetherlandinstitute.org/history-and-heritage/additional -resources/dutch-treats/peter-schagen-letter/.

10 "must be a very mean fellow": De Vries, quoted in Jameson, *Narratives of New Netherland*, 209.

11 "I heard a great shrieking": quoted in Jameson, 227–28.

12 "under the blue canopy of heaven": quoted in Allen Trelease, *Indian Affairs in Colonial New York* (Ithaca, NY: Cornell University Press, 1960), 83, quoted in Anne-Marie Cantwell and Diana diZeregal Wall, *Unearthing Gotham*, 128.

12 Munsee deaths from epidemics: Cantwell and Wall, 142–43.

CHAPTER 2: HALF FREEDOM

13 "in passing through": Danckaerts, *Journal of Jasper Danckaerts*, 68.

14 "almost entirely taken up": Danckaerts, 64.

15 Dutch conflicted about slavery: Burrows and Wallace, *Gotham*, 32.

17 "We went from the city": Danckaerts, *Journal of Jasper Danckaerts*, 65.

17 "in all to about 6 acres": Stokes, *The Iconography of Manhattan Island*, vol. 6, 75.

18 "Groot Emanuel, negro": Reformed Dutch Church baptism records, quoted in Henry Hoff, "A Colonial Black Family in New York and New Jersey," 103.

19 slavery statistics: Burrows and Wallace, *Gotham*, 48–50, 55–56, 126; "Slavery in New Netherland," New Netherland Institute, https://www.newnetherland institute.org/history-and-heritage/digital-exhibitions/slavery-exhibit/; "1613–1865: Slavery and Freedom," Black New Yorkers website, accessed May 12, 2021.

21 "Well known in the colony": Stokes, *The Iconography of Manhattan Island*, vol. 6, 75.

21 "train the youth of the Dutch": "1613–1865: Slavery and Freedom," Black New Yorkers website, accessed May 12, 2021.

21 Andros returned to the Americas in 1686 to take over as governor of the Dominion of New England (a territory that included New England, New York, and New Jersey). Based in Boston, he again earned enemies, this time for his arrogant governing style, suppression of town governments, and enforcement of laws that restricted the colonists' ability to trade.

21 "30 Acres of Upland" awarded to Solomon Pieters in 1680: Stokes, *The Iconography of Manhattan Island*, vol. 6, 107; *Letters Patent, 1664–2017*, New York State Archives, Series Number: 12943, vol. 5, 6–7. (Numerous histories, including *Valentine's Manual of Old New York*, mistakenly state that the land was granted in 1670.)

22 value of Pieters' Bowery Ward property: New York Tax Lists 1695–1699, cited in Hoff, "A Colonial Black Family in New York and New Jersey," 103.

23 "Iron Tooles Implements": Hoff, 106.

23 Pieters family sells tract to John Horne: Stokes, *The Iconography of Manhattan Island*, vol. 6, 107.

24 "in Torment for Eight or ten hours": quoted in Burrows and Wallace, *Gotham*, 148.

24 "It is found by experience": quoted in Thelma Foote, *Black and White Manhattan*, 150.

25 Lucas Pieters living as indentured servant: Harris, *In the Shadow of Slavery*, 39.

CHAPTER 3: THE JOHN HORNE FARM

27 "Read and Write Perfectly": Philip Field Horne, "The Horne Family of Bloomingdale Road," 3.

29 "a sweet and rural valley": Washington Irving, *Knickerbocker's History of New York*, 388.

29 Manhattan denuded: Richard Howe, "Notes on the Deforestation of Manhattan."

30 Surveyor Casimir Goerck divided the Common Lands in 1796 into lots separated by three long parallel streets, called the East, Middle, and West roads—the future Fourth (Madison), Fifth, and Sixth avenues, respectively—to make the lots easier to sell.

31 "had a Small Patent": Stokes, *The Iconography of Manhattan Island*, vol. 6, 107.

31 "An admirable Beautifying wash": quoted in Burrows and Wallace, *Gotham*, 124.

32 sugar trade and slavery statistics: Burrows and Wallace, 119–20, 127; Harris, *In the Shadow of Slavery*, 29–31.

33 "I could not believe my eyes": quoted in Burrows and Wallace, *Gotham*, 231.

35 "around the tour by Horn's": Hopper Striker Mott, *The New York of Yesterday*, 58.

35 "venerable and stately sycamore trees": Mott, 6.

CHAPTER 4: THE MAKING OF BLOCK 825

37　"the end of the little old city": Stokes, *The Iconography of Manhattan Island*, vol. 1, 407–8.

38　"caused a good deal" "felt called upon": quoted in Stephen Jenkins, *The Greatest Street in the World*, 175.

39　"The natural inequalities": quoted in Paul Cohen and Robert Augustyn, *Manhattan in Maps*, 103.

42　"Following the old-time custom": Mott, *The New York of Yesterday*, 408.

43　"Sweep, O-O-O-O": Paul Gilje and Howard Rock, "'Sweep O! Sweep O!'"

43　"old and well-known": Jenkins, *The Greatest Street in the World*, 234.

45　"earn an honest living": Society for the Reformation of Juvenile Delinquents in the City of New York, *Tenth Annual Report* (New York: Mallon Day, 1835), 17, quoted in the preface to Austin Reed, *The Life and Adventures of a Haunted Convict*, xxix.

45　House of Refuge residents C.A., J.M.C., J.G., S.C.B., D.B.L., and J.P.: The Society for the Reformation of Juvenile Delinquents, *Documents Relative to the House of Refuge*, 60, 61, 91, 57, 93, 58.

46　"home still hanging": Reed, *The Life and Adventures of a Haunted Convict*, 10.

46　"grasped us and lock us": Reed, 28.

47　"Where I come from": quoted in William Bailey, *The Encyclopedia of Police Science* (Oxfordshire: Routledge, 1995), 357.

48　Curiously, the ghost of the House of Refuge reemerged on the Twenty-third Street block decades later. In the late 1800s, the New York Juvenile Asylum, a twenty-nine-acre residential school in Washington Heights, housed its reception branch at 30 West Twenty-fourth Street. The asylum had been founded in 1851 as a kinder, gentler alternative to the House of Refuge, but often failed to deliver on that promise. A case in point occurred in August 1890, when Mrs. Mary Schmaltz appealed to the mayor to help her recover her fourteen-year-old daughter Lizzie from the asylum. She had placed Lizzie there a year earlier, but when she went to the West Twenty-fourth Street office to retrieve her daughter, she was told she could not take Lizzie out due to "bad marks" against her. Lizzie's sister then abducted Lizzie from the school, and Lizzie told her family startling stories of being cruelly beaten with a strap and "walked upon" by a Miss Dick. The asylum denied the charges, and a man from the Society for the Prevention of Cruelty to Children took Lizzie back uptown. *New York Times*, Aug. 22, 1890.

CHAPTER 5: FROM PIGS TO OSTRICHES

50 "Knuckle down" "fen dubs" "fen everything": Gene Schermerhorn, *Letters to Phil*, 17.

53 "Nothing else is talked about": Philip Hone, *The Diary of Philip Hone, 1828–1851*, 462.

54 Knickerbocker Base Ball club: Burrows and Wallace, *Gotham*, 733.

55 Mildebergers ordered to move farmhouse: Stokes, *The Iconography of Manhattan Island*, vol. 4, 485; Mott, *The New York of Yesterday*, 6.

55 The irregularly shaped plot of land: The Mildebergers owned the southeastern side of the block, but the northeastern side at Twenty-fourth and Broadway was owned by Samuel Howland and his wife, Joanna Hone Howland. Miriam Berman, *Madison Square*, 36.

56 "This was the hostelry": Abram Dayton, *Last Days of Knickerbocker Life in New York*, 363–64.

57 K.K.K. sign: *Real Estate Record and Buyers' Guide*, Dec. 24, 1904.

59 John B. Monnot also purchased the Hone/Howland property at the northeastern corner of the block in 1853, making him the fourth owner of that piece of property. Berman, *Madison Square*, 36.

60 "blackguards, gamblers, rowdies" "indiscriminate admission": *New York Daily Times*, May 16, 1853.

60 "Amusements of the Ancient Greeks and Romans": *Literary World*, May 21, 1853.

61 "We don't know": *Constitution* (Middletown, CT), May 25, 1853.

61 "Vive la humbug": *Daily Picayune* (New Orleans), June 8, 1853.

61 "nothing more than a Bowery circus": *Sun* (Baltimore), May 21, 1853.

61 death of Augusta Taylor: *New York Herald*, July 7, 1853; *Boston Daily Bee*, July 11, 1853.

62 animals sold at hippodrome auction: *New York Times*, Nov. 13, 1855.

CHAPTER 6: ENO'S FOLLY

63 "the best specimen": *New York Times*, Aug. 23, 1859.

64 "staid puritanical character": Amos Eno to Lucy Phelps, Feb. 16, 1834, quoted in Char Miller, *Gifford Pinchot and the Making of Modern Environmentalism*, 44.

64 "small means, small credit": Joseph Scoville, *The Old Merchants of New York City*, 138.

65   "an interrogation point": *Commemorative Biographical Record of Hartford County, Connecticut* (Chicago: J.H. Beers & Co., 1901), 763.

65   value of Amos Eno's real estate holdings: *New York Times*, Feb. 22, 1898.

66   "No other single hotel": Moses King, *King's Handbook of New York City*, 200.

67   symbolism of America's luxury hotels: Molly Berger, *Hotel Dreams*, 2–10; Jefferson Williamson, *The American Hotel*, 38–40.

67   "When the new hotel": Anthony Trollope, *North America*, vol. 2, 396.

67   "An American hotel is to an English hotel": George Augustus Sala, "American Hotels and American Food," *Temple Bar Magazine* 2 (July 1861): 345, quoted in Berger, *Hotel Dreams*, 113.

67   "may not just *be* the American spirit": Henry James, *The American Scene*, 103.

69   "living fairies" "Here assemble": Reuben Vose, *Wealth of the World Displayed*, 184.

70   "staining or spoiling": *Harper's Weekly*, Oct. 1, 1859.

70   "Ill-breeding never appears": Junius Henri Browne, *The Great Metropolis*, 395.

71   "One is struck": A.C. and I.C., *The United States And Canada*, 17.

72   "Every man of taste": Vose, *Wealth of the World Displayed*, 181–82.

72   "I had, of course, a very gay winter": "Recollections of Mary Eno Pinchot," Pinchot Papers, quoted in M. Christine Boyer, *Manhattan Manners*, 52, from Nancy Jean Carrs, "Madison Square, The Eno Family and the Fifth Avenue Hotel" (unpublished manuscript, 1981). Mary Eno's oldest son, Gifford Pinchot, born in 1865, was a founder of the American conservation movement and the first chief of the U.S. Forest Service.

72   The Jerome family lived on Madison Square for only few years. In 1868 they leased their mansion to the Union League Club, which remained there until 1881. Later tenants included the Turf Club and University Club. The building was demolished in the late 1960s.

74   "Nothing to Wear": William Allen Butler, "157. Nothing to Wear," Bartleby.com, https://www.bartleby.com/102/157.html.

75   "intense grief": Ian Radforth, *Royal Spectacle*, 344.

77   "shampoo": *New York Times*, Oct. 17, 1860.

77   "He had the suite": Wetherbee, quoted in Fifth Avenue Bank, *Fifth Avenue*, 24.

CHAPTER 7: WAR

78   "Bay State boys!": *New York Times*, April 19, 1861.

79   "Immense crowd, immense cheering": George Templeton Strong, *The Diary of George Templeton Strong*, abridged version (Seattle: University of Washington Press, 1988), 188.

83 "We were all in all": Devlin, quoted in Eleanor Ruggles, *Prince of Players*, 126.

83 "The harlotry of the city": Strong, *The Diary of George Templeton Strong*, vol. 3, 521.

84 "Now for the Fifth-Avenue Hotel": *New York Times*, July 14, 1863.

85 "the rioters went away": Charles Carter, "The Passing of a Historic Hostelry," 964.

85 "surging, swaying" "whooping, yelling": William Stoddard, *Lincoln's Third Secretary*, 185.

86 John Andrews and prostitute: John Strausbaugh, *City of Sedition*, 286.

89 "There must be something dead": John Headley, *Confederate Operations in Canada and New York*, 272.

89 "three mammoth fat girls": *New York Times*, Nov. 22, 1864.

90 "I'm looking for who did it": Union Provost Marshal's File, Prison Records 1862–65, quoted in Nat Brandt, *The Man Who Tried to Burn New York*, 15.

91 Charles H. Foster's séances at 14 West Twenty-fourth Street: *New York Herald*, Sept. 11, 1874.

91 In May 1873 Edwin Booth auctioned off his fine black walnut furniture, many oil paintings, and two pianos from his home at 14 West Twenty-fourth Street (*New York Herald*, May 31, 1873), probably to help fund his struggling Booth's Theatre. The theater would go bankrupt a year later in the wake of the financial Panic of 1873, which began that September.

92 "In a deep trance": letter from Booth to Richard Stoddard, Nov. 18, 1863, quoted in Daniel Watermeier, *American Tragedian*, 104. In his letters, Booth refers to Foster by last name only, and Watermeier believes he is referencing, and misspelling the name of, another prominent medium, Thomas Gales Forster. Given the shared address, however, it is more likely that Booth is writing about Charles Foster.

92 Foster's pamphlets, filled with "his wonderful revelations, manifestations, sayings and doings," were available for fifty cents at the Fifth Avenue Hotel, according to classifieds that ran in the *New York Herald* in 1874. Two years earlier, Foster had been exposed as a charlatan, but his many ardent followers disregarded that news and continued to believe in him for many years.

92 "train began to move": *Century Illustrated Monthly Magazine*, vol. 77, 920.

CHAPTER 8: CRACKS IN THE VAULT

93 "SURE CURE": quoted in James McCabe, *Lights and Shadows of New York Life*, 620.

93   "Ladies cured at one interview": Anonymous, *The Gentleman's Companion*, 54.

93   "Monthly pills": quoted in Marilynn Wood Hill, *Their Sisters' Keepers*, 237.

94   rate of abortion in the 1850s: Hill, 237.

94   "Why do they persecute me so?": quoted in Karen Abbott, "Madame Restell."

94   Strong vs. Strong divorce case: *New York Times*, March 10, 17, 1865; May 6, 1865; Oct. 26, 1865; Nov. 24, 28, 29, 1865; Dec. 9, 13, 14, 17, 22, 27, 28, 1865; *New York Herald*, March 6, 17, 1865; Nov. 25, 1865; Dec. 16, 19, 1865.

95   Things weren't so simple: Naomi Cahn, "Faithless Wives and Lazy Husbands," 5–6, 34–35; Di Long, "Divorce in New York from 1850s to 1920s," 35–42.

96   "elderly, quiet mannered gentleman": *New York Times*, Nov. 28, 1865.

96   death of Mrs. Adams: *New York Times*, March 5, 1865, and March 17, 1865.

96   alleged abortion: *New York Times*, March 10, 1865, and October 26, 1865.

96   "I have meant to go": Strong, *The Diary of George Templeton Strong*, vol. 4, 54.

97   "nurses with infants": James McCabe, *New York by Sunlight and Gaslight*, 269.

98   "The guests of that most charming": Strong, *The Diary of George Templeton Strong*, vol. 3, 420.

98   "The performance was perfect": Strong, *The Diary of George Templeton Strong*, vol. 2, 212.

101   "Will you powder?": Deborah Davis, *Gilded*, 57.

101   "The whole secret of the success": Ward McAlister, *Society as I Have Found It*, 215.

103   "Their home was lavish": *New York Times*, July 30, 1870.

106   "No blood could ever be found" "He never seemed to find": quoted in Josh Nathan-Kazis, "A Death in the Family," 4.

CHAPTER 9: HOTEL LIVING

107   "She is no hair-lifting beauty": Clara Morris, *Life on the Stage*, 308.

109   "Take 'em!" "The street became demoralized": James Medbury, *Men and Mysteries of Wall Street*, 43, 254.

110   "Daniel says up": Wheaton J. Lane, *Commodore Vanderbilt* (New York: Alfred A. Knopf, 1942), 236, quoted in John Steele Gordon, *The Scarlet Woman of Wall Street*, 117.

111   "He who sells what isn't his'n": quoted in John Steele Gordon, *The Great Game* (New York: Scribner, 1999), 61.

112   "Alighting from our cab": C. B. Berry, *The Other Side: How It Struck Us* (New York: E.P. Dutton & Co., 1880), 14.

115 "Whenever I feel": A. Emerson Belcher, *What I Know about Commercial Traveling* (Toronto, 1883), quoted in Jefferson Williamson, *The American Hotel*, 174.

115 "entirely from that want": Trollope, *North America*, vol. 2, 401.

116 social criticism of luxury hotels: Berger, *Hotel Dreams*, 112–40.

116 unsavory mixes of classes: Berger, 133–35.

117 "King of the Banco Men": Herbert Ashbury, *The Gangs of New York*, 197–98.

118 "One of the oldest and cleverest": Thomas Byrnes, *Professional Criminals of America*, 327.

119 "If this printing press": William Croffut, *The Vanderbilts and the Story of Their Fortune* (Chicago: Bedford, Clarke, 1886), 91, quoted in Gordon, *The Scarlet Woman of Wall Street*, 171.

120 "She was tall": *New York Herald*, Jan. 18, 1871.

121 "[You] should be the last man": James Fisk's affidavit, *New York Times*, Nov. 19, 1868, quoted in Gordon, *The Scarlet Woman of Wall Street*, 202.

CHAPTER 10: DEATH ONSTAGE AND OFF

123 "the blonde, bustling": William Worthington Fowler, *Inside Life in Wall Street*, 477.

125 "What security" and ff.: Joseph Francis Daly, *The Life of Augustin Daly*, 87–88, 13.

128 "the rocking figure": C. D. Odell, *Annals of the New York Stage*, vol. 9, 152, quoted in Grossman, *A Spectacle of Suffering*, 10.

129 "Wife—whose wife?": Clara Morris, *Life on the Stage*, 308.

129 The fire at Daly's marked the thirty-fifth theater fire to blaze in New York since the early 1800s. Most of the fires were caused by stage lights hung too close to flammable draperies or scenery, or by gas-light explosions, and since many of the venues were built of wood, they burned fast. Not until 1887 were stringent laws passed ordering that theater floors and partitions be built of masonry or iron, and not until the early 1900s were laws requiring asbestos curtains, fire extinguishers, and emergency exits enacted.

129 "the greatest emotional actress": *Boston Transcript*, quoted in Grossman, *A Spectacle of Suffering*, 263.

130 "Immediately on entering": Mary Duffus Hardy, *Through Cities and Prairie Lands*, 302–6, quoted in Bayrd Still, *Mirror for Gotham*, 235.

130 Fifth Avenue Hotel fire: *New York Times*, Dec. 12, 1872, and Dec. 13, 1872.

131   The fire at the Fifth Avenue led to the inspection of other New York hotels, but little change came about until a catastrophic 1877 fire at the Southern Hotel in Saint Louis, Missouri, which took the lives of close to forty guests, many leaping to their deaths to escape the flames. Afterward, city officials around the country took a serious look at their hotels, and in January 1883, New York passed effective legislation requiring the installation of fire escapes. Hoteliers protested vigorously, but to no avail, and by late 1883, thirty-nine hotels, including the Fifth Avenue, had installed fire escapes.

131   "Oh, my dear": Edith Wharton, *Old New York: New Year's Day*, 11–12.

132   modern historians are not so sure: Gordon, *The Scarlet Woman of Wall Street*, 277; Edward Renehan, *Dark Genius of Wall Street*, 177.

132   "the Mephistopheles of Wall Street": Renehan, 180.

134   "Come along" and ff.: Testimony of Thomas Hart at the coroner's inquest, quoted in R. W. McAlpine, *The Life and Times of Col. James Fisk, Jr.*, 356–57.

134   Stokes would be tried three times. The first trial ended in a hung jury due to charges of jury tampering. The second found him guilty of first-degree murder, and he was sentenced to death, a verdict that his high-paid lawyers overturned. The third found him guilty of manslaughter, and he served four years in Sing Sing.

135   "Do you believe" and ff.: *New York Times*, Jan. 7, 1872.

135   "I cannot sufficiently": *New York Herald*, Jan. 8, 1871.

135   "The scene at the Fifth Avenue Hotel": *New York Herald*, Jan. 7, 1872.

135   "They remembered": *New York Herald*, Jan. 7, 1872.

136   "I wish it to be": *New York Herald*, Jan. 7, 1872.

CHAPTER 11: LADIES OF THE NIGHT

137   Lizzie: House of Refuge Case Histories, No. 17561 (vol. 37, 1877).

137   Maria: House of Refuge Case Histories, No. 17259 (vol. 36, 1876).

137   Fannie: House of Refuge Case Histories, No. 11667 (vol. 30, 1866).

137   Ann: House of Refuge Case Histories, No. 10400 (vol. 29, 1865).

139   "abandoned women" and ff.: *New York Daily Tribune*, Nov. 14, 1860.

139   "quite a private resort" and ff.: A Free Loveyer, *Directory to the Seraglios in New York, Philadelphia, Boston, and All the Principal Cities in the Union.*

139   three doors off Twenty-fourth Street: It is unclear whether the brothel was south of Twenty-fourth Street and therefore on the block, or on Sixth Avenue between Twenty-fourth and Twenty-fifth streets.

139 number of prostitutes: Lewis Morris, *Incredible New York*, 44; Timothy Gilfoyle, *City of Eros*, 57–59. The correct number probably lay somewhere in between the minister's and police estimates. Gilfoyle, who examines the subject in great depth, believes that perhaps 5 to 10 percent of all women between the ages of fifteen and thirty in nineteenth-century New York were prostitutes at some point, with that figure rising to above 10 percent during periods of depression.

140 "Impure women": McCabe, *Lights and Shadows of New York Life*, 314.

140 prostitutes on Broadway: Anonymous, *The Gentleman's Companion*, 9–11.

140 "maidenly reserve": Edward Crapsey, *The Nether Side of New York*, 139.

140 "loud-voiced and foul-tongued" "not hesitate": McCabe, *New York by Sunlight and Gaslight*, 253.

141 prostitutes for only a few years: Christine Stansell, *City of Women*, 171–92; Marilynn Wood Hill, *Their Sisters' Keeper*, 40–42, 46, 62.

142 "green and red fiery eyes": Hardy, *Through Cities and Prairie Lands*, 63, quoted in Still, *Mirror for Gotham*, 219.

143 "One is struck": McCabe, *Lights and Shadows of New York Life*, 506–7.

143 Hotel de Wood: *The Gentleman's Companion*, 36.

143 brothels on West Twenty-sixth and Twenty-seventh streets: *The Gentleman's Companion*, 38–41, 43, 47.

144 "cultured and pleasing companions": Ashbury, *The Gangs of New York*, 175.

145 "negress" "one of the toughest" "whose name": New York Press, *Vices of a Big City*, 57–58.

147 "The landladies, however": *New York Times*, May 4, 1892.

147 raid on Charley Walter's place: *New York Times*, March 10, 1900.

147 Gracie Irwin goes missing: *New York Tribune*, March 2, 1889; *Evening World*, March 2 and 20, 1889.

147 "ALL COME AT ONCE": *New York Tribune*, March 27, 1879.

148 Frank Hart's winnings: Matthew Algeo, *Pedestrianism*, 209.

148 attempted entrapment of Charles Sears: *Sun*, Dec. 12, 1886.

148 "notorious Sixth avenue resort": *Evening World*, March 20, 1889.

148 "comfortably installed" "at Auntie Caroline's": *Evening World*, March 2, 1889.

150 "bankers, express-men" "If a daughter": Matthew Hale Smith, *Sunshine and Shadow in New York*, 379–80.

150 "It is now too late": Smith, 386.

CHAPTER 12: AT THE END OF THE NIGHTSTICK

153   "There is more law": Ashbury, *The Gangs of New York*, 237.

154   "I have had chuck": *New York Times*, March 26, 1917.

154   "I'm so well known": *New York Times*, Dec. 27, 1894.

155   clubbings statistics: Marilynn Johnson, *Street Justice*, 19.

156   "the most conspicuously": *New York Times*, Sept. 23, 1878.

156   Gilmore's Garden: The New York and Harlem Railroad Depot closed in 1871, after the opening of Grand Central Station at Forty-second Street. Two years later, the old depot was leased to P. T. Barnum, who in turn leased it to military bandleader and showman Patrick Gilmore. Barnum's traveling circus appeared in the venue every spring, while Gilmore presented everything from beauty contests to sporting events the rest of the year. William K. Vanderbilt purchased the venue in the late 1870s and reopened it as the first Madison Square Garden on Memorial Day 1879. It continued to host Barnum's circus every spring, with the showman's annual march of the elephants through the city's streets becoming a New York tradition that lasted for over 130 years.

156   "sound of the heavy blows": quoted in Matthew Algeo, *Pedestrianism*, 127.

157   "Come out of here" and ff.: *New York Times*, March 18, 1879.

157   "What did you strike me for?" and ff.: *New York Times*, Oct. 30, 1879.

158   Williams's political support: Daniel Czitrom, *New York Exposed*, 52–58.

158   signers of petition supporting Williams: *New York Tribune*, Feb. 20, 1885.

158   "No officer of the law": *New York Tribune*, Feb. 28, 1885.

159   "a memento of the quickening": *New York Times*, May 27, 1885.

159   album paid for by madams and gamblers: *Report and Proceedings of the Senate Committee Appointed to Investigate the Police Department of the City of New York*, vol. 5, 5551.

159   "reward long deserved": *New York Times*, Aug. 10, 1887.

159   "Just ask the Mayor": *New York Times*, March 26, 1917.

162   "sun shone brightly": *New York Herald*, June 3, 1875.

162   After the eulogy, the Baron lay embalmed in a cemetery vault in Williamsburg, New York, for almost six months because America's first crematorium was still being built. His body finally joined his spirit on December 6, 1876.

163   "One hundred and seventy massive": *New York Times*, June 28, 1883.

166   "vile and abusive": Luc Sante, *Low Life*, 114.

167   Mary Cole's arrest: *New York Times*, Aug. 29, 1881.

167   "a vertical house of mirth": James Weldon Johnson, *The Autobiography of an Ex-Coloured Man*, 446–47.

CHAPTER 13: IS SHE A LADY OR IS SHE NOT?

169   "one of the most beautiful belles": *New York Tribune*, April 4, 1895.

170   "a piece of foolish extravagance": *The Granite Monthly, A New Hampshire Magazine*, Jan. 1, 1892, vol. 14, 119.

171   "man's mind": Walsingham, "Our Worldings" clippings.

173   "unassailable" and ff.: Frederick Martin, *Things I Remember*, 26, 67.

173   "All Rome is talking": Fanny Reed, *Reminiscences, Musical and Other*, 21.

173   "Mrs. 'Fifth-Avenue Hotel'": Maria Lydig Daly, *Diary of a Union Lady*, 320.

174   "strained their necks": *New York Times*, April 28, 1874.

176   "The man or woman": *New York Times*, July 30, 1878.

177   "Oh, you know": Edith Wharton, *The Age of Innocence*, 259–60.

178   "It is evidently Mrs S's fault": Louis Auchincloss, *Edith Wharton: A Woman in Her Time* (London: Michael Joseph, 1971), 44, quoted in Julie Ferry, *The Million Dollar Duchesses*, 138.

178   "an alleged preponderance": Shari Benstock, *No Gifts from Chance* (Austin: University of Texas Press, 2004), 46, quoted in Ferry, *The Million Dollar Duchesses*, 139.

178   The story of Wharton's breakup is obfuscated yet further by the 2009 discovery of letters she wrote to her German governess in the mid-1880s. In one, written when she was eighteen, she says that Stevens visited her five months after the breakup and gave her "such a pretty ring for Easter—a black and white pearl." In another, written two years later when she was already engaged to Teddy Wharton, she seems to be alluding to Stevens when she writes, "If my present happiness had come to me at eighteen, I should probably have taken it as a matter of course. But coming to me after certain experiences of which you know, it seems almost incredible that a man can be so devoted, so generous, so sweet-tempered & unselfish" (Rebecca Mead, "The Age of Innocence," *New Yorker*, June 29, 2009).

179   "Mrs. Paran Stevens Sues Again": *New York Times*, Oct. 15, 1893.

179   "fairly shuddered in his easy chair" and ff.: *New York Times*, Oct. 4, 1887.

180   "Mrs. Stevens is not an ordinary witness" and ff.: *New York Times*, Oct. 29, 1887.

180   "I will spend my life to ruin you!": *New York Times*, Feb. 22, 1887.

181   "Go! Leave this house" and ff.: *New York Times*, Nov. 22, 1891.

181   "It was her habit": Wharton, *The Age of Innocence*, 26–27.

182   "There is one house": quoted in Lloyd Morris, *Incredible New York*, 142.

183   "remarkable female" and ff.: *Harper's Weekly*, April 13, 1895.

183   "When, as the wife": *New York Times*, April 7, 1895.

CHAPTER 14: BETRAYAL

185 "The Wealth concentrated": Moses King, *King's Handbook of New York City*, 56.

185 "Crowds throng the sidewalks": James McCabe, *New York by Sunlight and Gaslight*, 153–54.

186 St. Vitus' dance, more scientifically known as Sydenham's chorea or rheumatic chorea, is a neurological disorder characterized by rapid, irregular jerking movements of muscle groups, mostly in the face, hands, and feet.

188 "that each piece on display": *New York Times*, Aug. 22, 1894.

189 "without risk of coming into contact": quoted in Charles Musser, *Before the Nickelodeon: Edwin S. Porter and the Edison Manufacturing Company* (Berkeley: University of California Press, 1991), 116–17.

192 "a lot of dirty little claimants": *New York Times*, Dec. 28, 1882.

196 "The Board of Directors": *New York Tribune*, May 14, 1884.

197 "Mr. Eno is not here" "Search the house!": *New York Times*, May 25, 1884.

197 "No, he is not there": *New York Tribune*, May 25, 1884.

198 "The Son of Man came eating and drinking": Lately Thomas, *Delmonico's*, 220.

198 "Early in his priestly career": Monsignor Michael Lavelle's eulogy at Father Ducey's funeral in 1909, quoted in the *Catholic News*, quoted in Alex Phelps, "Father Ducey," in "A Spring Scandal."

199 "The Rev. Father Ducey": *New York Times*, June 1, 1884.

199 "Neither [Eno] nor his wife": *New York Globe and Mail*, reprinted in *Frank Leslie's Illustrated Newspaper*, June 12, 1886.

200 aggressively set about replacing servants: Phelps, "The Prodigal Son Returns," in "A Spring Scandal."

200 "Integrity, tenacity, and judgment": *New York Times*, Feb. 22, 1898.

200 "I always found Mr. Eno a friend": *New York Times*, Feb. 25, 1898.

201 "stood for years like a closed vault": *New York Times*, Dec. 7, 1892.

201 "a relic of a past generation": *New York Times*, Feb. 10, 1907.

CHAPTER 15: ROUNDSMEN OF THE LORD

202 description of Comstock and chapter title: from Heywood Broun and Margaret Leech, *Anthony Comstock*.

203 "immoral book" and ff.: *Publishers Weekly*, No. 1316, April 4, 1897, vol. 51; *Sun*, April 10, 1897; *New York Journal and Advertiser*, April 9, 1897.

203 "over-doing in a purity convention": Broun and Leech, *Anthony Comstock*, 11.

204 "as you hunt rats, without mercy": quoted in Burrows and Wallace, *Gotham*, 1015.

205 "A bloody ending to a bloody life": Broun and Leech, *Anthony Comstock*, 156.

205 "I am taking my life" "world is not yet ready": Broun and Leech, 212; "Ida Craddock's Letter to Her Mother on the Day of Her Suicide," http://www .idacraddock.com.

206 "somewhat strained" "not very musical": *Chautauquan* 20 (1884–1885): 349.

207 "polluted harpies that, under the pretense": Charles Parkhurst, *Our Fight with Tammany*, 10, 18.

207 "screamed almost" and ff.: Charles Gardner, *The Doctor and the Devil*, 7–10.

208 "on each chair sat": Gardner, 16.

208 "sat in blissful ignorance": Gardner, 20.

208 "In each room sat a youth": Gardner, 58.

209 "a very hard man to satisfy" "show me something worse": Gardner, 64.

209 "down into the disgusting depths": Parkhurst, *Our Fight with Tammany*, 74.

210 "from her private carriage": *New York Tribune*, Aug. 11, 1894.

211 "was not afraid that the police": *New York Tribune*, Aug. 8, 1894; *New York Times*, Aug. 8, 1894.

211 "the notoriety arising from": *New York Tribune*, Aug. 11, 1894.

212 Mrs. Sallade's Donkey: *New York Tribune*, Aug. 24, 1894.

212 arrest of Richard E. Young: *Evening World*, Dec. 14, 1893.

213 "[His] recent troubles": quoted in Malcolm Goldstein, "On Beyonde Holcombe."

213 "opium chewing prevails here: Strong, *The Diary of George Templeton Strong*, vol. 1, 203.

213 "women of all classes" "pale and interesting": George Ellington, *The Women of New York*, 223.

215 "I suppose" and ff.: *Report and Proceedings of the Senate Committee Appointed to Investigate the Police Department of the City of New York*, vol. 5, 5526–74; the dialogue quoted here has been condensed.

217 "Inspector, you're a slick one": *New York Times*, May 25, 1895.

217 "Well, well, reform has gone to hell!": Esther Crain, *The Gilded Age*, 213.

218 "clumsiest execution in the history of Sing Sing": Stephen Chermak and Frankie Bailey, eds., *Crimes of the Centuries: Notorious Crimes, Criminals, and Criminal Trials in American History*, vol. 1 (Santa Barbara, CA: ABC-CLIO, 2016), 68.

CHAPTER 16: AMERICAN BEAUTY

The dialogue and many descriptions in this chapter come from Evelyn Nesbit's two memoirs and newspaper accounts of her court testimony. The wording of the dialogue and other details differ slightly from account to account, but their overall meaning is the same.

221 "Where are the rest of the people?" and ff.: *New York Evening Telegram*, Feb. 7, 1907, and *New York Evening Journal*, Feb. 7, 1907, quoted in Simon Baatz, *The Girl on the Red Velvet Swing*, 36–37; Nesbit, *The Story of My Life*, 74.
223 "There began a buzzing": Nesbit, 75.
223 "an abbreviated pink undergarment" and ff.: Nesbit, *Prodigal Days*, 41, and *The Story of My Life*, 75–77.
223 "I went . . . that night a child" and ff.: Nesbit, *The Story of My Life*, 73–77; and *Prodigal Days*, 33–34.
225 "Stanford White was a great man": Nesbit, *The Story of My Life*, 50.
227 "there was no fending him off" and ff.: Nesbit, *Prodigal Days*, 93.
228 "Drink this" and ff.: Nesbit, *Prodigal Days*, 108.
231 "Oh, Harry, what have you done?" and ff.: Paula Uruburu, *American Eve*, 284.
231 "No jury will convict me": *New York American*, June 29, 1906, quoted in Baatz, *The Girl on the Red Velvet Swing*, 125.
231 "Everything . . ." and ff.: Uruburu, *American Eve*, 334; Nesbit, *The Story of My Life*, 116.
232 "I can't go on!" and ff.: Douglas Linder, "The Trials of Henry Thaw for the Murder of Stanford White."
233 "The world didn't see what I remembered": *New York Journal American*, Sept. 14, 1955, quoted in Paul Baker, *Stanny*, 398.
234 "I was sorry for him": Nesbit, *The Story of My Life*, 226.
234 Nesbit did purportedly get one small moment of revenge against the Thaw family. According to her grandson, Russell Thaw, quoted in a *Los Angeles Times* article (Dec. 11, 2005), she donated the $25,000 she received from the Thaws at the trials' end to political anarchist Emma Goldman, who in turn gave it to John Reed, a leader of the American Communist Party.
235 Auction of White's collections: *New York Times*, April 5 and 6, 1907.
236 "All day long and far into the night": *New York Times*, April 5, 1908.
236 "'Fat?' said one of the auctioneer's men": *New York Times*, April 8, 1908.

CHAPTER 17: MODERN TIMES

238 $25,000 for Flatiron site: *New York Times*, Feb. 22, 1898.

240 "This is a question of personal *honah*": *Chicago Tribune*, May 19, 1901, quoted in Alice Alexiou, *The Flatiron*, 57.

241 "Lynch him! Kill him!": *New York Times*, July 7, 1901.

242 "It looked, from where I stood": Alfred Stieglitz, "The Flatiron," Art Institute of Chicago, https://www.artic.edu/artworks66315/the-flatiron.

245 "a little rattan stick": Henry Collins Brown, *Fifth Avenue Old and New*, 73.

245 "That very first traffic jam": John Montgomery, *Eno*, 8.

246 "On every hand curious figures": Theodore Dreiser, *Sister Carrie*, 327–28.

247 number of garment factories around Madison Square: Jerry Patterson, *Fifth Avenue*, 62.

247 historical and architectural details of buildings on the block: New York City Landmarks Designation Commission, *Ladies' Mile Historic District, Designation Report*, 873–902, 927–41.

249 "I am a working girl": Tony Michels, "Uprising of 20,000 (1909)," Jewish Women's Archive Encyclopedia, https://jwa.org/encyclopedia/article/uprising-of-20000-1909.

250 "white goods" protest: *New York Times*, Feb. 12, 1913.

250 American Museum of Safety: *New York Times*, May 5, 1915.

251 Soup carts in Belgium: *New York Tribune*, March 29, 1915.

252 Boy Scouts during World War I: *New-York Tribune*, April 14, 1917; May 19, 1919.

252 Silent Protest Parade: National Association for the Advancement of Colored People, "Silent Protest Parade Centennial," accessed May 12, 2021, https://naacp.org/silent-protest-parade-centennial/; *New York Times*, July 29, 1917; *New York Tribune*, July 29, 1917; *Evening Star* (Washington, D.C.), June 15, 1922.

CHAPTER 18: ON THE WEST SIDE

255 "new and improved style": *New York Times*, Nov. 25, 1900.

255 "I've been looking for you": *New York Times*, Jan. 21, 1921.

256 "the spitting crime" "the man who looks": *New York Times*, Jan. 6, 1901.

257 "was feeling now": *New York Herald Tribune*, March 26, 1934.

257 Sylvia Goldfarb: *New York Herald Tribune*, May 16, 1945.

257 number of illegal bars: Michael Lerner, *Dry Manhattan*, 138–40.

258 "white-coated fellows": *New Yorker*, Jan. 16, 1926, quoted in Lerner, 139.

258 "a hundred Eiffel towers": Philippe de Rothschild, *Paris–Paris: Instantanés d'Amérique* (Paris, 1931), 28, quoted in Still, *Mirror for Gotham*, 260.

258 New York as city of dreams: Ric Burns, "New York: Cosmopolis," episode 5, *American Experience: New York*, PBS Broadcasting.

260 Flanagan's testimony: Congressional Record, "Investigations of Un-American Propaganda Activity in the United States," Hearings Before a Special Committee on Un-American Activities, House of Representatives, Seventy-Fifth Congress, Third Session, 1939, 2839–2858.

262 "cardinal keystone of Communism": "Federal Theatre Project," The Living New Deal, https://livingnewdeal.org/glossary/federal-theatre-project-ftp-1935 -1939/.

262 "the set-up of the whole Arts": Congressional Record, "Investigation and Study of the Works Progress Administration," Hearings Before the Subcommittee of the Committee on Appropriations, House of Representatives, Seventy-Sixth Congress, First Session, 1939, 1084.

262 "had been known as far back as 1927": Congressional Record, "Investigation of Un-American Propaganda Activity in the United States," 2791.

262 "rather large number of the employees": Hallie Flanagan, *Arena*, 347.

263 "Only a watchman": *New York Times*, Aug. 1, 1939.

263 "one of the finest examples": *Real Estate Record and Buyers' Guide*, Oct. 3, 1908.

263 E. E. Cummings poem: "E.E. Cummings Told Him," *Latham's Quarterly*, 1944.

CHAPTER 19: TOYS, TOYS, TOYS!

The Toy Fair has been officially known by different names over years, including the New York Toy Fair, the American Toy Fair, the American International Toy Fair, and the North American Toy Fair, but throughout the decades most of the industry has referred to it simply as the Toy Fair. I have followed their example.

271 "the largest dealer in toys": *New York Times*, April 28, 1897.

271 "putter[ed] around the store": E. B. White, "F.A.O.," *New Yorker*, Feb. 28, 1931.

272 toy production increased by 500 percent: Richard Levy and Ronald Weingartner, *The Toy and Game Inventor's Handbook*, 52.

272 "exert[ed] the sort of": *Boston Post*, Oct. 25, 1918, quoted in Ellen Terrell, "A. C. Gilbert's Successful Quest to Save Christmas," *Inside Adams*, Library of Congress, Dec. 14, 2016.

273 statistics on the Toy Fair: *New York Times*, March 7, 9, and 19, 1948; March 7, 12, and 20, 1949; March 14, 1953; March 18, 1954; March 13, 1962.

276 Toy Center sold: *New York Times*, Dec. 3, 1950, and June 22, 2005; *New York Observer*, Oct. 30, 2007; CityReality.com, April 3, 2007; CityReality.com, Oct. 3, 2007.

CHAPTER 20: DARK DAYS

278 slashings in Madison Square Park: *New York Times*, June 29, 1981.

278 decline of manufacturing jobs: Rona B. Stein, "New York City's Economy—A Perspective on Its Problems," *Federal Reserve Bank Quarterly Review*, Summer 1977, 50.

279 homeless and welfare hotel statistics: Jonathan Kozol, *Rachel and Her Children: Homeless Families in America* (New York: Crown Publishers, 1988), 14–15; "Welfare Hotels," History of Poverty & Homelessness in NYC, http:// nychomelesshistory.org/#welfare-hotels; "History of Homelessness in NYC," City University of New York, https://homelessnyc.commons.gc.cuny.edu /2020/07/16/history-of-homelessness-in-nyc/.

280 "was found to be an undesirable": *New York Times*, Aug. 24, 1973.

280 welfare hotels north of Madison Square: *New York Times*, June 13, 1986; Aug. 31, 1983; Jan. 27, 1988.

282 "We used to laugh": Patti Smith, *Just Kids*, 9.

283 "Junkies would break the lock": Nathaniel Rich, "Where the Walls Still Talk," *Vanity Fair*, Oct. 8, 2013.

283 "Is this the shy pornographer?": Patricia Morrisroe, *Mapplethorpe*, 112.

287 "I'm looking for the unexpected": *ARTnews*, late 1988, quoted on Robert Mapplethorpe Foundation website, http://www.mapplethorpe.org/biography/.

289 "Robert and I lived here": Jack Walls, "For Robert," Visual Aids, https:// visualaids.org/blog/for-robert.

CHAPTER 21: TIME AWAITS

294 New York State third-largest tech sector: "The Technology Sector in New York City," Office of the New York State Comptroller, Report 4-2018, Sept. 2017, https://osc.state.ny.us/files/reports/osdc/pdf/report-4-2018.pdf.

294 jump in jobs: Flatiron/23rd Street Partnership, "Flatiron Quarterly District Market Snapshot," Q3 2019, https://www.flatirondistrict.nyc/uploaded /files/Reports%20&%20Data/Quarterly%20Reports/2019/Q3%20Final%20 Draft_10.29.2019.pdf.

294 42 West 24: "The History of Coworking," April 5, 2021, https://www.cowork
      ingresources.org; Carsten Foertsch and Rémy Cagnol, "The History of
      Coworking in a Timeline," Aug. 15, 2013, https://deskmag.com/en/coworking
      -spaces/the-history-of-coworking-spaces-in-a-timeline.

296 Freemason statistics: Masonic Services Association, https://www
      .msana.com.

298 "pure Italianness": *New Yorker*, August 11, 2002.

300 tourism figures: *NYC & Company Annual Report 2019–2020* and *NYC &
      Company Annual Summary 2013*, NYC & Company, https://business.nycgo
      .com/research/.

300 New York world's wealthiest city: Capgemini, "World Wealth Report 2019,"
      Barron's, Oct. 20, 2019.

300 poverty rate: "The New York City Government Poverty Measure, 2018,"
      Mayor's Office for Economic Opportunity."

300 hotel rooms: Flatiron District/23rd Street Partnership, "The Flatiron District:
      Hospitality Hotspot," *Flatiron: Where Then Meets Now*, Fall 2018, 9, https://
      www.flatirondistrict.nyc/uploaded/files/2018_FWTMN_FINAL.pdf.

301 number of homeless in Flatiron District: interview with Urban Pathways,
      Feb. 25, 2021.

301 vacant retail space: "Retail Vacancy In New York City: Trends and Causes,
      2007–2017," Sept. 25, 2019, Office of the New York City Comptroller, https://
      comptroller.nyc.gov/reports/retail-vacancy-in-new-york-city/.

303 foot traffic: Flatiron/23rd Street Partnership, "Flatiron Plaza Pedestrian
      Counts," Q1 2020 and Q4 2020, https://www.flatirondistrict.nyc/about-the
      -bid/reports-and-data.

305 "The past and present wilt": Walt Whitman, "Song of Myself," verses 51–52,
      https://www.poetryfoundation.org/poems/45477/song-of-myself-1892-version.

BIBLIOGRAPHY

BOOKS

A.C. and I.C. *The United States and Canada: As Seen by Two Brothers in 1858 and 1861*. London: Edward Stanford, 1862.

Alexiou, Alice Sparberg. *The Flatiron: The New York Landmark and the Incomparable City That Arose with It*. New York: Thomas Dunne Books, 2010.

Algeo, Matthew. *Pedestrianism: When Watching People Walk Was America's Favorite Spectator Sport*. Chicago: Chicago Review Press, 2014.

Anonymous. *The Gentleman's Companion*. New York, 1870.

Ashbury, Herbert. *The Gangs of New York: An Informal History of the Underworld*. New York: Paragon House, 1990.

Baatz, Simon. *The Girl on the Velvet Swing: Sex, Murder, and Madness at the Dawn of the Twentieth Century*. New York: Mulholland Books, 2018.

Baker, Paul. *Stanny: The Gilded Life of Stanford White*. New York: Free Press, 1989.

Ballon, Hilary, ed. *The Greatest Grid: The Master Plan of Manhattan, 1811–2011*. New York: Museum of the City of New York and Columbia University Press, 2012.

Batterberry, Michael, and Ariane Batterberry. *On the Town in New York: The Landmark History of Eating, Drinking, and Entertainments from the American Revolution to the Food Revolution*. New York: Routledge, 1999.

Benjamin, Marcus. *A Historical Sketch of Madison Square*. New York: Meriden Britannia Company, 1894.

Bentley, Joanne. *Hallie Flanagan: A Life in the Theatre*. New York: Alfred A. Knopf, 1988.

Berger, Molly. *Hotel Dreams: Luxury, Technology, and Urban Ambition in America, 1829–1929*. Baltimore: John Hopkins University Press, 2011.

Berlin, Ira, and Leslie Harris, eds. *Slavery in New York*. New York: New Press, 2005.

Berman, Miriam. *Madison Square: The Park and Its Celebrated Landmarks*. Salt Lake City, UT: Gibbs-Smith, 2001.

Bolton, Reginald. *Indian Paths in the Great Metropolis*. New York: Museum of the American Indian, 1922.

Boyer, M. Christine. *Manhattan Manners: Architecture and Style, 1850–1900*. New York: Rizzoli International Publications, 1985.

Brandt, Nat. *The Man Who Tried to Burn New York*. New York: Berkley Books, 1990.

Broun, Heywood, and Margaret Leech. *Anthony Comstock: Roundsman of the Lord*. New York: Albert & Charles Boni, 1927.

Brown, Henry Collins. *Fifth Avenue Old and New, 1824–1924*. New York: Fifth Avenue Association, 1924.

Brown, Henry Collins. *Old New York: Yesterday and Today*. New York: Privately printed for *Valentine's Manual*, 1922.

Brown, Henry Collins, ed. *Valentine's Manual of Old New York*. New York: Valentine's Manual Inc., 1919–1928.

Browne, Junius Henri. *The Great Metropolis: A Mirror of New York*. Hartford, CT: American Publishing Company, 1869.

Burrows, Edwin, and Mike Wallace. *Gotham: A History of New York City to 1898*. New York: Oxford University Press, 1999.

Byrne, Christopher. *They Came to Play: One Hundred Years of the Toy Industry Association*. New York: Toy Industry Association, 2016.

Byrnes, Thomas. *Professional Criminals of America*. New York: Cassell & Company, 1886.

Cantwell, Anne-Marie, and Diana diZerega Wall. *Unearthing Gotham: The Archaeology of New York City*. New Haven, CT: Yale University Press, 2001.

Cellem, Robert. *Visit of His Royal Highness the Prince of Wales to British American Provinces of North America and United States in the Year 1860*. Toronto: Henry Rowsell, 1861.

City History Club of New York and Frank Bergen Kelley. *Historical Guide to the City of New York*. New York: Frederick A. Stokes Company, 1909.

Cohen, Paul, and Robert Augustyn. *Manhattan in Maps, 1527–1995*. New York: Rizzoli International Publications, 1997.

Crain, Esther. *The Gilded Age in New York: 1870–1910*. New York: Black Dog & Leventhal, 2016.

Crapsey, Edward. *The Nether Side of New York: or, The Vice, Crime and Poverty of the Great Metropolis*. New York: Sheldon & Company, 1872.

Craven, Wayne. *Gilded Mansions: Grand Architecture and High Society*. New York: W. W. Norton, 2008.

Czitrom, Daniel. *New York Exposed: The Gilded Age Police Scandal That Launched the Progressive Era*. New York: Oxford University Press, 2016.

Daly, Joseph Francis. *The Life of Augustin Daly*. New York: Macmillan, 1917.

Danckaerts, Jasper. *Journal of Jasper Danckaerts, 1679–1680*. Edited by Barlett Burleigh James and J. Franklin Jameson. New York: C. Scribner's Sons, 1913.

Davis, Deborah. *Gilded: How Newport Became America's Richest Resort*. New York: John Wiley & Sons, 2009.

Dayton, Abram. *Last Days of Knickerbocker Life in New York*. New York: G. P. Putnam's Sons, 1897.

Dorsey, Leslie, and Janice Devine. *Fare Thee Well: A Backward Look at Two Centuries of Historic American Hostelries, Fashionable Spas & Seaside Resorts*. New York: Crown, 1964.

Dreiser, Theodore. *Sister Carrie*. New York: Dover Publications, 2004.

Eliot, Elizabeth. *They All Married Well*. London: Cassell & Company, 1960.

Ellington, George. *The Women of New York, or The Under-World of the Great City*. New York: New York Book Company, 1869.

Eno, Henry Lane. *The Eno Family, New York Branch*. Princeton, NJ: Princeton University Press, 1920.

Ferry, Julie. *The Million Dollar Duchesses: How America's Heiresses Seduced the Aristocracy*. London: Aurum, 2018.

Fifth Avenue Bank. *Fifth Avenue: Glances at the Vicissitudes and Romance of a World-Renowned Thoroughfare*. New York: Fifth Avenue Bank, 1915.

Fisher, Harriet. *The Darlings of Vermont's Northeast Kingdom.* Charleston, SC: History Press, 2008.

Flanagan, Hallie. *Arena: The Story of the Federal Theatre.* New York: Random House, 1988.

Foote, Thelma Wills. *Black and White Manhattan: The History of Racial Formation in Colonial New York City.* New York: Oxford University Press, 2004.

Fowler, William Worthington. *Inside Life in Wall Street.* Hartford, CT: Dustin, Gilman & Co., 1873.

A Free Loveyer. *Directory to the Seraglios in New York, Philadelphia, Boston, and All the Principal Cities in the Union.* New York: Printed and published for the trade, 1859.

Fuller, Robert. *Jubilee Jim: From Circus Traveler to Wall Street Rogue.* New York: Texere, 2001.

Gardner, Charles. *The Doctor and the Devil, or Midnight Adventures of Dr. Parkhurst.* New York: Gardner & Co., 1894.

Gilfoyle, Timothy. *City of Eros: New York City, Prostitution, and the Commercialization of Sex, 1790–1920.* New York: W. W. Norton, 1992.

Gordon, John Steele. *The Scarlet Woman of Wall Street: Jay Gould, Jim Fisk, Cornelius Vanderbilt, the Erie Railway Wars, and the Birth of Wall Street.* New York: Weidenfeld & Nicolson, 1988.

Grossman, Barbara. *A Spectacle of Suffering: Clara Morris on the American Stage.* Carbondale: Southern Illinois University Press, 2009.

Grumet, Robert Steven. *The Lenapes.* New York: Chelsea House Publishers, 1989.

Hall, Max, ed. *Made in New York: Case Studies in Metropolitan Manufacturing.* Cambridge, MA: Harvard University Press, 1959.

Harris, Leslie. *In the Shadow of Slavery: African Americans in New York City, 1626–1863.* Chicago: University of Chicago Press, 2003.

Headley, John W. *Confederate Operations in Canada and New York.* New York: Neale Publishing Company, 1906.

Henderson, Mary. *The City and the Theatre: The History of New York Playhouses*. New York: Back Stage Books, 2004.

Hill, Marilynn Wood. *Their Sisters' Keepers: Prostitution in New York City, 1830–1870*. Berkeley: University of California Press, 1993.

Holloway, Marguerite. *The Measure of Manhattan: The Tumultuous Career and Surprising Legacy of John Randel Jr*. New York: W. W. Norton, 2013.

Homberger, Eric. *Mrs. Astor's New York: Money and Social Power in a Gilded Age*. New Haven, CT: Yale University Press, 2002.

Hone, Philip. *The Diary of Philip Hone, 1828–1851*. Vol. 1, edited by Allan Nevins. New York: Dodd, Mead and Company, 1927.

Howard University's New York African Burial Ground Project. *The New York African Burial Ground: Unearthing the African Presence in Colonial New York*. Washington, DC: Howard University Press, 2009.

Irving, Washington. *Knickerbocker's History of New York*. Chicago: W. B. Conkey Company, 1809.

Jackson, Kenneth, ed. *The Encyclopedia of New York City*. New Haven, CT: Yale University Press, 1991.

Jackson, Kenneth, ed. *The Great Metropolis: Poverty and Progress in New York City*. New York: American Heritage Custom Publishing Group, 1993.

James, Henry. *The American Scene*. New York: Horizon Press, 1967.

Jameson, J. Franklin, ed. *Narratives of New Netherland, 1609–1664*. New York: Charles Scribner's Sons, 1909.

Jenkins, Stephen. *The Greatest Street in the World: The Story of Broadway, Old and New, from the Bowling Green to Albany*. New York: G. P. Putnam's Sons, 1911.

Johnson, Clint. *"A Vast and Fiendish Plot": The Confederate Attack on New York City*. New York: Citadel Press Books, 2010.

Johnson, James Weldon. *The Autobiography of an Ex-Coloured Man*, reprinted in *Three Negro Classics*. New York: Avon Books, 1999.

Johnson, Marilynn. *Street Justice: A History of Police Violence in New York City*. Boston: Beacon, 2003.

Kaye, Marvin. *A Toy Is Born.* New York: Stein and Day, 1973.

King, Moses. *King's Handbook of New York City.* Boston: Moses King, 1892.

King, Moses. *Notable New Yorkers of 1896–1899: A Companion Volume to King's Handbook of New York City.* New York: Moses King, 1899.

Kraft, Herbert. *The Lenape-Delaware Indian Heritage: 10,000 BC to AD 2000.* Stanhope, NJ: Lenape Lifeways Books, 2001.

Kurlansky, Mark. *The Big Oyster: History on the Half Shell.* New York: Random House Trade Paperbacks, 2006.

Lardner, James, and Thomas Reppetto. *NYPD: A City and Its Police.* New York: Henry Holt, 2000.

Leadon, Fran. *Broadway: A History of New York City in Thirteen Miles.* New York: W. W. Norton, 2018.

Lerner, Michael. *Dry Manhattan: Prohibition in New York City.* Cambridge, MA: Harvard University Press, 2007.

Lessard, Suzannah. *The Architect of Desire: Beauty and Danger in the Stanford White Family.* New York: Dial, 1996.

Levy, Richard, and Ronald Weingartner. *The Toy and Game Inventor's Handbook.* New York: Alpha Books, 2003.

Lockwood, Charles. *Manhattan Moves Uptown: An Illustrated History.* Boston: Houghton Mifflin, 1976.

Martin, Frederick Townsend. *Things I Remember.* London: Eveleigh Nash, 1913.

Martineau, Paul, and Britt Salvesen. *Robert Mapplethorpe: The Photographs.* Los Angeles: J. Paul Getty Museum, 2016.

McAllister, Ward. *Society as I Have Found It.* New York: Cassell, 1890.

McAlpine, R. W. *The Life and Times of Col. James Fisk, Jr.* New York: New York Book Co., 1872.

McCabe, James. *Lights and Shadows of New York Life; or, the Sights and Sensations of the Great City.* Philadelphia: National Publishing Company, 1872.

McCabe, James. *New York by Sunlight and Gaslight: A Work Descriptive of the Great American Metropolis*. Philadelphia: Hubbard Brothers, 1881.

Medbury, James. *Men and Mysteries of Wall Street*. Boston: Fields, Osgood & Co., 1870.

Mendelsohn, Joyce. *Touring the Flatiron: Walks in Four Historic Neighborhoods*. New York: New York Landmarks Conservancy, 1998.

Miller, Char. *Gifford Pinchot and the Making of Modern Environmentalism*. Washington, DC: Island Press, 2001.

Montgomery, John. *Eno: The Man and the Corporation*. Westport, CT: Eno Foundation for Transportation, 1988.

Morris, Clara. *Life on the Stage: My Personal Experiences and Recollections*. New York: McClure, Phillips & Co., 1902.

Morris, Lloyd. *Incredible New York: High Life and Low Life from 1850 to 1950*. New York: Syracuse University Press, 1996.

Morrisroe, Patricia. *Mapplethorpe: A Biography*. New York: Da Capo, 1997.

Moss, Jeremiah. *Vanishing New York: How a Great City Lost Its Soul*. New York: Dey Street, 2017.

Mott, Hopper Striker. *The New York of Yesterday: A Descriptive Narrative of Old Bloomingdale*. New York: G. P. Putnam's Sons, 1908.

Nesbit, Evelyn. *Prodigal Days*. New York: Julian Messer, 1934.

Nesbit, Evelyn. *The Story of My Life*. London: John Long, 1914.

New York Press. *Vices of a Big City: An Expose of Existing Menaces to Church and Home in New York City*. New York: J. E. Clarke, 1890.

Parkhurst, Charles Henry. *Our Fight with Tammany*. New York: Charles Scribner's Sons, 1895.

Patterson, Jerry. *Fifth Avenue: The Best Address*. New York: Rizzoli International Publications, 1998.

Paxton, Bill. *A World Without Reality: Inside Marvin Glass's Toy Vault!* Self-published, 2019.

Radforth, Ian. *Royal Spectacle: The 1860 Visit of the Prince of Wales to Canada and the United States*. Toronto: University of Toronto Press, 2004.

Reed, Austin. *The Life and the Adventures of a Haunted Convict*. New York: Random House, 2016.

Reed, Fanny. *Reminiscences, Musical and Other*. Boston: Knight and Millet, 1903.

Renehan, Edward. *Dark Genius of Wall Street: The Misunderstood Life of Jay Gould, King of the Robber Barons*. New York: Basic Books, 2006.

Richardson, Douglas. *The Eno and Enos family in America; descendants of James Eno of Windsor, Conn*. Sacramento, CA: printed by the author, 1973.

Rosenberg, Charles. *The Cholera Years: The United States in 1832, 1849, and 1866*. Chicago: University of Chicago Press, 1987.

Ruggles, Eleanor. *Prince of Players: Edwin Booth*. New York: W. W. Norton, 1953.

Sanderson, Eric. *Mannahatta: A Natural History of New York City*. New York: Harry N. Abrams, 2009.

Sanger, William. *The History of Prostitution—Its Extent, Causes, and Effects Throughout the World*. New York: Harper and Brothers, 1858.

Sante, Luc. *Low Life: Lures and Snares of Old New York*. New York: Vintage Books, 1992.

Schermerhorn, Gene. *Letters to Phil: Memories of a New York Boyhood, 1848–1856*. New York: New York Bound, 1982.

Schermerhorn, Richard. *Schermerhorn Genealogy and Family Chronicles*. New York: T. A. Wright, 1914.

Schmidt, Leigh Eric. *Heaven's Bride: The Unprintable Life of Ida C. Craddock, American Mystic, Scholar, Sexologist, Martyr, and Madwoman*. New York: Basic Books, 2010.

Scoville, Joseph Alfred. *The Old Merchants of New York City*. New York: Carleton, 1863.

Shorto, Russell. *The Island at the Center of the World: The Epic Story of Dutch Manhattan and the Forgotten Colony that Shaped America*. New York: Vintage Books, 2005.

Singer, Herbert, and Ossian Lang. *New York Freemasonry: A Bicentennial History, 1781–1981*. New York: Grand Lodge of Free and Accepted Masons of the State of New York, 1981.

Smith, Matthew Hale. *Sunshine and Shadow in New York*. Hartford: J. B. Burr and Company, 1868.

Smith, Patti. *Just Kids*. New York: Ecco, 2010.

Stansell, Christine. *City of Women: Sex and Class in New York, 1789–1860*. Urbana: University of Illinois Press, 1987.

Stern, Sydney Ladensohn, and Ted Schoenhaus. *Toyland: The High-Stakes Game of the Toy Industry*. Chicago: Contemporary Books, 1990.

Still, Bayrd. *Mirror for Gotham: New York as Seen by Contemporaries from Dutch Days to the Present*. New York: Fordham University Press, 1994.

Stoddard, William O. *Lincoln's Third Secretary: The Memoirs of William O. Stoddard*. New York: Exposition, 1955.

Stokes, I. N. Phelps. *The Iconography of Manhattan Island, 1498–1909*. Vols. 1–6. New York: Robert H. Dodd, 1915–28.

Strausbaugh, John. *City of Sedition: The History of New York City During the Civil War*. New York: Twelve, 2016.

Strong, George Templeton. *The Diary of George Templeton Strong*. Edited by Allan Nevins and Milton Halsey Thomas. Vols. 1–4. New York: Macmillan, 1952.

Thomas, Lately. *Delmonico's: A Century of Splendor*. Boston: Houghton Mifflin, 1967.

Toy Manufacturers of the USA. *Official Directory of the American Toy Fair*. New York: Toy Manufacturers of the USA, 1950, 1954.

Trollope, Anthony. *North America*. Vol. 2. New York: Hippocrene Books, 1987.

Uruburu, Paula. *American Eve: Evelyn Nesbit, Stanford White, the Birth of the "It" Girl, and the Crime of the Century*. New York: Riverhead Books, 2008.

Valentine, D. T. *Manual of the Corporation of the City of New York*. New York: New York (City) Common Council, 1841–70.

Van der Donck, Adriaen. *A Description of New Netherland.* Edited by Charles Gehring and William Starna. Translated by Diederik Goedhuys. Lincoln: University of Nebraska Press, 2008.

Van Every, Edward. *Sins of New York as "Exposed" by the Police Gazette.* New York: F. A. Stokes Co., 1930.

Vose, Reuben. *Wealth of the World Displayed.* New York: Reuben Vose, 1859.

Wallace, Mike. *Greater Gotham: A History of New York City from 1898 to 1919.* New York: Oxford University Press, 2017.

Walsh, Tim. *Timeless Toys: Classic Toys and the Playmakers Who Created Them.* Kansas City, MO: Andrews McMeel, 2005.

Watermeier, Daniel J. *American Tragedian: The Life of Edwin Booth.* Columbia: University of Missouri Press, 2015.

Weisz, Peter. *The Lander Legacy: The Life Story of Rabbi Dr. Bernard Lander.* Jersey City, NJ: KTAV Publishing House, 2013.

Wharton, Edith. *The Age of Innocence.* New York: Collier Books, 1986.

Wharton, Edith. *Old New York: New Year's Day.* New York: D. Appleton, 1924.

Williamson, Jefferson. *The American Hotel: An Anecdotal History.* New York: Alfred A. Knopf, 1930.

Wulffson, Don. *Toys! Amazing Stories Behind Some Great Inventions.* New York: Square Fish, 2014.

ARTICLES, REPORTS, RECORDS, AND PAPERS

Abbott, Karen. "Madame Restell: The Abortionist of Fifth Avenue." *Smithsonian Magazine,* November 27, 2012. https://www.smithsonianmag.com/history /madame-restell-the-abortionist-of-fifth-avenue-145109198/.

Amos Eno Papers. 1857–1880. Columbia University.

André, Elizabeth Mary. "Fire Escapes in Urban America: History and Preservation." PhD thesis, University of Vermont, February 2006.

Cahn, Naomi. "Faithless Wives and Lazy Husbands: Gender Norms in Nineteenth Century Divorce Law." *University of Illinois Law Review* (2002): 651–98.

Carter, Charles. "The Passing of a Historic Hostelry." *Scrapbook* 5, no. 6 (June 1908), 958–67.

Christoph, Peter R. "The Freedmen of New Amsterdam." In *A Beautiful and Fruitful Place: Selected Rensselaerswijick Seminar Papers*, vol. 1, February 1983. New Netherland Institute. https://www.newnetherlandinstitute.org/files/7313/5067/3659/6.2.pdf.

Dodge, Henry Irving. "Forty Years on Twenty-Third Street." In *Valentine's Manual of Old New York 1924*, edited by Henry Collins Brown. New York: Chauncey Holt Co., 1923.

Dunne, Dominick. "Robert Mapplethorpe's Proud Finale." *Vanity Fair*, February 1989, 124–87.

Eno-Enos Family Miscellany. New York Public Library.

Fifth Avenue Hotel. Hotel Files, New-York Historical Society.

Freedman, Paul. "American Restaurants and Cuisine in the Mid-Nineteenth Century." *New England Quarterly* 84, no. 1 (March 2011): 5–59.

Freedman, Paul, and James Warlick. "High-End Dining in the Nineteenth-Century United States." *Gastronomica* 11, no. 1 (Spring 2011): 44–52.

Gilje, Paul, and Howard Rock, "'Sweep O! Sweep O!': African-American Chimney Sweeps and Citizenship in the New Nation." *William and Mary Quarterly* 51, no. 3 (July 1994): 507–38.

Goldstein, Malcolm. "On Beyonde Holcombe: Ladd & Coffin." http://1898revenues.blogspot.com/p/on-beyond-holcombe.html.

Hart, Nathaniel, ed. *Documents Relative to the House of Refuge*. New York: Mahlon Day, 1832.

Hoff, Henry B. "A Colonial Black Family in New York and New Jersey: Pieter Santomee and His Descendants." *Journal of the Afro-American Historical and Genealogical Society* 9, no. 3 (Fall 1988): 101–34.

Horne, Philip Field. "The Horne Family of Bloomingdale Road." Unpublished manuscript, New-York Historical Society. Bronxville, NY: Private printing, 1974.

Howe, Richard. "Notes on the Deforestation of Manhattan." Gotham Center for New York History, March 1, 2012. https://www.gothamcenter.org/blog/notes-on-the-deforestation-of-manhattan.

Linder, Douglas. "The Trials of Henry Thaw for the Murder of Stanford White." www.famous-trials.com/thaw/405-home.

Long, Di. "Divorce in New York from 1850s to 1920s." Unpublished master's thesis, University of Georgia, 2013.

Nathan-Kazis, Josh. "A Death in the Family." *Tablet Magazine*, January 13, 2010. https://www.tabletmag.com/sections/community/articles/a-death-in-the-family.

New York City. Department of Buildings, Building Information System.

New York City. Records of Assessment, New York City Municipal Archives and Records Center.

New York City Landmarks Designation Commission. *Ladies' Mile Historic District, Designation Report*. Edited by Marjorie Pearson. Vols. 1–2. New York, 1989.

New York City Landmarks Preservation Commission. *Madison Square North Historic District Designation Report*. Edited by Matthew Postal. New York, June 26, 2001.

New York State. *The Greatest Reform School in the World: A Guide to the Records of the New York House of Refuge*. New York: New York State Archives, 1989.

New York State. New York House of Refuge Inmate Case Histories. New York State Archives, Albany.

New York State, Committee on Police Dept. of the City of New York, Jacob Cantor, Clarence Lexow, and New York State. *Report and Proceedings of the Senate Committee Appointed to Investigate the Police Department of the City of New York*. Albany, NY: J. B. Lyon, 1895.

New York State Department of State. *Letters Patent, 1664–2017*. New York State Archives, Series Number: 12943. Vol. 5, 6–7.

New York State Historical Society. "Moving Buildings." *Heritage: The Magazine of the New York State Historical Society* 6, no. 4 (March–April 1990), 8–9.

Phelps, Alex. "A Spring Scandal." In "Shards, Fragments of a Life." FranKanTru Productions, 2003. www.frankantru.com/familyhistory/aspringscandal.

Serratore, Angela. "A Preservationist's Guide to the Harems, Seraglios, and Houses of Love of Manhattan: The Nineteenth Century New York City Brothel in Two Neighborhoods." Unpublished master's thesis, Columbia University, 2013.

Sprague, Stuart. "Lure of the City: New York's Great Hotels in the Golden Age, 1873–1907." *Conspectus of History* 1, no. 4 (1977), 73–84.

Wahba, Phil. "FAO Schwarz Closes: Read Fortune's 1940 Story about Its Rise." Fortune.com, July 15, 2015. https://fortune.com/2015/07/15/rise-of-fao -schwarz/.

Walsingham. "Our Worldlings." Collection of clippings and notes about Mrs. Paran Stevens, New York Public Library.

Werner, H. R. "Dr. Parkhurst's Crusade." *New Yorker*, November 19, 1955, and November 26, 1955.

Wilds, Ellen. "The Eno Embezzlement Case." In Their Own Words: Diaries, Memoirs, and Letters of the Past. Webmouse Cyberspace Publications, 2011. http://www.webmousepublications.com/itow/whoswho/phelps/doc-eno.html.

Wittenberg, Ernest. "The Thrifty Spy on The Sixth Avenue El." *American Heritage* 17, no. 1 (December 1965), 60–64.

MAPS AND DIRECTORIES

Atlas of the Entire City of New York. New York: G. W. Bromley & E. Robinson, 1879–1911.

Doggett's New York City Street Directory for 1851. New York: John Doggett, 1851.

Insurance Maps of the City of New York, Borough of Manhattan. New York: Sanborn, 1824–present.

Manhattan Address Telephone Directory. New York: New York Telephone Directory, 1930–1970.

Maps of the City of New York Surveyed Under Directions of Fire Insurance Companies. New York: William Perris, 1852–1862.

Maps of Farms Commonly Called the Blue Book, 1815. Laid out by John Randel Jr. Otto Sackersdorff, surveyor. New York, 1868.

Phillips Business Directory of New York. New York: Phillips & Co., 1910–1922.

Plan of the City of New York in North America: surveyed in the years 1766 & 1767. Bernard Ratzer, cartographer. London: Jefferys & Faden, 1776.

Trow's Business Directory. New York: Trow Directory, Printing and Bookbinding Co., 1874–1906.

SELECTED WEBSITES AND BLOGSPOTS

Black New Yorkers. Schomburg Center, New York Public Library. https://blacknewyorkers-nypl.org/.

The Bowery Boys. https://www.boweryboyshistory.com/.

City University of New York. "Cholera in New York." http://www.virtualny.cuny.edu/cholera.

City University of New York. "History of Homelessness in NYC." https://eportfolios.macaulay.cuny.edu.

Daytonian in Manhattan. http://daytoninmanhattan.blogspot.com/.

Ephemeral New York. https://ephemeralnewyork.wordpress.com/.

Flatiron/23rd Street Partnership. https://flatirondistrict.nyc.

History of Poverty & Homelessness in New York. http://povertyhistory.org.

Living New Deal. https://livingnewdeal.org.

Madison Square Park. https://www.nycgovparks.org/parks/madison-square-park/history.

Mannahatta Project. Eric Sanderson and Wildlife Conservation Society. https://welikia.org/m-map.php.

Nanticoke and Lenape Federation Learning Center. https://nanticokelenapemuseum.org.

New Netherland Institute. https://www.newnetherlandinstitute.org/.

INDEX

A NOTE ON THE AUTHOR

CHRISTIANE BIRD is the author of *The Sultan's Shadow*; *A Thousand Sighs, A Thousand Revolts*; and *Neither East nor West*, among other titles. She has worked on staff for the New York *Daily News* and has written for the *Wall Street Journal*, the *Washington Post*, the *Los Angeles Times*, and the *Miami Herald*, among other publications. She holds a BA in literature from Yale University and an MALS in American Studies from Columbia University. She lives in New York City with her family.